Motor Learning and Control for Dance

Principles and Practices for Performers and Teachers

Donna H. Krasnow, PhD

York University, Toronto, Canada, Professor Emerita
California Institute of the Arts, Valencia, California

M. Virginia Wilmerding, PhD

University of New Mexico

**Human
Kinetics**

Library of Congress Cataloging-in-Publication Data

Krasnow, Donna.
 Motor learning and control for dance: principles and practices for performers and teachers / Donna H. Krasnow, PhD, York University, Toronto, Canada, Professor Emerita, California Institute of the Arts, Valencia, California, M. Virginia Wilmerding, PhD, University of New Mexico.
   pages cm
 Includes bibliographical references and index.
 1. Dance--Study and teaching. 2. Dance--Physiological aspects. 3. Motor learning. 4. Movement, Psychology of. I. Title.
 GV1589.K73 2015
 793.307--dc23

                          2014039680

ISBN: 978-1-4504-5741-5 (print)

The web addresses cited in this text were current as of February 2015, unless otherwise noted.

Acquisitions Editor: Gayle Kassing, PhD; **Developmental Editor:** Melissa Feld; **Managing Editor:** Karla Walsh; **Copyeditor:** Joanna Hatzopoulos Portman; **Indexer:** Alisha Jeddeloh; **Permissions Manager:** Dalene Reeder; **Graphic Designer:** Denise Lowry; **Cover Designer:** Keith Blomberg; **Photograph (cover):** Albert David, Bangarra Dance Theatre, with Miranda Coney, The Australian Ballet, in Stephen Page's *Rites*. Photography by Jim McFarlane; **Photographs (interior):** Jake Pett, photographer, unless otherwise noted. Figure 7.6 (top left and right, bottom left), Alexander Yakovlev/fotolia.com; figure 7.6 (bottom right), © Human Kinetics; p. 119, Hulton Archive/Getty Images; Chapter 10 opener, courtesy of Lee K Choo; p. 148, AP Photo/Bizuayehu Tesfaye; figure 10.2, courtesy of José Limón Dance Company, photographer Walter Strate; figure 10.4, courtesy of Pat Berrett, photographer; figure 12.1, reprinted, by permission, from D. Krasnow et al., 2012, "Examination of weight transfer strategies during the execution of grand battement devant at the barre, in the center, and traveling," *Medical Problems of Performing Artists*, 27(2): 74-84; figure 12.4, photo and image from a study by Krasnow, Wilmerding, Stecyk, Wyon, and Koutedakis 2012; p. 227, courtesy of Lee K Choo; p. 235, Canadian Contemporary Dance Theatre performing *Nine Person Precision Ball Passing*, by Charles Moulton. Photo by David Hou; p. 263, photos from a study by Krasnow, Wilmerding, Stecyk, Wyon, and Koutedakis 2012; p. 270, courtesy of Lee K Choo, **Photo Asset Manager:** Laura Fitch; **Photo Production Manager:** Jason Allen; **Art Manager:** Kelly Hendren; **Illustrations:** © Human Kinetics, unless otherwise noted; **Printer:** Edwards Brothers Malloy

Printed in the United States of America   10 9 8 7 6 5 4 3 2 1

The paper in this book is certified under a sustainable forestry program.

Human Kinetics
Website: www.HumanKinetics.com

United States: Human Kinetics, P.O. Box 5076, Champaign, IL 61825-5076
800-747-4457
e-mail: humank@hkusa.com

Canada: Human Kinetics, 475 Devonshire Road Unit 100, Windsor, ON N8Y 2L5
800-465-7301 (in Canada only)
e-mail: info@hkcanada.com

Europe: Human Kinetics, 107 Bradford Road, Stanningley, Leeds LS28 6AT, United Kingdom
+44 (0) 113 255 5665
e-mail: hk@hkeurope.com

Australia: Human Kinetics, 57A Price Avenue, Lower Mitcham, South Australia 5062
08 8372 0999
e-mail: info@hkaustralia.com

New Zealand: Human Kinetics, P.O. Box 80, Torrens Park, South Australia 5062
0800 222 062
e-mail: info@hknewzealand.com

E5990

Contents

When dancers perform, they often demonstrate impressive skills that seem far removed from ordinary movement. However, these skills have more in common with ordinary movement than awed audience members may realize. Simple skills such as walking, riding a bike, and brushing your hair share basic motor control principles with complex dance activities such as multiple pirouettes, large jumps and leaps, rhythmic tap dance sequences, falls to the floor, and lifts. To develop these complex skills, dancers must dedicate years of practice and receive support from teachers, artistic directors, choreographers, and other movement practitioners. In recent decades, research in the fields of motor development, motor control, and motor learning has begun to influence understanding of dance practice and how to enhance the training of dancers. While some dance training environments have welcomed new research information, others have been reluctant to shift emphasis, believing that doing so could compromise the artistic and challenging nature of the practice. This book bridges the gap between these two environments.

The first of its kind, this book introduces the foundations of the three areas of motor behavior—motor development, motor control, and motor learning—from the perspective of dance. It takes past and current research in motor learning and provides practical applications to dance instruction and performance. For example, research can inform dance teachers about the timing of introducing skills. When teachers understand how to introduce skills at appropriate developmental stages, they can create class plans that are better suited for their dance students. Research has also provided a more specific picture of how elite dancers perform dance skills, thus allowing teachers and dancers to refine methods of learning and to improve their skills. This book presents dance science and motor behavior theory in a way that enhances and complements current training and educational practices while preserving artistic values.

Purpose

Currently, no other text concerning the three areas of motor behavior exists specifically for dancers. While many dance texts embrace some of the scientific principles of motor behavior, none offers a comprehensive treatise of this important information for the dance community. The motor behavior field has a unique role in the scientific studies of human behavior in that it expressly studies the profound connections of the musculoskeletal system (the muscles and bones that create movement) and the nervous system (the brain and its pathways to and from the body). Previously a dualism existed in scientific thought that treated the body and the brain as separate entities. Current thinking recognizes the continuous interweaving of physical and neurological functions. As dance training evolves and the interest in the mind–body connection develops, the knowledge of motor behavior is increasingly significant to the dance field. The study of motor behavior can assist dancers in learning and mastering new skills and in improving efficiency and integration of known skills, especially considering the complexity of dance practice and the ever-expanding array of dance styles and forms. Dancers and teachers can better understand movement from a scientific perspective, and motor behavior is essential in supporting this process.

This book is written for collegiate undergraduate and graduate students taking courses in dance performance and movement studies, including those in education programs. Students with no prior experience in kinesiology, physiology, psychology, biomechanics, or other basic sciences will find the information in this book to be challenging yet accessible. Students focusing on somatic practices will also find this book to be an excellent complement to their studies. Additionally, it is written as a guide for dance teachers and artistic directors to assist them in optimizing their methods for sharing their work with students and dancers. The book can inform anyone in dance and dance education about how the young dancer develops motor skills, how dancers control movement on all levels, and, most important, how motor skills are best taught and learned.

The content of this book covers motor development, motor control, and motor learning as they pertain to dance practice and dance training. The content is organized in this order so that the student begins with the early years of training and skill development, moves through the most current knowledge of how the brain and nervous system perceive the environment and control movement, and ends with the best ideas about learning and teaching dance movement. The theories, history, and basic concepts of these three interrelated fields of study are described in terms applicable to dancers, with examples from common dance practice settings and solutions for the training setting. Content is drawn from the broader motor behavior literature and distilled through the dance lens. We have examined both theoretical and practice-based research, and we present a straightforward and accessible text. We have chosen not to disturb the flow of the text with ongoing justifications, references, and dialogue concerning conflicting research conclusions. However, we have ensured that all of the material and final recommendations are supported by available research.

Organization

This book is organized into three sections. It begins with an overview of motor behavior and a brief history of somatic practices (chapter 1).

Somatic education has been a crucial component in bringing an awareness of motor learning ideas to the dance field; as such, it deserves special attention in a text for dancers. First, somatic practices provide an opportunity for dancers to work in a state of heightened awareness of sensory experiences and to explore novel options of how movement can be executed. Second, somatic practices can encourage periods of rest in a dense schedule of dance practice, which can foster consolidation of learning and potentially reduce fatigue-related problems.

Part I covers motor development from birth to early adulthood. A synopsis of the history and theories of motor development appears in chapter 2 so that the practical work in later chapters has a sound foundation. Following the theoretical framework, the study of postural control and balance (chapter 3) begins the in-depth examination of the motor development stages, because they underlie all dynamic dance movement. When dancers consider the idea of balancing, they think about skills such as balances on one leg, balances on the hands, and balances en pointe. However, all movement, especially movement in space, is a constant transition from one balance to the next and requires ongoing postural adjustments. Following the topic of balance control is an extensive look at the development of locomotor skills (chapter 4). All children first learn basic traveling skills such as walking, running, galloping, hopping, and skipping. Chapter 4 investigates these foundational locomotor skills and how they underlie a wide range of complex dance-specific skills such as combinations of elevation steps, traveling turns, and moving through space, coordinating multi-limb and multi-rhythmic steps. The final skills that develop in childhood and adolescence are the ballistic skills (chapter 5), which are probably the most difficult to teach and to learn in dance. This select group of skills includes athletic activities such as throwing and kicking, but the discussion in the text focuses on dance activities such as grand battement and frappé in classical dance, sharp and forceful movements in street dance, and zapateado in flamenco.

Part II explores motor control and the way that movement is planned, initiated, and finally executed. While dancers focus almost exclusively on muscles and joints when considering how movement occurs, it is essential that they understand the profound role that the nervous system plays in dance training. Chapter 6 discusses the brain and the central and peripheral nervous systems and explains how the nervous system organizes the coordination of movement. The text then moves to the important topics of attention and performance (chapter 7), with a particular focus on varying capacities for attention, and the effects of anxiety and states of arousal on dance performance. The text then investigates two different aspects of movement organization and control. The first emphasizes perception and the sensory systems—that is, how the senses such as sight, hearing, and touch receive information, which is then integrated into movement planning and responses (chapter 8). The second emphasizes central contributions to motor control (movement patterns developed in the brain that control movement) from the simplicity of walking and running to the complexity of high-level elite dance skills (chapter 9). The final chapter in part II, chapter 10 begins with an exploration of speed and accuracy of movement and how these two movement concepts interact. The chapter concludes with a discussion of coordination, rhythm, and musicality.

Part III investigates aspects and methods of motor learning for dancers of all ages. As with part I, it begins with the history and theories of motor learning, the stages of learning from beginner to elite dancers, and a look at learning styles (chapter 11). This broad-based knowledge prepares you for the practical applications to dance training that follow. The book then explores a wide variety of instructional strategies, including demonstration (modeling), verbal instruction, verbal cues, and feedback. It includes an extended discussion of how to determine the best approaches for learning dance skills, including the timing and frequency of feedback and the content of feedback (chapter 12). A study of motivation follows (chapter 13), encouraging you to consider ways to stimulate and inspire the dancer, suggesting optimal ways to structure dance classes to support

self-esteem and skill mastery. The book then introduces various conditions of practice, how variability enhances the learning experience, and the various methods of practice that enrich this experience (chapter 14). Additionally, the text examines dance-specific conditions, such as mirror use and improvisation, and how they can hinder or aid learning in dance practice. As explored in chapter 15, learning is measured in two ways: retention (how much dancers remember) and transfer (or how the learning of one skill influences the learning of a related skill or performance in a different setting). You will learn strategies for improving memory and the recall of dance skills and sequences, and how to learn skills in the most effective way to transfer them to a broad range of situations. Finally, the book describes modalities of mental practice and imagery and explains their uses in dance performance (chapter 16). This chapter encourages you to take a deeper look at somatic practice and its valuable contribution to the understanding of imagery and motor learning in dance.

Conclusion

Throughout each chapter, examples relating directly to dance practice are described. These practical examples use a variety of dance forms, including modern dance, ballet, contemporary dance, jazz, musical theater, tap, flamenco, classical Indian dance, street dance, and contact improvisation. These examples are designed to illuminate the theoretical aspects of motor behavior and to assist dancers and dance teachers in developing their practice and strategies. This text presents a unique exposition of motor development, motor control, and motor learning, providing a depth of understanding previously not offered in traditional dance training. It is not the intention to fundamentally alter or diminish the rich and varied landscape of dance training as it is presented in today's studios, colleges, universities, and professional training programs. Rather, this book adds to a wide palette of tools and strategies for learning the elegant artistry of dance.

Acknowledgments

There are so many people, past and present, who have contributed to our book. We would like to thank our families for their ongoing support of our work and the many teachers, researchers, and writers through the years who have inspired us. We would like to acknowledge Dr. Blake Martin for his invaluable contributions to the content and the visual images in the book, and for his wit through the process. We want to thank Jake Pett, New Mexico Dance Academy, and all of the dancers for making the photography possible. Finally, we would like to thank the staff at Human Kinetics for their assistance and trust in creating this work. It was a long journey, and we were glad to have so many people with us along the way.

Chapter 1
Foundations of Motor Behavior

*H*uman movement in the form of dance has existed for thousands of years. Relatively recently in human history, instructors and coaches began training people to enhance movement skills, and scientists and researchers have become interested in the study of movement. Dance teachers who work with children may have explored when to introduce certain aspects of training to their students. These teachers may have differing opinions on the subject. For example, teachers differ in determining at what age ballet students should start work at the barre or when they should start pointe work. Many dance schools differ in when they offer modern and contemporary dance classes, basing these decisions on their ideas about when dancers are ready to approach torso movement off the vertical—that is, movement with the spine bending in any direction away from the vertical axis. Other teachers and researchers have focused their attention on trying to understand precisely how elite skills are best executed. For example, for many decades people believed that deeper pliés resulted in higher jumps, but research has revealed that this is not the case. Even views about the best methods of instruction are varied. Some teachers emphasize repetition in the learning process, while others spend more time analyzing and describing new movements. All of these issues exist under the umbrella of motor behavior.

Motor behavior has a unique place in the human movement sciences. It is specifically interested in the connection between the mind and the body. This connection includes how the brain perceives, plans, and causes movement, and how the senses send essential information to the brain about the surrounding environment. Vision is a powerful tool in balance. To understand how powerful it is, try doing a simple one-legged balance with your eyes closed. Hearing has an important role, too. Consider how an urban dancer relies on the sounds of the music to establish the physical rhythm of the steps. In addition, the sense of touch is fundamental to the movement experience in contact improvisation. This two-way communication between the brain and the senses is constantly in play as you dance. Beyond the interplay of the brain and the senses lies an important feature called *focus* (attention). Awareness during learning and executing movement will critically affect how well a dancer will do. In somatic work, all of these aspects of how the brain functions during movement are called the *mind–body connection.* While many dancers have never formally studied motor behavior, most have some exposure to somatic education. The somatic practices have been the doorway for the dance community to understand just how essential awareness and the mind–body connection are in dance training. Teachers of dance technique with backgrounds in somatic education (somatic practitioners) were often the ones who initially added dance science courses into the broader dance curriculum. For this reason, this book examines somatic practices in far more depth than any current text on motor behavior.

Defining Motor Behavior

Motor behavior is a broad term that covers all aspects of human movement, including the fields of motor development, motor control, and motor learning. Each of these fields deals with a different perspective within motor behavior. **Motor development** involves three characteristics: (1) It describes ongoing change in movement function and ability; (2) it examines these changes throughout stages of life, from prenatal to senior years; and (3) developments are progressive and irreversible, and they result from changes within the person as well as from environmental interactions (Haywood & Getchell, 2009). **Motor control** explores how the nervous system organizes and directs the muscles and joints to produce coordinated movement, and how sensory information from the body (such as vision and hearing) and from the environment around the body is used to accomplish this task (Schmidt & Lee, 2011). **Motor learning** examines changes in a person's skill capabilities that are caused by experience or practice rather than development. These changes cannot be measured directly; rather, they are inferred by alterations in performance and are relatively permanent (Magill, 2011).

Dance teachers use motor learning principles while instructing students in a class.

Understanding motor behavior can enhance dance training. For those teaching young children through adolescents, knowledge of motor development is crucial in knowing when and how to introduce new skills. An understanding of motor control gives insight into how dancers perform elite skills, which allows educators to teach more effectively. For those teaching dancers of any age and any skill level, various strategies of motor learning—such as demonstration, feedback, and motivation—are essential tools.

Historical Development of Dance Pedagogy

Historically, dance pedagogy was primarily concerned with the structure of dance class and appropriate instructions about teaching dance vocabulary. Only the rare teacher considered the scientific basis of movement, how learning actually occurs, and how teaching methods could reflect individual learning strategies. In early dance programs in educational institutions of the 1920s and '30s, such as those created by Margaret H'Doubler, Bird Larson,

and Gertrude Colby, dancers learned anatomy because these programs were housed in physical education departments. As dance expanded in the educational setting, programs appeared in a variety of departments, including fine arts, theater, and music. Teachers were regularly hired from the professional dance environment, and often programs developed a conservatory approach. In the conservatory environment, the emphasis turned toward technique, choreography, and performance, and less time was devoted to understanding the dancer's unique anatomical structure or learning process.

A shift in pedagogical thinking occurred with the introduction of somatic practices, which were initially called the *body therapies* in summer dance intensives in the 1960s. One such dance intensive was the American Dance Festival, under the direction of Martha Myers, dean of the American Dance Festival School from 1969 to 2000. Somatic practices encouraged an integration of science into movement practice by introducing the process of exploring one's own anatomical capabilities and the act of acknowledging the nervous system as critical components for change. Academic post-secondary institutions and professional dance schools began to add the study of motor behavior to pedagogy courses to better prepare teachers for the challenges of student expectations and to recognize the variety of learning styles. It is now fairly common to find somatic practices and supplementary training based on somatic work in a variety of dance training settings. These methods broaden the learning environment and increase the tools available to the dance educator, particularly as they relate to motor learning.

Dance is unique in that it is both an art form and an athletic activity. In its early days in post-secondary education institutions, dance was housed in both fine arts and physical education departments. The study of motor behavior and how it affects physical development and learning has come much later to dance than to other athletic activities. Dance artists and educators were often wary of allowing any scientific analysis or viewpoints to inform teaching practices for a variety of reasons, including fear that it might interfere with the artistic mystique or because of a lack of understanding of scientific principles. The first major inroad to dance training from a motor learning perspective came from the influence of the somatic practices. Somatic education moved away from the rote, one-size-fits-all approach to skill learning and focused on the mind–body connection and individual experience. Because this evolution has been a major aspect of dance and its relationship to motor behavior, special attention is given in this text to the somatic practices.

Somatic Practice

The term *somatic* literally means "of the body"; it derives from the Greek word *soma*. In the 1970s, Thomas Hanna was the first to apply the term to movement education. Hanna described somatics as "the art and science of the inter-relational process between awareness, biological function and environment, all three factors being understood as a synergistic: the field of Somatics." Martha Eddy, the founder and director of the Center for Kinesthetic Education, defines three branches of somatics: somatic

psychology, somatic bodywork, and somatic movement. This latter branch has most affected dance education and is most closely connected to theories of motor learning. While it is not possible to go into detail in this chapter about all of the forms and developments in somatic movement and somatic education, this section provides an overview of these systems and their relevance to dance education.

While each of the somatic practices has a unique approach, they all share certain aspects. All place a focus on breath, alignment, and efficiency of movement. The personal and kinesthetic experiences are emphasized. Communication from the instructor or practitioner often includes guidance through touch as well as words, and experiential anatomy is a common tool. **Experiential anatomy** is a creative and practice-based learning approach using movement, touch, and other art forms to embody the understanding of anatomical principles. The issue of patterning for new movement choices (often called *movement reeducation*) is central.

Glenna Batson is an internationally known dance artist, educator, and physical therapist. She has been a recognized Alexander Technique teacher since 1989. She integrates dance, somatics, neuroscience, and rehabilitation medicine. She defines three areas of exploration in the somatic process: (1) novel learning context, (2) sensory attunement, and (3) augmented rest. The novel learning context emphasizes slowing down in order to focus attention on sensory information such as breath and muscle tension. It allows for personal exploration and a noncompetitive approach, and it encourages discovery of poor alignment and inefficient movement habits. From a motor learning perspective, this process can permit the nervous system to reorganize habitual patterns of muscle use that are interfering with effective movement. Sensory attunement focuses awareness on how one is doing the movement and not the form of the movement itself. This encourages shifting focus from the external references such as mirrors to the internal perception of movement. Sensory attunement is crucial to the process of becoming aware of how movement is experienced within the body's internal landscape, and is essential if change is going to occur. Augmented rest incorporates periods of rest into physical activity to assist in learning and retention of material and in processing new information.

Early Practitioners

In the early 1980s, Martha Myers published a series of articles in *Dance Magazine* highlighting four innovators who are considered the pioneers in somatic practice and whose systems are still commonly taught today: F. Mathias Alexander, Moshe Feldenkrais, Lulu Sweigard, and Irmgard Bartenieff. To further explore these innovators and their methods in greater detail, find their biographies in the websites listed in the following paragraphs.

F.M. Alexander developed his system as a response to his personal problems with chronic laryngitis. His system is known as Alexander Technique (www.alexandertechnique.com; figure 1.1). Alexander Technique is not a set of specific exercises; rather, it is a way of observing one's patterns in daily life and in skilled activity. This approach is sometimes referred to as *mindfulness.* The method addresses problems in posture by examining the relationship between the head, neck, and back and working toward a better balance between the large superficial muscles and the deeper postural muscles to rid the body of unnecessary tension. It allows

artists in many fields, including dance, to move with greater ease, balance, and coordination in any movement style or form. In the years since its development, musicians and actors have become particularly interested in Alexander Technique. It is taught at many prominent schools, including the Juilliard School of Performing Arts in New York, The New School for Drama in New York (formerly the Actors Studio Drama School), the Royal College of Music in London, The Boston Conservatory of Music, and The Royal Conservatory of Music in Toronto.

The Feldenkrais Method (www.feldenkrais .com) has two components. The hands-on work is called Functional Integration, in which the practitioner guides the participant through gentle touch. The active movement system in the work is called Awareness Through Movement (ATM). Unlike Alexander Technique, the Feldenkrais Method is a structured method of movement exercises in which participants are guided to pay attention to sensory feedback as they execute specific movements through a small range of motion. Its main goal is to reduce pain and movement limits and to enhance movement range and capacity. The movements often resemble those of an infant, explored with reduced effort and with a sense of play. Movement exercises are balanced with augmented

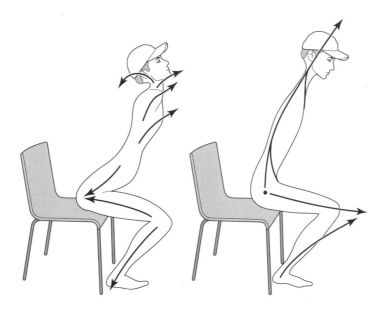

Figure 1.1 Alexander Technique: improving movement patterns in daily life.

rest, and imagery is sometimes employed. Hundreds of ATM lessons exist, ranging from very simple to difficult exercises in both structure and physical demand. This work is supported by systems theory (to be covered in chapter 2), in which practitioners can accomplish changes in motor behavior in an environment of exploration and by interrupting old patterns so that new ones can emerge.

Lulu Sweigard's method is termed *Ideokinesis* (www.ideokinesis.com). Its emphasis is almost entirely on imagery and not on movement exercises. Sweigard proposed that the imagery process is used to repattern the neuromuscular system to create new alignment and mechanical balance, and to encourage movement reeducation. Sweigard was taught and inspired by Mabel Todd, who suggested that reducing strain may minimize causes of injury to the body. Sweigard created the work termed *nine lines of movement* (figure 1.2), which documented her research and clarified specific goals for changes in alignment. She suggested that this visualization work be done with no movement to allow the neural system to eliminate unwanted tension. More research exists about Ideokinesis than about any other somatic practice. Seven decades of sport psychology research support the positive effects

of visualization and mental practice. Sweigard taught for decades in the Dance Division at the Juilliard School of the Performing Arts in New York, and the dancers attended her posture labs on a regular basis. Sweigard's work has had a profound impact on dance training. Her work has altered the language that teachers use in the dance class and informed teachers about movement efficiency through better alignment.

Irmgard Bartenieff (www.connectedmovement.com) was a dancer and choreographer who applied her training with Rudolf Laban to the field of physical therapy. She was a pioneer in the development of dance therapy. She was a dancer, cross-cultural scholar, and physiotherapist who worked with people with polio to improve their movement efficiency. In her early years as a therapist, she called her movement exercise *correctives.* Unlike the typical physical therapy of her time, her system emphasized body integration (also known as *total body connectivity*), which sees the body as a whole and acknowledges that all of the body parts constantly influence each other. Her series of exercises, called the Bartenieff Fundamentals, have become known as the Basic 6. They include two preparations (breath preparation and rocking preparation) and six exercises: (1) thigh lift (hip flexion), (2) pelvic

1. Lengthen the spine downward

2. Shorten the distance between the mid front pelvis and the twelfth thoracic vertebra

3. From the top of the sternum to the top of the spine

4. Narrow the rib cage

5. Widen the back of the pelvis

6. Narrow the front of the pelvis

7. From the center of the knee to the center of the femoral joint

8. From the big toe to the heel

9. Lengthen the central axis of the trunk upward

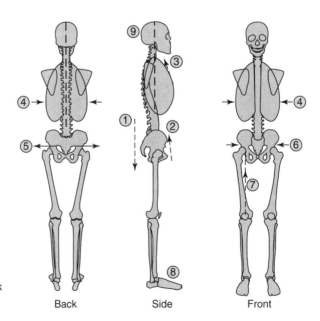

Back   Side   Front

Figure 1.2 Sweigard's nine lines of movement.

Reprinted from L.E. Sweigard, 1974, *Human movement potential: Its ideokinetic facilitation* (Allegro Editions).

forward shift, (3) pelvic lateral shift, (4) body half, (5) diagonal knee reach (knee drops), and (6) arm circles with diagonal sit-up. A typical class would start with easeful floor exercises and progress to complex phrases that change levels and move through space. It is probably the most physically active of the four traditional somatic practices. Central to her work are improvisation, breath support, and developmental processes. Other principles include core support, initiation and sequencing, spatial intent, effort intent, and weight transfer.

Additional Somatic Practices

Several additional somatic practices evolved from these early methods. Each of these practitioners worked with one or more of the originators in the field and found their own voice and methodology through somatic principles:

- Judith Aston and Dorothy Nolte—Rolf Movement Integration
- Bonnie Bainbridge Cohen—Body-Mind Centering
- Emilie Conrad—continuum movement
- Irene Dowd—neuromuscular retraining
- Sondra Horton Fraleigh—Shin Somatics

- Peggy Hackney—Integrated Movement Studies (IMS)
- Anna Halprin—expressive arts healing
- Joan Skinner—Skinner Releasing Technique (SRT)
- Elaine Summers—Kinetic Awareness
- Nancy Topf—Topf Technique

Each individual will discover a different approach within the range of somatic practices that appeals to the personality and movement preferences of that person. The goal would be to explore a variety of approaches and select the one that is most beneficial.

Systems With Somatic Influences

In addition, two other developments are related to somatic practices. One is the interest in Eastern movement forms such as tai chi chuan, yoga, and qi gong. These forms share advantages for dance training that are embedded in somatic practice, such as focus on breath, self-awareness, balance, slowing the pace of movement, and alignment. It is not unusual to find that some of the early somatic innovators studied one or more of these systems. For example, Bartenieff was involved with qi gong. Many professional

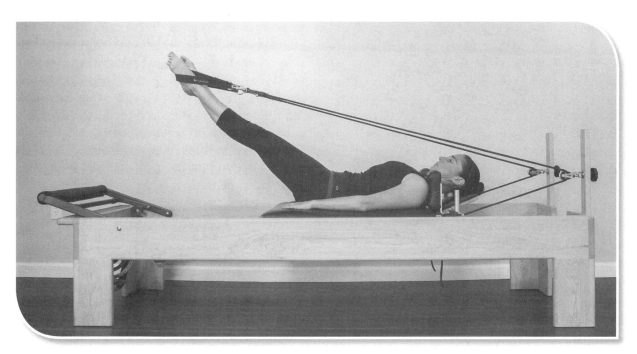

The Pilates Reformer can help dancers develop appropriate dance-specific motor control.

dancers practice these movement forms to supplement their primary dance training.

The other development is the evolution of Western-based somatic practice and the exploration of how it might merge with more active conditioning systems. These systems include C-I Training, Franklin Method, Gyrokinesis and Gyrotonic, Pilates (seen in the photo on the previous page), and Zena Rommett Floor-Barre Technique. While these systems are different from each other, they all incorporate principles of somatic practice into the work, and they focus on individual intention rather than external form.

Developed by Donna Krasnow, C-I (conditioning with imagery) Training (www.citraining.com) merges work from various conditioning systems and physiotherapy exercises with imagery and awareness from the somatic practices, primarily the work of Sweigard and Bartenieff. Exercises are done primarily on the floor and are set to musical rhythm to encourage transfer to dance performance. It emphasizes breath, whole-body integration and connectedness, and core support. Eric Franklin (www.franklinmethod.com) worked with Irene Dowd and Andre Bernard, and he developed his own method called the Franklin Method. It teaches dynamic alignment and using imagery and the brain to enhance function.

Gyrokinesis and Gyrotonic (www.gyrotonic.com) were developed by Juliu Horvath. He combined aspects of yoga, dance, gymnastics, and swimming to create these systems. Gyrokinesis is done on mats and stools, while Gyrotonic uses apparatus such as the Pulley Tower and the Jumping Stretching Board. Movements are spiraling and sequential, emphasizing awareness, breath, fluidity, and core-supported movement. Pilates (www.pilatesmethod alliance.org) is probably the most widely known method. Developed by Joseph Pilates in the first half of the 20th century, it emphasizes spinal and pelvic alignment, breath work, core support, and improved coordination. Pilates class sequences may use both mat work and various apparatus such as the Reformer and the Cadillac. Zena Rommett Floor-Barre Technique (www.floor-barre.org) was developed by Zena Rommett, a former dancer and dance teacher. Floor-Barre is executed on the floor and focuses on correct alignment and muscle efficiency. The family of somatic practices and related forms can be seen in figure 1.3.

Influences of Motor Behavior Studies and Somatic Practice on Dance Training

The somatic practices, and subsequently the study of motor control and learning, have had a pronounced influence on dance training. Early dance training focused on teaching dance vocabulary and preparing dancers to learn choreographic material for stage. Limited attention was given to teaching correct alignment and principles of anatomy and motor control, and there was almost no clear biomechanical application to dance practice. When Martha Myers introduced somatic practices (then known as *body therapies*) to the American Dance Festival, a shift in teaching methods began to occur. Myers brought practitioners of Alexander Technique, Feldenkrais Method, Ideokinesis, and Bartenieff Fundamentals to the American Dance Festival, founded in 1934, for several

The C-I Training system combines conditioning and imagery work to assist dancers in developing motor control that is useful in dance practice.

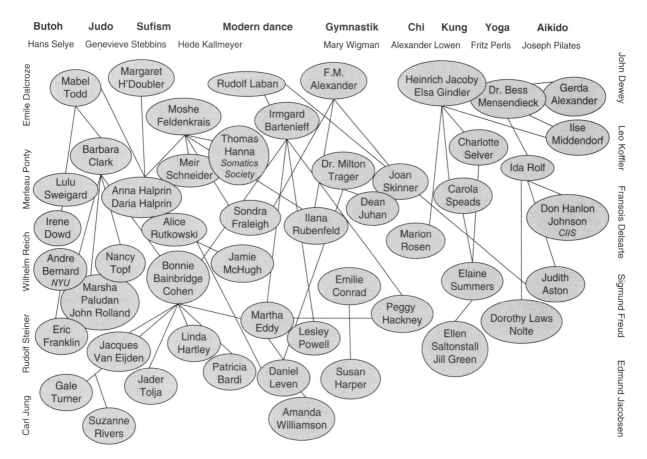

Figure 1.3 Founders of somatic movement trainings and their influences.

Reprinted from M. Eddy, 2009, "A brief history of somatic practices and dance: Historical development of the field of somatic education and its relationship to dance," *Journal of Dance and Somatic Practices* 1(1): 5-27. By permission of Martha Eddy.

summers. As a consequence of this program and other new and experimental approaches to teaching dance, dance teachers began to instruct dancers on correct alignment and movement practices, and eventually dance sciences and somatic education were introduced in dance training and academic settings.

Teachers such as Glenna Batson, Martha Eddy, Sylvie Fortin, Pamela Matt, Jennifer Scanlon, and Ann Vachon introduced somatic education directly into the dance technique class. Although they were not using somatic practices directly, other teachers began altering the focus of their classes to incorporate some of the somatic ideas. These influences began a shift in some technique classes from a rote, practice-driven, competitive setting to a motor learning laboratory that encourages individual exploration, problem solving, and experiential learning.

In addition to somatic education, educational settings started offering courses in dance

science in ever-growing numbers. Many of these courses focus on alignment and anatomy, but the underlying concepts of motor behavior are often included. Dancers are being instructed on the importance of the mind–body connection and how the brain is central to how the body moves. The physical facility of the dancer—flexibility, strength, endurance, joint structure, and general fitness—is certainly crucial, but how the brain and the body speak to each other is essential to the dancer's capacity for movement and the dancer's ability to learn new movement patterns. Teachers are relying on motor learning principles in the delivery of the dance class material. By expanding their strategies to include such techniques as better class organization, sound progressions of skill development, and a variety of correction styles, they are incorporating some of the best of what the science of motor learning has to offer.

In addition, conferences and journals have begun to emphasize new approaches and methods for training dancers. Arising in the 1980s and 1990s, conferences and journals devoted to issues of dancers and performing artists brought together educators, medical practitioners, and researchers to discuss how to improve the training and treatment of artists from the scientific perspective. The wealth of research and knowledge in the field of motor behavior from the sports realm began to infuse the dance science and education communities and to stimulate research and discussion of the uses of motor behavior theory in dance training. Today, the content of this text will inform teachers and dancers about the theories and discoveries in motor behavior and about how dance training and performance can be enhanced through this knowledge.

Summary

Motor behavior covers all aspects of human movement, including the fields of motor development, motor control, and motor learning. Historically, dance pedagogy focused on class structure and teaching dance vocabulary. With the introduction of somatic practices, dance training shifted to incorporate an emphasis on the process of self-exploration of one's anatomical capabilities and an acknowledgment of the nervous system as critical components for change. The early somatic practitioners are F. Matthias Alexander, Moshe Feldenkrais, Lulu Sweigard, and Irmgard Bartenieff. Later developments by teachers such as Bonnie Bainbridge Cohen, Irene Dowd, Peggy Hackney, and Joan Skinner drew from early systems and developed their own methods. Other teachers found ways to merge somatic principles with conditioning systems. Both somatic education and motor behavior have influenced dance training and education. Teachers and dancers now recognize that the physical facility of the dancer is certainly crucial, but how the brain and the body speak to each other is essential to the dancer's capacity for movement and the dancer's ability to learn new movement patterns.

Part 1

Motor Development

Chapter 2
Theories of Motor Development

*M*any people in various professions share an interest in motor development. Medical practitioners want to understand their young patients' stages of growth and want to know how to recognize delayed or atypical development. Schoolteachers can benefit from understanding the impact of motor development on cognitive function and learning. Anyone who trains young people in a sporting activity—such as in group sports, gymnastics, or figure skating—has a vested interest in understanding motor development. Dance teachers regularly use theories and ideas from motor development, whether they do it consciously or intuitively. For example, dance teachers of young children understand that they cannot teach skipping before the age when children are developmentally ready. They also need to understand when it is appropriate to teach dancers complex movements such as the fouetté sauté, which builds on the hopping ability while turning and executing leg gestures.

The field of motor development has been evolving for many years. If you study the history of the field, you can understand the full breadth and depth of knowledge of motor development. It is essential for dance teachers and other professionals who teach motor skills to accrue a broad theoretical background in motor development as well as in motor control and learning. Through this knowledge, they can understand the current research in these areas and apply strategies and methods in the practical setting.

In order to understand how motor skills develop from early years throughout a lifetime, several theories have been proposed over the past two centuries. Theories of motor development provide a context—a way to describe or define the complex process of acquiring human movement skills from the basics of sitting, standing, and walking to the changes in neuromotor behavior that occur at the end of a lifetime. Theories of motor development emerge from corresponding theories of motor control. Motor development is essentially the story of how humans develop and maintain motor control across the life span. In the sports literature, motor development is usually found in a separate textbook from motor learning and control. This textbook covers the entire spectrum of motor behavior for dancers and dance teachers. The developmental issues are especially important for dance teachers because of the young age at which most dancers begin their dance training. Therefore, this text begins with a look at motor development. The basis of the material in this chapter is what is now called *dynamic systems approach*, also known more simply as *systems theory*. In order to present a complete picture of how this theory evolved over time, the chapter provides a brief summary of the history of motor development theories and highlights some of the primary researchers in the field.

Early Theories of Motor Development

Motor development has its foundation in research dating back to the late 1800s. While some of this early work may seem simplistic by today's standards, the first pioneers in the field were able to construct broad and insightful theories with little previous science to support their ideas and using poor equipment to observe and analyze their research findings. Their dedication, imagination, and generosity and their early theories provide the underpinnings of current thinking about motor development. The following review of the early theories of motor development sheds light on today's concepts. Some of the earliest theories are in fact theories of motor control, but their importance in understanding motor development is paramount, and therefore they are included in this discussion.

Reflex Theory

Reflex theory is one of the earliest theories of motor control. This theory attempts to explain motor control based on the idea of movement responses as reflex-based responses. In simple terms, a reflex is an involuntary movement that occurs because of a particular stimulus. A common example is withdrawing your hand from a hot stove before the sensation of heat consciously registers. Sir Charles Scott Sherrington, an early and eminent researcher who described and studied reflexes, developed the hypothesis that reflexes act as building blocks of more complex movement. Sherrington published a series of lectures called "The Integrative Action of the Nervous System: A Centenary Appreciation" that he gave at Yale University in 1904, described in detail in Robert Burke's article on Sherrington in the journal *Brain*. In these lectures he summarized two decades of his research. Sherrington's view was that reflexes acted in sequence like chains and that the summation of a group of reflexes defined complex movement. Sherrington's work affected the course of neurophysiology, the area of scientific study that deals with the function of the structures of the brain and the nervous system. His work still influences theories of motor control today.

Researchers now recognize limitations to Sherrington's theory of motor control. For example, reflex theory cannot explain movement that happens in the absence of stimuli, such as the rhythmic sway of children during play. Nor can it adequately explain movement too fast for sensory information to trigger subsequent movement (such as typing) or certain rapid steps in tap dancing. It also does not account for people's ability to override reflexes, such as the ability of a dancer to continue dancing in extreme pain from injury. Finally, reflex theory cannot explain how people produce novel, unexpected movement seen in the improvisational and choreographic processes. While these examples are primarily limitations from a motor control perspective, they suggest that motor development has influences coming from a broader perspective than suggested in reflex theory.

Hierarchical Theory (Reflex/Hierarchical Theory)

Sherrington did extensive work on reflexes and motor control, but his work did not really propose a complete theory of how motor development occurs over the life span. Based on Sherrington's work, researchers studying human motor development began to propose the **hierarchical theory**, also referred to as **reflex/hierarchical theory**. This theory states that the nervous system is organized in a hierarchy and that as a baby develops, reflexes emerge in a certain order. Motor control emerges from reflexes nested at different hierarchical levels of the nervous system. As each reflex appears, the previous one no longer dominates as the source of movement control. For example, a reflex known as the asymmetric tonic neck reflex is present at 1 month old. When the child's head is turned to the side, the arm on that side straightens and the opposite arm bends. Researchers believed that this reflex preceded the development of hand–eye coordination. By 4 months old, the asymmetric tonic neck reflex begins to disappear. Instead the baby exhibits the righting reactions, which orient the head in space and help to keep the child upright. Figure 2.1 illustrates reflex/hierarchical theory, showing the progression of these reflexes as they appear in the early period of the child's life.

One of the researchers supporting reflex/hierarchical theory was neurologist John Hughlings Jackson, who claimed that the brain had higher, middle, and lower levels of control,

Children can develop motor skills through improvisation.

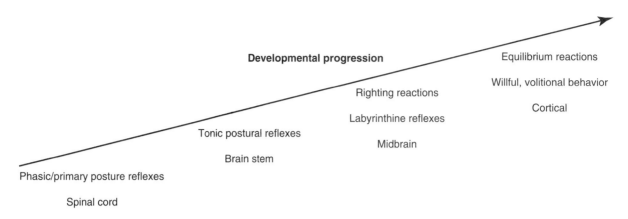

Figure 2.1 Reflex/hierarchical theory of motor development.

which were associated with various levels and areas of the brain. In this view, control is always top–down, never bottom–up. Together with neuropsychiatrists Sir David Ferrier and Sir James Crichton-Browne, Jackson was one of the founders of the influential journal *Brain*, which is still in publication today. Its inaugural issue was published in 1878.

Another researcher, Rudolf Magnus, found that lower-level reflexes occur in the adult only when higher (cortical) brain damage exists. Usually these lower-level reflexes would be inhibited, but the brain allows them to resurface when higher levels can no longer function. Neurologist Georg Schaltenbrand took the work of Magnus and described development in terms of the appearance and disappearance of reflexes in a set progression. He suggested that this process could be used to determine the neural age of a child. Stephan Weisz proposed a relationship between the development of reflexes and the natural stages of sitting, standing, and walking in the growing child.

Later researchers questioned the reflex/hierarchical theory because it failed to take into account differing development seen in children who have varying experiences and responses to an ever-changing environment and set of tasks. This exception is apparent in the advanced motor skills observed in very young children who receive elite training in dance, gymnastics, and other athletic endeavors. Reflex/hierarchical theory also failed to explain why lower-level reflexes were still in play in developed adults, such as withdrawing one's foot from a nail. This could be considered bottom–up action

and, according to the reflex/hierarchical theory, would not be present.

Maturational Perspective

Another theory that emphasizes the innate or genetic characteristics of the human system in motor development is known as **maturational perspective**, which was popular in the 1930s. Two of the early researchers in this field were Arnold Gesell and Myrtle McGraw. Both of these proponents of maturational perspective believed that the nervous system was the *one* system primarily responsible for the emergence of motor skills, and in fact no other system was significant. For example, while environment might play a role in the pacing of this development, it does not affect whether or not these skills will emerge. That occurrence is predetermined by the innate genetics of the person. While the influence of this perspective is still felt today, it is limited in its disregard of the multiple systems (such as cardiovascular, skeletal, endocrine, and muscular) that can affect development.

Information Processing Perspective

Another early motor development theory is called the **information processing perspective**, which looks at the brain as a computer that takes in information and processes it, with movement as the resulting output. Born in the 1970s, this theory was popular in physical education, emphasizing concepts such as feedback and knowledge of results, which are discussed in detail in chapter 12. The models designed in this theory are still of interest today because of the perspective they can provide about the most efficient output of the nervous system in determining movement patterns.

The information processing perspective has these four stages:

1. Thinking: This stage includes perception of the environment and storing of information.

2. Analysis of stimuli: This process adjusts new information through interpretation to complement previous experience.

3. Situational modification: In this stage, the person uses past experience to formulate a strategy for a new situation.

4. Obstacle evaluation: This stage allows the person to take into account any obstacles or problems that might be encountered. In the final stage, the current level of cognitive development and problem-solving abilities of the person will have an impact on how new situations are considered and managed.

While this theory can predict certain patterns of development, it lacks a broader perspec-

This child can explore imaginative ways to use a familiar toy.

tive that could explain some of the behaviors observed in developing children. In particular, because of its narrow perspective it cannot fully represent how the nervous system processes information during learning and development. One example is seeing a child use a toy in a new and imaginative way that is outside the child's experience or knowledge of that toy.

Behaviorism

During the first half of the 20th century, developmental theories were also evolving in the field of psychology. The basic tenet of **behaviorism** was that psychologists should focus on behavior that can be observed rather than try to understand or interpret what is happening in the mind. These theories influenced motor development theories. Two of the more prominent ones are discussed next.

Radical behaviorism was developed by Burrhus Frederic (B.F.) Skinner, who claimed that changes in behavior and learning result from reinforcing consequences, whether these consequences are positive or negative. Skinner was not interested in considering thinking, perception, or emotion. He conducted research on animals on operant conditioning (also called *operant response*). After the research subject had a response, Skinner delivered either reinforcement (positive) or punishment (negative) to affect future behavior.

Social learning theory was proposed by Albert Bandura. Bandura stated that people learn new information and movement skills by watching other people. He was particularly interested in the willingness of humans to imitate the behavior of others, especially aggression. Bandura defined certain steps in the learning process:

1. Attention: In order to learn any behavior, you must first pay attention. Negative mental states (sleepy, anxious, distracted) will be detriments to learning.

2. Retention: The learner must be able to retain (remember and later recall) what has been learned.

3. Reproduction: The observed behavior must be translated into action or behavior.

4. Motivation: There must be some reason that the learner wants to model the observed behavior.

Skinner, Bandura, and other behaviorists influenced the current theoretical approaches to motor development by bringing behavior, responses to others, and environment into the construct.

Current Theory of Motor Development: Ecological Perspective

With the rich background of reflex and hierarchical theories, maturational and information processing perspectives, and behaviorism in psychology, researchers in motor development began to think about ways to integrate all of these ideas into new models. They wanted to understand how development could be predetermined by reflexive and genetic factors and yet be responsive to the task and the surrounding environment. The contributions to the field described in this section have led to the current approaches in the understanding of life span motor development.

The recent approaches to the fields of motor development and motor control have roots in the 1960s with the work of James and Eleanor Gibson and continued to grow through the work of their students in the 1980s. The broad term for the resulting theories is the **ecological perspective**. It emphasizes the interactions between the individual, the environment, and the task, as illustrated in figure 2.2. This was the first time that the environment was considered as an important factor in motor development and control. In this view, actions need information from the environment (perceptual information) that is specific to the desired motor action.

The ecological perspective differs from the maturational perspective in two ways. First, it emphasizes that multiple systems can affect development and that the nervous system is not solely responsible for developmental changes. Second, because the influences on development continue throughout a lifetime, the ecological perspective sees motor development as occur-

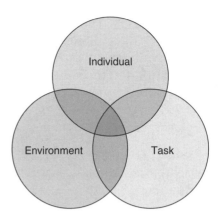

Figure 2.2 Ecological perspective.

ring throughout the entire life span, whereas the maturational approach sees it ending with the end of puberty.

In addition, the information processing perspective claims that all decisions are made from a central executive (the brain). However, in the ecological perspective, perception influences how muscles self-organize into groups, creating a much simpler and more efficient process, because fewer decisions are directed by higher brain centers. This can be observed in the organization of the muscles in the foot, ankle, knee, and hip in walking patterns, which are described in detail in chapter 4.

The ecological perspective has two branches. One focuses on motor coordination, and it is called the *dynamic systems approach* or, more simply, *systems theory*. The other is concerned with perception, and it is called the *perception–action approach*. This approach shifts the view of the nervous system and motor development from one of a reactive sensorimotor system to that of a perception–action system that satisfies the movement goals through investigation of the environment. The concepts supported by the two branches of the ecological perspective are shown in figure 2.3. The left side of the figure expresses the structural and coordinative aspects of movement, while the right side exhibits the perceptual factors that influence movement.

Dynamic Systems Approach

The **dynamic systems approach** began with the work of researchers such as Nikolai Bernstein, Peter Kugler, Scott Kelso, and Michael Turvey,

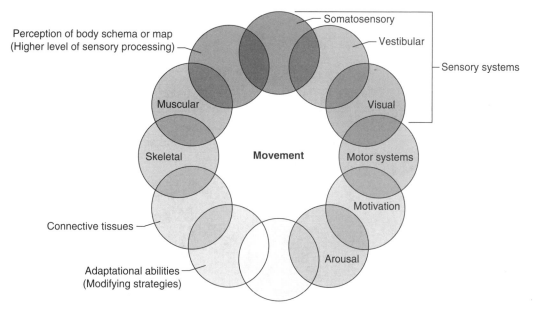

Figure 2.3 Ecological perspective: dynamic systems approach and perception–action approach.

who suggested that the human body's physical structure, in conjunction with the physical environment, constrains or restricts motor behavior. For example, even though adults are still capable of crawling, the structures of their lower extremities (hip, knee, ankle, foot) encourage walking instead. This phenomenon is sometimes called *spontaneous self-organization*. The researchers in the field call it *soft-assembled* rather than *hardwired*, because people do still have the flexibility to make choices if they want to alter their patterns of locomotion. Another way of saying it is that people are attracted to certain movement patterns rather than others, but the choices remain. You can still choose to crawl if you want to do so or if the environment compels this action (such as getting underneath a fence).

An important concept in systems theory is the idea of rate limiters (also called *controllers*). Rate limiters are any of the systems that contribute to the development of motor patterns. These limiters might include the muscular and skeletal systems, the sensory systems, or motivation. Because the various systems do not all develop at the same rate, any one of the systems might slow down the emergence of a motor pattern. A person will demonstrate a new skill, such as walking, when the slowest of the rate limiters reaches the appropriate level. In the case of walking, the infant's muscular strength must reach a certain level before the body can support weight and move through space. Similarly, a dancer cannot achieve a turn on one leg until she can achieve the appropriate body and limb position needed for the turn.

In terms of the lifespan perspective of systems theory, the rate limiters can work in reverse. When a system deteriorates to a critical point, movement function will be negatively affected. For example, when arthritis in the hip develops to a certain extent in the older dancer, high leg extensions will no longer be possible, even if the muscles surrounding the hip still have sufficient strength and flexibility.

Perception–Action Approach

The second branch of the ecological perspective is the **perception–action approach**, which states that the development of perception and the development of movement cannot be separated. This implies that one cannot study movement without considering the environment. James J. Gibson described the function that an object can provide, calling it *affordance*. For example, the floor is horizontal and affords a person a walking surface, whereas a wall affords a place to lean. It should be noted that when people are determining whether or not an

Dancers can choose to do movement material on the floor even if it would normally be done standing.

object provides affordance, they make subjective determinations. If an adult and a toddler approach a flight of stairs, the adult will walk up the stairs, but the toddler may choose to crawl if the stairs are too steep for walking. The term *body scaling* is used to describe this use of intrinsic (relative to the individual's body) rather than extrinsic (objective) dimensions. Similarly, temporary conditions can alter one's perception of affordance. If a dancer is seriously injured, he may decide that normal walking up a flight of stairs is not possible, and he may alter his locomotor pattern to step up with one foot and then step together on that stair.

Impact of the Ecological Perspective

Over time, the ecological perspective has become increasingly popular. It has altered the questions motor behavior theorists are asking. How does environment influence motor development and control? What are the rate limiters to varying motor patterns as the child develops? As the questions change, the research is evolving to accommodate these new ideas, but the earlier researchers were essential in

arriving at current perspectives. Throughout this text, the ecological perspective continues as the basic theoretical construct on questions of dance training and motor learning. However, the text continues to address issues of reflexes, brain hierarchy, maturation, and information processing as they are pertinent and apply to questions of motor learning for dancers.

Summary

Sherrington's reflex theory and the reflex/hierarchical theory explain all motor control and development as reflex based. When reflecting on them today, it is easy to see the limitations and oversimplification of these early models. The maturational perspective and the information processing perspective added ideas about contributions from individual genetic makeup and brain processing to these first ideas. Behaviorism added yet another layer to the growing theoretical construct, emphasizing responses to others and the environment in how people learn. Finally, from this rich groundwork of research and hypotheses emerged the development of the ecological perspective, incorporating dynamic systems approach and perception–action approach. These two approaches are two prongs of this idea: The individual, the task at hand, and everything in the environment contribute to motor development across the life span. Each infant comes into the world with potential. What the infant perceives (and how the infant responds) contributes to how he or she will organize and develop movement skills and choices. At this point in time, the ecological perspective and variations on this theory are generally the most broadly accepted by motor behaviorists. However, ongoing research continues to evolve the understanding of how humans acquire motor skills in the developmental years and beyond, and the field will continue to add new and expanded theories to explain motor development.

Chapter 3
Development of Postural Control and Balance

*I*t is awe-inspiring to watch elite dancers achieve extraordinary balances. Whether it is the classical dancer perched on one pointe shoe in arabesque, or the jazz dancer suspended in a layout, or the street dancer in stillness on one hand, seeing high-level balancing skills is inspiring. Whether working with small children or preprofessional dancers, teachers can excel in encouraging the development of high-level balancing skills through enlightened training methods.

The moment dance students step into their first dance class, they begin to experience the demands of learning new ways to stand and maintain good alignment. They are asked to stand in unfamiliar positions, and they are asked to balance on two legs and one leg in various and challenging poses, including inverted and off-vertical positions. Most dancers would say that balancing is being able to get into a shape, probably on one leg, and maintain it for a period of time. Many dancers do not realize that balance is happening every moment that they are dancing—and every moment they are not dancing as well. Gravity is an ever-present force, and the human body, whether in static stance or in dynamic motion, must actively resist this force or fall down. This ability of the body to oppose gravity and balance moment by moment is called *postural control*. When dancers understand postural control, they can train more effectively for the demands of dance.

Defining Postural Control

Postural control underlies all motor skills that involve standing, moving through space, or manipulating objects such as balls or other props. Without postural control, the simplest activities would be impossible. For example, even lifting a glass of water could cause you to fall over! Dancers often use the terms *alignment* and *posture* interchangeably. However, in motor behavior, these terms refer to very different aspects of movement. **Postural control** is the ability to acquire, maintain, or regain a state of balance during physical activity. **Balance** can be defined as the ongoing loss and recovery of equilibrium during dynamic movement. The two important aspects of postural control are stability and orientation. **Stability** is the ability to maintain the center of mass over the base of support. **Center of mass** is the central point in the body with equal mass in all directions, also called the center of gravity. In women the center of mass lies in the pelvis, and in males it tends to be higher, toward the sternum. **Orientation** is the relationship of the body to the environment, and of the parts of the body to each other. If one lacks either stability or orientation, movement in space is an impossible task. In addition, postural control assumes a complicated interaction of both neural (the brain and its sensory input) and physical (musculoskeletal) systems. In other words, the brain must interpret information it is receiving about the body's positions and its movement through space, and the body must be able to generate enough muscle force to produce the desired movement.

An example of the concept of stability in dance is the difficulty of maintaining balance in fifth position en pointe in ballet. It is simpler en relevé, and it is simpler still on the whole foot. In each successive case, the base of support is larger, making it easier to maintain the center of mass over the base of support. Another example would be a headstand in street dance. This task is easier using the hands on the floor to create a tripod for balance rather than attempting to balance on the head alone.

A dance example of the concept of orientation would be a développé devant on a raked (sloped) stage. While raked stages are less common in the United States, dancers in Europe still dance on them regularly. Also, dancers working outdoors and in unconventional environments, including street dancers, encounter uneven ground or sloping surfaces. Even dancers on conventional flat stages could step on a cord, a part of a costume, or another dancer's foot, thereby having to manage a nonlevel surface. In order to achieve balance in these conditions, the brain must assess the difference in gravitational pull on the various body parts because of the slope of the stage. In particular, when doing développé devant facing the audience on a raked stage, the angle of the standing ankle will be very different than on a flat stage. The muscles of the standing leg will need to organize differently to achieve the développé. In fact, the gravitational relationship of many of the body segments will be different on this rake than on a flat surface. It should be clear from this example that postural control varies depending on the environmental context. Consider how this movement would be further affected by gravity while wearing a heavy costume or attempting to hold a partner in the air and move across the space.

Keep in mind that most dancers use the word *posture* to mean something entirely different than this motor control definition of postural control. When dancers and dance teachers refer to good posture, they are actually talking about **alignment**, and specifically a particular linear organization of the body parts with respect to gravity and the dance aesthetic. It is a myth that good alignment and good technique are interdependent. It is not the case that someone with poor alignment (e.g., swayback, round shoulders, forward head) will necessarily have a lower level of skill. A body can have well-developed postural control and balance but have poor alignment. A common example is a dancer in extreme lumbar lordosis (swayback) who can balance and turn with ease. Why, then, do teachers spend so much time correcting alignment? Beyond the aesthetic beauty of the well-aligned form, good alignment encourages efficiency—less muscular effort to achieve the task at hand. Less effort can translate into less wear and tear over time and possibly reduced injury rates, which creates a more sustainable dance practice. This chapter focuses on the development of the postural control mechanisms and not on correcting alignment problems. Regardless of how well aligned dancers may be, teachers need to understand postural control and how to encourage effective balancing strategies to create highly skilled dancers.

Understanding Postural Reflexes

In order to fully understand balance and postural control, you must know what postural reflexes are. Simply defined, **postural reflexes** are responses that occur when groups of mus-

Postural reflexes will help this dancer prevent falling to the floor.

cles (sometimes called *muscular synergies*) prepare for or react to disturbances using an automatic sequence in order to maintain equilibrium. Consider standing on a moving bus, facing the front of the bus. When the bus takes off, the body begins to fall backward. To maintain balance, the muscles at the front of the legs and spine will engage in a particular automatic sequence. If the bus comes to an abrupt stop, the body will begin to fall forward. The muscles at the back of the legs and spine will engage in a particular automatic sequence to maintain balance. These reactions are not done consciously, but they are necessary for preventing falling in dance and in daily life.

Responses to Equilibrium Disturbances

The body can respond to disturbances to balance in two ways. One way is to respond to unexpected (unplanned) disturbances, and the other way is to respond to expected (planned) disturbances. Dancers use both types of responses. If one dancer is in a balance and another dancer unexpectedly runs by too closely, the momentum of the passing dancer could cause the balancing dancer to fall. The necessary muscles of the balancing dancer will activate *after* the disturbance in order to maintain the balance. On the other hand, if one dancer is balancing while expecting another dancer to approach and lean on him or her, the necessary muscles of the balancing dancer will activate *before* the other dancer arrives, preparing for the disturbance. These two examples demonstrate ways that dancers need good postural responses for a variety of challenging conditions. While these responses are reflexive and cannot be trained in the dance class, the dancer's overall organization and skill development can take advantage of these reflexes.

Responses to Falling on Level Surfaces

In the 1960s, it became possible to look at muscle use through advanced electromyography equipment. **Electromyography (EMG)** is the process of measuring electrical activity created by muscles during action, which gives information about when muscles contract and how much of each muscle is being recruited. The photo of the dancer responding to an unexpected disturbance is an example of **compensatory (reactive) reflexes**. These reflexes activate the postural muscles in response to the disturbance. They are sometimes called *feedback control.* When the body is falling backward, the muscles at the front of the legs and torso respond by contracting. They do so in a particular sequence (distal to proximal; from the periphery to the center of the body) and in a particular timing, measured in milliseconds. The sequence is tibialis anterior muscles at the front of the ankles, followed by quadriceps at the front of the thighs, followed by abdominals at the front of the torso. When the body is falling forward, the muscles on the back of the legs and torso respond. They do so in the same sequence (distal to proximal) and in the same timing. The sequence is gastrocnemius (calf muscles) at the back of the ankles, followed by hamstrings at the back of the thighs, followed by erector spinae at the back of the torso. These two cases are identical to how the body responds when you

are riding on a bus. The first case is like the bus taking off, which causes the body to fall backward, and the second case is like the bus screeching to a halt, which causes the body to fall forward. Any time dancers are starting to lose balance by falling forward or backward, these same postural reflexes will activate. A fascinating fact about the timing of the postural responses is that they are remarkably uniform for all adults, assuming no neural illnesses or deficits (such as cerebral palsy) exist. This similarity is not dependent on the person's size, weight, or activity level.

Discovery of Responses to Equilibrium Disturbances

Lewis Nashner is an inventor and researcher who investigated postural reflexes. Nashner and NeuroCom International, the company he founded in 1984, have invented concepts and technology that help people all over the world understand balance for normal function and aid in rehabilitation of balance disorders. Through research conducted in the mid-1970s and beyond, Nashner and his colleagues were the first to describe what are now called *postural reflexes*. He created a mechanical device called the **perturbation platform**, which is used to test responses to disturbances. To begin the test, the participant stands on the platform. In the early studies, two optional movements would occur. The platform could suddenly jerk forward or jerk backward, and the participant was not told in advance what was going to happen. This motion was known as *platform translation*. The platform replicates what is described in the earlier examples about riding the bus. Nashner and other researchers subsequently did many other studies using the perturbation platform to test postural reflexes under varying conditions.

Responses to Sloping Surfaces

Sometimes balance is disturbed not by falling backward or forward, but by the person unexpectedly encountering a surface that suddenly slopes up or down. This situation might occur if someone walks into a dark theater or a dancer is working on an inclined surface, and suddenly the angle of the floor changes. When the floor angles downward, the first result is that the front of the ankle elongates. This elongation signals to the brain that the body is falling backward, when in fact it is falling forward because of the slope of the floor. This incorrect response causes the anterior muscles (specifically the tibialis anterior at the front of the ankle) to *fire*; that is, neurons (nerve cells) send impulses (messages) to the muscle fibers, and these fibers contract, causing the body to fall even further forward. Through repeated experience the brain learns that the appropriate response is to engage the posterior muscles (specifically the gastrocnemius at the back of the ankle) to halt the forward fall. The muscles in question are identical to the muscles that respond in platform translation (described in the previous section); in this case, the change of the slope of the surface is called *platform rotation*. This information is significant to dancers because the postural responses are not hardwired; they are not destined to react the same way over and over regardless of the circumstances. So, through experience and training, dancers can learn to adjust the postural responses to varying conditions. Figure 3.1 shows the perturbation platform in both the platform translation and the rotation conditions.

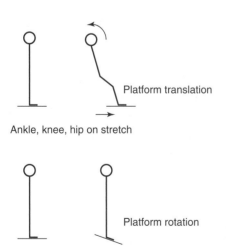

Platform translation

Ankle, knee, hip on stretch

Platform rotation

Ankle only on stretch

Figure 3.1 Anterior ankle stretch in both platform translation and rotation conditions. In the platform translation, the anterior muscles contract. In the platform rotation, the posterior muscles contract.
Created by Donna Krasnow.

Responses to Expected Equilibrium Disturbances

Most people have experienced the surprise of lifting a suitcase that they thought was full but discovering that it was empty as they flew in the opposite direction. The brain evaluates situations that will affect balance before they occur, and it determines how to adjust the body's center of mass accordingly. In dance, partners must anticipate the additional weight that they will carry at the moment of a lift in order to make a smooth transition.

When a person lifts an object or a dancer lifts a partner, muscles of the arms and chest primarily do the lifting while the postural muscles support balance. The postural muscles fire before the arm and chest muscles. Even when a person expects the change in weight, the body uses the same postural muscles and the same timing and sequencing as in the case of unexpected disturbances. Researchers use the term **anticipatory postural reflexes** (also called *feedforward control*), because the muscular activity occurs before the disturbance. However, if a person is leaning on a bar or other external support when lifting the object, the postural muscles of the legs and spine do not fire in anticipation. The body simply relies on the external support, and the postural muscles are not required to maintain the balance. Figure 3.2 shows both conditions—without support and leaning on a support. Lewis Nashner and his colleague Paul Cordo used EMG equipment to record muscle use in the two conditions. In figure 3.2*a*, the person is standing freely, and the postural leg muscles can be seen activating before the arm muscles fire. In figure 3.2*b*, the person is leaning on a bar, and the postural leg muscles are quiet; only the arm muscles show activation.

This knowledge has important implications for the use of the barre in ballet and other dance classes. If holding on to the barre is similar to leaning on an external support, it may be impeding the postural responses needed to maintain balance during dance movement. In other words, the muscles of the standing leg and trunk are not firing at the barre in the same way that they would activate in center practice. This subject

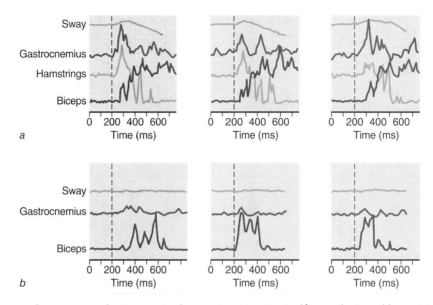

Figure 3.2 Postural responses that occur in the gastrocnemius (calf muscles) and hamstrings (at the back of the thigh) during arm-pulling movement (using the biceps of the arm): *(a)* responses when the body is unsupported, and *(b)* responses when the body is supported by leaning on a bar.

Reprinted, by permission, from P.J. Cordo and L.M. Nashner, 1982, "Properties of postural adjustments associated with rapid arm movements," *Journal of Neurophysiology* 47(2): 287-302.

is explored further in the discussion of transfer of training in motor learning (see chapter 15).

Changing Support Surfaces and Equilibrium Disturbances

Sometimes dancers are required to dance on various surfaces, such as on a slope. Three different strategies cover various types of disturbances to equilibrium. (Note that the word *strategies* does not necessarily mean conscious choices.) The first strategy is called the *ankle strategy*. This strategy was described in the Responses to Sloping Surfaces section; the ankle muscles fire first, followed by the thigh and torso muscles. This strategy occurs when the perturbation is small and the support surface is firm. If the perturbation becomes larger, the second strategy, called the *hip strategy*, takes over. In this instance, as the body falls forward in a larger motion, the hip joints flex and the anterior muscles (quadriceps and abdominal muscles) engage. In the case of the body falling backward in a larger motion, the muscles that respond in order to regain equilibrium are the posterior muscles (the hamstrings and erector spinae). The hip strategy has these two notable differences: The ankle muscles are not involved, and the muscles are opposite from

The dancers' balancing strategies are very different when dancing on the slope of the hill rather than on a flat surface.

the ankle strategy; that is, when the body falls forward a small amount, the posterior muscles react (ankle strategy), but when the body is falling forward a large amount, the anterior muscles react (hip strategy).

This information affects dancers in two main ways. First, dancers often deal with big challenges to balance in dance movement. When these challenges occur, the ankle strategy is not sufficient for dealing with such large disturbances. Second, the hip strategy takes over when the base of support changes. When standing on the whole foot on a normal surface,

the ankle strategy is sufficient to handle disturbances to balance. When standing on a narrow beam or when on relevé and en pointe, the body must rely on the hip strategy. Unlike life outside of dance, when dancers are dancing, they spend a great deal of time in conditions that have large perturbation to balance or require the use of varying bases of support. Figure 3.3 shows the case of the body falling forward with varying bases of support. In *a* and *b*, the support base is normal, and the body is falling forward. The muscles that engage are the posterior ankle, thigh, and torso muscles. In *c* and *d*, the support

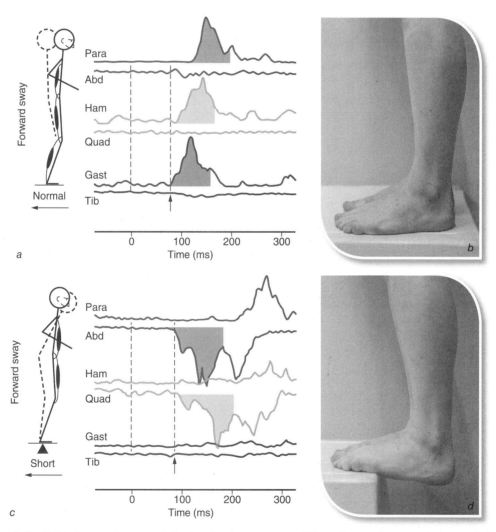

Figure 3.3 With forward sway of the body, the strategy differs depending on the size of the disturbance and type of surface. *(a, b)* In the ankle strategy, the posterior muscles in all three levels of the lower extremities and body contract: gastrocnemius in the calf, hamstrings in the thigh, and paraspinal muscles in the back of the trunk. *(c, d)* In the hip strategy, the anterior muscles in only two areas contract: quadriceps in the thigh and abdominals in the anterior trunk.

(a) and *(c)*: Reprinted, by permission, from F.B. Horak and L.M. Nashner, 1986, "Central programming of postural movements: Adaptation to altered support-surface configurations," *Journal of Neurophysiology* 55(6): 1369-1381.

base is much smaller, with the body still falling forward. In this case, the muscles that engage are the anterior thigh and torso muscles.

When the disturbance becomes even larger, the body uses a third strategy. It takes a small step to regain equilibrium. This strategy is called the *stepping strategy*. The stepping strategy also has a relationship to the phases of a dance class and to dance performance. In center work the goal is to avoid having to take a step to regain lost balance, while in traveling work the intention is to achieve large steps, which can happen more effectively if the center of mass is falling off the base of support with control. In order to develop optimal balancing skills, dancers need to practice all three of the strategies during training.

When the direction of the disturbance is altered, the postural responses change, including activating different muscles. Various studies have demonstrated that postural reflexes are adaptable and vary during changes to support surfaces, size of disturbance, and direction of disturbance. All of these modifications to conditions can be seen in the demands placed on dancers, including work en pointe, large shifts of weight in space, and rapid movements in a variety of directions. The chapters on motor learning (part III) explore the question of how practice and training influence a dancer's postural responses.

Perturbation While Moving Through Space

When a dancer is moving in space and something happens to create a disturbance to balance, such as catching a partner while traveling, the same postural muscles fire as described previously, and they use the same timing and sequencing. The difference is that the postural muscle activity only occurs on one leg—the leg that bears the weight at the moment of the disturbance (also known as *stance phase*). The postural response is not observed in the non-weight-bearing leg (known as the *swing phase*). The movement that the traveling dancer is executing does not need to be interrupted even as the postural muscles fire, so that dancer does not have to stop traveling in order to catch the partner.

Sensory Systems and Postural Control

Going onstage for the first time is an exciting, yet eye-opening experience for all dancers. They do not expect the difficulty of performing well-rehearsed choreography in lighting that compromises vision. Simple turns and balances can suddenly become a struggle. Dancers are often unaware of the relationship between the sensory systems and postural control. Awareness of this relationship can help them better prepare for onstage performance.

Defining the Three Sensory Systems for Balance

The sensory systems (modalities) involved in balance are the visual system, the vestibular system, and the somatosensory system (which includes proprioception, as seen in figure 3.4). Each system makes a unique contribution to balance. The brain must decipher and integrate information from each of these systems in order to achieve balance. It can examine all of the sensory information simultaneously in the cerebellum, and it attempts to select what is important and relevant for maintaining balance.

Vision involves both seeing as well as processing what has been seen. It includes the eyes, which are the receptors that receive the visual information and transmit it to the brain, and the occipital or visual cortex in the brain, which interprets the information, known as *visual perception*.

The **vestibular system** has its receptors in the inner ear, and it is mainly concerned with providing information about the head's position in space and about quick changes in direction of movements of the head. Fluids in the ear's semicircular canals make contact with nerve cells called *cilia* (hair cells). Varying degrees of excitation to these cells send signals to the brain about position and direction changes. Other structures that complement the semicircular canals are the otoliths (organs in the inner ear that sense gravity and linear acceleration) as well as vision and proprioception.

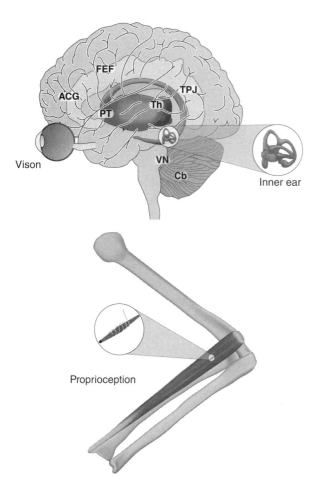

Figure 3.4 The three balancing mechanisms—the visual system, the vestibular system, and the somatosensory system—integrate, and the multiple sources of information are interpreted in the cerebellum. The vestibular system is zoomed in on at the far right, the spindle fibers of the proprioceptive system are in the lower section, and vision is on the left. These three systems contributing to balance converge on a number of brain areas. These brain areas are the anterior cingulate gyrus (ACG), the frontal eye fields (FEF), the putamen (PT), parts of the thalamus (Th), areas in and around the insula and temporo-parietal junction (TPJ), the vestibular nucleus (VN), and areas within the cerebellum (Cb).

Created by Blake Martin.

Proprioception is one of the three parts of the **somatosensory system**. Each part has a distinct pathway in the spinal cord to the brain, and each part targets a distinct area of the brain. The first is called *discriminative touch*, which includes light touch, pressure, and vibration perception and enables people to describe the shape and

texture of an object even if they cannot see it. Further, touch contributes to balance through sensory receptors on the bottom of the feet, which is particularly useful for regulating foot position on uneven or irregular surfaces. The touch of even a single finger on a surface dramatically reduces body sway, which is small movement of the center of gravity even when standing still. This light touch on a supportive surface alters disturbance to balance, suggesting that using the barre with even the lightest touch or one finger makes it easier to maintain control. The second group is called *nociception* (ability to sense pain or harm) and includes the sensations of temperature, itch, and tickle. The third is **proprioception**, which includes receptors for what happens below the body surface. These receptors can be found in muscles, fascia, tendons, ligaments, and joints. Some scientists believe these receptors are also in the skin. For example, they give the brain information about muscle stretch, joint position, and tendon tension. Proprioceptive information is received by various areas of the brain, which need moment-by-moment feedback on what the muscles and joints are doing. The areas of the brain that deal with motor control are discussed in more detail in chapter 6.

Each of the three systems provides different information that allows the brain and the nervous system to create the necessary muscle responses to achieve balance. In instances where the information is contradictory, the brain can determine which information is more vital to the situation. A common example is sitting in a still car when the car next to you begins to move slowly. Initially your vision tells you that you are moving, but your somatosensory information can sometimes make it clear that you are stationary, inhibiting an inappropriate response. When dancers complete a series of rapid turns such as chaînés or spins on the head, the initial sensation from vestibular information is that they are still turning. However, visual and somatosensory information inform the dancers that the turning has stopped. In both of these instances, the brain activity to make these determinations happens unconsciously. Figure 3.4 shows the three sensory systems related to balance, and where they integrate in the brain.

Integration of the Three Sensory Systems

It is crucial that the three sensory systems related to balance integrate in the developmental years and that the brain has areas dedicated to resolving sensory conflict. Without this important feature, adults would not be capable of balancing when contradictory sensory information occurs.

Adults usually rely on proprioception in most instances to manage disturbances to balance. However, because the three sensory systems are integrated, vision and vestibular functions can mediate or take over when proprioception is compromised. When dancers are standing on a narrow support or working on relevé or en pointe, ankle joint input becomes limited. A similar situation exists when a dancer experiences a severe ankle sprain. In these instances, the dancer needs to rely on visual information to maintain balance.

Input that can alter balance also includes somatosensory information about the environment, such as the nature of the surface experienced by the soles of the feet and ankles. A simple dance involving balance that a dancer has performed many times in the studio can suddenly become more difficult if performed on a grassy lawn or if restrictive shoes are added.

In addition to the information provided by vision and proprioception, vestibular inputs provide a reference system about the body's relation to gravity. A dancer can maintain a fixed body position, but be lifted off the ground, and have her relationship to gravity altered. Although her joint angles and muscle lengths remain the same, and although she may have her vision blocked, she is still receiving information about her position in relation to gravity from the vestibular system, and she is not disoriented when she is returned to the ground. Just as proprioception is more important than vision for balance in ordinary conditions, proprioception is also more important than the vestibular system.

Discovery of the Mechanisms of Sensory Integration

In the 1970s and 1980s, Lewis Nashner and colleagues did experiments examining balance in a range of environmental conditions, again using the perturbation platform and also using a device called the *moving room*, a three-sided enclosure with movable walls. Figure 3.5 shows a representation of the moving room.

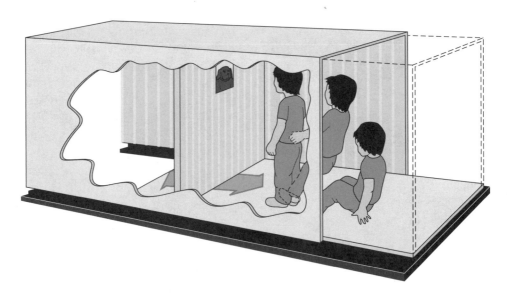

Figure 3.5 Schematic representation of the moving room. The small "room" (made up of four walls and a ceiling) is moved toward the child, and the child falls backward. This response would occur if the child perceived the optical flow produced by the room movement as forward sway rather than as room movement.

Reprinted from B.I. Bertenthal, J.L. Rose, and D.L. Bai, 1997, "Perception-action coupling in the development of visual control of posture," *Journal of Experimental Psychology: Human Perception and Performance* 23: 1631-1634. By permission of B.I. Bertenthal.

In the studies of Nashner and his colleagues, either visual input was disrupted, somatosensory (proprioceptive) input was disrupted, or both were disrupted. All possible combinations of disruption created these six conditions:

- *Condition 1* represents normal conditions with the eyes open, the room stationary, and the platform stationary.
- In *condition 2*, the eyes are closed but the room and platform remain the same.
- In *condition 3*, the eyes are open but the room sways (also called *vision servoed*).
- In *condition 4*, the eyes are open and the room is stationary, but the platform moves (also called *somatosensory input servoed*).
- In *condition 5*, the eyes are closed and the platform moves.
- In *condition 6*, the eyes are open but both the room and the platform move.

The results suggest that with either visual or somatosensory input reduced, body sway increases, and with both reduced, even greater sway exists. Figure 3.6 displays the amount of sway in each condition. For each condition, as the amount of sway increases, the difficulty for the participant to maintain balance increases.

In summary, all three sensory systems—visual, vestibular, and somatosensory—are essential for maintaining balance in all conditions of stance and locomotion. Strategies can alter based on the task or on the environment. The three systems are integrated or organized; regarding balance, a hierarchy exists that ensures the best responses. Under ordinary conditions for adults, the nervous system gives more weight to the somatosensory input than to visual or vestibular contributions. Because dancers work in conditions that can compromise vision, they need to have excellent proprioceptive and vestibular responses as well as good use of visual cues.

Development of Postural Control and Dance Training

As people develop from birth to the end of the life span, postural control goes through many stages. In the early years of dance training

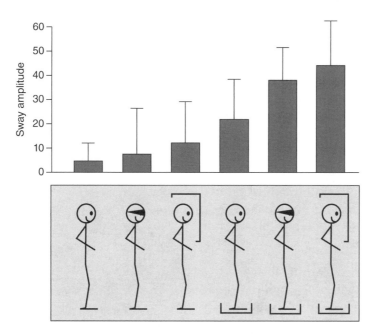

Figure 3.6 The six conditions used by Nashner and colleagues, testing the various disturbances to balance. Note that as each condition is increasingly more difficult, the amount of sway (shown in the bar graphs) increases. From left to right: eyes open; eyes closed; eyes open, room sways; eyes open, platform moves; eyes closed, platform moves; eyes open, room sways, and platform moves.

Created by Blake Martin.

(from 3 years old to adolescence), the changes are profound. Understanding these changes can inform teachers about good instructional techniques. For example, when compared to adults, children 12 years of age and younger rely predominantly on vision for balance. Therefore, during the early years of training, disrupting vision during complex movement can hinder the development of good balance.

Developing Postural Control From Birth to Early Adulthood

The years from birth to early adulthood are characterized by exploration and by periods of regression (apparent decreases in skills). This experimental approach is evident in the development of general skills for all children as well as dance-specific skills for young dancers. All typically developing children show certain patterns in their development of postural control.

Postural control develops through a **cephalocaudal** (head-to-tail) progression. Over time, organization evolves that relates sensory information to the motor actions that control body positioning and movement. Here is an overview of this organization:

- Control begins in the head, and the first sense mapped to head control is believed to be vision.
- With independent sitting, infants learn to extend rules for head control to the trunk muscles, and they coordinate the sensorimotor information involving the head and trunk.
- Senses are initially patterned to actions individually, then multiple senses are mapped together, allowing for coordinated postural control.

It is common in motor learning to see a pattern of one system developing, then the rules of this system transferring to the next emerging system, and finally multiple systems being organized together. In this way, the body can experiment with one area in simple ways before tackling the complexity of managing multiple senses or body areas.

Birth to Independent Standing

Although infants do not dance, it is informative to consider some of the developmental transitions during the time from birth to independent standing and early walking. Patterns of progression, plateaus, regression, and further improvement occur repeatedly through childhood and adolescence. In addition, the rate limiters at each stage can provide insight into what occurs in adolescence, which is a critical time in the training of most dancers.

In the 1970s and 1980s, many researchers studied the reflex responses in infants and young children in a variety of conditions, including the moving room and the perturbation platform. The results of these studies are summarized in the following text and tables. Infants have no organized neck muscle activity until 2 months of age, because they lack the strength and the ability to organize responses to perturbation. It could also be because of what is called **reciprocal excitation**, in which both agonist and antagonist muscles respond simultaneously to reflex stimulation. Agonist and antagonist muscles are muscles that are

The young child develops postural control in the early stages of walking.

on opposite sides of a joint and cause opposite movements, such as the quadriceps extending the knee and the hamstrings flexing the knee. Reciprocal excitation occurs before 2 months of age, and it prevents appropriate reflex responses. In these first months, infants have not yet calibrated the neck muscles to give a correct response to visual input. However, by 2 months old, they develop a correct neck response to light stimulation, and by 3 or 4 months, visual and vestibular stimuli are being controlled in a coordinated fashion. Thus, the child first develops control between one sense and the head, then learns to coordinate the senses together.

By the time young infants can sit, the neck muscles are responding appropriately to visual stimuli. However, in the seated position, the head rules have not yet transferred to the trunk when dealing with visual input. The developments seen in table 3.1 occur from 5 to 9 months old when placed in the moving room.

During these same months, the infants demonstrate head and trunk responses when dealing with perturbation to balance, and the responses seen in table 3.2 are observed.

As infants begin to prepare for independent standing, rate limiters include muscle strength and motor coordination. The sensory systems are sufficiently developed in advance of the appearance of independent standing, but the infant will not stand until sufficient strength and coordination exist.

As infants make the transition from sitting to standing, the EMG responses to perturbation are fascinating to observe. Infants change from no organized muscle responses to the full postural reflex synergies in less than 1 year. Table

Table 3.1 Infant Trunk Responses to Visual Stimuli When in the Moving Room

Age	Trunk muscle response
5 months	No response
7 months	Responded as long as the whole room moved
9 months	Responded if only the side walls (periphery) moved

Table 3.2 Infant Trunk Responses to Perturbation

Age	Response
2 months	No organized response
3-4 months	Neck muscles showed direction-specific responses, which were appropriate in 40-60% of trials.
5 months	In addition to consistent neck muscle responses, trunk muscles responded in about 40% of trials.
8 months	Good neck and trunk activity shown in 100% of trials.

3.3 demonstrates how the system builds these synergies one step at a time.

The postural reflex synergies (tibialis anterior → quadriceps → abdominals) are also demonstrated by placing infants in the moving room, supported by their mothers. The moving room tests infants' responses to visual stimuli, and these studies indicate that infants respond to this stimulus as well as to perturbation. Hence, at an early age the child has developed the rules for coordinated vision and muscle response.

Even in very young children, certain characteristics of muscle responses, such as encouraging muscle synergies, are trainable. However, at this age response time cannot be altered through training, because there is no way to accelerate the process of **myelination**, which is the growth of the insulating fatty sheath around the nerve cells responsible for the speed of neural transmission. It is important to understand which aspects of development respond to training and which aspects cannot, because some of the rate-limiting factors cannot be accelerated.

Postural Responses in Early Childhood

Postural responses in upright stance go through major changes from the early years of the toddler to prepubertal years. During this time, a key regression phase occurs. From 4 to 6 years old, balance is erratic and unstable, showing less control in some ways than 1- to 3-year-old children. Researchers and educators debated

Table 3.3 Infant EMG Responses in Developing Postural Reflexes

Age	Phase	Response
2-6 months	Pre–pulling to stand	No organized muscle responses to platform perturbations
7-9 months	Early pulling to stand	Muscle responses are emerging (ankle muscles begin to activate). With forward perturbation tibialis anterior response occurred, and with backward perturbation gastrocnemius response occurred.
Varies with individual	Mid–pulling to stand	More synergy development was observed, such as tibialis anterior coupled with quadriceps (anterior muscle responses) and gastrocnemius coupled with hamstrings (posterior muscle responses).
9-11 months	Late pulling to stand and independent standing	Full postural synergy was present: Tibialis → quadriceps → abdominals, with forward platform movement; and Gastrocnemius → hamstrings → trunk extensors, with backward platform movement

whether this regression occurred because of physical changes or other rate-limiting factors. Two researchers, Anne Shumway-Cook and Marjorie Woollacott, explored these questions in their studies on young children. They have also coauthored textbooks, including *Motor Control: Theory and Practical Applications* (Shumway-Cook & Woollacott, 2001). Shumway-Cook is interested in the physiologic basis for balance disorders, and her clinical practice focuses on the management of the patients with balance and mobility impairments. Woollacott is the director of the Motor Control Laboratory at the University of Oregon, and she has done extensive research on balance function in both young children and the elderly.

Shumway-Cook and Woollacott did a landmark study observing three age groups on the perturbation platform. On the platform, normal adults show distal to proximal (from the periphery to the center of the body) synergies with no coactivation. **Coactivation** is the simultaneous contraction of both the agonist and the antagonist during a given movement. The results of this study influenced the understanding of postural response development for decades, and they are still relevant today. Noteworthy in the study was the regression phase seen in children aged 4 to 6. Table 3.4 indicates the responses seen in the three age groups.

These results raised the question of what is happening in 4- to 6-year-old children. Shumway-

Table 3.4 Postural Responses in Three Age Groups From 1 to 10 Years Old

Age	Response
15-31 months (1-3 yrs)	There was muscle co-activation; that is, responses could be seen in tibialis anterior → quadriceps, but also in gastrocnemius → hamstrings at the same time; also there were slow muscle responses to the disturbance.
4-6 years	A lot of variability existed in this age group—very erratic responses, which looked like a regression in development. Also, there were slower responses and a longer delay between lower and upper leg muscles activating, and there was a bending at the knee joint.
7-10 years	Responses in this age group were similar to those of adults, except that response times were slightly longer.

Cook and Woollacott decided to look at the intersensory integration of these age groups, using the perturbation platform with a protocol similar to that used by Nashner and seen in figure 3.6 on page 33. **Intersensory integration** refers to the processes in the brain that can take sensory information from more than one sensory modality and organize the input to create an appropriate response by the muscles. Recall that the six conditions in Nashner's early study establish the subject's ability to integrate the three major balance modalities—vision, vestibular, and sensorimotor—and to adapt to various conditions, depending on the type of sensory input and the nature of the disturbance. The study by Shumway-Cook and Woollacott used only conditions 1, 2, 4, and 5: Condition 1 represents normal conditions with the eyes open, the room stationary, and the platform stationary. In condition 2, the eyes are closed, but the room and platform remain the same. In condition 4, the eyes are open and the room is stationary, but the platform moves (also called *somatosensory input servoed*). In condition 5, the eyes are closed, and the platform moves. They did not use the two conditions with the moving room (also called *vision servoed*). The results of this study can be seen in table 3.5.

The researchers concluded that the 4- to 6-year-old children seem to be in the process of learning to integrate somatosensory, visual, and vestibular information, and they mature at around 7 years old. In fact, children aged 4 to 6 have responses that are slower and more variable than 1- to 3-year-olds, 7- to 10-year-olds, and adults—an apparent regression in development. The reason for this variability might be related to disproportionate growth and body changes during the period between 4 to 6 years, which can cause discontinuous changes in development. In motor learning and control, **discontinuous** refers to a plateau in behavior followed by a sudden change, such as the shift from supported walking to independent walking. However, more recent research has demonstrated that what is observed in 4- to 6-year-old children is much more likely because of nervous system changes than physiological changes. In other words, the neuromotor system is in a way experimenting with different strategies, which results in the variability of responses. By approximately 7 years old, both the integration and hierarchy of postural responses to disturbances to balance are established.

The Adolescent Years

The research discussed in the previous section suggests that postural reflexes are similar between 7- to 10-year-olds and adults. However, various aspects of postural control develop later. Some aspects of maturation may occur by 12 years of age, and other aspects can mature as late as 16 years of age. In a few instances, aspects of control are not fully developed until adulthood.

For example, in conflicts between vision and somatosensory systems, children aged 12 and younger were deficient in the somatosensory modality, meaning that they were predominantly reliant on vision as compared to adults. Postural sway with eyes open and eyes closed

Table 3.5 Postural Responses in Three Age Groups Under Varying Conditions

Age	Response
1-3 years	This age group would not tolerate the testing conditions, and they refused to perform; instead they cried.
4-6 years	This age group had good responses with normal vision and normal platform, and they had fair responses with eyes closed and normal platform. However, they had serious problems with normal vision and platform moving (1 out of 4 children fell), and none could balance with eyes closed and platform moving (4 out of 4 children fell).
7-10 years	This age group showed responses similar to those of adults, except response times were slightly longer.

As children develop higher levels of dance skills, they are capable of more structured and difficult balances.

showed both differences due to age (groups ranging from 10 years to 15 years) and due to gender; boys develop more slowly than girls. Children performed balancing tasks more poorly with cognitive loading, such as counting backward while balancing, or attending to concurrent feedback, such as listening to corrections from the teacher while doing physical activity.

The growth spurts that occur in the adolescent years have an impact on motor development issues. Growth spurts usually occur at ages 11 to 14 and can last 18 to 24 months. As changes occur in body mass, limb length, and proportions, there is variability in balance and coordination. For dancers these changes can cause decreases in skill levels, and movements such as balances and turns can be negatively affected.

Clearly, what is now known about postural control and its development from birth to adulthood can influence approaches to dance training. The next section suggests ways to organize dance classes and the content of these classes for varying age groups.

Implications of Postural Control Research for Dance Training

Understanding the developmental progression of the postural reflexes helps dance teachers to structure classes in more effective ways. Elements to consider include when to present material, how to organize the dance class, and how content can best reflect the stages of development of the dance students. Some of these ideas are examined from the perspective of technical training, and the potential role of improvisation in dance training is discussed.

Implications for Technical Training

Up to this point, the text has described and clarified the balancing systems of the body and their development. This section provides information and suggestions for dance teachers about how to optimize these systems in the dance training process. The importance of the development of the three balancing systems—visual, vestibular, and sensorimotor—and the integration of these systems can provide guidance about the timing for introducing technical work.

Consider the following time line, which is based on the motor development literature, as optimal in terms of the young child's experience in dance classes. For dancers aged 3 and 4, the dance class content should be primarily creative play. It is an excellent way for the young child to expand physical capabilities while exploring imagination. For dancers aged 5 and 6, dance classes can begin to introduce the very beginning stages of technique, such as body part articulation, standing alignment, and basic locomotor steps. However, most dance classes for this age group should still involve creative movement. By the time the child is 7 or 8 years old, the emphasis of the class can begin to shift toward training in dance technique. Young dancers should have their first classes with time spent at the barre no earlier than this age, and creative play should still be incorporated into class on a regular basis. They can learn and accomplish basic dance vocabulary. In addition, they can begin to spend more time learning movement material set by the teacher but still be given time for creating their own dance material. By the time dancers reach 10 to 12 years old, classes can become more technique based as the need for skill acquisition increases. This is the age when most professional dance schools audition and accept dancers for elite training. Throughout adolescence it is not uncommon for dancers to spend many hours in highly structured classes learning elite skills. In ballet training a large portion of the class would be spent at the barre, and most of the work would be executed with the spine in vertical stance. It would benefit these adolescent dancers to continue exploring creative movement and use of the torso in nonvertical shapes in both stance and locomotion, regardless of the dance form they are learning.

By ages 7 or 8, the three balancing systems have just achieved adultlike integration in the dancer. This is an ideal time to challenge the three systems for optimal development. Young dancers could benefit from spending time disrupting the visual and vestibular systems in simple ways, hence enhancing the sensorimotor system. In other words, positioning the head off

Because of the narrow base of support, pointe work demands not only strength and good alignment but also high levels of balancing skills.

the vertical (away from the upright position) and changing visual focus, even when traveling in space, could potentially create dancers with better proprioceptive responses and hence better balance. Further, because aspects of postural control continue developing throughout adolescence, teachers might want to consider continued challenges to all three systems. That is not to suggest that the traditional format of the dance class needs to change in any drastic way. Rather, it means that teachers may include simple additions to class content in order to assist dancers in coping with challenges to balance, especially when it is time for the dancers to go onstage and perform with reduced visual input from the effect of stage lighting.

For example, asking dancers to close their eyes for simple balances is an excellent way to remove visual input. Clearly this strategy would need to be done progressively, starting with closing the eyes standing in parallel position, then closing the eyes in a first position plié, then moving to relevé in first position, then adding closed eyes to balances on one leg, and finally working with the eyes closed in taking single steps (transferring the weight through space). An added benefit to this process is that it creates an internal body awareness that is not always achieved with the eyes open, when concentration is divided between seeing other dancers and self-reflection. Another strategy is to add an off-center (away from vertical) torso movement to a traditional step, such as side bends involving the head off the vertical with a traveling waltz step, or with younger children, simply running across the space. In modern and contemporary classes, sometimes off-vertical head movement is done in center practice but not in traveling material, especially with younger dancers. Adding this element to the traveling work would be an excellent way to increase challenges to the balancing systems.

These guidelines for dance training development have been suggested based on the motor development literature. It would benefit the dance community for dance-specific research in this area of pedagogy to validate these principles.

Use of Improvisation

Improvisation has been a valuable asset in the creative arts for centuries. Many choreographers use improvisation both in their own movement explorations and in the rehearsal process with their dancers. However, motor development research might suggest other valuable reasons for including improvisation as a consistent part of dance training, regardless of the form or genre being studied.

Several differences are apparent between learning set material and exploring improvisation in the dance class. First, in set material, dancers must consider multiple elements, such as counts, directions, shape design, dynamics, and technical challenges such as balances. With improvisation, the number of components can be reduced, and dancers can focus on balancing strategies. Second, compensatory and anticipatory postural control responses are different strategies for coping with disturbances

to equilibrium. In general, when dancers are executing set material, they know where they are headed and can anticipate the balancing challenges. Improvisation provides unplanned, surprising challenges to the dancer, and balance can be tested and developed in conditions that have not been predetermined, triggering the compensatory responses. Third, use of focus in the traditional class can be limited, often involving verticality of the head and straightforward focus. Improvisation provides an opportunity to disrupt the habitual use of focus, possibly allowing the motor system to establish new mechanisms for integrating visual stimuli, and challenging the vestibular and sensorimotor systems. Fourth, in the traditional technique class, few opportunities are provided for dancers to interact with each other in novel movement sequences and settings. Improvisation can provide an environment in which unplanned interactions with other dancers can occur: Spatial conflicts, movement dialogues, and tasks such as copying and mirroring are an opportunity to explore spontaneous visual and kinesthetic responses to external stimuli.

Recent research in neuroimaging has demonstrated that more areas of the brain are active, and exhibit higher activation, when visualizing improvisational movement than when visualizing set, traditional movement. Both novice and elite dancers participated, and these studies suggest a relationship between visualizing improvisational movement and creative thinking.

Studies observing music improvisation found heightened activity in several areas of the brain, including the following: the area involved in conflict monitoring and decision making, and the area involved when people speak and understand language, and when people hear and understand music; this last area is the same as the area involved in the creation of music. While this research has not been duplicated on dancers, it does suggest that improvisation might enhance areas of the brain that could contribute to heightened motor skills.

In some dance schools and programs, improvisation is included in the ongoing training of dancers. However, it is easy to add the occasional improvisational game in a technique class, encouraging novel body positioning in relation to gravity, and creating the element of surprise in balancing tasks. An added benefit is that it gives the dancers a brief rest period from learning set material and can assist in preventing mental fatigue in class. It also begins to encourage and nurture the next generation of choreographers.

Summary

Postural control underlies all movement and allows the body to acquire, maintain, or regain a state of balance during activity. People have both compensatory and anticipatory responses to disturbances to balance, and these responses adapt to changes in support surfaces, the direction of the disturbance, and the challenges of moving through space. The three sensory systems—visual, vestibular, and sensorimotor (part of the somatosensory system)—are the important environmental contributions to postural control, and they integrate during the early years. Control begins in the head, then moves to the trunk during sitting, and finally extends to the lower extremities for independent standing. Children demonstrate what seem to be periodic regressions in motor behavior, but in fact these regressions represent times of developing new strategies for using sensory information and executing motor skills. Certain rate-limiting components must reach a point of development before postural control at the next level can emerge. Teachers can modify dance training to incorporate these ideas about motor development and to create classes that optimally enhance balancing mechanisms. They can also incorporate dance improvisation to further contribute to this process. Even the balances seen during improvisation can be extraordinary and demand excellent balancing mechanisms, although they are unplanned. The postural reflexes add a new dimension to the appreciation of the body's ability to regain and maintain equilibrium in motion as well as in stillness. Moment by moment, the brain and the nervous system take in vast amounts of sensory information from the environment, interpret this information, and translate it into messages to the muscles to support the ongoing task of balancing.

Chapter 4
Development
of Locomotor Skills

*T*he process of dance training often involves executing movement that is static in space. For example, ballet dancers might execute movements while remaining stationary in the center or at the barre. However, performing most dance forms entails moving through space. Even forms considered stationary, such as tap dance and street dance, include movement that travels from one point to another. When the youngest dancers start training (usually at about 3 or 4 years old), they are still developing the fundamental locomotor skills that all children develop at this stage. These universal steps are the foundation for all of the movement forms and locomotor skills that dancers will learn later in their training. Because the focus of this text is dance, the discussion is limited to children who are able to dance without any disease, injury, or disability that could affect these stages of development. Only the views of child motor development for the general population are covered. For those teachers interested in teaching dance to children with special needs, Theresa Purcell Cone and Stephen Cone have written the excellent text *Teaching Children Dance*, which addresses this population.

Because this text is for dancers and dance educators, you might expect to examine locomotor skills starting at the ages of 3 or 4 (the earliest ages when children begin their dance experience). However, observing how infants develop locomotor skills from birth can teach you a lot about locomotor development. One critical factor is the issue of motivation. It is the desire to achieve a goal that actually compels the beginning of locomotion. A second reason for considering infants is because of what it illuminates about the learning process. It was through observations of infants that some of the early proponents of the dynamic systems approach found evidence of the importance of interacting with the environment to learn motor skills.

The first part of the chapter describes the work of Esther Thelen and its importance to understanding early motor development. The second part examines the motor milestones of early locomotion, including some of the studies done with infants. The third part of the chapter describes sensory and cognitive contributions to locomotion and the common locomotor skills seen in children: walking, running, jumping, hopping, galloping, sliding, and skipping. The fourth part of the chapter considers adolescents and their growth spurts. The fifth and final part of the chapter discusses dance training and age-appropriate movement skills. Each section considers the importance of understanding these phases in designing effective dance training. Throughout this discussion, the themes of postural control and sensory input from the environment remain relevant.

The Work of Esther Thelen

Esther Thelen was a developmental psychologist in the late 20th century and one of the more influential researchers in the field of motor learning. She was president of the Society for Research in Child Development, and she had a profound effect on how people think about the formative years of children's motor skills. Her research focused on the study of the emergence of kicking, stepping, and walking in infants. While she was also interested in the development of eye–hand coordination and reaching, the focus of this chapter is on her studies that relate to locomotion.

Thelen based her work on the dynamic systems approach of Nikolai Bernstein and the further elaborations of this theory by Scott Kelso, Michael Turvey, Peter Kugler, and other colleagues. Before discussing Thelen's research and how it expanded on ideas in the dynamic systems approach, it is helpful to review this summary of the fundamental concepts of the theory as discussed in chapter 2:

- Moving and developing systems are self-organizing.
- During individual development (called **ontogeny**), skills emerge in a nonlinear manner; that is, some factors develop faster than others, and the skills will not manifest until the slow or rate-limiting factors mature.
- Behavior shifts in a discontinuous fashion; that is, from a developmental perspec-

tive, rudimentary behavior will plateau until the more complex behavior suddenly appears.

Studies in Kicking and Stepping

Thelen documented the occurrence of repetitive motions in infant behavior. She observed that rocking preceded crawling and kicking preceded walking. One significant feature of her early studies of repetitive motions is that these behaviors allow infants to be actively involved in their learning process. She was particularly drawn to kicking for a number of reasons. First, infants often repeat kicking, allowing for ongoing observation. Second, kicking resembles stepping activity. Thelen was intrigued that kicking behavior continues and increases, whereas stepping vanishes within the first three months. Some researchers suggested that brain maturation was inhibiting the **stepping reflex**, which refers to movements traveling forward that occur when the infant is held upright and inclined forward with the feet touching a flat surface. Thelen found a different answer to this puzzle.

Along with Esther Thelen, researchers Donna Fisher and Robyn Ridley-Johnson conducted a longitudinal study of infants at 2, 4, and 6 weeks of age. As infants gained weight, the stepping reflex began to disappear, and the chubbier infants were the first to lose the reflex. When weights were added to the legs of the infants still stepping, they stepped less. Finally, when the infants were partially submerged in water, stepping increased and flexion in the joints of the legs was greater. Therefore, the absence of stepping is not a brain maturation change as previously proposed, it is a result of physical changes in weight relative to strength.

Other studies by Thelen and colleagues present evidence that development is nonlinear and self-organizing. They observed periods of greater instability during transitional periods in the infants' behavior, with an eventual trend toward enhanced organization. Thelen investigated infants starting at 1 month old, and she conducted a longitudinal study every month for 7 to 10 months. In this study, the infants were supported by an adult while their feet were placed on a moving belt. The study

These children are in the early stages of acquiring jumping skills, which follows kicking and stepping activities.

incorporated these elements, which led to the understanding of dynamic systems approach concepts as they relate to developing children:

- A variable that examined the phase relationship of the legs in the walking cycle demonstrated the integrated responses of the leg muscles.
- Control parameters, such as muscle strength, influenced when changes in movement behavior can occur.
- Evidence of nonlinear changes, such as abrupt shifts in motor patterns, was observed through increases in stepping at various stages.
- Evidence of self-organized behavior was observed; the infants could step on the treadmill but not in other contexts.

Regarding nonlinear changes, in the early months the infants did few steps on the treadmill, and most of the infants experienced a sudden increase in frequency by around 3 months. Regarding self-organization, the motion of the treadmill stimulated the appearance of the stepping behavior when it would not normally be seen otherwise. In other words, the treadmill literally assembled walking behavior for the infants. It is interesting that although these infants demonstrated varying forms of stepping patterns during the study, they did not actually walk until they had explored and experimented for months. Further studies also reinforced the idea that development is individual, and each infant experiments and selects personal strategies regarding locomotion.

Toward the end of her career, Esther Thelen became a practitioner of the Feldenkrais Method. As discussed in chapter 1, the Feldenkrais Method is one of the somatic practices; it is a structured method of movement exercises in which participants are guided to pay attention to sensory feedback as they execute specific movements with a small range of motion. Thelen was drawn to the Feldenkrais Method because it uses novel and simple movement exercises to bring increased awareness and retrain old habitual patterns. She was drawn to the exploratory nature of the process, which allows the person to experiment with movement possibilities and choices. The Feldenkrais work embraced the same principles driving Thelen's approach toward motor development. From a similar perspective, in an article written for her students, Thelen compared motor development to improvisational jazz music. Like the musician, infants create new movement choices through their individual investigations, so practitioners must look at the whole pattern as it emergences rather than the note-by-note sequence.

Impact of Thelen's Work

The influence of Thelen's work and ideas on researchers that followed cannot be understated. Two observations highlight her importance to the field. First, she did rigorous studies of infants about aspects of motor learning in the young child that were not previously understood by the scientific community. Second, at the time when dynamic systems theory was developing, she helped support this theory by providing empirical evidence of its actuality in infant behavior. Thelen's work provides a basis for understanding the motor milestones and later locomotor patterns in the progression of motor development from infant to child.

Motor Milestones

In order for children to be able to walk, they pass through **motor milestones**, which are certain stages through which children must progress. Each of these stages allows the child to gain essential motor skills that lead to complex behaviors. These fundamental steps are a series of benchmarks in every child's motor development. While individual variation exists in the specific timing of these milestones, the order of acquiring the skills is similar across all typically developing children.

Components Affecting Changes in Motor Milestones

Several developing motor systems determine at what point a particular milestone will emerge. The first is the central nervous system. The **central nervous system (CNS)** comprises the brain and the spinal cord, and this system must have the capability to direct the muscles to organize and to engage in various locomotor behaviors. Second, the muscles must achieve sufficient strength and endurance to accommodate each task. As Thelen and colleagues demonstrated, when the infants' legs weighed more than their strength could handle, stepping ceased to occur. Third, the development of posture and balance is absolutely essential in support of locomotion and the emergence of motor milestones. Although at a certain point infants' legs have sufficient strength for independent stance, they will not walk until they have achieved postural control. Fourth, the brain's ability to process information from the senses must improve in concert with the neuromuscular and physical changes. In each instance of the transitions between motor milestones, the last (or rate-limiting) component must reach a level of maturity for the behavior to manifest.

In the past century the time lines for motor milestones have not substantially changed. From 2004 to 2006 the World Health Organization supported a series of studies in five countries with 816 children. They observed sitting without support, creeping, standing with assistance, walking with assistance, standing alone, and walking alone. The ages at which milestones appeared had not altered (except by a few weeks in the earlier stages) since landmark studies done in the 1930s by Nancy Bayley and the 1960s by Mary Shirley. Even with changes in factors such as nutrition, the basic sequencing and timing of the motor milestones have remained fairly constant.

Birth to Walking

The motor milestones observed from birth to walking in young children are crawling, sitting, creeping, pulling to stand, independent stance, and walking. Seen at about 2 months, **crawling** is a form of locomotion using both arms and legs with the chest and abdomen on the floor. Independent sitting occurs at 6 or 7 months. While

infants can sit supported at an earlier age, they will not sit independently until postural controls for the head and trunk are established. Seen at 8 to 10 months, **creeping** also uses both arms and legs, but the torso is now lifted off the floor. Various transitions occur during the creeping phase, including a period of rocking back and forth in the creep position. Pulling to stand occurs at 9 or 10 months. During the pulling-to-stand stage, the full postural reflex synergies evolve, making adjustments to standing disturbances possible. Independent standing emerges at 12 or 13 months. Because the postural responses are the last component to mature in this phase, the child is finally capable of standing without support. Finally, independent walking is seen at 14 to 18 months. These age parameters are averages of several developmental assessment scales, and differences in individual children can be expected. Average ages for various motor development milestones are illustrated in figure 4.1.

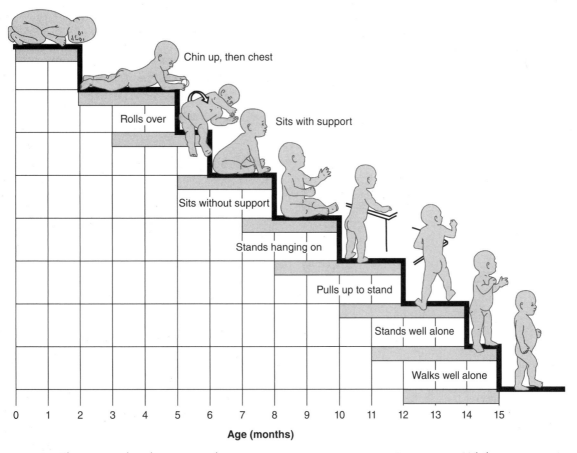

Figure 4.1 The motor development milestones occur at various approximate ages. While a range exists in which children exhibit these milestones, all children typically go through each stage in this successive order.
Created by Stuart Pett.

Assessment Tools

Several assessment tools are useful for evaluating the progression of locomotor skills. Most practitioners use the norms established by Myrtle McGraw, a psychologist interested in the study of motor milestones. She was known for her study of twins and for her 1943 book titled *The Neuromuscular Maturation of the Human Infant.* Her assessment norms included the skills of sitting, standing, walking unsupported, reaching forward, and moving from a sitting to standing position. A major function of various assessment tools is to determine when children are exhibiting abnormal development. Some of these tools include the Gross Motor Function Measure, the Peabody Developmental Motor Scales, the Bayley Scales of Infant Development, and the Movement Assessment of Infants. The Gross Motor Function Measure was originally designed to examine development in children with neurological and genetic disorders, such as cerebral palsy and Down syndrome. The Peabody Developmental Motor Scales tool was designed to look at children from birth to 5 years old, with tests examining these categories: reflexes, stationary (body control and equilibrium), locomotion, object manipulation, grasping, and visual–motor integration. The Bayley Scales of Infant Development tool is used primarily to assess the motor (fine and gross), language (receptive and expressive), and cognitive development of infants and toddlers from birth to 3 years old. In addition to examining children with disorders, these tools became important in understanding the stages of development in typical infants and children.

Transitional Phases

In the training of dancers, progress is not linear. All dancers experience periods in which their skill levels seem to either stagnate or even regress. An example of this phenomenon is what can occur to dancers regarding their ability to turn. Dancers can go through phases in which the capability to turn seems to diminish, and then reappear at a later time. Similarly, in childhood and adolescent motor development, progress is not linear. The common developmental skills that all children experience go through phases of regression and advance.

Arnold Gesell was a psychologist and pediatrician who greatly influenced the field of child development. He made use of one-way mirrors when observing children. He invented the Gesell dome (a one-way mirror shaped as a dome), under which children could be observed without being disturbed. Gesell formulated the **law of developmental direction**, which stated that the direction of development is from head to foot as well as proximal to distal in each segment. He also remarked on the nonlinear nature of the emergence of skills, noting periods of advancement, then apparent regression, followed by another phase of advancement. An example he described is that of crawling, which begins with **homolateral** arm and leg use (using the same-side arm and leg) and then changes to **contralateral** arm and leg use (opposite-side arm and leg). When the infant advances to creeping, the symmetrical pattern reappears (apparent regression), and later, the asymmetrical use of the arms appears in creeping. The asymmetrical pattern is seen as the predecessor to arm use in walking and is therefore seen as superior to the symmetrical pattern.

Another example of the regression of control as the infant makes the transition to a new phase is that of independent sitting. Sway in sitting actually increases just before the ability to stand independently, demonstrating that the system is learning new strategies for postural control, called **recalibration of the sensorimotor system**. As the infant prepares for bipedal locomotion (walking), the systems must recalibrate, causing the increased swaying in sitting behavior. As infants experience longer periods of stance and develop toward walking, their postural sway begins to resemble that of adults.

Independent Walking

Once independent walking emerges in the young child, it is a behavior that will persist for most of that person's lifetime. In fact, a surprising constant is the timing pattern exhibited. In this pattern, a particular phasing occurs between the legs. When the left leg is halfway through its full cycle, the right leg is beginning its cycle, and periods of two-legged support alternate with periods of one-legged support. This timing manifests early in a child's locomotion, and while factors such as speed or length of stride might alter, the coordination of the walking pattern is constant for most of the lifetime.

Early Walking

Most of the child's strategies during early walking are to enhance balance. These tactics include small steps with little joint extension, flat feet, feet wide apart with toes pointing outward to increase the size of the support, no torso rotation, and arms held high with the elbows slightly bent. At this stage no arm swing occurs with walking, and each step is a solo step rather than a continuous series of steps. The rate limiters for the appearance of early walking include strength and coordination. Certainly, strength in the legs must develop to the point that the child can stand on one leg and be able to balance on one leg during weight transfer to the other foot. Both the coordination to move the legs in an alternating pattern and sufficient trunk control to support an upright torso must be present before independent walking can emerge.

Progression of Walking Skills

While some of the features exhibited in early walking optimize stability, changes occur that favor mobility as the child gains more experience. The length of the stride increases with more muscle force, more leg extension, and longer legs. The foot pattern shifts from flatfoot to heel-to-forefoot organization. The toeing-out pattern (walking with the toes pointing out instead of forward) is lessened; at the same time, the base of support decreases in the side-to-side (lateral) plane. A particular coordination in the knee called **double-knee lock** emerges. It has three phases: (1) an extended knee when the heel contacts the support surface, (2) a slight flexing of the knee as the weight transfers to the foot, and (3) the knees extend again during push-off, the phase in which the foot pushes away from the floor to propel the body forward. Finally, the upper body starts to rotate in opposition to the pelvis, balance improves with less leaning forward of the trunk, and oppositional arm swing appears, generated mostly at the shoulder. These components of

walking skills can all be seen by about age 4. As range of motion and leg length increase, strides continue to lengthen. Pace accelerates, and marked improvement occurs in rhythm and coordination up to age 5.

Running

It is intuitively understood that running is faster than walking, and other similarities as well as differences exist. Both walking and **running** share the same timing pattern explained in the section on independent walking, but running includes a period during which neither foot is in contact with the support surface—a period of flight. After children have been walking for 6 or 7 months, they begin to run. By 2 years old, they are competent runners. At first, the attempt to run is nothing more than accelerated walking. At this point children demonstrate a regression in the use of wide support base, landing on flat feet, lack of knee flexion during one-legged support, and arms held high. This regression, which is an attempt to make the effort easier, disappears as the child has more practice running. Because the timing pattern is similar with walking and running, coordination is not the rate limiter. However, because of the flight phase, strength in the legs is definitely an issue in advancing to running, and balance on one leg is a factor in the landing phase. Similar to the changes that occur in the skill progression of walking, as children become more skilled in running, stride length increases, there is less lateral leg movement, heel-to-toe organization and narrowing of the support base reemerge, and the trunk establishes a forward lean. In the use of the arm swing, the elbows form a right angle.

Running is significant to dancers for two reasons. First, it is the initial step in child development that has a flight phase, and therefore it precedes much of the elevation vocabulary in dance. Second, if children develop poor skills, inefficient patterns, or poor biomechanics in running, it can impact all of the later traveling material in dance classes. Several approaches to somatic practice acknowledge this deficit. Irmgard Bartenieff developed her Fundamentals of Movement to encourage adults to revisit early developmental patterns in order to improve inefficient movement habits in adulthood.

Bonnie Bainbridge Cohen's work in Body-Mind Centering also examines motor development and motor milestones in the infant and young child and seeks ways of exploring movement in adulthood that relate directly to the developmental phases. It also explores patterns of movement that inhibit the development of more integrated and complex skills. Somatic practices in general can address some of the inefficient movement habits found in dancers by returning to the simplicity and foundational work of early childhood development. For example, it is common in Bartenieff classes to do foundational skills such as hip flexions and arm circles that children use to acquire more complex locomotor patterns.

Other Locomotor Skills

The locomotor steps that children explore after they are able to run serve as foundations for many of the movements that can be enhanced through dance exposure. From the elegant elevation of the classical dancer to the fast footwork and level changes of the street dancer, the basics are derived from early locomotor skills. A major transition that occurs after children can run is moving from symmetrical to asymmetrical traveling steps.

In addition to walking and running, locomotor skills seen in children include jumping, galloping, hopping, and skipping. These skills have been researched far less than walking and running, but observations and studies exist that can benefit those interested in dance. Some of these skills are not evident until the years when children begin their dance experiences, and understanding the timing for the appropriate introduction of these skills is paramount. Generally, girls execute locomotor skills earlier than boys, and understanding this gender difference is also crucial to how teachers approach dance instruction.

Experience with various locomotor skills can affect balance skills in developing children. Marjorie Woollacott, Jodi Jensen, and Maria Roncesvalles are researchers in the motor development of children. These three researchers studied 61 children from 9 months to 10 years of age, classified as walkers, runners-jumpers, gal-

Young boys develop the same locomotor skills at later stages than girls, but they can still benefit from involvement in dance classes.

lopers, hoppers, and skippers. When they tested the children with a variety of support surface perturbations, children with more locomotor experience regardless of age had enhanced balance, demonstrating faster recovery to the perturbation as well as greater strength. In fact, these children began to match the responses of adults. How children gain proficiency at jumping, galloping, hopping, and skipping informs teachers about the effective progression of dance education. The jump, gallop, hop, and skip are illustrated in Figure 4.2.

Jumping

The skill of **jumping** involves pushing off the ground with both feet and landing on both feet, as seen in figure 4.2a. Children exhibit the simplest forms of jumps by age 2. The way that children initiate their first experiences with jumping is by moving off a surface like a step and landing on the surface below. They explore higher and higher levels, teaching the

After children develop the ability to jump, they develop the locomotor skill called galloping.

motor system how to land. Eventually the child masters jumping forward and jumping over obstacles, usually by the age of 3. The vertical jump appears before the horizontal jump, and in the early stages, how the body bends in preparation is shallow. The hips and knees are still slightly flexed during the jump, and elevation is minimal. Also, the takeoff is asymmetrical, meaning that a slight step might precede the elevation. As the jumping technique improves, the preparatory bend deepens, the joints of the lower leg extend completely during elevation, and the takeoff and landing become symmetrical. As the horizontal jump improves, a 30-degree lean of the trunk occurs, and the 3-year-old child can now choose to alter this angle to create either a horizontal or a vertical jump. The transition from beginning jumping to accomplished jumping also involves changes to arm use. The strategies in the early jumping phases do not support the action of the legs, whereas later, the arms assist in the elevation.

From ages 3 to 7, jumping continues to improve. For most children in this age range, the action and coordination of the legs are more advanced than in the arms. However, the general coordination patterns for both the vertical and horizontal jump are similar from age 3 to adulthood. As with running, not all children acquire effective skills in jumping in the formative years and even into adolescence, and teachers must be able to analyze and assist their students' development of jumping abilities.

The main rate limiter for jumping is muscle force in the legs. Without sufficient strength, the child cannot thrust the body into the air against gravity. The body can walk and run simply by falling forward, but this use of momentum will not achieve a jump.

Galloping

Galloping is an asymmetrical traveling step that consists of a step on the leading foot followed by an elevation step with the back foot as it chases the front foot. The same foot always stays in front. Galloping is illustrated in figure 4.2*b*. Sometimes this step is done to the side, in which case it is referred to as *sliding.* With all of the asymmetrical steps that children learn, they will initially lead with their dominant leg. Rather than insist that young children in dance classes complete these tasks on both sides, in the early stages children should be allowed to select the lead leg.

Children begin to gallop sometime between ages 2 and 3, after they have been able to run for about 6 months. Early research revealed some controversy about whether or not hopping preceded galloping, but sufficient evidence now exists that hopping appears later. Galloping is the first asymmetrical step that children exhibit. It has already been stated that children lead with the dominant leg in galloping before achieving the skill with the nondominant leg. Coordination is the rate limiter for galloping. The even timing pattern described for walking and running must shift to accomplishing two different tasks on the right and left leg that take different amounts of time. These tasks also require different muscular force, and coordinating this asymmetrical use of the muscles is challenging.

Hopping

Hopping is an elevation step pushing off one foot and landing on the same foot, as seen in figure 4.2*c*. Hopping requires enough muscular

Figure 4.2 Jump, gallop, hop, and skip. Each of the successive stages of locomotor movement develops a different set of skills for the young child. *(a)* Jumping relies on two feet for the takeoff and landing. *(b)* Galloping demands movement through space. *(c)* Hopping requires the strength of takeoff and landing on one foot. *(d)* Skipping demands the coordination of alternating legs.

Created by Stuart Pett.

strength in one leg to project the body into the air, and it requires the balance necessary to land on a small support base. Hopping is an essential skill for dance practice, because it is the first one-legged elevation step and therefore integrates strength with balance. Children first begin to hop at about age 3-1/2. Very few children younger than 3 years can hop repeatedly. In the initial stages, the legs are not very efficient in getting the child off the floor, similar to early attempts to jump. The arms tend to be underutilized. As the child improves at hopping, the gesture leg leads the pelvis, the pushing leg fully extends, the arms move in opposition, and the landing uses a soft knee bend. As with galloping, children are able to hop on the dominant leg before they can hop on the nondominant leg. Hopping skills continue improving past the age of 5. The primary rate controller is the development of the balancing mechanisms available to support the weight on one leg for a series of hops. In addition, because the legs do not alternate as they do in running, the same leg must be able to produce force repeatedly.

Skipping

Skipping is a continuous series of a step followed by a hop, using alternating legs, as seen in figure 4.2*d*. Skipping appears sometime between 4 and 7 years old and is the last developmental locomotor step to appear. Only about half of all 5-year-olds can skip. In fact, research has suggested that less than 20% of 4-year-olds can skip, but over 90% of 6-year-olds can skip. Often children first demonstrate a step–hop only on one side (the dominant leg), followed by a simple running step on the nondominant leg. Even after they begin to skip, children show occasional breaks in the pattern, with a step or gallop on the nondominant leg inserted. In the initial stages of hopping, the movement is disjointed, and later the action becomes smooth with softer landings and a more even rhythm. At first the arms are not used in a coordinated manner, but children develop an oppositional use of the arms to the legs. The complexity of this skill determines the age at which skipping appears. Force and balance are not rate limiters, because the child is already hopping, so elevating and landing on one leg are already possible.

Because of the coordination demands of alternating legs, children learn to hop before learning to skip.

Sensory and Cognitive Contributions to Locomotion

Sensory and cognitive contributions to locomotion are just as important to the dancer as their contributions are to postural control. Imagine trying to travel through space without any sensory information and without the cognitive ability to process that information and solve problems or make relevant decisions. Dancers are often unaware of the contributions of the sensory systems and cognitive processes to locomotion.

When examining the development of the growing child and adolescent, movement and perception are undeniably linked. The maturation of the senses and balancing mechanisms (vision, vestibular, somatosensory—which includes proprioception and hearing) happen simultaneously with motor skills, and cognitive skills develop at the same time. **Cognitive skills** are the mental skills that include problem solving, attention, memory, learning reasoning, and decision making. The question for movement educators is how the senses contribute to the progression of motor skills throughout the years from birth to young adulthood. The next section explores the link between senses and motor skills.

Animal Studies

Numerous studies involving animals have helped to determine how the senses, particularly vision, relate to motor development. One selected study demonstrates the importance of physically engaging with the environment to fully acquire a range of sensorimotor interactions.

Richard Held and Alan Hein work at the Department of Brain and Cognitive Sciences at Massachusetts Institute of Technology (MIT). Richard Held's laboratory works on issues of visual development of infants and children, and Alan Hein works with animals in the acquisition and maintenance of visually guided behavior.

They used kittens to examine visual influences on navigating in the environment and to explore the need for environmental interaction in order to map vision and motor control together in the brain. They hypothesized that the animals need experience during development to be able to correlate active movement with the visual field. They performed a study using 10 pairs of kittens. The kittens were raised in the dark, except for one hour each day, in which they were placed in a gondola apparatus (figure 4.3). The control kittens could physically move and respond to the visual stimuli from the environment, but the experimental kittens could only see the environment and not move in relation to it. They were passively moved in small carts so that they experienced cues of optic flow, but these cues were not integrated with locomotion and interaction. After several weeks, the kittens were returned to normal conditions. The control kittens were developmentally typical, but the experimental kittens could not navigate in the environment when locomoting independently, and they proceeded to bump into everything. Tests of visually guided paw placement, discrimination on a visual cliff, and the blink response were normal for the control kittens but not for the experimental kittens. Hence passive locomotion with vision related to the environment is not sufficient to map the visual and locomotor spaces. The happy ending is that the experimental kittens could locomote independently without bumping into walls and objects within 48 to 72 hours.

Sensorimotor Integration in Independent Stance and Walking

As children progress from the ability to stand independently to walking skills, responses to visual input change. When prewalkers are tested using vision and no vision, no differences in muscle responses are found. However, as children make the transition to walking, they show much more muscle response with optical flow, which can come from using film or light techniques that create the illusion of movement on a still surface. In particular, the visual feedback cues the gastrocnemius muscles in the calves to contract as if the body were losing balance. This result demonstrates that visual cues affect postural muscle responses in children once they make the transition to walking.

Another observable difference between independent standers and new walkers is amount of sway, touching and not touching a surface. The independent standers have significantly less

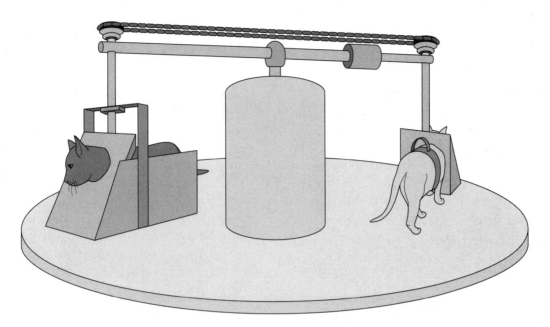

Figure 4.3 The apparatus used by Held and Hein related movement development to visual feedback. The kitten on the left is being moved passively, while the kitten on the right is actively interacting using visual feedback.

From R. Held and A. Hein, 1963, "Movement-produced stimulation in the development of visually guided behavior," *Journal of Comparative and Physiological Psychology* 56: 872-876, fig. 1. Copyright © 1963 by the American Psychological Association. Reprinted with permission.

sway when touching a static surface than when standing freely. The walkers demonstrated no differences in sway whether or not they were touching a surface.

Early Walking and Haptic Exploration of the Environment

Toddlers relate to the environment as they begin moving through changing conditions. New walkers must begin to navigate an environment with obstacles, changing floor angles, and stairs. When they encounter an obstacle, toddlers place their feet directly on the object rather than step over it. Similarly, they place their feet on the edge of a stair rather than on the flat surface. When dealing with changing floor angles, they do not maintain constant speeds as adults do. They decelerate while walking up, and they accelerate while walking down. Initially all of these responses to varying conditions were seen as poor motor control. It is now believed that this represents what is known as **haptic exploration**; that is, the child is intentionally exploring the environment through the sense of touch to gain greater coordination

and understanding of changing circumstances. Further, vision plays an important role during this developmental phase. Infants spend more time visually exploring obstacles than adults do. The haptic and visual explorations go hand in hand so that the infant can verify and understand the nature of the obstacle. In this way, future encounters with similar obstacles can be navigated with visual exploration only.

Head and Trunk Organization

Throughout the life span, the relationship of the head to the trunk can vary depending on whether the frame of reference is the support surface or the vertical line of gravity. When the frame of reference is the support surface, the body organizes from the lower half of the body to the head. In stance, this orientation is from the feet to the head. In locomotion, it is from the hips to the head. The postural responses reverse when the body is relating to the line of gravity (from head to feet). Further, two different ways that the head can relate to the trunk are observed. One is called **en bloc**, meaning that the neck muscles are held stable relative to the trunk. The other is called **articulate**, meaning that the neck muscles remain fluid and not statically held on the trunk.

From the period of independent stance to about age 6, children generally demonstrate the en bloc mode to maintain control of balance. By age 7, children more commonly use the articulated mode and can control balance without having to freeze the head on the trunk. The relationship of the head to the trunk continues to develop varying strategies into adulthood.

Sensory and Cognitive Development With Locomotion

Throughout the life span, sensory, cognitive, and motor skills continually evolve. The changes are dramatic in the earliest years; maturity of these components occurs in early adulthood, as late as 25 years old. While it is possible to discuss each of these three areas separately, their interrelationship throughout the aging process should be emphasized.

Sensory Development

From early childhood to adulthood, the senses continue to mature. In terms of postural control and locomotion, the critical sensory systems are visual, vestibular, and somatosensory. While all of the systems are developing and being mapped to the motor system, each has a different timeline for maturation.

It has been observed that while somatosensory function in relation to balance appears quite early and matures by 3 to 4 years of age, visual function in relation to balance and locomotion matures much later, reaching adultlike characteristics by age 15. Vestibular function matures later, and even by age 15, the vestibular system does not function as it does in adults. At 7 to 8 years of age, girls show vestibular function superior to that of boys, and boys under 10 years old exhibit more sway and greater instability than do girls of the same age. Research using adults has demonstrated that when the visual and somatosensory systems give conflicting information, the vestibular system arbitrates and resolves the conflict. However, the ability to manage multisensory cues and conflicting sensory information is not present in childhood. This information is useful for understanding age limits to multisensory organization when teaching dance. Dance teachers must recognize all of these age landmarks in order to be effective. See the section titled Age-Appropriate Movement and Dance Training for further discussion on this topic.

Recently, interest in the adolescent years has been increasing. Understanding the profound changes in all facets of adolescent behavior—motor, sensory, cognitive, physiological, and psychological—has begun to influence every aspect of training and education for this age group. Researchers Catherine Quatman-Yates, Carmen Quatman, Andrew Meszaros, Mark Paterno, and Timothy Hewett did a systematic review of articles examining sensorimotor development in adolescence published in 2012. They began with 2,304 articles, and based on selection criteria they reduced the number of articles to 33. They revealed several aspects of changes throughout adolescence. While 14- to 16-year-olds can already perceive static objects and have good peripheral vision, dynamic perception continues maturing up to age 16. Proprioception also continues maturing as late as 12 or 13 years of age, but adolescents react more slowly to movement than do adults. In studies examining neuromuscular control during jumps, it was found that after puberty, girls had decreased control in landings, while boys did not exhibit this regression and sometimes even improved their skill level. Coordination shows continued improvement in the adolescent years, including changes in speed, direction, muscle tension, and timing, but considerable variability in same-age children persists. Further, coordination in some tasks (e.g., repetitive) matures by 12 to 15 years, while coordination in more complex tasks might not mature until age 18. Anticipatory strategies also continue to develop through adolescence, and these strategies occur more quickly.

The few studies that deal with regression to sensorimotor capabilities yield evidence that regression occurs. In particular, young people go through phases in which they select accuracy and control over speed and flexibility in movement choices. As mentioned previously, some aspects of neuromuscular control, such as knee joint action in landings, go through periods of regression in the transition from prepuberty to puberty. Finally, adolescents may demonstrate increased reliance on vision and regress in their use of proprioceptive information. It is critical that dancers and dance teachers recognize regression phases and acknowledge the need to modify or alter work during these periods.

Cognitive Development

Cognitive development deals primarily with development of mental processes such as conscious thought, reasoning, abstract thought, and problem-solving abilities. Two areas of the brain that are crucial for movement and for planning movement are the frontal cortex and the cerebellum. These two areas mature relatively late, well into adolescence and early adulthood. Therefore, one can assume that this lengthy maturation of cognitive function has an impact on motor skills. For this reason, it is important to reduce the amount of cognitive loading (the total extent of conscious mental activity at any given instant in time) for adolescents during movement acquisition. For example, it may not be effective to give adolescents corrections about alignment while they are attempting to learn a new and complex dance skill.

While it is recognized that complex cognitive skills take time to evolve, the time needed to demonstrate complex motor skills is often neglected. Too often those who teach dance, gymnastics, and other athletic activities to children expect execution of highly difficult skills that are beyond the capacity of their students. Those educators who understand the relationship of movement to cognition advocate a process called *active learning*, in which students are encouraged to actively and physically participate in the learning process rather than passively listen to the teacher. However, note that adolescents demonstrate poor ability to assess risk or to see complex outcomes from choices. What seems like a good idea for a dance move for an adolescent might be very dangerous, and teachers can help youth to navigate these situations. For example, the weight support on the head and hands seen in street dance may be too demanding for some children and adolescents.

As evidence continues to accumulate, the profound interrelationship of motor, percep-tual, and cognitive skills becomes apparent. Trying to separate these three components of human interaction with the environment is an artificial approach to understanding how people learn to move. The focus of this text will continue to be on motor skills, but keep in mind the importance of all of the functioning systems for achieving advanced motor control.

Physiological Development: Adolescent Growth Spurts

Physiological changes in the adolescent years powerfully affect motor skills. **Physiology** is the study of the human body and its systems. While anatomy focuses on form, physiology is concerned with function. In particular, adolescents often go through growth spurts, in which dramatic physiological changes can occur in short time periods. Most growth spurts occur between ages 11 and 14, and they last for approximately 18 to 24 months. Girls can experience growth spurts earlier, and boys later. Changes include increases in height, weight, and arm and leg length. The proportion of limbs to torso also changes, because the arms and legs grow more rapidly than the torso. These physical developments affect coordination and balance. The growth of the limbs can be asymmetrical, such as one leg growing faster than the other. Bone growth precedes muscle growth, and for a period of time, the muscles are short relative to the length of the long bones. This relationship can affect strength and flexibility. Areas where muscle tendons attach to bone can become vulnerable to injury. Finally, for girls other changes occur during puberty with the onset of menarche, including breast development and proportion changes, which can affect motor skills.

All of these changes can affect dance skills as well. It is not uncommon for technique and control to regress. Diminished strength and flexibility can cause decrements such as early fatigue and lower leg extensions. Poor equilibrium and coordination can create problems for turns and balances. Good alignment is difficult to establish, especially in the pelvis and spine, because of both the physical and coordination deficits. The effects of all of these problems on the psychological state of the adolescent should not be underestimated.

Major changes also occur in brain growth and development preceding puberty and into adolescence. Although the brain reaches 95% of its adult volume by age 5, major changes continue for several years. The frontal lobes, which are the center of organization and planning, impulse control and reasoning, do not fully develop until early adulthood. Similarly the corpus callosum, noted for its connection to intelligence and self-awareness, continues growing into the 20s. The parietal lobes, which integrate visual, auditory, and tactile information, are still maturing into the mid-teen years. The cerebellum is another part of the brain still developing well into adolescence. Its role in motor skills as well as cognition is still being explored. During this time period, the brain is undergoing changes in which unused connections are removed and used in alternative ways. For example, the adolescent who ceases playing soccer and focuses on dance practice will develop brain connections that encourage dance coordination. In other words, the brain is specializing in behavior that is the most practiced and rewarded. Skill development and maintenance during adolescence has great perseverance into adulthood.

The adolescent years are a time of major changes to many systems. Knowledge of the impact of these transitional stages is crucial for developing sound pedagogical strategies for teaching dance. Figure 4.4 emphasizes the changes in proportions that occur from birth to adulthood that influence the various stages of motor development. It is apparent from the proportionately large head of the infant why standing would be impossible at this age, even if the coordination were present. The change in leg length between ages 2 and 5 clearly supports the emergence of the locomotor steps. Even in the teen years, the lack of physical maturity and the lack of adultlike proportions are evident. The next section presents specific recommendations for dance training during the developmental years.

Age-Appropriate Movement and Dance Training

Dance training can be more effective when teachers and dancers understand the landmarks in various stages of motor development and the age limits to multiple sensory inputs. Many phases in this process exist, but this section focuses on two distinct time lines, the early childhood years and the adolescent years.

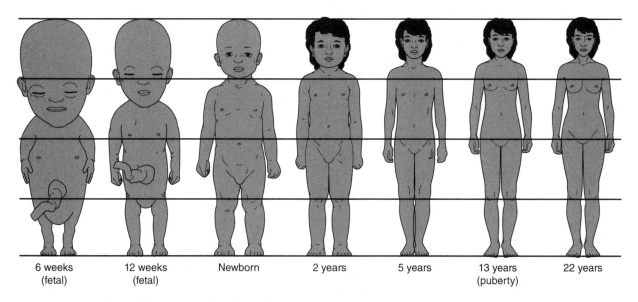

| 6 weeks (fetal) | 12 weeks (fetal) | Newborn | 2 years | 5 years | 13 years (puberty) | 22 years |

Figure 4.4 These figures are placed on the same scale to more clearly show changes in proportions through maturation. Note that the two on the left are pre-birth, which is why the umbilical cord is seen.

Adapted from Piek 2006.

Childhood and Prepuberty

Dance classes can begin for children as young as 3 or 4 years old. Typical children in this age range are already walking, running, and jumping competently. From age 3 to 7 jumping continues to improve, so it is an excellent time to explore this skill. One of the more engaging ways to work on jumping skills is through jumping over objects, both real and imaginary. Muscle force is the main rate limiter in jumping, so be aware of the potential to overtax the legs in these games and exercises.

Galloping also emerges at a fairly young age (between 2 and 3 years old). The main difference between galloping and the previously mentioned skills, such as walking and running, is that galloping is asymmetrical. Further, most children gallop with the dominant leg in front considerably sooner than with the nondominant leg. This preference suggests that the youngest students should be allowed to select the leading leg and not be pressured to perform the task on both sides. By age 4, children can be asked to gallop on either side.

Hopping should not be introduced until children are fairly comfortable galloping. Hopping does not emerge until 3-1/2 years of age, and it continues improving past age 5. Like galloping, it is asymmetrical, and children use the dominant leg initially. Because this skill requires more strength and balance in one leg, these aspects should be considered carefully in designing class material for children. An additional factor is the underuse of arms in the early stages of hopping. Asking children to fully engage their arms during this phase only overwhelms them.

Skipping appears sometime between 4 and 7 years old, and only about half of all 5 year olds can skip. Recall that less than 20% of 4-year-olds can skip. Regardless of the amount of instruction and practice that they are given, 4-year-old children will not accomplish skipping. Forcing this skill in this age group merely serves to discourage the children. Once again, the favoring of the dominant leg appears; children often step–hop on the dominant leg and take a running step on the nondominant leg. Children need to practice the leg action in skipping until they are comfortable with the skill before they are asked to integrate oppositional arms.

In each of these asymmetrical locomotor steps, consider allowing young children to select their preferential leg; do not impose a structure of performing on both sides. Note that children use the en bloc strategy for the neck and trunk until about age 7, so to expect movement of the head in opposing directions to the torso is unrealistic in the early years of dance class.

Much of the research highlighted in this chapter emphasized the late development of the ability to manage multisensory (visual, vestibular, and somatosensory) input. It is imperative that younger children be given movement of sufficient simplicity that the various modalities are not in conflict. For example, if giving material that involves moving through the space, it is best to have them keep the head vertical on the spine. This suggestion also supports the heavy reliance on visual information in young children.

Finally, girls develop more quickly than boys in a number of cognitive and motor skills. It may be wise to give boys different variations of class material that is appropriate for their stage of development. This differentiation needs to be handled sensitively so that young boys do not feel self-conscious. In addition, boys are often stronger than girls of the same age, so they can be encouraged to jump, skip, and hop higher and further than the girls as a way to compensate for poorer coordination. This strategy is a way of supporting boys in class and encouraging their confidence.

Chapter 3 described some of the potential benefits of using improvisation in dance classes. Improvisation is commonly found in classes for children ages 3 to 7, often called creative movement classes. However, by age 8 or 9, children regularly move into more highly structured technical classes. While the importance for children to begin gaining technical skills is acknowledged, the value of continued improvisational movement should be recognized. Aside from the creative expression it affords children, its use in motor skill development is apparent from all of the information provided in this chapter. From unexpected challenges to balance to disrupting habitual movement patterns, improvisation can serve as a remarkable tool in dance training.

Adolescent Years

Because of the changes resulting from growth spurts in this age group (as explained earlier in the chapter), adolescent dancers need special consideration. Teachers can modify class material either for the entire group or for specific dancers going through a growth spurt. It is also a good idea to place limits on work such as jumping, pointe work on one leg, stressful partnering work, and movements that stress the knees, including grand pliés and floor work. Teachers can emphasize work that develops core support, alignment, kinesthetic awareness, and artistry. Balancing work can focus on proprioception, such as simple balances with eyes closed rather than difficult positions and turns. Growth spurt periods can also be good times to introduce supplementary conditioning and expand continued improvisational work into composition and choreography. This age group should avoid excessive flexibility exercises, because muscles have limited strength especially during growth spurts, and the tendon attachments are weaker at this age. Encourage adolescents to make informed and responsible choices about how they will modify class. Remain aware that students will go through regression phases, and help them understand that this is temporary. Skills will return, but the dancers should not stress and strain the body to achieve what cannot occur during these transitions.

Aside from acknowledging the growth spurts, adolescence can be an ideal time to begin challenges to multisensory input. Now is the time to add complexity that challenges the three mechanisms for balance. You can give traveling material with the head and torso away from the upright alignment, even with the body turning. As vestibular and visual systems are disrupted, proprioception is further challenged. Both improvisation and closed-eye balances work to heighten proprioception and to prepare dancers for work onstage when lighting diminishes visual acuity.

Summary

The motor milestones delineate how young children progress through the stages of crawling, sitting, creeping, pulling to stand, independent standing, and finally independent walking. Esther Thelen was one of the early researchers who documented child development through the lens of dynamic systems theory. Thelen and later researchers demonstrated the complexity of the many systems that act as rate limiters and must reach a threshold level of maturity for children to reach the next milestone. After walking, children begin to run, jump, gallop, hop, and skip. Each of these transitions requires increasing levels of muscle strength, coordination, balance, and control. Sensory and cognitive systems develop in concert with the motor system. Children can be observed interacting with the environment to map sensory perception to motor control and integrate cognitive abilities simultaneously. As children reach adolescence, they face other transitions during the development of motor, sensory, and cognitive skills, including growth spurts and subsequent physiological and cognitive challenges. At each stage of motor development, distinct variability in same-age children persists, and the needs, skills, and potential of each child must be acknowledged. Understanding and applying theories of motor development can greatly enhance dance training from the youngest years to early adulthood.

Chapter 5
Development of Ballistic Skills

*B*allistic movements in dance provide pleasure and excitement for viewers and dancers alike. Audiences cheer the extended circling leaps of the male ballet dancer and marvel at the fast ballistic zapateado of the flamenco dancer and the nerve tap of the tap dancer. In more recent years, locking and waacking from street dance have intrigued young audiences with sharp attack and rapid level change. Ballistic movements in dance can be some of the most difficult material to learn and to teach. In addition, the explosive nature of these skills causes dance teachers to have concerns regarding safety and injury prevention. This chapter describes the development of ballistic skills through childhood and adolescence.

Much of what is known about ballistic skills is derived from sports. Tasks such as throwing and kicking balls, and striking with a bat or racket, all involve ballistic actions using the arms or legs. **Ballistic skills** are skills in which a person provides impetus to an object or body part through forceful and rapid exertion, setting the object or body part into motion along a specific trajectory. In sports, ballistic skills usually involve object manipulation, whether throwing an object such as a ball or striking an object with another implement such as a racket. In dance, ballistic skills include single-leg actions such as grand battement and frappé in ballet; elevation steps such as leaps in ballet, modern, and contemporary dance; thrown limb gestures in street dance; zapateado in flamenco dance; and foot stamping in classical Indian kathak dance. In these instances, the object set into motion is the human body or a body part. Little research exists on the motor development and control of ballistic skills in dance. Most teachers instruct about these skills based on their own personal training and educated guesses. Therefore, the information from sports serves as a foundation for this material, and conclusions for dance based on sports knowledge are suggested.

Defining Ballistic Movement

To accurately define ballistic movement, one must understand how the muscles function during ballistic movement. With this understanding, dancers and teachers can design methods to create the most effective motor strategies. Sometimes teachers attempt to teach ballistic actions in dance by teaching them slowly, hoping to achieve good form. Their intention is to accelerate these slow versions, and the ballistic action will be present. However, this method is not a successful teaching strategy, because the motor programs for slow and fast versions of the same movement are completely different.

Ballistic movements can be defined by the amount of time they take to occur. Generally, a rapid movement of the limb is considered ballistic if it takes less than 150 milliseconds (ms). Some examples include striking a key on a typewriter, which takes fewer than 100 ms, and swinging a bat in baseball, which takes fewer than 140 ms. A specific pattern of agonist–antagonist activity can be described; it is called the **triple-burst (triphasic) EMG pattern**, three phases of agonist–antagonist–agonist muscle activity that control ballistic movements. The **agonist** in a movement is the muscle creating the action. The **antagonist** is the muscle that creates the opposite movement; in most movements it relaxes while the agonist fires. For example, when you extend (straighten) your elbow, the agonist is the triceps group, and the antagonist is the biceps group, which would flex (bend) the elbow. In a ballistic movement, an initial burst of muscle activation occurs in the agonist. This burst is followed by a period in which the agonist is inhibited and the antagonist fires in order to decelerate the limb. In the third phase, the agonist fires again while the antagonist is inhibited. This last phase is believed to cause **clamping** of the movement, or completing the intended action in a smooth, controlled manner. In the previous example, this pattern would be a burst of the triceps, followed by firing of the biceps as the triceps stops firing, followed by another activation of the triceps. Figure 5.1 shows the three phases described in an electromyograph (EMG): first the triceps burst, then the biceps burst, and finally the second triceps burst.

The various hypotheses about how control in the three stages is accomplished are complex, and they are still in discussion. A known fact is that fast and slow movements are controlled by the nervous system in different ways. With a few notable exceptions such as checking a

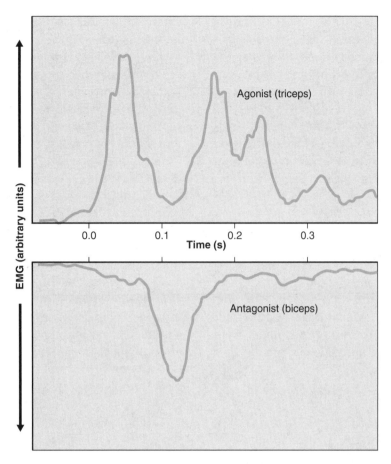

Figure 5.1 Electromyographic results from agonist (upper trace) and antagonist (lower trace) while the subject produces the movement, a ballistic extension of the elbow.

Adapted from W.J. Wadman, 1979, "Control of fast goal-directed arm movements," *Journal of Human Movement Studies* 5: 10. By permission of W.J. Wadman.

baseball swing, once a ballistic movement has been initiated, it cannot be stopped or corrected in the middle of execution.

Sports Activity Using Ballistic Movements

It is clear that major differences exist between those sports that involve contact with equipment and activities such as dance, which rarely uses external objects in a ballistic way. When dancers use props, it is usually a manipulation of an object as part of the dramatic intention, and it is handled with less force. Despite the differences, similarities exist in the stages of learning that young children experience as they explore ballistic activity, regardless of the movement form.

Because so many sports include these movements, extensive research on ballistic movements in sports has been conducted.

Upper-extremity ballistic movements are found in sports such as baseball, tennis, handball, volleyball, basketball, golf, racquetball, field and ice hockey, and polo. Lower-extremity ballistic movements are found in sports such as soccer, rugby, football, track and field, and martial arts. Often examined are throwing, striking (both sidearm and overarm), and kicking. Each of these forms of ballistic movement can provide insight into developmental stages, and these insights can be applied to dance.

Ballistic Skills in the Upper Extremities

Some of the earliest expressions of ballistic movement in children occur with the upper extremities. Children begin throwing objects using an overarm throw before the age of 3. Ballistic skills in the upper extremities can be divided into throwing and striking. While many types of throws exist, the one most commonly studied is the overarm throw with one hand, as seen in figure 5.2. The basic mechanics of the overarm throw apply to other types of throws. Striking can be divided into sidearm striking and overarm striking. While throwing and striking objects are rare in dance, these skills are briefly reviewed with an emphasis on what can apply universally to all ballistic movement and specifically to dance movement.

Overarm Throwing

When determining the best ways to learn and teach a skill, one should be able to assess that skill. Often when people assess throwing skills in sports, they use **end-product assessments**, which measure results such as accuracy, distance, or velocity. However, even with a skill as result-driven as throwing, problems with assessing only quantitative aspects arise. For example, because same-age children are different heights and at different strength levels, distance can be dependent on individual variation and may not reflect actual differences in skill. For this reason, assessments must include qualitative aspects of the skill, such as the sequencing of the various components in the movement pattern.

In early overarm throwing, children tend to use the arm only, and they do not include stepping and torso actions that contribute to the momentum. In skillful throwing, the thrower uses a sequential pattern to achieve the task, which includes a forward step with rotation of the pelvis, rotation of the upper trunk with arm swing, inward rotation of the arm with extension of the elbow, a release of the ball, and a follow-through movement. This pattern of rapid actions in a particular sequence is a highlight of all ballistic movements. For example, in grand

Figure 5.2 Adolescents are involved in many sports activities that involve the ballistic skill of throwing.

battement in dance, skillful execution would begin the pattern with weight transfer to the standing leg. Leg action of the gesture (kicking) leg immediately follows, and, as the leg reaches a certain height, the pelvis begins to rotate and tilt to accommodate increased height. Later in the sequence, the standing knee slightly flexes to allow pelvic movement. If arm gestures are involved, they initiate with the leg but arrive slightly before the leg action is completed. As in the sports example, it would not be informative to judge the skill execution of grand battement only by measuring its height. This qualitative assessment of sequencing is equally important.

Clear and detailed procedures exist for observing overarm throwing. The observer should focus on one component or a small number of components at a given time. In addition, the observer should determine what the best angle is for viewing a given component. In the grand battement devant, if trunk alignment is the primary focus, the observer should watch the dancer in profile. If the leg's relationship to the midline of the body is the focus, the observer should watch from the front. Specific and detailed observational procedures have not been delineated in dance as they have been in sports.

Striking

Striking always involves using an upper extremity or an implement to make contact with an object and determine a new trajectory. While striking is uncommon in dance, applications to ballistic movements of the arms in various dance forms are suggested. Far less information exists about striking than about throwing and kicking. Two forms of striking exist: sidearm and overarm. Because striking actions are so rare in dance, the two forms are not considered separately. Instead, the basic underlying principles of both are combined.

The sequencing for striking actions includes a preparatory backswing with a step forward, rotation of the pelvis, rotation of the spine with arm swing, contact, and finally follow-through. As with throwing, the beginner shows little torso involvement in the strike. It is later in the development of striking skills that weight transfer from one foot to the other and the use

of pelvic and spine rotation contribute significantly to the momentum.

It is interesting to observe how many preparatory actions occur just before the actual contact of the arm or implement with the object. This preparation is an essential aspect of ballistic movements, including striking as it relates to athletic activities. Street dancers anticipate ballistic arm movements with torso support, just as modern dancers use a preparatory plié before jumping and hopping. In traveling elevation work such as leaps, the timing of the push-off step and of the arms is critical in creating both height and distance. Flamenco and tap dancers must employ a preparatory flexion of the lower-extremity joints as well as torso support before fast and ballistic footwork. Without anticipatory preparations, ballistic movements in dance would not have the necessary force or control to succeed.

Tossing

Tossing or throwing lifts are examples of the rare instances in which dancers use ballistic movements to throw an object, in this case another dancer. While little research exists on the subject of tossed lifts, it can be hypothesized that the sequencing and the core support are similar to that of the athlete throwing an object. One of the primary differences is that in the dance case, the object is closer in size and weight to the thrower than in most sports, and the distance the object travels is much shorter. Often, because of choreographic choices, the thrower is not permitted to take steps before or after the throw, which can affect the mechanics of the throw. Sometimes the thrown dancer is caught by the initial partner, and sometimes by a third dancer. While the trajectory of the flying dancer differs in these two types of throws, the basic form and sequencing of the ballistic throwing action is similar. The sport in which thrown lifts involving humans are observed is in pairs ice skating, but rarely do dancers land from thrown lifts on the ground unsupported, as the skaters do.

Another consideration for dancers comes from the sports setting. Coaches and trainers who work with children are cognizant of the importance of size-appropriate implements. If the balls or striking implements are too large for the child, the motor patterns will be poorly learned. Similarly, if dance teachers ask children to practice elevation steps using the barre, the height of the barre is critical. If the barre is too high, poor upper-extremity use will be automatically embedded in the motor memory for this skill. Figure 5.3 illustrates this problem.

Figure 5.3 The problems of working at a barre that is too high for this child's proportions are apparent in the child's poor arm organization and alignment.

Ballistic Skills in the Lower Extremities

Dance is rife with examples of lower-extremity ballistics. Ballistic skills include single-leg actions such as grand battement and frappé in ballet; elevation steps such as leaps in ballet, jazz, modern dance, and contemporary dance; zapateado in flamenco dance; the nerve tap in tap dance; foot stamping in classical Indian

kathak dance; and sharp leg actions of locking and waacking in street dance. In sports, kicking is the most observed lower-extremity ballistic action. The following two sections examine two forms of kicking: kicking with an object and kicking without an object. Subsequent sections discuss vertical elevation steps and striking foot movements.

Kicking With an Object

Athletes generally have two ways to propel an object using the legs. One way is called kicking—contact with a ball that is on the ground, either stationary or moving toward the player. The other way is known as punting—to hold and then drop the ball, followed by striking the ball with the foot. Because kicking has been more widely studied and punting is mechanically similar to kicking, this discussion focuses on kicking with some additional comments about punting at the end. As with throwing and striking, general principles of kicking can motivate a discussion of dance-related lower-extremity ballistics, which do not use objects.

Similar to upper-extremity ballistic actions, early attempts at kicking display single actions instead of sequences of actions. Form in the body, such as a bent knee at the moment of ball contact, may be undefined, and often a retraction rather than follow-through occurs with ball contact. The trunk and arms are not involved. In proficient kicking, the sequence of movements includes a preparatory windup, sequential movements of the kicking (gesture) leg, full range of motion at the hip for the end of the kick, trunk rotation, and arm opposition. Observers look for specific components, including range of motion of the kicking leg, extension of the kicking leg, range of motion in the trunk, and oppositional use of the arms. Research has found that only about 10% of children aged 7 to 9 show skilled kicking. This fact suggests that children do not necessarily acquire skillful kicking motor patterns before 10 years of age. As with throwing, children will not automatically demonstrate the patterns of skilled kicking.

Punting is similar to kicking with a few exceptions. First, the ball is not on the ground but rather is dropped by the athlete before contact. Second, the ankle of the kicking leg remains dorsiflexed during ball contact, whereas in punting, the ankle plantar flexes prior to and during contact with the ball. Third, during the punt a hop occurs on the supporting foot after ball contact. Comparing these actions to grand battement devant, the dancer would have a pointed foot (plantar flexed ankle) but would optimally not hop after the battement. In this way, battement combines some of the features of the two actions of kicking and punting.

Kicking Without an Object

Kicking without objects occurs in sports, such as the leg action to clear a hurdle in track and field or the crescent kick or side kick found in martial arts. However, with most sporting events, each of these steps serves a functional purpose: to clear a physical object or to confront an opponent. In dance, while height is certainly valued, elevation steps involving kicking have a major aesthetic component. In fact, dancers sometimes sacrifice some of the height of a jump to achieve a particular form. Kicking in dance can include movements such as battement done in stationary stance, or movements that lead to traveling elevation steps, such as leaps. Both initiate with a ballistic leg action, but they have different goals.

Studies in dance have frequently examined either impact forces in landings or the biomechanics of various dance movements. In dance, very little discussion about motor strategies or sequencing patterns exists as it does in sports. One area of patterning that has been observed in dance outlines how dancers transfer weight from two feet to one foot for grand battement. In this instance, the sequence is initiation of the transfer of weight to the standing leg, followed by gesture leg movement along with torso support and increased spine extension, and then pelvic rotation and tilt to accommodate greater range of motion. Various researchers and teachers have suggested that this sequencing is relevant to high leg kicks in any direction. One of the characteristics seen in beginners is initiating the kick by rotating or inclining the pelvis too early in the sequence. This strategy can result in both instability and poor form. An instructional technique to ensure proper sequencing is to emphasize the lateral shift of the pelvis

without tilting during weight transfer in simpler movements that lead up to high kicks. Examples include tendu, dégagé, and rond de jambe. Even in some jazz forms in which considerable pelvic movement is permissible in battement, this motion of the pelvis should not initiate the kick, rather it should occur later in the sequence. The following theory based on the triple-burst EMG pattern is proposed for the grand battement devant:

1. The weight begins to transfer to the standing leg, and the muscles that extend the torso further activate to prevent the torso from flexing during the battement, as shown in figure 5.4a.

2. The initial burst of the hip flexor muscles (such as the iliopsoas) begins the action (phase 1 of the triple-burst EMG pattern), as shown in figure 5.4b. The gesture leg is beginning to move forward, and the burst of the hip flexors has already begun.

3. As the gesture leg approaches the full height of the battement, the hip extensors (hamstrings) fire to decelerate the leg (phase 2 of the triple-burst EMG pattern), as shown in figure 5.4c.

4. The hip flexors then do a second burst to smooth or coordinate the action (phase 3 of the triple-burst EMG pattern), as shown in figure 5.4d. The leg has reached full height, and the hip flexors are clamping to smooth the endpoint of the battement.

Leaping (grand jeté) is an elevation step from one foot to the other foot that travels in space and is initiated with a kick of the leading leg. The leap is shown in figure 5.5. In some respects a leap can be considered running with an emphasis on the flight phase. A leap can go in any direction—front, side, or back. The lead leg either does a straight-leg ballistic kick or a développé action starting with a bent knee that finishes extended, called saut de chat. Other variations include stag leaps, in which the lead leg remains flexed at the knee, and leaps with both legs bent. In each case, the initial movement of the lead leg is ballistic. Since this particular aspect of leaping has not been studied in dance, the following theory based on

Figure 5.4 The triple-burst pattern of grand battement devant involves the following stages: *(a)* the moment of weight transfer, *(b)* the gesture leg moving forward, *(c)* the gesture leg just before reaching full height, and *(d)* the moment of full height of the gesture leg.

Figure 5.5 This leap in midflight is initiated with a kick of the leading leg, providing some of the momentum for the height and distance of the leap.

the triple-burst EMG pattern is proposed for the forward leap with straight legs:

1. The initial bursts of the hip flexor muscles and the knee extensor muscles begin the action (phase 1 of the triple-burst EMG pattern).

2. The torso moves from a slightly backward lean to a forward lean to assist in propelling the body forward in space.

3. The arms begin a swing, often oppositional, that contributes momentum to the action.

4. At end range (that is, the full height) of the lead leg, the hip extensors fire to decelerate the leg (phase 2 of the triple-burst EMG pattern).

5. The hip flexors of the lead leg then do a second burst to smooth or coordinate the action (phase 3 of the triple-burst EMG pattern).

A pattern involving eccentric control (muscle tension as the muscles is lengthening) follows for the landing phase, but this part of the leap is not the focus of this chapter.

When beginners have not achieved this clean triple-burst pattern, a jerk can occur at the top of the leap, leading to an uncoordinated and unaesthetic result as well as poor movement efficiency. The complexity of both the sequencing and number of body components involved, plus the speed at which each step must occur, makes accomplishing this task with proficiency quite advanced. Young or inexperienced dancers can certainly attempt leaps, but it is unrealistic to expect success in every aspect of this task. The focus should initially be on the sequencing pattern; later, other aspects can be addressed.

Another type of ballistic kick to consider is the group of gestural kicks seen in street dance or capoeira that resemble martial arts kicks, as seen in figure 5.6. These kicks are similar in the triple-phase EMG pattern to the grand battement already described. The differences are fundamentally aesthetic, including whether internal or external hip rotation occurs and

Figure 5.6 In street dance, kicking with the lower extremities is a common movement used as a gesture rather than for elevating off the floor.

whether or not the foot is pointed or flexed. In addition, far more torso compensation is permissible in street dance.

Vertical Elevation Steps

The question arises as to whether or not vertical elevation steps such as jumps and hops are ballistic leg actions. Certainly the push-off phase uses the same kind of ballistic or forceful thrust to propel the body into the air as seen in phase 1 of the triple-burst EMG pattern. However, the entire triple-burst EMG pattern does not occur in vertical jumps. Despite this difference, many researchers still consider vertical jumps to be ballistic actions. Because the pushing action sends the body straight up into the air, gravity acts to dissipate the force naturally, and there

is no need for the antagonist muscles to fire to decelerate the action or for the agonist to do a second firing to clamp the movement. In learning and teaching vertical jumps, encouraging this initial ballistic phase is essential, and the component of power must be part of the dancer's training. Figure 5.7 shows two variations of vertical elevation: jumping from two feet to one foot (sissonne) and jumping from two feet to two feet (sauté).

Striking Foot Movements

Several dance forms include various kinds of striking foot movements. Unlike the movements of grand battement and leaps, these foot actions have an external object as a target, which is the floor. The various striking foot movements in

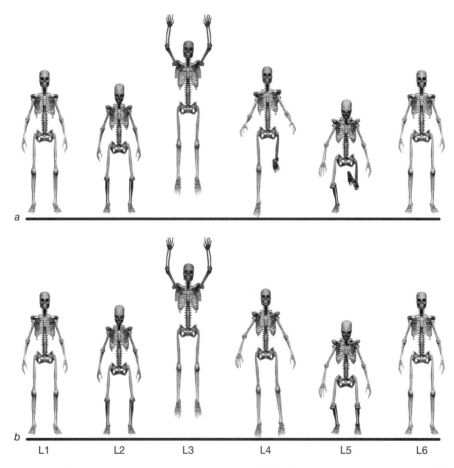

| L1 | L2 | L3 | L4 | L5 | L6 |

Figure 5.7 Phases of elevation steps. *(a)* In the sissonne, L2 is the push-off phase, and L3 is the instant of elevation, followed by a single leg landing in L4 and L5. *(b)* In the sauté, L2 is the push-off phase, and L3 is the instant of elevation, followed by a two-legged landing in L4 and L5.

Reprinted, by permission, from G. Leporace et al., 2011, "Activation of hip and knee muscles during two landing tasks performed by male volleyball athletes," *Revista Brasileira de Medicina do Esporte* 17(5): 324-328. Available: www.scielo.br/scielo.php?script=sci_arttext&pid=S1517-86922011000500006&lng=en&tlng=en. 10.1590/S1517-86922011000500006.

dance have differing aesthetic goals. Because of limited research, it is unknown at this time whether they fulfill the triple-burst EMG pattern, but explanations for the various movements are suggested.

One common example in ballet is called frappé, which is the past tense of the French word *frapper*, meaning "to strike." The importance of frappé is that it is considered to be a preparation for many elevation steps in ballet because of the quick and powerful attacking action of the foot. A frappé is done with the gesture foot starting at the ankle of the standing leg, followed by a ballistic action of striking the ball of that foot against the floor. As with leaps, the frappé can happen in any direction, but for simplicity, the side direction has been selected for description. Figure 5.8 illustrates the stages described next.

1. In the initial stage (phase 1), bursts from the agonist muscles involved occur, including hip flexors and abductors (such as the iliopsoas and tensor fasciae latae), knee extensors (quadriceps), and ankle plantar flexors (gastrocnemius); see figure 5.8a. The gesture foot is just beginning to move away from the standing leg.

2. At the moment of contact of the ball of the foot with the floor, the muscles in action amplify (increase their contraction) as a result of the resistance of the floor; see figure 5.8*b*.

3. This high-intensity agonist activity is followed by phase 2, activation of the antagonists (such as the hamstrings and adductors) to decelerate the striking leg; see figure 5.8*c*.

4. In phase 3, the agonists will fire for the second time, to clamp or smooth the foot and leg actions and allow for a clean stop at end range; see figure 5.8*d*. This moment of the movement is literally milliseconds later than figure 5.8*c*, and it is not discernible to the naked eye.

If the tempo is reduced and the motion becomes sustained instead of ballistic, the frappé will not serve as a jump preparation, and will have little use in the ballet vocabulary.

The striking foot actions in flamenco, kathak, tap, and stepping (which has its origins in gumboot dance from South Africa) share the common goal of making sound. In each of these forms, the foot hits the ground in a ballistic action to create rhythmic patterns that can be heard. It is probable that phases 2 and 3 of the triple-burst EMG pattern do not occur. Because of the intended speed and repetition of the foot action, the foot retracts actively from

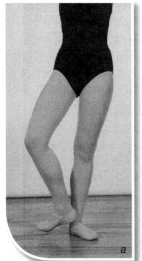 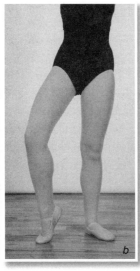  

Figure 5.8 The triple-burst pattern of the frappé involves the following stages: *(a)* the gesture leg beginning to move away from the standing leg, *(b)* the moment of contact of the gesture foot with the floor, *(c)* the gesture foot approaching full extension, and *(d)* the moment of full extension of the gesture foot and leg.

the floor rather than being decelerated by the antagonist. These actions are similar to vertical jumping in that the initial attack is ballistic, but forces or resistance outside the body absorb the momentum.

Implications for Dance Training

Young dancers love dance class. Most of all, they love those portions of class that are ballistic, including all of the big jumps and leaps that move across the floor. The excitement of learning new steps that elevate, and new ways to extend range of motion, has drawn young dancers to class for generations. The teacher's goal is to encourage and nurture this joyfulness while imparting information about correct execution and injury prevention.

Children are less likely to develop proficiency in ballistic skills than in any other kind of movement skills, even if practiced regularly. Dance teachers tend to introduce new skills for students through a variety of strategies, including slowing the tempo. Unfortunately, teaching ballistic movements at a slow pace does little to instruct how to accomplish these tasks. Through the understanding of the speed and sequencing of muscle use in ballistic actions, teachers need to realize that instruction should first encourage the ballistic pattern, and proper form can be achieved later.

Introducing Ballistic Movement to Young Children

It is essential that young children be allowed to experience early jumping and leaping activities in ways that encourage exploration. Concentrating too soon on correct form can detrimentally affect the ability to develop proficient ballistic patterns—in other words, the triple-burst pattern involving agonist and antagonist muscle actions. Imagery is an effective tool to use at this age. Games in which children soar over imaginary objects and obstacles can encourage the sensation of flight. Use of the arms can be included if they are described in terms of momentum and not shape design and formal-ized positions. In addition, improvisations can be structured that include ideas of throwing, tossing, and kicking imaginary objects, allowing children to employ a learning discovery situation for ballistic movement. Regardless of age, early experiences with elevation and other ballistic movements need to start with a realistic approach to the necessary speed and force.

Adolescence and Ballistic Movement

Adolescents who have already begun their dance training confront different difficulties with ballistic movements as they go through growth spurts. Activity must be modified to accommodate the physiologic and neurological changes that are occurring without activity becoming so restrictive that the dancers are frustrated. Loss of flexibility in muscles around the hips would require reducing range of motion in battement. One option is to have the dancers do battement in attitude position (bent knee of the gesture leg) so that they can experience the thrusting action without risking muscle tears. Also, various jumps and leaps can be modified by simplifying the complexity of combinations, reducing beats, minimizing multiple leg and arm positions, and taking care regarding numbers of repetitions. Keep in mind the dancers' need for continued jumping and other ballistic movements during this time period. These movements should not be removed entirely, both for morale reasons and so that the dancers continue developing proficiency in ballistic patterns. Finally, this is an age in which dancers are increasingly attracted to street dance. As with other ballistic movements, the dancers should not be restricted from these dance activities, but they can be informed about potential risks.

Stretching and Ballistic Movement

The aesthetics of many dance forms require greater flexibility than the natural range of motion for nondancers, so dancers spend a great deal of time stretching. However, stretching before performing ballistic movement can have a negative impact on the muscles' ability to fire in the ballistic pattern. In fact, stretching can alter balance, proprioception, reaction time, power, vertical jump height, and muscle force generation. These negative effects can last anywhere from 15 minutes to 2 hours, and they are not dependent on the type of stretching, such as static or dynamic. While a few studies including some dance research on this subject give differing evidence, these studies follow protocols that digress from the abundant sports literature. Therefore the overwhelming evidence supports avoiding lengthy stretches preceding ballistic movement.

Dancers should be do their stretching after activity, when they are warm and will not be required to participate in ballistic movements and choreography, as seen in figure 5.9. For the extremely flexible and hypermobile dancers, stretching at any time should be avoided, other than brief stretches to release tension after immediate activity. Given the effects of stretching on ballistic movement, the tradition of a long, extended period of stretching at the end of barre before center work is a questionable practice.

It is exhilarating to perform ballistic activities. Whether it is finding new heights in elevation work, or achieving new speed at nerve taps and zapateado, or acquiring new complex patterns in arm motifs in street dance, experiencing the intensity and power of ballistic actions is deeply satisfying. When dancers can learn and accomplish the sequencing of ballistic movement patterns, they can arrive at new levels of these skills. In addition, as they incorporate the timing of the arms and torso to create greater force and momentum, the movements become even more heightened and exciting. Teachers working with dancers of any age or level can inspire high skill levels in these difficult but fulfilling dance steps.

Figure 5.9 If dancers spend too much time in static stretching preceding activity, it can compromise ballistic actions required in dance.

Summary

Ballistic skills are a unique set of dance movements that involve a specialized triple-burst EMG pattern involving the agonists and antagonists of a given movement. In sports, ballistic activities in the upper extremities include throwing and striking. Lower-extremity ballistic movements include kicking with and without objects. The studies of these skills in sports suggests information that is useful in analyzing dance skills, including battement, leaps, frappé, foot strikes for rhythm and sound, tossed lifts, locking, and waacking. This knowledge can greatly enhance how teachers approach designing class material and imparting their expertise about these important dance skills. Each age group of dancers, from the youngest children to adolescents to professionals, has unique needs and desires, and the teacher's role is to nurture the dancers in their journey.

Part II

Motor
Control

Chapter 6
Organization of Motor Control

*H*ow is movement produced? To answer this question, most dancers might describe the way their muscles cause changes in body shapes and dynamics. Dancers who have had courses in experiential anatomy or kinesiology might say that movement is really about the joints of the skeleton and that muscles move bones to cause movement. While these descriptions are true, movement is initiated because the nervous system, comprising the brain and its pathways, sends messages to the muscles. Without nervous system activity, no movement could occur. The study of **motor control** explores how the nervous system organizes and directs all of the body's muscles and joints to produce coordinated movement, and how sensory information from within the body, such as vision and hearing, and from the environment around the body are used to accomplish this task (Schmidt & Lee, 2011). Sometimes movement relies primarily on instructions from the brain; other times, information from the environment that is taken in through the body's senses is necessary in order to accomplish movement tasks. In both cases, the brain and its pathways are essential for executing movement.

When getting feedback about their movement, dancers receive verbal instructions and corrections in many ways. Some teachers use demonstration, some use imagery, some describe goals, and some tell dancers which muscles to use. Dancers can get confused about which approach is best and about whether different tactics are better in certain circumstances. Knowing the best way to communicate in order to clarify instructions to dancers begins with understanding how the brain and the nervous system function. When dance teachers understand motor control, they can develop language that elicits the most efficient and clear movement response from their students.

For example, when a person is walking on uneven surfaces and begins to twist an ankle, it is messages from the spinal cord and not conscious messages from the brain that determine the appropriate reaction. The response of the muscles to contract and protect the ankle from injury is immediate and much faster than the brain receiving the sensory information of the stretch and deciding how to respond. The human body is remarkable. It has many reflexes to protect itself, as well as a clear organization of the brain to handle various tasks. On the other hand, if dancers are supinating (also called *sickling*) on relevé, the teacher can cue them through imagery to consciously organize the ankle in correct alignment. This process uses some of the same muscles, but it has different neural pathways for the muscle initiation. Understanding this division of roles can help teachers more effectively design their language and instruction. This chapter begins by describing the nervous system, including the brain, and how movement is organized. It then describes the various reflexes of the movement system and discusses their impact on flexibility and alignment. Finally, it explores the implications and suggestions for dance training.

Nervous System

The human nervous system is both marvelous and complex. The mastermind of the nervous system is the brain. Scientists have only recently begun to uncover some of the functions of the deeper areas of the brain. Modern technology is capable of mapping parts of the brain that were little understood or even misunderstood for centuries. **Positron emission tomography (PET)** and **functional magnetic resonance imaging (fMRI)** are two methods of differentiating layers of the brain and seeing the functional processes that are occurring in it. Through use of these tools, scientists are beginning to uncover the extraordinary capacity of the human brain to absorb, process, and retain information, and direct the human body to function in the world.

Overview of the Nervous System

The nervous system is divided into two parts. The brain and the parts of the nervous system that reside in the spinal cord are collectively called the **central nervous system (CNS)**. The parts of the nervous system that lie outside the spine and connect to the muscles and organs are collectively called the **peripheral nervous system (PNS)**. All messages from the PNS to muscles originate in the CNS, either at the brain level or the spinal cord level. This complex messaging system comes down to the single-cell level, called the neuron, which is the basis of the entire nervous system.

Neurons

The most basic cell in the nervous system is called a **neuron**, or nerve cell. The neuron has a cell body, which contains the nucleus. The nucleus is the part of the neuron that controls the overall functioning of the cell, and it is one of the contributing factors to the internal chemical balance that determines when the neuron fires. The neuron also has **dendrites**, treelike extensions that branch out from the nucleus to receive impulses (messages) from other neurons. Each neuron can have many dendrites. At the other end of the neuron is the **axon**, also called a *nerve fiber*, which is responsible for sending the message to the next neuron or possibly on to muscle fibers. Each neuron has only one axon, but the axon can have several terminals (branches). Many axons are coated with layers of **myelin**, the insulating fatty sheath around the nerve cells responsible for the speed of neural transmission. At birth, the nerve cells have very little myelin, and messages to muscles are relatively slow. Myelination is the growth of this insulating fatty sheath, which facilitates coordination by accelerating transmission of messages to the muscles. In certain neurological disorders, such as multiple sclerosis, the myelin is scarred and lost, accounting for the loss of muscle control and coordination in people with this condition. Figure 6.1 displays the various parts of the neuron and the direction of neural transmission. The connections from axons to dendrites are called **synapses**.

Three main types of neurons exist, and they can be defined by their functions. **Sensory neurons** (also called **afferent neurons**) send impulses (messages) from the body to the CNS, giving the brain information about the environment through sight, sound, touch, smell, and taste. Sensory neurons are the least numerous of all types of neurons. **Motor neurons** (also called **efferent neurons**) send impulses from the CNS to the skeletal muscles to create movement. **Interneurons** are only found in the brain and spinal cord. They act as connectors between sensory neurons and the spinal neurons ascending to the brain, or between neurons descending from the brain and motor neurons, or between neurons within the brain itself. Interneurons are the most numerous of the three types of neurons.

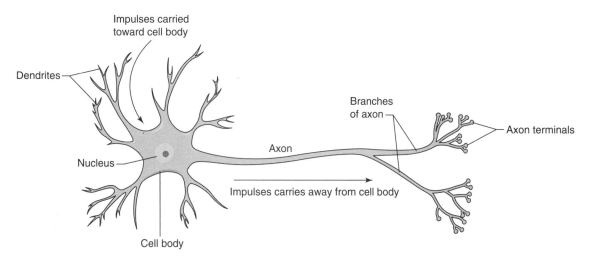

Figure 6.1 The neuron (nerve cell) is the simplest component of the nervous system, which carries all of the messages between the brain and the body.

Reprinted, by permission, from K.M. Haywood and N. Getchell, 2014, *Life span motor development*, 6th ed. (Champaign, IL: Human Kinetics), 91.

Brain

The brain is divided into parts both anatomically and by function. The brain includes the forebrain, the cerebellum, the brain stem, and the limbic system (figure 6.2), along with some of the main subdivisions of these four parts. Each of these parts contributes significantly to motor control. Other important groupings of nerve cells are the basal ganglia and the corpus callosum, which contains axons of important nerve cells. These two areas also have functions that relate directly to movement. For the purposes of this text, select areas of the brain that relate directly to motor control are described. For example, autonomic functions, such as heartbeat and breathing, are discussed only in terms of their relationship to movement.

Forebrain

The **forebrain** is the largest and most forward part of the brain. It is responsible for all conscious thought as well as control of attention. A person does not require use of the forebrain to remain alive, because the brain functions that sustain life lie in other portions. The forebrain is further divided into the cerebrum and diencephalon. These two areas have functions that are critical to the ability to plan, coordinate, and execute movement.

Cerebrum

The **cerebrum** is crucial in both the planning of movement and the integration of sensory and motor functions. It consists of two halves, the right and left hemispheres. In a very broad sense, the left hemisphere generally controls

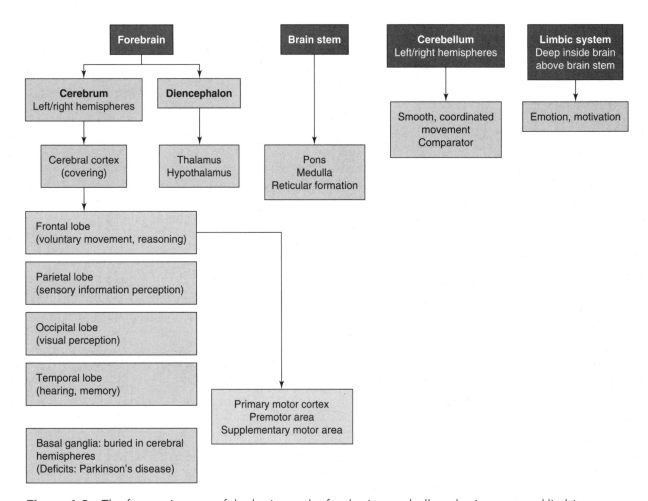

Figure 6.2 The four main areas of the brain are the forebrain, cerebellum, brain stem, and limbic system. Each area makes a contribution to the control of movement.

more academic or analytic functions, and the right hemisphere deals with more creative processes. Recent research acknowledges that far more overlap of function exists, and this left/right division is not absolute. Figure 6.3 is a lighthearted representation of the functions of the two hemispheres. As acknowledged previously, much overlap exists between functions of the left and right hemisphere. Nonetheless, this image offers a simplification of the hemispheres.

The cerebrum has been divided into several numbered sections, called Brodmann areas. These areas were originally defined by the German anatomist Korbinian Brodmann and published in 1909. While some of this numbering has been further delineated and refined, and other systems related to function are developing, the Brodmann system is still in use today.

The **corpus callosum** is a very dense bundle of strongly myelinated axons that connects and integrates the two hemispheres of the cerebrum. It has been demonstrated that musical training alters the development of the corpus callosum during the early part of life. One of the benefits is an increased coordination of hands and changes in motor and auditory function, which would assist in future musical training. One study found that children who began musical training before the age of six (minimum 15 months of training) had an increased volume of their corpus callosum and adults who began musical training before the age of 11 also had increased bimanual (two-hand) coordination. Dance teachers might consider adding specific musical training for their dance students.

The **cerebral cortex** is a thin layer of nerve cell bodies. Also known as the **gray matter**, it is an undulating, gray-colored mass that covers

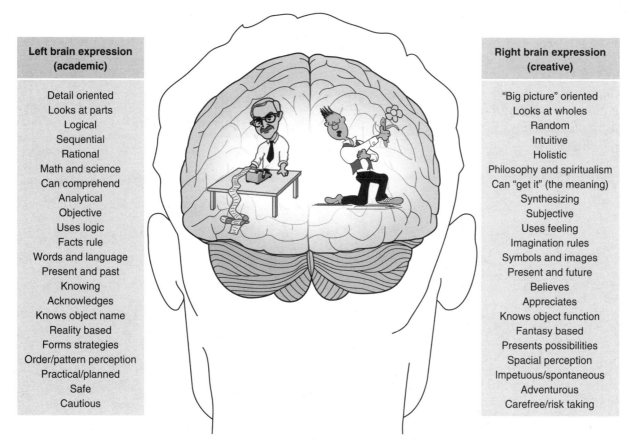

Left brain expression (academic)

Detail oriented
Looks at parts
Logical
Sequential
Rational
Math and science
Can comprehend
Analytical
Objective
Uses logic
Facts rule
Words and language
Present and past
Knowing
Acknowledges
Knows object name
Reality based
Forms strategies
Order/pattern perception
Practical/planned
Safe
Cautious

Right brain expression (creative)

"Big picture" oriented
Looks at wholes
Random
Intuitive
Holistic
Philosophy and spiritualism
Can "get it" (the meaning)
Synthesizing
Subjective
Uses feeling
Imagination rules
Symbols and images
Present and future
Believes
Appreciates
Knows object function
Fantasy based
Presents possibilities
Spacial perception
Impetuous/spontaneous
Adventurous
Carefree/risk taking

Figure 6.3 The left hemisphere of the brain generally controls more academic or analytic functions, and the right hemisphere deals with more creative processes. However, far more overlap of function exists, and this left/right division is not absolute.

the hemispheres of the brain. Each ridge of the cerebral cortex is called a **gyrus**, and each groove is called a **sulcus**. These gyri and sulci give the brain a far bigger surface area than if it laid flat, allowing for many more brain cells in a smaller area. The brain's **white matter** lies underneath the cortex and is made of a layer of myelinated nerve cells. The white matter quickly transmits signals and coordinates communication between different brain regions.

The cerebral cortex is further divided into four portions, called *lobes* (figure 6.4). The **frontal lobe** is the largest of the four lobes and the most anterior portion, in front of the central sulcus. It contains areas that are essential to the planning and control of voluntary movement, reasoning, and the inhibition of socially unacceptable behavior. It is strongly connected to the limbic system, the seat of emotions. The **parietal lobe** is posterior and adjacent to the frontal lobe, and it is the key area for the perception and integration of sensory information, including heat, cold, pressure, pain, and the position of the body in space. It communicates closely with the primary motor area in the frontal lobe, and it is associated with attention and intention to movement. Another way of saying this idea is that the parietal lobe is concerned with the *how* of movement. The **occipital lobe** is the most posterior section, and it is crucial to visual

perception, which is why it is sometimes called the *visual cortex.* The **temporal lobe** is located laterally, and it deals with memory, abstract thought, and judgment. It also contains the hearing processing center, and it is concerned with the *what* of movement.

Four areas within these lobes are fundamental to the study of motor control. Within the frontal lobe, three areas that are crucial are the primary motor cortex, the premotor area, and the supplementary motor area. The **primary motor cortex** (Brodmann's area 4) sends messages to specific skeletal muscles in all parts of the body. This area is essential for initiating movement, for postural coordination, and for fine motor skills, such as the finger movements for playing a piano or putting on stage makeup before a dance performance. The **premotor area** (part of Brodmann's area 6) organizes movement before initiation and handles rhythmic coordination. It is also involved in how learning can be accomplished by observing others. The **supplementary motor area (SMA)**, which is part of Brodmann's area 6, plays an important role in executing already-learned sequential movements, in preparing and organizing movement, and in bimanual coordination.

Within the parietal lobe, the **somatosensory cortex** is the fourth area in the cerebral cortex involved in movement. It plays a major role in

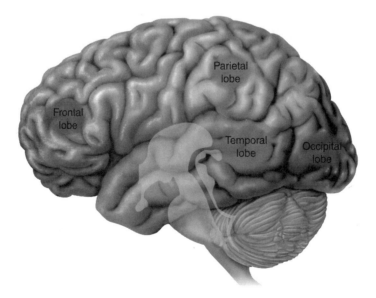

Figure 6.4 The spatial relationship of the four lobes of the cerebral cortex: frontal, parietal, occipital, and temporal.

visual and auditory attention. It interacts with the three motor areas described previously by integrating sensory information into the planning stages of movement as well as during movement. Figure 6.5 shows the areas of the cerebral cortex related to movement planning and execution: primary motor cortex, premotor area, supplementary motor area, and somatosensory cortex.

In addition to the four areas described, several association areas exist throughout the frontal, temporal, and parietal lobes. These areas are also involved in the planning stages of movement, and neuroscientists think that the first formulation of the movement plan begins in the association areas. The development of the plan is influenced by sensory information at this level of the brain.

When doing simple tasks such as reaching and tapping, scans of the brain show that activity is greatest in the primary motor cortex and primary somatosensory cortex. However, when doing complex tasks there is activity in these two areas plus the SMA. When visualizing a task, the brain activity is only found in the SMA. These scans verify the roles of these areas of the brain in the planning and execution stages of movement. For example, if dancers are learning and executing a complex dance phrase, the first part of the process involves visualiz-

ing doing the movement as they observe the demonstration. In this phase, the SMA is very active. Next, the brain begins to organize the movement before any initiation, which involves the premotor area. The movement plan is sent to the primary motor cortex, which is responsible for sending the actual messages to the skeletal muscles to execute the dance phrase. Other areas of the brain are involved as well, including receiving important sensory information from the primary somatosensory cortex.

Sensory homunculus and **motor homunculus** are graphic ways to represent the anatomical segments of the brain directly responsible for movement and for the exchange of sensory and motor information (figure 6.6). They show the primary somatosensory cortex and the primary motor cortex, and they show the extent to which these regions correspond to various body areas. It is interesting to note how much of the motor cortex is devoted to the hands and face.

One other structure within the cerebral cortex is extremely important to movement initiation and coordination. The **basal ganglia** are buried deep in the hemispheres of the brain and consist of four clusters of nerve cells: the caudate nucleus, the putamen, the substantia nigra, and the globus pallidus. The basal ganglia are critical in the control of antagonist muscles during movement and in the control

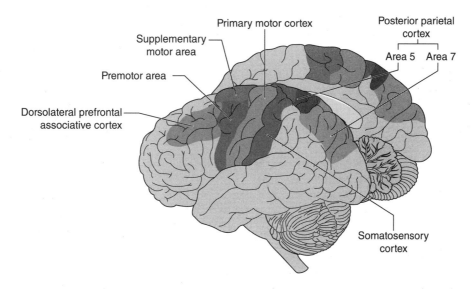

Figure 6.5 Four areas of the cerebral cortex are important to learning. Three lie in the frontal lobe (primary motor cortex, premotor area, and the supplementary motor area), and the fourth is in the parietal lobe (somatosensory cortex).

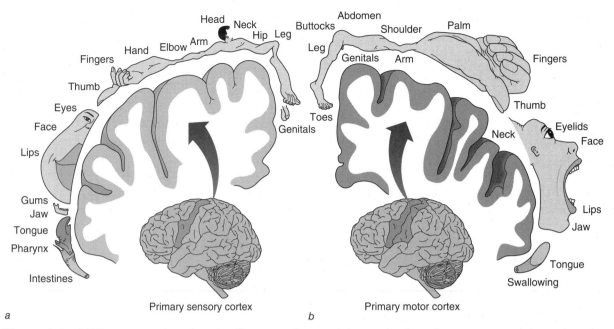

Figure 6.6 *(a)* The sensory homunculus illustrates the spatial organization of somatosensory input into the parietal lobe by body area. *(b)* The motor homunculus illustrates the spatial organization of motor output from the frontal lobe by body area.

(b): Reprinted, by permission, from B. Abernethy et al., 2013, *Biophysical foundations of human movement*, 3rd ed. (Champaign, IL: Human Kinetics), p. 236.

of force. Deficits or injury to the basal ganglia cause diseases such as Parkinson's disease and Huntington's disease, which result in serious motor disorders, including loss of spontaneous movement, the occurrence of involuntary movements, and posture disturbances. For people with typical motor development and control, the basal ganglia are responsible for the initiation of movement and for smooth, coordinated movement.

Diencephalon

The **diencephalon** lies between the cerebrum and the brain stem, and it contains the thalamus and hypothalamus. The **thalamus** is a complex computational relay station, and it sorts important information from insignificant information. Almost everything going into and out of the cerebral cortex passes through the thalamus. It also plays a role in attention, mood, the perception of pain, and regulating arousal, and it is very involved with the motor systems. The **hypothalamus** controls regulation of body responses to temperature, hunger, thirst, and stress. While the diencephalon is not directly related to movement planning and

execution, issues of attention, mood, and stress certainly can affect dancers' motor control and learning; if it is damaged, huge motor deficits can occur.

Brain Stem

The **brain stem** connects directly to the spinal cord and has three areas that are involved in movement. The **pons** controls body functions such as chewing, swallowing, salivating, and breathing, and it may be involved in balance control. The **medulla** or **medulla oblongata** interacts with the pons and controls functions such as breathing and heartbeat. The **reticular formation** is a link between sensory receptors in the body and motor control centers in the brain. It plays an important role in regulating CNS messages to the body, hence affecting skeletal muscle activity and muscle tonus. For example, when a dancer is feeling anxious, muscle tone and tightness increase.

Cerebellum

The **cerebellum** fine-tunes motor control, giving smoothness of motion and exactness of positioning, and it controls the force and range of movements. Sometimes called the *little brain*, the cerebellum has two hemispheres like the cerebrum, and it lies behind the cerebral hemispheres near the brain stem. It contains 10% of the brain by volume, but it has 50% of the neurons. It acts as a movement error-detection and correction system, and therefore it is sometimes called *the comparator*. The cerebellum accomplishes this role by comparing the motor plan being sent to the muscles with the sensory information coming into the brain about what is actually happening. It then signals the muscles about necessary adjustments in order to accomplish the task. In addition, posture control, balance, muscle tonus, and learning of motor skills are part of cerebellar function, as are certain types of cognition, such as language.

Limbic System

The **limbic system** is the most ancient area of the brain, and it is crucial to the formation of memories and to the desire or motivation to act. The fight-or-flight response originates in this area of the brain. In association with the hypothalamus, it is regarded to be the primary center of emotions. Since the hypothalamus controls the autonomic and hormonal systems, its association with emotions is not surprising. Almost all emotions are associated with a response of body organs, such as muscle constriction, heart rate alterations, and changes to breathing and blood pressure. The frontal lobe of the cerebral cortex is also strongly connected to the limbic system, and therefore movement and emotional response are powerfully interconnected. However, this connection is poorly developed in adolescents, meaning that rational thinking does not temper many of the emotional decisions of teenagers.

It should now be clear that the brain regulates almost every level of movement organization and execution. What dancers call *muscle memory* actually refers to that phase of motor learning when controlling actions shifts from the conscious planning areas of the brain to the automatic patterning that can be done without intentional thought. Dancers realize how much

practice it takes to arrive at the point where they no longer need to focus their attention on movement components such as turnout and pointed feet. However, many of them do not realize that all of these dance-specific patterns are stored in the brain, available to access simply by recalling the whole task. If dancers had to direct each muscle in a complex movement such as tour jeté, it would be impossible to accomplish the skill. Fortunately, the brain has organizational levels that manage the movement components as dancers perform combinations.

Organization of Movement

The complexity of the brain and the nervous system can be overwhelming, and yet various brain functions rarely interfere with each other or become muddled with the millions of neurons firing. A hierarchy of motor control exists from the lowest level of spinal cord reflexes to the highest level of cerebral planning and reasoning. All of these levels of organization interact, and all of the descending messages eventually lead to the muscles. In addition, movements can be defined from the simplest reflex action, such as catching the ankle that is twisting, to the most sophisticated and complicated functions, such as playing a Beethoven sonata on the piano or dancing a lengthy toda in classical Indian khatak dance.

Organization of the Motor System

The *motor system* refers to all of the parts of the CNS involved with movement. Three levels of hierarchy exist in this system, and they are each responsible for different aspects of organizing and controlling how movement is executed. In addition, the motor system has features that refine how movement is coordinated and assist in distributing the various tasks of motor control to the appropriate area of the brain.

Three Levels of Hierarchy

The organization of movement is controlled at three levels in the CNS, sometimes referred to as a *hierarchy*. These levels are the spinal cord, the brain stem, and the cortical or cerebral cortex motor areas in the frontal lobe. The higher centers give general commands but do not specify the details of motor action or muscle selection. Parallel organization also exists, so higher levels can act directly on the lowest levels of function.

The lowest level of the nervous system hierarchy is the spinal cord. The spinal cord has neural pathways that mediate automatic reflexes, such as the stretch reflex or withdrawing the hand from a hot stove. It also contains neural pathways responsible for what are called **central pattern generators** that create rhythmic patterns such as walking, running, and other rhythmic behaviors. The same interneurons that cause reflex actions are also involved in voluntary movements. All of these various levels of control converge on the motor neurons innervating and activating the muscles. This sum of information flow is called the *final common path*.

The brain stem is the second level of hierarchical control. It integrates visual and vestibular information with somatosensory contributions, all of which are important for control of posture. Along with other areas in the brain, the brain stem is also critical for eye- and head-movement control, such as spotting turns in dance. None of this coordination occurs on the conscious level.

The third and highest level of the hierarchy is the cerebral cortex. Within the cerebral cortex, the premotor area and supplementary motor area are important for coordinating and planning complex sequences of movement, while the primary motor cortex sends the actual plan down to muscles. After leaving the brain, the messages traveling to the muscles by way of the primary motor cortex use the same final common path as the reflexes. However, they originate from a different source. The messages from the higher levels are typically generated from conscious thought, while the reflex messages are entirely nonconscious and emanate from the spinal cord.

Each of the three levels of hierarchy receives messages from the periphery by way of sensory neurons, and each level can discriminate in terms of how it uses this information. For example, the higher level can override a reflex if necessary, such as running into a burning building to save someone. Dancers can override pain messages and continue dancing even though the reflex level is signaling the injured muscle to shut off.

Additional Tasks and Features of the Motor System

The motor system has three additional tasks. The first is to convey accurately timed commands to many groups of muscles at the same time. The second is to consider the distribution of body mass and to make appropriate postural adjustments for the situation. The third is to take into account the mechanical arrangement of muscles, bones, and joints so that the correct movement can be accomplished.

Finally, the motor system relies on two organizational features. One is the continuous flow of sensory information about events in environment, position, and orientation of the body and limbs, and the degree of contraction of muscles. All of these factors influence the ongoing messages to the muscles. The other feature is the hierarchy of control levels that receive information relevant to function so that higher levels dealing with strategic issues do not monitor moment-to-moment details. Rather, they leave those details to lower levels. The higher levels must interpret the sensory information in order to make comprehensive decisions about motor control.

Three Classes of Movements

Movements can be divided into three broad, overlapping classes: voluntary movements, reflex responses, and rhythmic motor patterns. Both in everyday life and in dance performance, the body uses all three types of movements regularly. Complex turns and jumps are voluntary movements, while running across the dance floor is a rhythmic motor pattern.

Voluntary movements are the most complex actions. They are movements such as playing the violin, performing a pirouette, or spinning on the head. Voluntary movements are purposeful. They are intentional responses to a stimulus or a choice, and they are goal directed. These movements are sometimes called *willful* or *volitional.* They are largely learned and improve with practice so that eventually, if practiced enough, they can be accomplished with little or no conscious thought.

Reflex responses are the simplest motor behaviors. They are actions such as withdrawing the hand from a hot stove or the well-known knee-jerk reaction to the doctor's hammer. They are the least affected by voluntary controls, and they are rapid, stereotyped, and controlled in some way by an external stimulus. Stereotypic responses are patterned and always repeat in the same way given a particular stimulus.

Rhythmic motor patterns are somewhere in between voluntary and reflex. They are actions such as walking, running, and chewing. They combine features of voluntary and reflex actions. Their initiation and termination are voluntary, but once initiated, they continue in a reflex manner until stopped.

People develop basic motor control at a very early age, and much of it is so automatic that its complexity at the brain level is unrecognized. Most dancers start dancing at a young age (as early as 3 or 4 years old), and by the time they are consciously aware of what they are doing, much of the highly skilled movement they achieve has already reached the automatic phase of learning. For example, teachers do not need to expressly articulate how to do arm and leg opposition in locomotor movement. This motor pattern has already been developed during the early years of walking. Dancers can use this opposition easily, and they can apply it to complex dance movements without analyzing or breaking down the specific components and muscles being used. Teachers can use methods that encourage dancers to rely on the brain's natural wisdom to organize and execute movement, or they can interfere with this magnificent system by overloading dancers with instructions to try to move muscle by muscle. The goal of the teacher must be to define movement tasks and goals in terms that the conscious mind can assimilate, and then let the brain and its systems take care of the details.

Reflex Mechanisms and Their Effects on Flexibility and Alignment

Although the previous section delineated voluntary movement, reflex responses, and rhythmic motor patterns, reflexive behaviors underlie most voluntary movements. When dancers are doing complex dance phrases, alignment and flexibility are components that are strongly influenced by the reflex mechanisms in the body. Dance teachers often see dancers with lumbar hyperlordosis (commonly called *swayback*), and they give corrective exercises to alter this problematic alignment. Swayback is aesthetically unpleasing in most dance forms, and it predisposes dancers to injuries. However, even after dancers conscientiously perform various corrective exercises, they can still find themselves in this incorrect alignment. The key to comprehending this problem resides in the understanding of the reflexes. Although dancers cannot consciously regulate the reflex level of motor control, methods involving awareness, breath, relaxation, imagery, and somatic work can utilize the reflexes to make changes to alignment as well as to address flexibility. Once dancers have this understanding, they can alter their alignment or range of motion using means other than conscious muscle contractions.

Numerous neural reflexes influence how muscles respond to stimuli without conscious control. All muscle action, conscious or nonconscious, is the result of neurons firing and sending messages to muscles. Sometimes these muscle responses are called **reflexes**, a term used to describe a muscle response to a message that comes not directly from the brain but from a stimulus, such as touch, heat, pain, or stretch. The stimulus causes a neuron to fire, sending a signal to a neuron in the spinal cord, which in turn sends a message to the muscle. Because this pathway does not have to travel to the brain and back to the muscle, a reflex is faster than a conscious message sent from the brain to a muscle.

Basic Reflex Arc

Several reflexes exist that influence movement organization, alignment, and automatic responses to environmental factors. Each reflex has variations that make it unique, but they all follow a basic template, called the reflex arc. The **reflex arc** comprises the neurological components that create a response to a stimulus consisting of a receptor neuron, an interneuron, and a motor neuron.

- The *receptor neuron* lies in the muscle, tendon, or joint, such as a neuron in the muscle that responds to fast or extreme stretch. When it is stimulated, it fires and sends its signal along the pathway to another neuron in the sequence that will eventually reach the muscle fiber. The degree of stimulation needed to cause the neuron to fire is known as its **threshold**.

- The *interneuron* lies in the spinal cord. It is an intermediary neuron between the receptor neuron and the neuron that acts on the muscle fibers. It might be **excitatory** or **facilitatory**, encouraging muscle response and thereby causing the muscle to contract. It might be **inhibitory**, reducing muscle response, and thereby causing the muscle to stop contracting or reduce the level of contraction.

- The *motor neuron* is the final component in the reflex arc. It is the nerve cell that fires and sends its message directly to the muscle fibers.

Figure 6.7 illustrates the basic reflex arc. The right side of the drawing is where the muscle lies. The box inside the large circle represents the spinal cord inside the spine. The receptor neuron reacts to a stimulus. In the case of movement, it might be the dancer stretching too rapidly or an ankle twisting in a bad landing. The receptor neuron fires on the interneuron, the nerve in the spinal cord, which then sends its signal to the muscle by way of a motor neuron, either to contract or to stop contracting, depending on the type of interneuron it is (excitatory or inhibitory). This model is the basis for several reflexes.

Myotatic (Stretch) Reflex

The simplest of the reflexes is the **myotatic reflex**, also called the **stretch reflex**. It is strongly activated by rapid or extreme stretch of a muscle, such as a bouncing hamstring stretch or a twisted ankle. The stretch reflex arc does not contain an interneuron, which means that it is a two-neuron system; thus, it is the fastest reflex in the body. The stretch-sensitive receptor in the muscle is activated when stretch is either too rapid or too extreme. It fires directly to the motor neuron, causing the muscle fibers that have been stretched to contract. This reaction protects the muscle from injury. Ballistic stretches trigger this reflex. It is not a good idea to activate this system when working on increasing flexibility. Most dancers understand that hard bouncing, extreme force, or ballistic stretches can possibly tear muscles and are therefore dangerous. Many people do not realize that these forms

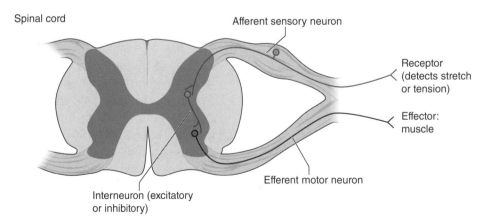

Figure 6.7 The basic reflex arc represents a model of the simplest form of the various reflexes. It contains a receptor in the muscle (the sensory neuron), an interneuron in the spinal cord, and a motor neuron that sends its message to the muscle.

of stretches cause the muscles to contract for protection from injury, and therefore they are not useful as stretches at all; once a muscle is contracting, it cannot stretch. However, keep in mind that bouncing *conditioning* is useful for conditioning tendons for repeated or sudden loading, and it is often used for people in racket sports. It might be useful for Irish or Scottish dancers or those practicing Bournonville ballet.

The stretch reflex is illustrated in figure 6.8. It is similar to the basic reflex arc (figure 6.7), but no interneuron fires. The speed of this reflex has saved many ankles from sprains. One more term in the diagram needs to be defined: the use of the word *alpha*. The neurons of the alpha system fire on muscle fibers called **extrafusal fibers**. These muscle fibers are **striated** throughout their entire length, which means that they have contractile proteins that interlock throughout the entire the fiber and give it a striped appearance. Most muscle fibers in the body are extrafusal fibers.

Autogenic Inhibition Reflex

The **autogenic inhibition reflex** functions to allow the muscle to adjust its level of contraction. The receptors in this case are called **Golgi tendon organs (GTOs)**, and they can be found in the tendons of the muscle. These neurons are also responsive to stretch, but because they are in the tendons, they react to or sense muscle tension. When the muscle contracts and gets shorter, the tendon actually stretches and lengthens. This stretch of the tendon also stretches the GTOs, and the GTOs in the tendon respond, sending the message to small inhibitory interneurons in the spinal cord. These interneurons can then adjust, altering the level of muscle contraction by reducing or inhibiting messages to the motor neurons. Figure 6.9 illustrates the Golgi tendon organs in the tendon of the muscle.

Originally researchers thought that this was another of the body's protection mechanisms, stopping the muscle from contracting to such an extreme that it could damage the tendon by overstretching it. They believed that GTOs only provoked a reflex when the tendon was stretched to the extreme, firing on the interneuron to inhibit the muscle completely. Scientists now know that this is not the case. Rather, GTOs contribute to the monitoring and control of muscle activity over the whole range, not just the extremes, so in fact, nothing can be stated clearly about the GTOs functioning as a protection mechanism. They supply information about muscle tension or force, and therefore these neurons act to assist in producing smooth, coordinated movement in complex activities by regulating tension across the entire musculotendinous unit. Figure 6.10 shows the pathways of the autogenic inhibition reflex. Two main differences exist between the stretch reflex and the autogenic inhibition reflex. First, the receptors in the autogenic inhibition reflex (GTOs) are in the tendon of the muscle, not the muscle itself as in the stretch reflex. Second, the autogenic inhibition reflex has an interneuron, and because it is inhibitory, the muscle relaxes rather than contracts as a result. The interneuron is colored white to indicate that it is inhibitory.

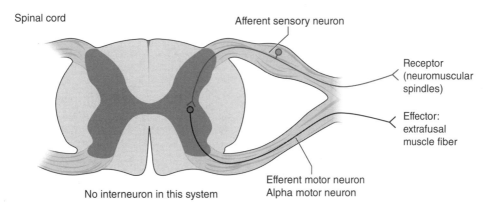

Figure 6.8 The myotatic (stretch) reflex is the fastest reflex in the body, because it has no interneuron. It is a protection mechanism to prevent injury caused by fast or extreme stretch.

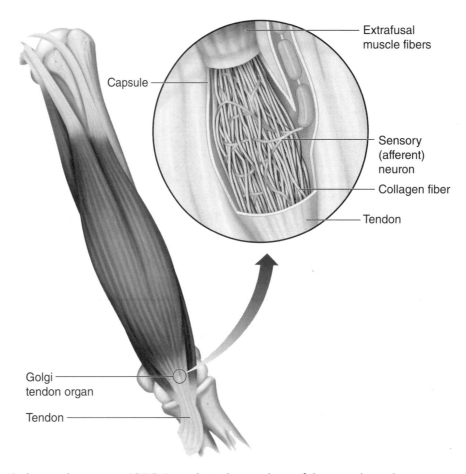

Figure 6.9 Golgi tendon organs (GTOs) reside in the tendons of the muscle and are responsive to stretch of the tendon.

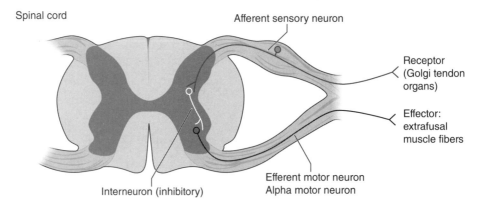

Figure 6.10 The autogenic inhibition reflex has neurons in the muscle tendon that respond to stretch, and contribute to the control of muscle activity and coordination.

Reciprocal Inhibition Reflex

The **reciprocal inhibition reflex** is used to inhibit (relax) the antagonist muscle when the agonist muscle is contracting. In this reflex, interneurons are going to the agonist (working muscle) and the antagonist (opposing muscle). For example, the hamstrings are the antagonist group to the quadriceps. As the agonist (quadriceps) receives messages to contract, the antagonist (hamstrings) is receiving simultaneous messages to relax. In other words, a strong contraction of the quadriceps will cause relaxation of the hamstrings. This effect can be used during **proprioceptive neuromuscular facilitation (PNF)**, a form of stretching using muscle reflexes and responses to aid in flexibility gains. In this case, the dancer would contract the quadriceps during a hamstring stretch. The interneuron firing on the motor neurons going to the agonist is excitatory (telling the quadriceps to contract), while the interneuron firing on motor neurons going to the antagonist is inhibitory (telling the hamstrings to relax). Some people find this method effective for working on flexibility. Another example is low-back stretching. The dancer would contract the abdominal muscles while sitting and hanging forward over the legs, which are extended out in front of the body. As the abdominals contract, a message is sent to the low back muscles telling them to relax, hence making it easier to stretch them. Figure 6.11 illustrates the reciprocal inhibition reflex. As in figure 6.10 of the autogenic inhibition reflex, the inhibitory interneuron to the antagonist is white. The interneuron telling the working muscle to contract is colored black to indicate that it is excitatory. The reciprocal inhibition reflex is different from the previous two reflexes in that it has two interneurons and two targeted muscles, agonist and antagonist.

Gamma Efferent System

Another system involving neural reflexes can influence flexibility, and it can explain why some people are very flexible in passive stretches but demonstrate much less range of motion in dynamic action. The main system controlling muscle tone (resistance in muscles to stretch) is the gamma efferent system. This system is crucial to the understanding of changes in flexibility and alignment. The key component in this system is called the **muscle spindle**, which consists of three components: special muscle fibers called intrafusal fibers, the gamma motor neuron, and the gamma sensory neuron (figure 6.12). They are responsible for regulating stretch in the muscle on an ongoing basis. In fact, the muscle spindle is the stretch-sensitive receptor in the stretch reflex in figure 6.8, but discussion of this structure has been saved for this section because of its relationship to more complex neural reflexes and muscle tone.

Most of the fibers in the muscles are extrafusal fibers, striated throughout the length of the fiber. When extrafusal fibers contract, the entire fiber shortens in length. An **intrafusal fiber**, however, is striated only at the ends and consequently does not contribute to overall force production (contraction) in the muscle. When they receive a message to contract, only the end portions of intrafusal fibers shorten. In the center of the intrafusal fiber is a sensory portion, sensitive to the length, speed, and rate of change of the muscle. While the extrafusal fibers receive a signal to contract and produce force by way of the alpha motor neuron, the intrafusal fibers receive a separate signal to contract by way of the gamma motor neuron. Another difference is that the extrafusal fibers

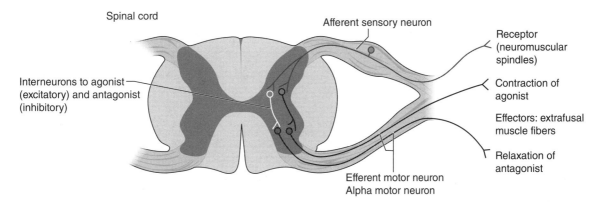

Figure 6.11 The reciprocal inhibition reflex is used to inhibit (relax) the antagonist of a muscle while the agonist muscle is contracting. Interneurons go to the agonist (working muscle) and the antagonist (opposing muscle).

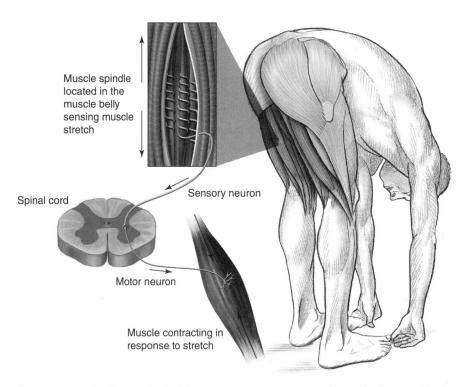

Figure 6.12 The muscle spindle consists of three components: special muscle fibers called intrafusal fibers, the gamma motor neuron, and the gamma sensory neuron. They are responsible for regulating stretch in the muscle on an ongoing basis, as can be seen in the stretched hamstrings.

receive messages from the primary motor cortex and other brain areas, whereas the intrafusal fibers receive messages from various areas of the brain such as the cerebral cortex and the reticular formation. A third difference relates to the sensory component of intrafusal fibers. Unlike the extrafusal fiber, the noncontractile center portion of the intrafusal fiber is wrapped by the spindle or gamma sensory neuron, which is sensitive to stretch. Whenever the center, noncontractile portion changes length, whether due to a contraction caused by the gamma motor neuron or when the muscle is passively stretched, tension on the gamma sensory neuron sends a novel signal to the spinal cord. The signal is then sent to the brain, contributing to body position sense, and the signal can also fire the alpha motor neurons of the same muscle. When the length of the muscle or the velocity of the position change is extreme, the sensory signal at the level of the spinal cord causes all the fibers of that same muscle to protectively contract to prevent damage. This is known as the myotatic (stretch) reflex, which is discussed more thoroughly in the previous

section on reflexes. On a moment-to-moment basis, gamma motor neurons have a usual rate of activity, so that contractile activity of intrafusal fibers typically matches the contractile activity of the extrafusal (force-producing) fibers. However, if the rate of gamma firing is increased relative to the rate of alpha motor neuron firing, the central sensory portion of the intrafusal fiber is under greater relative tension, causing it to be more sensitive. Conversely, if the relative rate of firing is lower than the rate of alpha motor neuron firing, the center sensory portion is under less tension and therefore is less sensitive. Figure 6.12 illustrates one of the muscle spindles located in the hamstrings.

In other words, relatively higher gamma motor activity results in increased muscle tone, called **hypertonia**. Relatively lower gamma activity results in decreased muscle tone, called **hypotonia**. Optimal tone is a dynamic balance between the two. For flexibility training it can be useful to induce a degree of hypotonia to enhance stretching. When the muscle is hypertonic, the least stretch of the muscle causes the gamma sensory neuron to fire, resulting in a contraction of the whole muscle. In a relaxed state, using imagery and breath, the brain can change the rate of gamma firing, allowing the intrafusal fibers to relax. In this hypotonic state, the whole muscle can stretch much further, because the stretch reflex is much less likely to be stimulated under the same length or rate of change. Some people have very hypertonic systems once they start moving, and the gamma efferent system does not allow range of motion. Learning to change the relative rate of gamma or alpha firing from the brain can be a long process of repatterning—first in a slow, relaxed context, such as in the somatic practices or a hatha yoga class, and then eventually in a more dynamic environment, such as in a dance class.

Gamma Efferent System and Alignment

The gamma efferent system explains how a dancer can be much tighter in movement than while passively stretching, but this system also affects alignment. When examining the problem of hyperlordosis (swayback) in the lumbar spine, the explanation is often given as tight hip flexors (possibly psoas or rectus femoris), tight lumbar extensors, and weak lumbar flexors (abdominals). These muscle imbalances may in fact be present. However, there may also be a neurological contribution to the swayback alignment.

If this swayback alignment is one that is familiar to the body because it has been patterned over a long period of time, then gamma motor activity to the various muscles is set so that the muscles are preset to maintain their various lengths. Dancers can override the nonconscious messages to the hip flexors and lengthen them to move toward neutral pelvis. One way to accomplish this change would be to increase abdominal or gluteal activity with conscious thought, bringing the pubic bone forward and reducing anterior pelvic tilt and hip flexion. This increased length also serves to lengthen all the muscle fibers in the hip flexors, including the intrafusal fibers, putting the gamma sensory nerves on stretch. As soon as the conscious mind goes to another movement task, such as relevé or chaîné turns or jumps, the conscious effort to use the abdominal or gluteal muscles diminishes. At that point, the stretched gamma sensory neuron fires, causing a contraction of

extrafusal fibers that exist in the hip flexors and returning them to the shortened, habitual length. A similar analysis can be made for the lumbar extensors, which return to their shortened, habitual length (hyperlordosis of the spine) and the abdominals, which return to an elongated state and allow the anterior pelvic tilt. Each time the dancer consciously contracts muscles to try to place the pelvis into neutral alignment, the gamma system acts to return it to the anterior tilt (swayback) that has been patterned for years. This is why it can take months of vigilance, imagery, quiet awareness work, and sensations of being in what at first feels like the wrong alignment for a time, before the brain's programming is literally rewritten, and gamma motor output to the intrafusal fibers in the key muscles is reorganized and adjusted. Stretching and strengthening the appropriate muscles may not be enough. This proposed situation of stretching and strengthening being insufficient to create alignment changes has not been documented in the research. However, teachers are familiar with dancers who do corrective exercises and yet do not change habitual patterns, and given what is known about the gamma efferent system, it is reasonable to hypothesize a neural contribution to changing habitual patterns.

The pathways of the gamma efferent system are illustrated figure 6.13. Messages from areas of the brain (1) go to the gamma motor neuron (2), which sends messages to the intrafusal fibers in the muscle (3). The gamma sensory neuron (4) wrapped around the intrafusal fiber is stretch sensitive, and it signals length, velocity, and change in the muscle. It reaches its threshold and fires on the alpha motor neuron (5), which then tells the extrafusal fibers in the same muscle (6) to contract, thus regulating how much or little that muscle can stretch at any given time. It is no wonder that dancers can become frustrated trying to make changes to alignment. However, once they understand the complexity of the gamma efferent system, they can be more attentive and perhaps even more patient.

Muscle Spindles and Golgi Tendon Organs Work Together

Along with the reticular activating system and various interneurons, the muscle spindles and

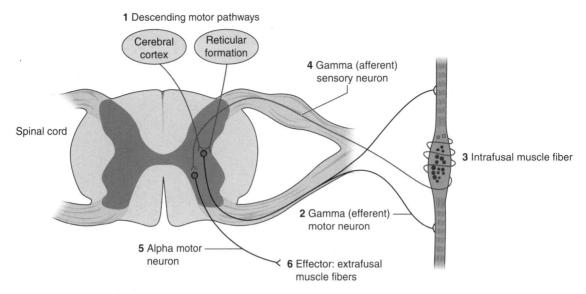

1 Descending motor pathways

Cerebral cortex

Reticular formation

4 Gamma (afferent) sensory neuron

Spinal cord

3 Intrafusal muscle fiber

2 Gamma (efferent) motor neuron

5 Alpha motor neuron

6 Effector: extrafusal muscle fibers

Figure 6.13 The gamma system is a complex organization that regulates alignment and muscle tension. Messages go from the brain (*1*) by way of the gamma motor neuron (*2*) to the intrafusal muscle fibers (*3*). The gamma sensory neuron responds (*4*), and it sends its message to the alpha motor neuron (*5*), which contracts the extrafusal muscle fibers (*6*).

the Golgi tendon organs act together to create smooth, coordinated movement. The muscle spindles are excitatory or facilitatory, while the GTOs are inhibitory. Like a dance between two partners, these structures (in association with brain areas such as the cerebellum and basal ganglia) constantly interact to ensure that muscle length changes are fluid, not jerky, and movement is coordinated. This relationship is at a nonconscious level, and it is one of the wonders of the neuromuscular system.

Gamma Efferent System and Flexibility Training

The two main forms of PNF stretching are called *contract–relax (CR) stretch* and *contract–relax with agonist contraction (CRAC) stretch.* Using the example of hamstring stretches, in the CR stretch, the hamstrings are first contracted near their end range of motion and then voluntarily relaxed while being stretched a bit further. While it was originally thought that the GTOs were responsible for the relaxation phase of this stretch, it is now believed that other sensory receptors account for the increased range of motion. In the CRAC stretch, in phase 1 the hamstrings are first contracted near their end range of motion, just as in the CR stretch. In

the next phase, the hamstrings are voluntarily relaxed while being stretched a bit further, and at the same time the quadriceps are contracted. It is during phase 2 that the reciprocal inhibition reflex plays its role, because the quadriceps contraction encourages further hamstring relaxation. However, these effects do not last long, and it is likely that the sensation of relaxation persists, encouraging continued release by the dancer stretching. While all of the neural mechanisms contributing to PNF stretching are not yet fully understood, these methods can be successful ways to increase flexibility for dancers and can be explored as part of the dancer's personal conditioning work.

A long history exists in most dance forms to address issues of alignment and flexibility. These two aspects of the dancer's anatomical attributes can be modified, but the methods of achieving changes are still controversial. Initially it was believed that the process was entirely mechanical. The traditional approach has been to force the body into correct alignment through conscious muscle contraction and to use extreme stretches to achieve the desired outcome for flexibility. Dancers trained in this traditional method use far too much muscle tension to organize the body. In the long term, this approach has little success and takes its toll in wear and tear. With the understanding of the neural components of both alignment and flexibility, dancers and dance teachers can use the nonconscious reflex mechanisms inherent in the body to make changes that create efficiency and optimal function. One of the values of somatic practice as part of dance training is its emphasis on encouraging reorganization of the nervous system to affect alignment. For example, in Ideokinesis, the dancer visualizes the movement, either as movement within the body or in space, without any conscious attempt at muscular effort. This approach reprograms unnecessary and unwanted muscular tensions, and it can allow for new alignment and movement patterns to develop.

Implications for Dance Training

Dance teachers can apply the knowledge about the neural mechanisms related to alignment and flexibility to create far more effective training procedures for their dancers. When recognizing an alignment problem, teachers must first assess whether any physiological imbalances, such as weak abdominals or tight hip flexors, need to be addressed. If this is the case, they can recommend appropriate corrective work. Several excellent texts are available to provide exercises (see Bibliography). Beyond the physical corrective work, addressing the neural components of misalignment must be done using tools beyond conditioning exercises.

One highly valuable tool is imagery. Imagery serves three functions. First, it avoids using conscious muscle contraction to change skeletal organization, which is not effective given what is known about the gamma efferent system. Through the use of imagery, the conscious centers of the brain can see the task, allowing the nonconscious centers to make the muscle selections. The process of how this works is discussed in detail in chapter 16. Second, images allow the brain to organize multiple muscle groups simultaneously, something that conscious muscle selection cannot do.

Third, imagery uses multiple brain areas, creating associations that reinforce the learning, potentially making learning more permanent. As many neuroscientists say, *Neurons that fire together, wire together.* Imagery can be particularly effective with young children and adolescents. For young children, working with the imagination and game playing is natural to their everyday lives, and they respond to imagery without inhibition. For adolescents, during growth spurts the neural system is already making considerable shifts and adjustments, and imagery can assist this process without overloading the brain with attention to multiple specific muscles. Further, this is a time of potential frustration resulting from the loss of skill and range of motion, and working with imagery can provide an enjoyable means of addressing problems without fixating on technical detriments.

Another useful tool for alignment correction is somatic practice. Somatic education uses many of the key elements to which the gamma efferent system responds, such as breath, awareness or mindfulness, relaxation, and slowing down the pace of material to allow for thoughtful attention. Adding somatic education classes can be a valuable asset to a dance program. Similarly, many somatic-based conditioning and movement systems exist that can appeal to young dancers. They are more diverse and integrated directly into technique classes than the early somatic practices, but they still contain the awareness and imagery elements.

Flexibility work should be done after activity, when the body is warm. It can include static and dynamic stretches, as well as the PNF techniques of CR and CRAC stretching. Utilizing both physiologic and neural mechanisms can create the best overall means for achieving flexibility. Bouncing and extreme stretching should be avoided, and dancers can be instructed about the consequences of these methods.

Dancers are creatures who live in the body and luxuriate in kinesthetic and visceral experiences. It is easy for dancers and dance teachers to diminish the role of the brain and the nervous system in every skill that they accomplish. When dancers think of brain activity, it is usually in the context of learning and memorizing exercise sequences and choreography. However, the way dancers perceive, interpret, and direct movement has a profound effect on how the muscles are used and how the body organizes. All aspects of dancers' training, from skill acquisition to alignment to flexibility, are directed by the interaction of sensory and motor mechanisms at the brain level. Teachers can enhance this magnificent system through instructional techniques that recognize and incorporate knowledge of the neural components of movement.

Summary

Motor control explores how the nervous system organizes and directs all the muscles and joints to produce coordinated movement, and how sensory information from the environment is used to accomplish this task. The smallest component of the nervous system is the neuron. The central nervous system comprises the brain and the neurons of the spinal cord, while the peripheral nervous system is composed of all the neurons functioning outside the spinal cord in the periphery of the body. The brain can be divided into the forebrain, the brain stem, the cerebellum, and the limbic system. The cerebrum is part of the forebrain, and it is divided into four lobes. The frontal lobe is responsible for voluntary movement and reasoning. The parietal lobe is involved in sensory information perception. The occipital lobe or visual cortex deals with visual perception. The temporal lobe is involved in hearing and memory. The brain stem controls autonomic functions such as chewing, swallowing, breathing, heartbeat, and muscle tone. The cerebellum is a comparator of the movement plan and what is occurring, and it also works with the basal ganglia in creating smooth, coordinated movement. The limbic system is the center of emotions and motivation. Movement is organized in three levels of a hierarchy: from low to high are the spinal cord, the brain stem, and the cerebral cortex. The three classes of movements are voluntary, reflex, and rhythmic motor patterns. Several reflexes control movement at the nonconscious level: the myotatic reflex, the autogenic inhibition reflex, the reciprocal inhibition reflex, and the gamma efferent system. The gamma efferent system has a profound impact on both alignment and flexibility, and dancers and dance teachers can use this knowledge to improve learning strategies. Somatic and somatic-based practices and PNF stretches are systems that dancers can employ to further the development of efficient alignment and excellent flexibility for dance.

Chapter 7
Attention and Performance

*A*ttention is one of the many factors that affect motor control and performance in everyday life and in dance. For example, some people who travel along a regular route that has become automatic can have the uncanny occurrence of arriving at their destination with no recall of how they got there or what they saw along the way. When people text or talk on the phone while driving or even while walking, they are more likely to get into a collision. At some point in their training, all dancers experience times when concentration in class is poor because of personal distractions and, as a result, performance and learning of motor skills suffer. Sometimes dancers in class suddenly become alert to the teacher's verbal cues when they hear their own name included in the comments, thereby enhancing their performance of the dance activity. Performers all experience stage fright—that moment before the audience when suddenly the skill seems far more difficult than in rehearsal, attention lags, and performance deteriorates. And most dancers have experienced that special audition when performance is enhanced due to increased concentration from the excitement and anticipation.

All of these seemingly unrelated scenarios relate to aspects of attention, an umbrella term that covers issues of distraction, automatic or habitual activities, performance nerves, and multitasking. Understanding the various aspects of attention can enhance dance training by helping dancers learn how to focus their minds and concentrate their efforts in class and performance. As part of their training, dancers can enhance attention to improve their motor control in dance skills.

Defining Attention

Simply put, **attention** is concentrated mental activity. Attention has been an area of consideration in the field of psychology dating back to the late 1800s. The prominent experimental psychologist William James described attention as selecting one stream of thought out of the simultaneous multitude of ideas in the brain at a given moment. In his view, attention included aspects of concentration, consciousness, and

focus, requiring that some issues be set aside in order to deal with the selected thoughts. A dance example might illuminate some of the various aspects of attention. When dancers are performing on stage, they must know the choreography and be aware of where they are in the sequence at a given moment in time. They must be listening to the music to ensure that they are synchronized with the sound score. They must be conscious of the other dancers and be responsive to any sudden and unexpected changes. They must be aware of the stage environment and make sure that they are in the correct spacing so that they are in the lighted areas of the stage. For entrances and exits, they must observe the curtains and legs in order to enter the wings cleanly. Depending on skill level and the complexity of the choreography, they give more or less focus to accomplishing the movement tasks. If attention fails in any of these performance aspects, the dancing suffers. Clearly attention is not one simple idea; many aspects contribute to it.

Types of Attention

First, attention is **selective**, which suggests that a person can choose to focus on one idea or source of information while ignoring another. For example, a dance student can choose to observe the teacher demonstrating while ignoring the two students talking beside her. Attention is **divisible**, meaning it can be separated among alternating sources of information, such as listening to the music in class while also hearing the teacher's corrections. However, relative to handling a single source of information, the ability to manage both sources is reduced. On the other hand, attention is **shiftable**, so dancers can also choose to move back and forth between two sources, first concentrating on the music while ignoring the teacher and then concentrating on the teacher's comments while not listening to the music. Shifting between sources can be voluntary (such as deciding to listen to the teacher) or involuntary (such as attending to a distraction—for example, the other students' conversation). Attention is also **sustainable**, keeping the focus on just one source for a prolonged period of time. Finally, attention is **limited**, which means that in terms

The posing dancer is distracted by the moving dancer, and attention and performance can diminish as a consequence.

of motor behavior, a person can only effectively achieve a finite number of activities at one time. When attention becomes divided, effectiveness is greatly hampered.

Controlled and Automatic Processing Mechanisms

Some activities demand considerable conscious thought, while others seem to be automatic or habitual. Dancers commonly use the term *muscle memory* to refer to movements that can be executed without attention, as if the muscles themselves had learned the movements. However, anatomy and physiology make it clear that the muscles do not actually have memories. Rather, the way information is processed by the brain falls into the categories of controlled or automatic mechanisms. This division is a continuum; many movements have varying aspects of control and automatic function.

The terms *controlled processing* and *automatic processing* are relative terms used to describe a range of differing categories for cognitive activity involving movement. **Controlled processing** is a volitional (willful) choice and can be easily ceased or prevented. It is also relatively slow and requires attention. Finally, controlled processing is **serial processing**, which means that one thought or part of the process happens after another in a sequence. For example, when people drive to a new location and are seeking the address by building number, they must carefully read the posted numbers one by one to find the correct address. Similarly when dancers in class are seeing a combination for the first time, they must concentrate on learning the sequence of steps and body positioning.

Automatic processing is not a volitional choice, and often it cannot easily be prevented. It is relatively fast and does not require attention. Finally, automatic processing is **parallel processing**, which means that thoughts and processes can happen simultaneously. For example, when people drive the same route to the same place daily, it requires so little conscious thought that they are often unaware that they have made the trip. When dancers are seeing a demonstration of a combination that

Dancers need sufficient attention to learn complex combinations in the class setting.

they have done many times, they can mark it along with the teacher without thinking about it. No process is entirely automatic and free from all conscious involvement.

The cognitive processes involved in motor skills can become faster and more efficient with extensive practice, which allows trained performers to focus on other aspects of the skill. With beginners, the processing of counts for a dance combination can demand considerable attention, so they often fail to see other aspects of the movement, such as the spatial design. More advanced dancers can process the count structure rapidly and without much conscious attention, therefore they can simultaneously observe many other aspects of the combination, such as body positioning, spatial design, and movement quality.

Interference and Attention

A term commonly heard in today's culture is *multitasking*. It is not uncommon to see someone walking down a busy street, avoiding cars and obstacles, texting on the phone, and looking for a favorite coffee shop all at the same time. People assume that the brain can simultaneously manage several thoughts and activities and do all of them well (figure 7.1).

Researchers use the term **task interference** to refer to one thought competing with another for

Figure 7.1 A lighthearted view of the current dilemma of multitasking in today's busy society.

attention. For example, if a dancer is executing a flamenco dance and suddenly catches her heel in her skirt, causing a loss of balance, attention to this problematic circumstance will interfere with concentration on the dance steps. One of these four solutions could occur:

- The dancer could continue dancing and ignore the skirt with no change in performance.
- The dancer could give complete focus to the skirt and stop dancing.
- The dancer could keep dancing but try to get the skirt off her heel, and both actions could be poorly done.
- The dancer could see that the skirt was about to get caught and alter the dance steps to avoid the problem altogether.

This scenario can illuminate the nature of attention and its limits. In fact, if two activities can be executed at the same time *and* each could be done by itself, it means that at least one of them requires little or no attention, which is called **automatic action**. The flamenco dancer might be so experienced and professional that she can kick the skirt away without premeditated thought. However, if adding a second task means that the first task is compromised, it means that both require attention.

The criterion of interference has been used in research for quite some time to determine whether a task requires attention. Typically researchers start with a primary task—a task of interest that they wish to assess. They then add a attention-demanding secondary task to see how it affects the primary task. If the primary task is unaffected, they conclude that it does not require attention from the subject. For example, in research about balance, adults can balance on one leg and do cognitive tasks such as counting backward at the same time, but when children try it, they usually fall over. Hence, balance is more automatic for adults than for children, although even for adults, it is challenging to do two tasks together, and one task might suffer.

An important consideration in this area for dancers is the attention it requires to alter or correct alignment problems. While some dance teachers do not place much emphasis on align-

ment, others stress the importance of alignment and see it as a major goal of the dance class. In this context, consider alignment as the primary task and simple or complex movement as the secondary tasks. If dancers can apply alignment corrections in simple slow work such as pliés, but revert back to their habitual alignment in a complicated combination, it indicates that they must still invest substantial attention to the primary task. Teachers should be understanding of this situation, and they must limit their expectations regarding complex material. After dancers have considerable practice in the slower context with the corrections, the new alignment becomes more habitual. At that point, the dancers are capable of doing complex combinations while using the corrected alignment simultaneously.

Two types of task interference can occur. **Structural interference** occurs when physical

The flamenco dancer will need to make fast decisions if her skirt becomes caught under the heel of her shoe.

or neurological events cause the decrease in attention. For example, physically the hand cannot hold on to the barre and manipulate a prop at the same time. Neurologically, dancers cannot see the teacher demonstrating and see themselves in the mirror at the same time. The process would be divided and therefore slowed down. **Capacity interference** occurs when no structural interference arises but the mental capacity to attend to multiple events is not available. Currently a debate is ensuing about whether hands-free phone communication while driving is superior to handheld devices. While hands-free phones do not create structural interference, the issue of capacity interference has not been resolved.

Understanding the types of attention and sources of interference explain some of the questions posed about attention limits. Researchers can address other questions by examining theories that describe and define theories of *capacity* or *resources for attention*. These theories can give dancers and dance educators a sound basis for determining how to hone concentration in the dance context.

Theories of Capacity or Resources for Attention

It can be perplexing to understand why attention can be so different in various circumstances. Concentration can be sharp during a dance audition, heightening the capacity to learn material. Dancers may wonder how they can listen to music and listen to corrections seemingly at the same time, or they may wonder how they can ignore pain from an injury and continue dancing. Theorists generally agree that

limits exist in a person's potential attention to a task at a given moment in time. Possible limitations include amount of information from the environment, number of tasks to be attempted simultaneously, and levels of fatigue or arousal. For example, when dancers are fatigued from a late-night rehearsal, concentration in the next morning's dance class is negatively affected.

Various theoretical models agree that limitations to attention exist, but they differ in their perspectives about what the innate capacity for attention in a person might be. At this point in time, no single theory of attention satisfies all of the observed aspects. Each of the theories described next—filter, central-resource capacity, multiple resource, and attention-selection—provides an understanding of some feature or features of attention. Due in part to wide-ranging definitions and the many aspects of cognitive thought involved, each of these theories offers insight into the complexity of attention.

Bottleneck Theories and Filter Theories

Bottleneck theories and **filter theories** suggest that in the early part of processing information, many functions can occur because it is happening in the large part of the bottle. Further down the line, the bottleneck is reached, and information not needed at that time is filtered out (figure 7.2). Various filter theories differ regarding the point at which the bottleneck occurs.

Psychologist Alan Welford was the first to suggest the early filter theory, which states that all information processing needs attention, and a single channel exists for these cognitive

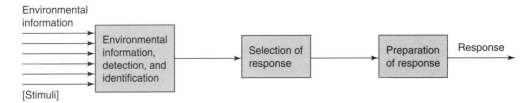

Figure 7.2 In filter theories, the information needed for a particular task is selected, then unnecessary information is filtered out.

Reprinted, by permission, from R.A. Magill, 2011, *Motor learning and control*, 9th ed. (New York: McGraw-Hill Companies), 196, © McGraw Hill Education.

events. Therefore a person can only attend to one thought or handle one stimulus–response task at a time. A secondary task at any point would interfere, so filtering of competing thoughts occurs early.

Late filter theories suggest that filtering occurs at a much later stage. In the 1970s, Steven Keele was a pioneer in the study of the neural processes that underlie the interaction of attention and motor control. His theory placed the bottleneck at the very end of the process. Unlike in the single channel view, multiple events are processed simultaneously for several stages. At a late stage, these events connect with memory. It is not until this point that a single event needs full attention, and other events are filtered out.

Other theories say that the filtering point can change depending on the circumstances. Despite these differences, all of the filter theories conform to the idea that the capacity for attention is fixed, and when the capacity is surpassed, performance starts to deteriorate. More recent theories suggest that the fixed capacity idea does not sufficiently explain all possible performance situations.

Central Resource Capacity Theories

In capacity theories, attention is viewed as a resource. **Central resource capacity theories** suggest that all activities needing attention compete within one centralized base for attention resources. One of the major influences affecting attention in these theories is arousal. **Arousal** is a person's general state of excitability, reflected by physiological responses such as heart rate and respiratory rate. Both low and high levels of arousal result in poor performance, whereas moderate levels create the best performance (figure 7.3). In other words, if dancers are either very tired or highly anxious, they are likely to perform badly.

A resource capacity theory proposed by Nobel laureate Daniel Kahneman continues to influence the understanding of attention today. Figure 7.4 illustrates factors that influence available capacity and regulate how they are used in Kahneman's model of attention.

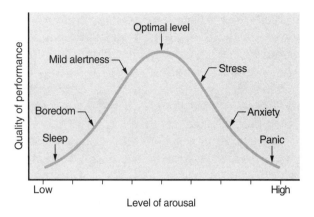

Figure 7.3 An inverted U graph shows the relationship between arousal levels and performance.

The box near the top of figure 7.4 represents the available resources and the capacity for attention. Unlike the fixed theories of capacity, in Kahneman's model, attentional capacity is flexible and not fixed, which is represented by the squiggly line inside the box. In this model, attention is mainly affected by levels of arousal.

Miscellaneous determinants and miscellaneous manifestations of arousal are at the top of figure 7.4, going into and out of the available

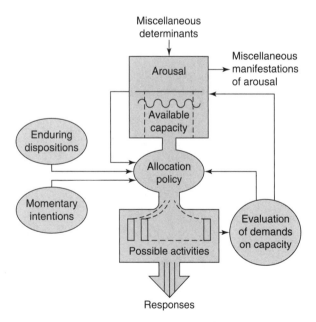

Figure 7.4 Kahneman's model of attention is far more complex than earlier theories, and it includes a flexible model of capacity for attention as well as several factors that influence attention.

Reprinted from D. Kahneman, 1973, *Attention and effort* (Upper Saddle River, NJ: Pearson Education). By permission from author.

capacity box. **Miscellaneous determinants** are elements that can affect arousal levels, such as amount of sleep and food before dancing. **Miscellaneous manifestations of arousal** are blatant actions, such as fidgeting resulting from overarousal, and generally have a negative effect on performance.

The circle on the right side of figure 7.4 is called **evaluation of demands on capacity**, which is an assessment of the requirements made on attention resources. Demands on capacity must be evaluated in order to determine whether two or more tasks can be handled at the same time, or whether one task is so demanding that taking on a secondary task will not be possible. For example, knowing that the dance performance is only two days away can increase dancers' arousal and inspire how keenly they concentrate in rehearsal. Sometimes evaluation of demands can be imposed from an external source, such as teachers announcing that they are assessing a combination in class that day to determine which dancers will be cast in the concert.

The ellipse in the center of figure 7.4 (called **allocation policy**) represents the decision maker, controlling how much attention will be given to each of several tasks, which will be affected by various factors. These factors, enduring dispositions and momentary intentions, are seen in the ellipses to the far left in the figure and are defined next.

Enduring dispositions are those events that involuntarily and automatically draw dancers' attention, distracting them from the focal task. Two types of events have this effect. One type concerns visual or auditory novelty. For example, if dancers are in class and the piano tuner unexpectedly walks in to work on the piano, the tuner's physical presence will visually distract the dancers. If the tuner is allowed to tune the piano, the sounds will create an auditory distraction. The second type of enduring dispositions relates to meaningful events. This type is so common that it is referred to as the *cocktail party phenomenon*. Everyone has experienced this phenomenon when attending a social event. In spite of being engrossed in a conversation, if a person hears his or her own name in another discussion, it will immediately draw the attention away from the original conversation. In dance class or rehearsal, dancers might

All dance forms require attention to many factors, including body shape, rhythm, use of space, and organization of the limbs with the trunk.

be attending to the corrections being given but have their attention suddenly distracted by hearing conversations that are meaningful to them for personal reasons. Enduring dispositions are also referred to as *bottom–up* (from the periphery to the brain), because the external stimulus is affecting or altering the attention.

Momentary intentions reflect a person's conscious decision to focus on one idea or task at a given time that relates to specific goals. Dancers may be executing a dance combination, and the teacher may ask them to focus on the musicality and rhythm of the phrase and not be especially concerned with the body shapes. Notice that evaluation of demands also influences allocation. In the dance example, because the dancers know that the teacher's instructions are of value, they will select to pay attention to this goal. Momentary intentions are also referred to as *top–down* (from the brain to action), because the internal goal is driving the attention.

The final box at the lowest point of figure 7.4 is called **possible activities**, which represents all of the possible choices regarding cognitive processes or tasks that the dancers might choose to address. In the example, dancers can choose to attend to the teacher's comments, but they may switch attention to a struggle with balance and then return to focusing on the instructions.

Kahneman's model of attention provides many useful tools in thinking about how attention is limited and how it becomes allocated efficiently. In the bottleneck theories, some of the information cannot pass on to the next level of processing because of the bottleneck. In Kahneman's model, however, it is because demands exceed attentional capacity, and choices are made based on a variety of influences determining allocation. None of the theories and models described so far explains why people can sometimes seem to do two activities at once, but at other times they cannot. This seeming contradiction is clarified in multiple resource theories.

Multiple Resource Theories

In **multiple resource theories** several resource capacities exist, and each has its own limitations. Each resource is particular to a singular aspect of performance. A popular multiple resource theory was proposed by the psychologist and researcher Christopher Wickens. He claimed that three different resources exist for processing information: input and output modalities, stages of information processing, and codes of processing information. **Input and output modalities** are the receptors of incoming information (input), such as vision and hearing, and the outgoing motor messages (output), such as muscles of the limbs and speech. **Stages of information processing** are the various cognitive steps, such as perception, memory, and response. **Codes of processing information** are ways of categorizing information, such as verbal codes and spatial codes. If two tasks do not compete within one of the three resource areas, but rather they exist in two separate resources, then the activities can be done simultaneously without detriment to performance.

For example, a person can drive a car and memorize the driving route at the same time, because the visual and motor requirements (input and output modalities) and the perception and memorization of the route (information processing) are separate pools of attentional resources. On the other hand, driving and putting on makeup using the mirror both require visual and motor attention; therefore, they cannot be done well as the same time. Similarly, in a dance rehearsal of a duet, the partners cannot be expressively focusing on each other or the space while at the same time critically examining their performance in the mirror, because both require visual focus and attention. However, they can achieve the choreography and focus on each other, because these tasks require different attentional resources. If the choreography is new to the dancers or is extremely complex, one of the tasks—either focusing on each other or completing the choreography—might suffer.

Multiple resource theories explain how dancers can achieve high-level activity while attending to various elements at the same time. If dancers need to coordinate new patterns of arms and legs and complex torso actions simultaneously, this multiple attention process might not be highly successful. On the other hand, dancers seem to be capable of listening

At times, the mirror can be a distraction rather than an aid to the dancer.

to music, attending to the motor patterns of known choreography, and concentrating on a dramatic metaphor at the same time. However, it is currently unknown how fully each of the various activities can be achieved. This result would depend on many aspects, such as how automatic one or more of the activities are for the dancers.

Action Selection Theories

One other approach to attention allocation disagrees with capacity theory. In **action selection theories**, selection is the basic system for determining attention, not capacities that limit the thought process. For example, when runners are in a race, and one runner falls, a teammate may select at that moment to stop and assist the injured friend. At that point, all other cognitive processes are prevented from interfering, including attention to pacing, obser-

vation of positioning in the group, and distance to the finish line. This narrow focus does not result from a lack of attentional resources; it is because once this selection is made, based on the immediacy of the event, the other possible processes cannot easily occur. Theories based on action selection are reflective of the ideas from the ecological perspective. Interaction with the environment and events in the environment determine certain responses requiring attention, thus precluding other demands on focus and concentration.

Competing for Attention

In a previous example, a flamenco dancer had to choose between dealing with a costume malfunction and continuing her dance performance. Another way of expressing this problem is to say that the two events were competing for attention. Selective attention is called **intentional** when people choose between competing events, as did the flamenco dancer in the example. Because the person is choosing where to place attention, the term *top–down* is used for this type of attention. On the other hand, selective attention is called **incidental** when events are considered regardless of intentions. Because the event or stimulus draws attention, the term *bottom–up* is used in this instance. An example of incidental attention is the case of dancers whose hair falls into their faces while they are dancing. In spite of teachers asking dancers not to fix their hair while executing dance combinations, the urge to attend to the distraction is unavoidable and is usually done with little or no conscious thought. Three effects uncovered through research clearly outline some of the issues with intentional and incidental attention.

The Stroop Effect

It is not uncommon for situations to occur in which a stimulus suggests one response, but the actual event needs a different response. This phenomenon is called the **Stroop effect**. It was discovered by psychologist John Ridley Stroop, who developed a method of testing competition for attention. In his simple test, a subject is asked to look at words on a screen and name the color of ink in which a word is printed. In the congruent condition, the meaning of the word matches the color; so, for example, the word *red* is in red ink. In the incongruent condition, the color and meaning are not matched, so the word *red* might be in blue ink. The color recognition in the congruent case is very fast, whereas it is delayed in the incongruent case. In other words, when the meaning of the word differs from its color, the meaning and the color are in competition, and the meaning interferes with color recognition, thus slowing down the response. The average person is unable to ignore the meaning of the word and simply respond to the ink color. This particular attentional effect is specific to semantic content.

The Cocktail Party Phenomenon

Another example of competition for attention is the cocktail party phenomenon that was described as part of the enduring dispositions in the Kahneman model. It was first described by British cognitive scientist Colin Cherry in 1953. In spite of being engrossed in a conversation, if a person hears his or her own name in another discussion, it will immediately draw the attention away from the original conversation. Note that this occurrence does not only say something about competition for attention. It also describes a situation of incidental attention, because the person is distracted whether or not they intend to change focus. Hence, when the stimulus is particularly important, it is permitted to move along the attentional pathways for further processing. The earlier dance example considered dancers hearing the teacher's corrections when their name was included, which would be intentional attention. In addition, a dancer would also hear other dancers talking on the other side of the room if that dancer's name were part of the conversation, which would be incidental attention. In both instances, the name recognition creates competition for attention. However, in one case the dancer selects to listen, and in the other case the situation creates an unintended distraction.

Inattention Blindness

A third example of competition for attention is the case of what is commonly called *looked but failed to see*. **Inattention blindness**, also called **cognitive tunneling**, refers to failing to see something in the environment because the focus is so engrossed in a selected event. Unfortunately, it is possible for a teacher of dance or any subject to fail to observe students bullying another student because the teacher's attention is on the lesson plan or another active group of students. In a dance class, a teacher might fail to see a dancer become injured because of concentrating on another student or group of students. Similarly, dancers might fail to see an obstacle on the floor when executing a series of chaîné turns and concentrating on spotting. In each of these cases, the incident or object that is not observed is in the field of vision yet not perceived. These situations are not cases of negligence, but they are incidences of inattention blindness that all people experience as part of selective attention.

Tap dance requires strong attention to rhythm in the music as well to as spatial awareness.

It is clear from these examples of the Stroop effect, the cocktail party phenomenon, and inattention blindness that attention can be altered or restricted by a variety of competing events. With an awareness of these issues, dancers can learn to intentionally and selectively focus on what is important in their environment and enhance their training through well-developed concentration.

Attention During Movement

Most dancers would claim that they are concentrating while dancing, regardless of their skill level. The question researchers often ask is how to determine what the content of the conscious thought processes are. Beginners need to focus on specific movement components of the work, such as pointed feet and turned-out hip joints in ballet or which part of the foot is hitting the floor in tap and flamenco. For advanced dancers, these aspects become automatic, and they can think about fine-tuning the rhythm,

artistic expression, their relationship to other dancers, and environmental issues such as spatial design. In driving, a beginner needs to consider the most basic aspects, such as steering and staying in the lanes, using the turn signals, and moving the foot from accelerator to brakes. When drivers are more experienced, they are better able to attend to road conditions, what other drivers are doing, planning future actions, and talking to a passenger. Although both the beginner and the advanced driver are doing the same motor skills, their attention is on very different aspects of the activity.

Attentional Focus

Disagreement exists among dance teachers about how to direct students' attention when they are learning and executing dance movements. Some teachers emphasize a focus on the specific movement components, and some direct attention to particular muscles, while others draw the attention to the overall movement goal or outcome. Most experienced dancers would not achieve multiple turns if they thought about the placement of the gesture foot or the straightening of the supporting leg as they go from plié to relevé. Instead skilled dancers concentrate on elements such as the initiating push-off, spotting the environment, musicality, and the landing. Researchers call this difference of approach internal versus external focus. **Internal focus** refers to concentrating on the specific movement components of the task. **External focus** refers to concentrating on the effects of the movements—the general outcome. It can also refer to focus on the external environment, such as the floor, props, stage space, and wings. When dancers work on lifts, they concentrate on getting the partner off the ground, not on the movements of their shoulder joints. While most research supports external focus for skilled performers, competing theories exist about what is best for beginners.

Early Theories

German psychologist James Cattell theorized about focus of attention in the late 1890s, but his work was not translated into English until 1947. In his words:

In the practiced automatic movements of daily life attention is directed to the sense impression and not to the movement. So, in piano playing, the beginner may attend to his fingers but the practiced player attends only to the notes or to the melody. In speaking, writing and reading aloud, and in games and manual work, attention is always directed to the goal, never to the movement. In fact, as soon as attention is directed to the movement, this becomes less automatic and less dependable. (Cattell, 1893, as cited in Woodworth, 1947, p. 253)

The Russian motor learning researcher Nikolai Bernstein corroborated Cattell's work and agreed that external focus of attention is a better strategy for advanced performers. In his words:

Consciously watching the movements of a teacher and intent attention towards one's own movements make sense only at the beginning of the process of skill development, when the motor composition of the skill is being defined. After the automations have already been elaborated and switched out of consciousness, it is useless and even detrimental to chase them behind the movement curtain. One needs to trust the level of the muscular-articular links; most of the time, our confidence is justified. (Bernstein, 1996, p. 203)

In the language of today's motor control theories, Cattell and Bernstein are stating that external focus is more appropriate than internal focus, except perhaps for the novice learning a new skill. In the case of the beginner, attention to movement components may be an essential part of the early learning process. However, they would claim that for the highly skilled person, focusing on these movement details would cause a disruption to automatic or habitual movements. This observation would help to explain why the advanced dancer does not need to attend to the movement components such as pointed feet and turnout, while some beginning dancers do need to concentrate on these movement components to achieve success.

Somatic Approaches

Movement educator and early somatic practitioner Mabel Todd was a pioneer in dance education in observing similar ideas to those of Cattell and Bernstein. In her words:

When "doing exercises" under instruction we are apt to think that we move or direct the moving of muscles. What actually happens is that we get a picture from the teacher's words or his movements, and the appropriate action takes place within our own bodies to reproduce this picture. The result is successful in proportion to our power of interpretation and amount of experience, but most of all perhaps to the *desire to do*. In any case, the final response is automatic and not the result of any consciously directed movement of particular muscles. It is the result of a combination of reflexes, no one of which can be selected as in itself "causing" the movement, or pattern of movement. (Todd, 1937, p. 33)

Note that Todd is taking this idea one step further, and she is pointing out that focus or attention to particular muscles is detrimental at any stage of learning new movement. When motor control theorists discuss internal focus and the beginner's need to think about movement components, they do not mean to think about particular muscles. In other words, when beginning dancers are thinking about straightening their legs in relevés or kicks, they may need to think about the movement component of an extended knee, but it is not useful to consciously direct the quadriceps to contract. No baseball coach would direct his pitcher to think about contracting the main chest muscle, the pectoralis major, when throwing the ball, nor would the football kicker think about his hip flexors when sending the ball to the goal posts. Todd's method for altering alignment, using visualization techniques of whole-body organization rather than directing individual muscles, is illustrated in figure 7.5.

Movement educator Lulu Sweigard furthered Todd's work after studying with her extensively. Sweigard studied anatomy and the nervous system, and she stated that thinking about directing individual muscles was indeed problematic. She claimed:

Our voluntary influence on movement is limited to controlling starting, stopping, direction, range, speed, and force. We can and do set the goal for movement, but this is where voluntary control ends. The choice of muscles whose coordinated work will

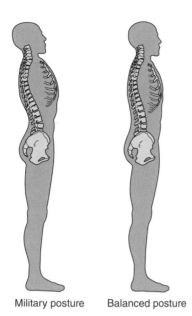

Military posture   Balanced posture

Figure 7.5 Through visualizing the elongation of the low back, the softening of the front of the rib cage, and floating the top of the head upward, the inefficiency of the "military posture" can be changed to a more "balanced posture."

achieve the goal and the selection of the nerve pathways over which the messages travel to these muscles reside in the nervous system. We can voluntarily interfere with this process and redirect our movement if the goal is not being achieved, but we cannot voluntarily impose controls on muscle coordination and hope to attain efficiency. (Sweigard, 1974, p. 4)

Sweigard's Ideokinesis was developed from her study and understanding of anatomy and the nervous system, and her nine lines of movement present an excellent approach to rebalancing and re-coordinating the muscles related to alignment. These images can provide the dancer with a method to influence alignment patterns without consciously attempting to control or engage muscles to achieve the goal.

Currently, several movement educators have embraced these ideas and continue to develop approaches that incorporate Sweigard's principles, including well-established educators Irene Dowd, Eric Franklin, and Donna Krasnow. Other educators have continued the work of a wide range of early somatic practices, such as Glenna Batson utilizing the Alexander Technique and Sylvie Fortin incorporating Feldenkrais work in her dance technique classes. What all of these and many other dance educators share is the principle of using imagery and awareness to alter alignment and movement patterns rather than consciously directing muscle use.

Recent Theories

While considerable research supports the idea that focus on specific movement components is detrimental to the skilled performer, the conclusions of studies on beginners and the use of internal focus are not unanimous. Some theorists think that even at the beginning level, it is best to approach learning a new skill by using external focus. The **constrained action hypothesis** states that using internal focus constrains (limits) the motor system because the learner is trying to assert conscious control, which disrupts the automatic processes of the motor control system. Several studies have supported this hypothesis. They consistently demonstrate that when performers at any skill level direct their attention to movement outcomes rather than specific components, they achieve greater success. This view is called the **action effect hypothesis**.

At this point in time, it is clear that disagreements exist about approaching learning new skills and the use of internal and external focus. Therefore, it is advisable for teachers to balance their comments and directions to the beginning dance student and encourage both internal and external focus. Further, it is recommended that internal focus only be used when the beginner is struggling with a specific movement component and it needs to be addressed. For example, when beginners first learn triplets in modern dance, they often have bent knees on the two relevé steps. It would be appropriate to remind the dancers to stretch their legs (straighten their knees), which brings the attention to a specific movement component and uses internal focus. No research or movement theories suggest that it is appropriate to attempt to control or direct individual muscles in learning or executing dance movements.

Fields of Attention

While internal and external uses of focus are directional concerns, the width of focus can also be a consideration. The term *width* indicates that attention can be broad or narrow, with reference to the environment and mental pursuits. **Broad focus** refers to directing attention to a large environmental area or on many components that need concentration. **Narrow focus** refers to directing attention to a small environmental area or fewer cognitive components. For example, when quarterbacks in football first take control of the ball, they use a broad focus to scan the field and seek open receivers. However, if no one is open, quarterbacks narrow the focus to their immediate surrounding to look for a break in the line and run the ball through the space between players. In dance, when dancers are doing unison ensemble choreography with a large group, they use broad focus. However, when a dancer is catching a leaping partner, the focus narrows. In choreographic situations where the environmental and mental activities are continually shifting, ability to rapidly switch from broad to narrow to broad focus becomes important. However, in a situation where dancers need to concentrate on intricate steps that do not rely on being in unison with other dancers, it is best to sustain attention narrowly for an extended period. Figure 7.6 shows the interaction of direction of focus and width of focus.

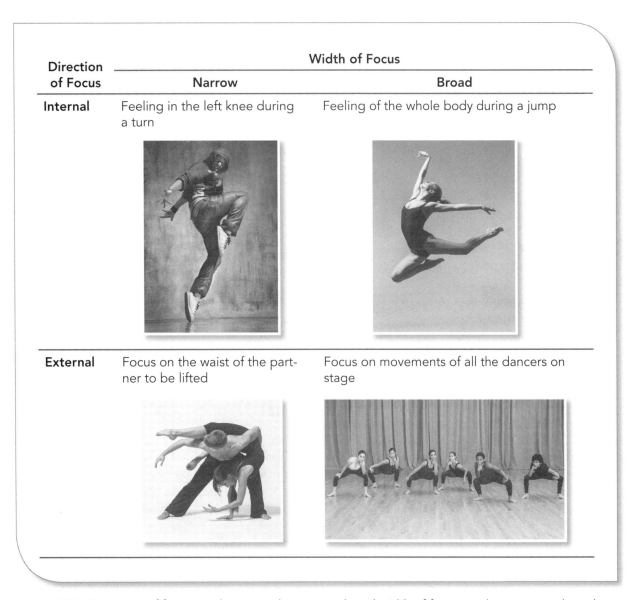

Direction of Focus	Width of Focus	
	Narrow	Broad
Internal	Feeling in the left knee during a turn	Feeling of the whole body during a jump
External	Focus on the waist of the partner to be lifted	Focus on movements of all the dancers on stage

Figure 7.6 Direction of focus can be internal or external, and width of focus can be narrow or broad.

Attention Under Pressure

At some point in most of their performance experiences, most dancers know what it feels like to perform under pressure. It might be during a major dance concert, a competition, an examination, an audition, or a workshop with a master teacher. It might involve a small jury of a few faculty members or a large audience. Monetary gain or elevated prestige before one's peers may be involved. In each instance, tremendous pressure exists to perform well. When dancers fail to meet expectations when dancing under pressure, the term *choking* is sometimes used. Performance anxiety can cause choking.

Performance anxiety, also called *stage fright*, involves a conflict between the desire to publicly perform in one's art and the fear of being inadequate and experiencing public humiliation. It has been a subject of discussion in the realm of the performing arts for some time, dating back to the 1960s. While much of the research has been conducted on musicians, these results apply to dancers and have been largely confirmed by recent research on dancers. The anxiety manifests in several physiological factors or somatic symptoms such as trembling, nausea, racing heart, shallow breathing, and loss of motor control. It also has cognitive components such as excessive worry and negative self-image, and these cognitive effects seem to be more debilitating to dancers than the somatic symptoms. It should be noted that in addition to these effects causing detriments to performance abilities, performance anxiety has also been linked to dance injuries. For all of these reasons, teachers and dancers should take this condition seriously and put strategies in place to assist dancers.

Sometimes the condition is treated with chemicals known as beta-blockers. Beta-blockers have shown some success in treating musicians with performance anxiety, especially in reducing blood pressure and heart rate. A problem for dancers using beta-blockers is the reported increase in fatigue during long aerobic dance pieces and reduced muscle power in anaerobic (short bout) activities, such as a series of jumps. The other approach to helping dancers deal with performance anxiety is the use of coping strategies. Positive coping strategies can include planning (seeing oneself succeeding), seeking support (talking through the issues and emotions), humor, positive self-talk, and efforts to enhance self-confidence (reaching a high point of preparedness for the event). Dancers can also use forms of meditation, visualization, breathing techniques, somatic work, and other methods of focusing the mind and calming the physiological processes just before the event. Negative strategies include self-blame, denial, venting of emotions, and use of alcohol and drugs to mask the emotions or physical symptoms. Finally, it has been observed that females and males equally experience performance anxiety, and earlier intervention is more successful than later intervention.

Some of the studies done on performance anxiety suggest that one cause of this unfortunate reaction is the tendency to revert to internal focus in the performance setting. When advanced dancers with high-level skills suddenly begin to focus on movement components and conscious movement control, skills decline. This response to dancing under pressure is another important reason to encourage external focus in dance training and rehearsals. These preparatory phases need to foster the physical, emotional, and cognitive processes that replicate the actual performance event so that dancers are prepared for the pressures of the stage environment.

Attention and the Ironic Effect

Another outcome of attentional focus, called the **ironic effect**, involves causing a motor action by mentally concentrating on avoiding it. Dancers know the frustration of saying the words *Don't fall over on this balance*, then observing their balance deteriorate with each subsequent attempt. Focusing on an undesired result or action is counterproductive, and it is not the best way to achieve success. Dancers must learn how to replace the negative thoughts with positive goals and imagery. This mental dialogue is known as *positive self-talk*. An important part of training for optimal motor control involves understanding the psychological effects of inappropriate attentional strategies, such as concentrating on what not to do. Sometimes teachers give corrections to dancers by telling them *not* to do a particular action. For example, in développés, teachers might give the correction *Don't lift your hip.* It would be better to find language that creates a positive goal to achieve, such as *When the leg is rising, imagine the sitz bone on that side of the pelvis sinking heavily toward the floor.* In this way the dancer can focus on a positive outcome rather than attempt to stop an undesired action.

Attention and Anxiety

Anxiety can occur in any situation, not only in stage performance. Anxiety and stress can cause dancers to become too highly aroused, and the result is diminished performance skills, as seen in figure 7.3. When this state becomes severe, it is referred to as **hypervigilance**, or panic. Some of the contributing factors might be a sudden and powerful stimulus, a perception that an outcome could be life-threatening, and the sense that time to handle an important circumstance is running out. Often in these situations people revert to their most common response—their highly practiced action. Dancers comment that in the midst of a panic response, their muscles seem to freeze and they cannot move with any kind of control. Physiological responses, such as hyperventilation and severely increased heart rate, also occur. Some of the methods suggested for dealing with this response are slow and deep breathing, imagery involving calming environments, and meditation techniques. Dancers who experience any of the effects of anxiety, whether in the performance venue or in daily activities, should seek assistance in developing appropriate coping strategies. Teachers can facilitate this process by developing a resource list of personnel who have the professional expertise and experience with dancers.

Attention and Injury

While extensive research has not been done on the use of attentional focus, emerging studies suggest that dancers may become more frequently injured as a result of attentional deficits. The mechanism of injury resulting from reduced or distracted attention has not been uncovered, but teachers should be sensitive to times when dancers have lowered attentional focus and the risks that these situations may present. Teachers should reduce the complexity and difficulty of class material during times of increased stress leading to diminished attention, such as just before performances. In addition, research on ballet dancers suggests that external focus during rehabilitation exercises is more effective than internal focus. These results are consistent with studies on nondancers looking at enhanced balance skills when external focus is used in the training. Clearly the theme of attention has implications for both the occurrence and rehabilitation of injuries for dancers.

It comes as no surprise that the world of athletics has seen increasing numbers of sport psychologists who emphasize concentration, attention, focus, and motivation. The importance of attention in all of its varying meanings cannot be overstated. Dealing with attentional deficits and learning to concentrate while avoiding distractions are paramount to the success of the performer in any discipline. Because dance psychology is such a young field, attention and motivation have not yet become primary in the goals of dance psychologists. Perhaps in the near future, dance psychology can branch into this important subject of attention, and researchers can use the depth of their expertise to heighten the cognitive skills of dancers.

Summary

Attention is defined as concentrated mental activity. Characteristics of attention include selective, divisible, shiftable, sustainable, and limited. The brain uses controlled (volitional) mechanisms as well as automatic (habitual) mechanisms to direct movement. *Interference* refers to one thought competing with another for attention. Both structural and capacity interference can affect success in motor skills. Several theories exist that describe attention capacities: bottleneck theory, filter theory, central resource capacity theories, multiple resource theories, and action selection theories. With wide-ranging definitions and many aspects of cognitive thought involved, each of these theories offers insight into the complexity of attention. Selective attention can be either intentional or incidental, depending on whether the focus of attention is deliberate or unintended. Three effects uncovered through research clearly outline some of the issues with intentional and incidental attention: Stroop effect, cocktail party phenomenon, and inattention blindness. Attention can be organized according to direction (external or internal) and width (broad or narrow). Additional areas of consideration are the effects of pressure, the ironic effect, and anxiety. Finally, although research is limited in this area, it suggests that dancers are more susceptible to injury when attention is poor, and teachers can encourage external focus during the rehabilitation process.

Chapter 8
Motor Control and the Sensory Systems

*I*magine a dancer named Anna involved in her daily dance class. She is bombarded with an overwhelming amount of sensory information. She can see the teacher demonstrating the combinations, and she can see the other students marking along. Anna can see her own image in the mirror as well as the musician accompanying the class. If the studio has windows, she can see anything occurring outdoors. All of these sights are in a myriad of colors, shapes, and sizes. Anna can hear the music coming from the piano or drums and the teacher's voice giving instructions and corrections. She can hear any outdoor noises, such as birds or automobiles, as well as indoor sounds such as people passing in the hallway. She can hear the sounds of the other dancers' feet as they travel and jump, and she can hear any comments or questions that they vocalize. Anna can feel the surface of the floor on her feet or through her shoes, and she can feel the texture of her clothing on her body. She can feel the barre under her hand if this is a ballet class, and she can feel any ties or clips holding her hair. When moving, she can feel any hairs that fall onto her face, and she can feel any surface irregularities on the floor, such as tape strips. Anna can smell the bread baking in the delicatessen next door, and if she skipped breakfast, this wonderful sensory experience can be very distracting. She might even be aware of the taste of her toothpaste remaining in her mouth or of the gum she chewed before class. In the summertime, Anna might be aware that the studio is too hot, and perhaps she'll notice the pain from her recent ankle sprain that is bothering her. Unconsciously her proprioceptive system is relaying information to her brain about muscle, tendon, joint, and ligamentous changes while she moves. If she begins to lose her balance, the incoming information will elicit a reflexive response to protect her from another injury.

In order for dancers like Anna to improve motor control, it is essential to understand how the brain deals with this magnitude of sensory information and determines how to use it. Understanding this complex coordination of incoming data and outgoing responses requires an examination of the sensory contributions to motor control. These contributions include input from the visual, auditory, vestibular, and somatosensory systems. In some circumstances, the brain does not need to use incoming sensory information to initiate and execute movement. In other circumstances, the sensory information is required in order to accomplish the task. These two conditions are known as open-loop and closed-loop control systems, or simply open-loop and closed-loop systems. This chapter begins with a comparison of these two systems. It follows with a description of the body's sensory systems and finally describes their implications for dance training.

Open-Loop and Closed-Loop Systems

When dancers are doing rapid, large jumps, such as the calypso leap in jazz dance, they have no time after the movement initiation to adjust or alter the motor plan. Dancers can hear corrections, but they cannot apply this information until they initiate the next leap. On the other hand, if jazz dancers are doing a lyrical movement, such as a slow jazz layout, they have sufficient time to correct the movement while it is occurring.

The calypso leap is an example of an **open-loop system**. This system does not use feedback (incoming information) during the movement to change the motor plan while it is being executed. In an open-loop system the movements are typically rapid, all necessary information is included in the instructions, and once triggered they proceed to completion. A typical sports example is an archer releasing the arrow to the target. In contrast, the slow jazz layout is an example of a **closed-loop system**. This system does use feedback during the movement to change the motor plan while it is being executed. In a closed-loop system the movements are typically slower, and feedback is compared to the initial plan during movement to make any necessary adjustments in order to complete the task. A typical sports example is a male gymnast doing an iron cross on the rings. A closed-loop system is illustrated in figure 8.1.

The first item at the top of figure 8.1 is the system goal, which is what the dancer is trying

The large, quick calypso leap is an example of an open-loop movement.

The slow jazz layout is a closed-loop system, because the dancer has time to use feedback for correction during the movement.

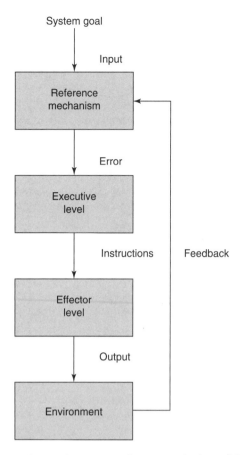

System goal

Input

Reference mechanism

Error

Executive level

Instructions   Feedback

Effector level

Output

Environment

Figure 8.1 Elements of a typical closed-loop control system. Note that the closed-loop system can use feedback during the movement to modify the end result.

Reprinted, by permission, from R.A. Schmidt and T.D. Lee, 2011, *Motor control and learning: A behavioral emphasis*, 5th ed. (Champaign, IL: Human Kinetics), 136.

to achieve, such as a contraction in a Graham technique class. The **reference mechanism** is the standard or the iconic representation that the system needs or desires to achieve. In the case of the Graham contraction, this standard would include the spatial relationship of the shoulders to the pelvis and the curved shape of the spine. The reference mechanism is compared to the feedback from the environment to detect error. For the contraction, this feedback would be the sensory data from the body about its position, the relationship of the body parts to each other, and the muscles creating the curve.

The difference between what the system wants to achieve and what the feedback relays about what is actually occurring is called the **error**. In the dance example, error might include sensory information that the shoulders have

come forward of the pelvis and that the lower back is not sufficiently curving. Information about the error is passed along to the **executive level**, which is the place where decisions are made to reduce error. For the contraction, the executive level determines how to move the body so that the shoulders align on top of the pelvis and the low back increases its curvature. The executive level sends instructions to the **effector level**, which is the stage where the actual changes to the motor plan can occur. The effector level sends messages, called *output*, which go to the environment, and the movement is then altered. In the Graham contraction, the environment is the body, and the output alters the muscles in order to improve the movement. This closed-loop process can continue until the dancer is satisfied with the contraction.

In an open-loop system, the reference mechanism and the feedback (on the far right of figure 8.1) are missing. While the reference mechanism for the movement might exist and feedback might be occurring during the movement, they cannot be used in cases of open-loop control. The executive level is preprogrammed to relay the instructions to the effector level at given times, and the effector sends the output to the environment with no possible way to modify or alter the instructions, even if problems arise with the plan. In the example of the calypso leap, if the dancer overturns the direction of the leap, this error cannot be corrected in midleap; the step will be completed as it was initiated. While some sensory information is involved in certain aspects of open-loop activities—such as orientation relative to space, obstacles, and visual and auditory cues needed for initiation of ballistic movements—generally sensory feedback is more involved in closed-loop activities with slower movements. Because the focus of this chapter is on sensory systems and their effects on movement, the discussion centers on closed-loop control.

Visual System

Vision is profoundly important in the control of movement. While dancers can function with their eyes closed or in very poor lighting conditions, movement control is certainly compromised. If it were not the case, stage managers would not need to use glow tape on the stage for dancers to place themselves in the dark. In adults, vision is supplementary to proprioception in maintaining postural control and balance during stance. However, children rely almost exclusively on vision when they first begin to stand and locomote. The balancing mechanisms (vision, vestibular system, and proprioception, as defined in chapter 3) are not yet integrated in children, and they use the one that matures earliest, which is vision. Even though postural control shifts from being primarily visual in childhood to being primarily somatosensory in adulthood, the importance of the use of vision throughout the lifetime cannot be underestimated. In addition, the way vision is used varies depending on the circumstances, such as whether the focus is about object manipulation, observing others in motion, or maneuvering through a crowded environment.

Central and Peripheral Vision

Experienced dancers know how to maintain their focus directly forward and still see all of the dancers around them in order to maintain their relationships in time and space. This ability is possible because of two types of vision, which are defined by scientists in specific numerical terms. **Central vision** can consciously perceive information only in the middle 2° to 5° in the visual field. It requires contrast and adequate light, and is needed for object identification and conscious awareness of the environment. Further, central vision is in color. **Peripheral vision** perceives information outside these limits, and it can range to 200° horizontally and 160° vertically. It does not need focus and can function in low light. Peripheral vision is very poor at color recognition.

Two examples can clarify how dancers use these two types of vision. Suppose a dancer in *A Chorus Line* must reach for a hat being handed over by an offstage technician before an entrance. The dancer must first focus on the hat using central vision, giving the dancer information about the size, shape, and distance of the object. Next, the dancer sees the moving hand reaching for the hat using peripheral

The famous Nicholas Brothers used both central and peripheral vision in navigating the complex environments used in their dance performances.

vision, providing feedback about the reaching action. As the hand gets closer to the hat, the dancer uses central vision again to take hold of the object just before entering the stage. The second example involves locomotion. In the film *Stormy Weather*, the Nicholas Brothers tap dance while leaping over bandstands and going up and down oversized stairs. Their central vision directs them so that they maintain a clear path throughout the dance. Their peripheral vision gives them continuous information about the environment, such as the location and size of the bandstands, the height of the stairs, and the musical instruments that they must avoid hitting. Peripheral vision is particularly important in assisting them in completing the spatial movement in the dance without being affected by the constantly changing obstacles.

Peripheral vision uses **optical flow patterns**, a term that refers to the patterns of light rays as they strike the eye. The use of the word *flow* suggests that these patterns are dynamic. As dancers move through the environment, or as they see other dancers moving in the environment, the patterns of light shift relative to each object and to the eye, and they are specific to the moving environmental features or people. This resulting information allows the dancer to achieve the set goals and complete the dance without colliding with objects or moving dancers in the space. For example, when dancers are entering a performance space, other dancers moving in their field of vision cause shifts in light patterns in their periphery, allowing the entering dancers to avoid hitting the onstage dancers even though they are not looking directly at them.

Research has proposed that two anatomical systems exist and function simultaneously. The **focal vision system** identifies the details of objects using central vision, and the **ambient vision system** identifies location of objects and motion in the larger environment using peripheral vision. For example, a street dancer would use focal vision to stare down another dancer standing directly in front of him, but he would use ambient vision to maintain an awareness of the audience and objects surrounding him in the space. The focal vision system relies on the **fovea** of the eye (shown in figure 8.2), which is in the center of the posterior retina and there-

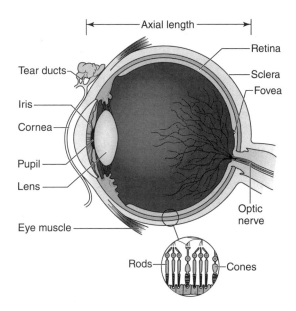

Figure 8.2 In the process leading to vision, *light* enters the eye through the *cornea*, then passes through the *pupil* (in the center of the *iris*) and the *lens*, which focuses it onto the *retina*. Directly behind the lens and on the retina is a depressed spot called the *fovea*, which lies at the center of the visual field.

fore requires good lighting. The ambient system relies on the entire retina, and therefore it is less affected when lighting is poor. This system helps people maneuver at night, and it is also essential to dancers in conditions of very low lighting onstage.

In dance training it is advantageous to encourage the use of peripheral vision so that dancers can adapt more easily to conditions of low light in performance settings and be aware of dancers around them onstage. This dance-specific visual training can include dancing without mirrors and verbal cueing from the instructor about nearby dancers during movement. The constant use of mirrors and disregarding or blocking out other dancers in the periphery can lead to heightened use of central vision.

Coordinating Vision and Movement

All dancers rely on vision during movement execution. Eye–hand coordination is essential when dealing with props such as candles and canes, costume pieces that are manipulated such as scarves and skirts, and partner work. Dancers also use visual information to correct movement in progress. Vision is particularly important during locomotion for a variety of reasons, such as avoiding collisions and determining spacing. All of these aspects of vision have been explored in the sports research and in dance training and education.

Eye–Hand Coordination

When dancers work with props or costume pieces that are moved, the hands and eyes need to work together to achieve the task. Research into eye–hand coordination is far more relevant to the wide variety of sports that involve object detection and manipulation, such as working with balls and targets. However, because of the use of props in many dance forms, it is essential to understand this particular coordination. **Perceptual-action coupling** refers to the spatial and temporal coordination of the hands and eyes or feet and eyes to achieve movements

Eye–hand coordination is particularly important when working with props or costume pieces.

involving objects. This coordination is necessary in both the initiation of the movement and to provide feedback that the action has been successful. In the case of the dancer in *A Chorus Line*, perceptual-action coupling first initiates the reach for the hat and then lets the dancer know that the hand has successfully arrived and grasped the hat. Another level of difficulty is added when dancers are engaged in complex choreography while manipulating objects, such as Fred Astaire using his cane in *Top Hat*. Because eye–hand coordination is not commonplace in dance, dancers need to spend additional time in rehearsals practicing these skills when they are needed.

Corrections to Movement Based on Vision

The issue of whether or not sensory feedback is used to correct movement in progress was discussed in defining open-loop and closed-loop systems. In order for the use of visual feedback to be possible, sufficient time is necessary between movement initiation and the feedback processing. If the time is insufficient, the feedback can be used to improve the next attempt. In sports, research has been conducted for over 100 years to determine the minimum time required for visual feedback to be used in movement correction. In spite of the abundant research, it is not possible to determine what that minimum time might be. It is estimated to be 100 to 160 milliseconds. A shorter time interval would result in the visual feedback not being useful for corrections of movements in process because of lack of time. For example, when capoeristas (practitioners of the Brazilian martial art and dance form capoeira) initiate very fast kicking movements, these kicks cannot use visual feedback to correct the height or direction of the kick. The one exception to this time limit is when the person anticipates the need to make corrections; in this case, it might be less time than the 100 to 160 milliseconds. For example, in a martial arts duo, if one person is anticipating a particular move by a partner, it might take an even smaller time interval for the receiving person to see the cue and alter a movement pattern accordingly. This reduced time is particularly true of high-level athletes, such as martial artists and hockey goalies, who are capable of anticipating opponents' movements using cues from the torso and orientation in advance of limb movements.

Time to Contact a Moving Object

When dancers or athletes must intercept a moving object or catch an object while in motion, they must be able to determine the time needed to arrive at the same point in space as the object at the right time. For dancers, this catching or intercepting behavior happens only sporadically in the work they do, such as the occasional choreography that involves catching props or (more commonly) in partnering work when partners are moving toward each other, whether in set work or contact improvisation. In sports, however, this phenomenon is common. The other difference between dance and sports in this regard is that in many types of sports, the time to contact is unpredictable because the arrival of the object is unplanned. For example, when outfielders in baseball are catching balls hit by batters, they must determine how fast and how far to run to intercept the ball. Similarly, in volleyball the speed and pathway of the ball over the net is intentionally random. In the ballet *The Nutcracker*, the sword is often thrown to the lead soldier; while this is planned and expected in the choreography, the soldier must still determine the speed and path of the sword, because variation is inevitable.

In sports, this theme of time to contact is so common that extensive research exists about how it is accomplished. In the early 1970s David Lee, director of the Perception-Movement-Action Research Consortium at the University of Edinburgh, defined a variable called *tau* (τ), which he mathematically described and quantified. The mathematical formulas are beyond the scope of this text. **Tau** determines a relationship between object size, its velocity and acceleration, and the distance between the object and the person. The brain does not do these calculations consciously; rather it takes in the visual information and makes determinations based on the sensory information and experience. In other words, the performer does not need to know cognitively the object's distance and speed to determine time to contact. If dancers are

doing partner catches or work with props, they must be provided with numerous variations of the tasks. Dancers who are very advanced and have performed in many pieces have probably already had enough variety to develop skill at determining distance and speed of the partner. However, younger or less-experienced dancers should have variation built into the training situation, either in rehearsals or in separate partnering or contact improvisation classes. In this way, they can develop sufficient experience to be flexible in any choreographic situation.

Importance of Vision During Locomotion

The use of vision while traveling in space changes according to the environment. When dealing with a smooth surface, the movement is controlled by rhythmic motor patterns that are regulated in the spinal cord and take little conscious thought. In this instance, vision is used to observe and foresee changes in the surrounding environment and to assess direction of travel and avoid objects. When the surface is irregular, vision is used to determine how and when to alter stride length to accommodate changes in the surface. For example, when dancers see wavy irregularities in a linoleum dance floor, they often adjust their stride length so that they do not end up having to balance on the uneven portion of the flooring.

In addition, vision is necessary when the body positioning must change in the middle of a traveling movement. Dancers need to judge their speed relative to the distance they must travel before the change is required. If the cue to make a change in body positioning is the moment of passing another dancer or a set piece, or to arrive at a certain spot for a lighting cue, then the use of vision is necessary in making this determination. Another use of vision for dancers requires judging stride length of runs preceding an exiting leap into the wings. Particularly for dancers who tour in professional companies, as stages change size and dimensions, dancers must continually alter the stride length to adapt to the various spaces and to adjust orientation relative to props and other dancers. For all of these reasons, vision is an essential tool.

Vision is just one of the sensory systems that assist in motor control in both daily life and in dance performance. It not only stands alone as an important sensory system, but it also works in concert with other sensory modalities, such as the auditory system, the vestibular system, and the somatosensory system. In exploring each of these systems, dancers can learn how to optimize the use of sensory information and how to depend on the efficient integration of all of the sensory modalities.

Auditory System

The **auditory system** is the sense of hearing, using the ears as receptors and the temporal lobe of the brain for processing. Dancers use their sense of hearing as another way to learn about their environment and direct their movements. At times dancers cannot see other dancers on the stage, but they can detect their location through the sound of their footsteps and even their breathing. Dancers use sound in darkness before and after a piece to find their place onstage and avoid collisions with other dancers. Most important, dancers are among the few athletes, such as figure skaters and rhythmic gymnasts, who time their activity to music. The sensory information derived from music tells dancers whether their timing is correct in terms of the choreography and whether they are maintaining their temporal relationship to other dancers. Music can even provide feedback about the level of arousal or anxiety of the dancer. Most dancers have experienced performances in which the music sounds slower than normal, and it is an indicator that the dancer is in a high state of arousal.

Hearing can also give dancers information about their own movement execution. The sound of landings can let dancers know whether they are properly using their muscles to soften the landing or if they are crashing and out of control. Attending to the sound of one's own breath can give the dancer information about tension in the chest and rib cage.

Vision is clearly more important than sound in navigating the environment, but the auditory system is a vital part of the sensory information used in movement execution for dancers. While visual information is more valuable, auditory information reaches the brain more quickly. Further, judgments about the environment can be made using the acoustic flow field in a similar fashion to the use of the optical flow field. The **optical flow field** is the apparent motion of objects and surfaces that an observer sees in a specified visual area. The term **acoustic flow field** refers to the various sounds occurring in the observer's environment. An effective tool in dance training is to ask dancers at times to move or perform combinations in silence to accentuate the importance of auxiliary sounds in the dance environment and sounds created by the dancers' movements.

Vestibular System

Dancers rely on yet another sensory mechanism to assist them with ongoing balance. The **vestibular system** has its receptors in the inner ear. It works in conjunction with other senses and is mainly concerned with providing information about the head's position in space and about quick changes in the direction of movements of the head. At times, dancers cannot rely on vision or proprioception to tell them where they are in space. For example, in a pas de deux the female dancer can maintain a fixed body position, yet be lifted off the ground and have her relationship to gravity altered. Although her joint angles and muscle lengths remain the same, and although she may have her vision blocked, she will still be receiving information about her position in relation to gravity from the vestibular system, and she will not be disoriented when she is returned to the ground.

Anatomy of the Vestibular System

The vestibular system lies in the innermost area of each ear, and it is essential to the control of posture and balance. Five sensory organs—the three semicircular canals and the two otolith organs—send signals to the brain about movements of the head. Movements of the human body consist of rotations (circular movements) and translations (linear movements). The three **semicircular canals** measure the change in velocity of rotational movements of the head or body. The semicircular canals on the left and right side work in concert with each other; they do not work independently. Each pair is responsive to one plane of movement; when the head moves independently from the body, this movement involves either neck flexion/extension (forward and backward bend), neck lateral flexion (side bend), or neck rotation. The two **otolith organs**, called the *saccule* and the *utricle*, measure the change in velocity of linear movements caused by gravity or body movement. The otolith organs register how the head is oriented relative to gravity because of the constant linear force that gravity exerts. The saccules are responsive to vertical changes of the head, in particular the effects of gravity, such as being in an elevator or jumping. The utricles respond to horizontal plane movement, such as the acceleration of a car or low

runs. The vestibular system is pictured in figure 8.3.

In all of these sensory organs, cilia (discussed in chapter 3) detect motional change. For the semicircular canals, motion causes thick fluid within these organs to move and create deformation of these cells, which then fire and send their signals to the brain. For the otolith organs, the picture is slightly more like a stone sitting on a stiff brush. The stones cause the bristles to bend because of inertia, which causes the signals. These cells are so sensitive to head movement that they can detect changes as small as 0.1° per second. In fact, the tiny head motions that occur during postural sway are sufficient to activate these cells.

Vestibular System Interactions With Vision

The vestibular system's effectiveness is heightened by ways in which it interacts with other

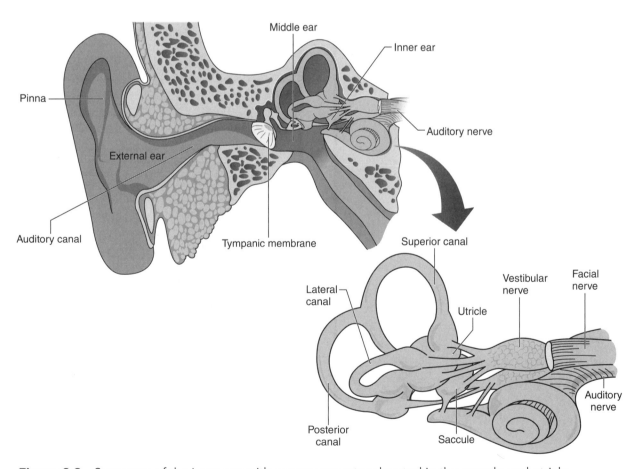

Figure 8.3 Structures of the inner ear, with sensory receptors located in the saccule and utricle.

senses, especially vision. One example is the **vestibular ocular reflex (VOR)**, which stabilizes the eyes during head movement. This reflex is especially important during very fast movements of the head, such as dancers' use of spotting when doing multiple turns. Dancers must rely heavily on vision when they are learning dance forms that mainly use turns with the torso and the head upright. The dancers are taught strategies such as spotting to preserve spatial orientation and balance. However, modern dance and street dance turn with the torso off the vertical, and vision can actually hinder the skill. When turning with the torso off the vertical, what dancers see can be confusing because it is misaligned relative to normal vision. It can be disorienting to see the environment in upside-down positions, so dancers must rely more heavily on somatosensory feedback than vision during these movements. In the dance class setting, it is crucial that the teacher first determine that the students are secure in the off-vertical position before they attempt to turn in it. Then dancers can attempt turning, and finally they can achieve turning with simultaneous locomotion. Integrating postural control into locomotion while reducing assistance from vision can be a frightening experience. It is a mistake to introduce turning with the torso off the vertical too soon, because it can foster a fear of falling.

In most situations that dancers encounter, if visual and somatosensory information are in conflict, the vestibular system takes precedence and resolves the conflict. Consider a street dancer outside at night with limited vision and dealing with constantly changing terrain. At this point visual information would be limited and somatosensory information from the ankles would be unpredictable. The dancer would be dependent on the vestibular system for maintaining balance. The same situation would occur with a dancer in dark lighting on a raked stage.

The vestibular system of the dancer should be conditioned to many peculiar relationships to gravity. It is not uncommon for a much-practiced, automatic balance to fall apart when a dancer is lifted, placed in an upside-down position, and then returned to the ground. It becomes even more disorienting when the lifter spins with the partner in the air. Dancers (both

In street dance, the head and torso are often in a different orientation to gravity than typical walking, and the dancers must rely more on somatosensory feedback than on vision.

the one doing the lifting and the one being lifted) should not attempt this task at full speed and with multiple turns until they are experienced. The more accustomed a dancer becomes to being lifted off the ground and turned upside down, the better the brain becomes at interpreting the spatial information provided by the vestibular system.

While vision is clearly the predominant sense in terms of the body's relationship to the environment, the vestibular system plays an important role in balance, posture, and dynamic motion through space. Its role in maintaining a clear relationship to gravity at all times is essential in the dancer's ability to do complex and often disorienting movement. Given the addition of many circumstances in which dancers must work in low or no lighting and on unusual surfaces, the vestibular system is the dependable partner to the visual system.

Somatosensory System

The **somatosensory system** is divided into three parts: discriminative touch, pain (nociception) and temperature, and proprioception. Each of these sensory modalities contributes to the dancer's experience of the environment and affects movement choices and responses. Dancers are dependent on the tactile sensation of the floor to determine the use of footwork in training and the tactile sensation of a partner's hands connecting to the body before a lift. Dancers rely on proprioception to make corrections to balance and prevent falls and to correct shape or movement for choreography. Dancers are aware of changes to flexibility in differing temperature conditions, and they can adapt movement range accordingly. Finally, dancers can use important pain messages that indicate injury or fatigue to let them know when to modify the intensity of practice.

The three sensory modalities are divided in terms of how they are sent to the brain and in what areas of the brain they are processed (see chapter 3). The first modality, **discriminative touch**, includes touch, pressure, and vibration perception. It allows dancers to find their costumes in the dark by the feel of the fabric or to know when they are in contact with another dancer without vision. The second modality is pain and temperature, and it includes the sensations of itch and tickle. Dancers become so familiar with varying types of pain that they are even aware of the difference in sensation between a sore muscle and a damaged tendon. The third modality is called **proprioception**, which includes receptors found in muscles, fascia, tendons, ligaments, and joints and gives the brain information about muscle stretch, joint position, and tendon tension. These sensors primarily send messages to the somatosensory cortex, which relays the information to the cerebellum, the area of the brain needing ongoing feedback on what the muscles are doing in order to serve its function as a detector and corrector of errors.

Adaptation to Sensory Information

When dancers put on their leotards, they are initially aware of the sensation of the cloth on their skin, but this sensation fades in a short period of time. Similarly, a shower or hot tub might feel very hot upon entry, but it soon feels comfortable. The receptors that send messages about touch and temperature are rapidly adapting. On the other hand, when dancers become injured, the sensation of pain does not immediately recede. Some of the proprioceptors are also slowly adapting, such as the sensation of the muscles contracting to hold the leg at full height for an extended dance adagio. Slowly adapting receptors continue to react throughout the extent of the experience. The purpose of rapidly adapting receptors is to provide information about changing sensory stimuli. They fire rapidly when first triggered, but then they stop firing until the stimulus either increases or decreases. The purpose of slowly adapting receptors is to keep the brain informed about the body and its surroundings.

Cutaneous Receptors

Cutaneous receptors are located in the skin, and they serve to inform the brain about touch, pressure, pain, heat, cold, and chemical stimuli such as odors, acids, solvents, and other irritants. The most important of these receptors to dancers are touch, pressure, and pain. Temperature becomes a critical factor only when dancers are required to dance in environments that are too hot or too cold for healthy practice. The areas of the body with some of the highest numbers of cutaneous receptors are the fingertips, so it is possible to easily detect information about object surfaces through touch. Other areas with numerous cutaneous receptors are the palms of the hands, the lips, and the soles of the feet. Cutaneous receptors in the soles of the feet contribute to the control of posture and locomotion and are therefore important to dancers. Because of the various adaptation characteristics of receptors, dancers can distinguish between a quickly applied touch, such as a light tap to suggest an alignment correction, or a slow touch, such as extended stroking of the arm from a dance partner.

Proprioceptors

The main proprioceptors in muscles and tendons are the muscle spindles and the Golgi tendon organs. Simply stated, **muscle spindles** are responsive to length, speed, and rate of change of the muscle, and **Golgi tendon organs (GTOs)** are responsive to muscle tension or contraction. (For details on how they function, see chapter 6.) To summarize, muscle spindles have an important role in movement and postural control, and they are the basis for the stretch reflex. They affect dancers' alignment, flexibility, and ongoing sensitivity to stretch during dynamic motion. As with cutaneous receptors, some muscles have far more muscle spindles than others. Those muscles responsible for fine motor control, such as the muscles that control the hands, are more highly saturated with muscle spindles. GTOs contribute to the monitoring and control of muscle activity by sensing muscle tension through the stretch of the tendon. By supplying information about muscle tension, they assist in producing coordinated movement in complex activities. In addition, the GTOs assist in assessing the weight of held objects or force applied to thrown objects. Along with the reticular activating system in the brain and various interneurons, the muscle spindles and the GTOs act together to create smooth, organized movement of multiple muscles. These structures constantly interact to ensure that muscle length changes are fluid (not jerky) and movement is coordinated.

Muscle spindles and GTOs play a role in postural control and automatic movement regulation. When functioning in this capacity, the signals are nonconscious. For example, when a dancer begins to land in poor lower-leg alignment and risks twisting an ankle, the stretch reflex that realigns and protects the ankle is not a conscious choice, nor is the dancer consciously aware that it is happening until after the fact. This characteristic of some of the reflexive and motor control aspects of proprioceptors is very different from the conscious awareness of touch or temperature.

The other category of proprioceptors is the group known as joint receptors. These receptors serve to provide an awareness of limb position and movement and have a role in sensing extreme ranges of motion. Joint receptors send messages about mechanical changes in the joint capsule that surrounds the joint and the nearby ligaments, including changes linked to pain. Most of these receptors are located in areas within the joints, allowing them to fire in extreme range of motion. In this way they serve to detect when joints are reaching and possibly going beyond safe limits, helping to protect them from injury. Recent studies suggest that they also have an important modulatory role working alongside the muscle spindles and GTOs in refining and adjusting the signals of these other proprioceptors. In this way, several different types of proprioceptors work together to ensure smooth, coordinated movement.

Conscious Perception of Movement

So far in the discussion of the somatosensory system, the focus has been on the nonconscious functions of the various receptors. Conscious perception of certain aspects of the system is also important in motor control. The dance teacher can use cutaneous and proprioceptive cues to assist dancers in recalling motor patterns. Dancers can use the conscious awareness of limb position to be highly accurate in creating shape design during dynamic movement. They can also create a range of dynamic qualities in movement through the awareness of levels of muscle tension. Finally, dancers with a perception of subtle differences in sensation have a better ability to detect and correct movement errors.

The term **kinesthesis** (also called **kinesthesia**) is used to describe the conscious sensation of movement. The ability to coordinate multiple body parts in complex coordination requires this conscious perception of movement sensation. Other than the hands and fingers, cutaneous receptors do not signal joint movement and position, although certain aspects can give information about motion. For example, when dancers slide a foot along the floor as in a tendu, the cutaneous receptors provide information that the foot is moving. In general, the importance of the cutaneous receptors in kinesthetic awareness is restricted to fine motor control. However, they do provide information about movement through sensation ranging from skin moving along a surface to changes in skin tension as one changes position, such as the skin tightening over the knee during grand plié.

Muscle spindles are the most important source available for kinesthetic awareness of joint position and movement, providing ongoing information about changes in muscle length. The main source of the awareness of muscular effort is the GTOs, through signals relating to changes in muscle tension. The muscle spindles and GTOs work collaboratively to create the richness of what is known as kinesthetic awareness.

Perception of the sensory inputs plays an important role in the comprehension of limits to stability. Usually, one's perceived limits of stability are equal to the actual mechanical limits, but this is not always the case. For example, older adults often have a reduced perception if they have fallen and are afraid of falling again. Occasionally, if a dancer has worked en pointe and suddenly is asked to work in bare feet, she maintains her perception of reduced stability limits even though the actual limits are now increased. Limits of stability can change from one situation to another; that is, they alter as task or environment alter, as demonstrated in figure 8.4.

Use of Feedforward Information

In some circumstances, dancers use information before executing a movement plan, which is called **feedforward information**. A copy of the motor plan for a given movement, known as the **efference copy**, is sent to areas of the brain that process sensory information. One role of the efference copy is to prepare the brain for incoming feedback during movement execution. The efference copy signals that active movement has actually occurred, and it is also used for error detection and correction. Similar to the reference mechanism in figure 8.1, the efference copy allows the brain to compare what is planned to what is occurring once movement is initiated. Through this process, movements can be improved using this feedforward information. Finally, the efference copy, as part of feedforward control, saves time when dancers are aware of the possibility of certain changing circumstances, such as moving from dancing on a hard surface to dancing on grass. The brain can predict the necessary changes to dynamic control in order that dancers do not fall over. The efference copy also acts as part of feedback control. For example, if dancers thought the stage were dry and anticipated their feet sticking, but they discovered that the stage was wet, they might begin to slip and to slide. The efference copy would allow them to make very quick judgments and rapidly regain balance and control.

As it should now be apparent, dancers can use sensory information in various ways. First, it provides knowledge of body position, which includes the relationship of body parts to each

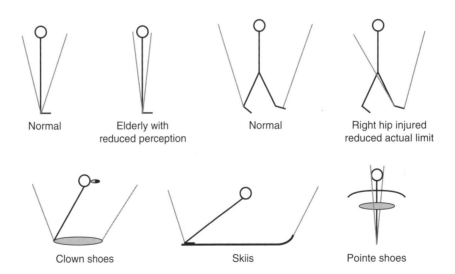

Figure 8.4 Differing limits of stability: perceptual and mechanical.

Created by Donna Krasnow.

other and the relationship of the body to the external environment. This knowledge helps dancers create the intended lines in their dance forms and it directs them in complex patterns in the space. It also allows dancers to make corrections and determine why errors occurred for future attempts. Second, sensory information is essential in planning actions relative to the environment, both temporal and spatial. For example, dancers need to create a movement plan that allows them to stay synchronized with the music and to travel sufficiently to reach a certain point in space in relation to the other dancers. Third, sensory information is essential in both learning new movement and relearning movement that may have been lost as a result of injury. For example, injury rehabilitation for an ankle sprain relies on conscious proprioception to establish good alignment for preventing injury recurrence. Use of the somatosensory system, both conscious and nonconscious, is fundamental to dancers and their abilities to plan, execute, and correct dance movements from simple exercises to complex choreography involving music, other dancers, and dramatic interpretations.

Issues in Dance Training

Knowledge of the sensory modalities gives dance educators and dancers a wealth of information about crafting dance training and practice. When teachers understand how motor control is strongly influenced by the extensive incoming sensory data, they can design and implement specific approaches to various skills. This section presents several examples, but teachers and dancers are encouraged to be creative and thoughtful in devising their own approaches.

Enhancing Use of the Senses

While the use of visual, auditory, and vestibular systems often occurs at the nonconscious level, researchers believe that people can develop cues and instruction to enhance the use of these systems. For example, dance teachers can discuss the concept of spatial awareness as part of training. Although open spaces and studios are less defined spatially than a stage with wings, dancers should learn to judge and modify stride length in preparation for various performance spaces. Teachers can encourage an awareness of the distance dancers travel in a given combination and how to adjust stride length to either increase or decrease traveling work. This skill is particularly important for dancers who present the same choreography in a variety of performance spaces. Similarly, teachers can encourage dancers to become aware of the subtle sounds of other dancers breathing to enhance group timing. Synchronization of breath timing can be especially helpful when working with no music, or with music that does not have a clear rhythmic beat, such as some contemporary scores. Finally, enlisting improvisations that encourage the head to be off the vertical in dynamic and traveling material can allow dancers to attend to unusual balancing situations. Bringing conscious attention to nonconscious sensory information can aid dancers in a fuller use of their sensory modalities in their dance practice.

Visual System

Several aspects of vision can be considered as part of training dancers. Peripheral vision is extremely important to dancers. They must be aware of the dancers and objects around them as well as precisely where they are in the performance space. If dancers regularly take class or practice without considering these elements, the transition to performance is difficult and can be overwhelming. Teachers can remind dancers to consider these aspects and become aware of the dancers around them even in simple center work combinations. The constant use of mirrors gives the impression that dancers are seeing the dancers around them, but it is illusory. Focus with mirrors uses central vision, and it actually weakens or reduces peripheral vision. At least some of the classes should be done with the mirrors covered or the dancers positioned to face a different direction.

While most dances use music for temporal cueing, dancers can also be trained to be sensitive to relying on visual prompts. Teachers and choreographers can remind dancers to see what is happening in the choreography at a specific point in the music, and sometimes choreographers want changes to occur using visual cues in the absence of musical cues. This strategy requires that dancers are seeing what is happening around them, attending to the surrounding environment, and at the same time concentrating on their own dancing.

Lifts that are done while one or both dancers are traveling in space are quite difficult. The dancers must integrate lifting techniques with the ability to determine time to contact. In other words, the two partners must calculate the exact point in space and time that they will meet to do the lift. Most beginners stop when they come together and then execute the lift. Experienced dancers make a smooth transition from the traveling steps into the lift. In training traveling lifts, the lift portion should be practiced first, then the traveling steps preceding the lift can be added as a second component.

Auditory System

In addition to relying on hearing for timing and cues, dancers can use sound to instruct them about their dancing. The sound of landings from elevation steps can indicate whether the landing is soft and fluid or abrupt, failing to use the controlled mechanisms of eccentric contractions in the primary muscles. If the landing is abrupt, the sound is much louder than a properly executed landing. While some choreography intentionally uses stomping for sound effect, the general training for dancers is to reduce the impact of landings.

For some dancers, hearing music and understanding its structure are natural and easy. For other dancers, the training needs to incorporate this awareness. Musical aspects that are critical for dancers are rhythm, melody, and the idea of phrasing. Rhythm provides the sense of meter (amount of time between beats) and the measure (the segment of time defined by a given number of beats). Melody adds the element of pitch to rhythm; it indicates when the pitch of the music is rising and falling. Phrasing is perhaps the most difficult musical concept to teach. The phrase is to music what the sentence is to speaking, and it merges all of the ideas of

musical structure with nuance and meaning. One of the classic ways of teaching phrasing is to start with breath. Encouraging dancers to use the natural inhalation and exhalation of the breath helps them find ways to phrase their movements. Another teaching tool is to remove the music and have dancers use audible breath or vocalization to find the phrase in the dance movement.

Vestibular System

When dancers cannot rely on vision or proprioception to tell them where they are in space relative to gravity, the vestibular system takes on heightened importance. As previously mentioned, during lifts in ballet, a female dancer can maintain a fixed body position yet be lifted off the ground and turned upside down, and her relationship to gravity can be altered. Although her body shape remains the same and her visual field may change, she still receives information about her position in relation to gravity from the vestibular system. In training dancers for lifts, teachers should begin with those lifts in which the lifted dancer is vertical in relationship to gravity. In this way, vision is not disrupted, so the lift is a less disorienting experience. Later, lifts that are upside down can be added to the repertory. Eventually, use of the vestibular system can be enhanced to include lifts that are upside down while turning and traveling in space; that is, dancers can become better at interpreting and using information from the vestibular system.

The technique of spotting involves two aspects that can assist in maintaining balance in turns. First, the focus is consciously reduced to seeing one spot directly in front of the dancer at the start and finish of each turn, especially during multiple consecutive turns. Second, when rapidly rotating the head, the spinning of the fluids in the sensory organs within the inner ears is reduced, because the head is turned quickly and then stopped, preventing the fluids from continuing to spin. Thus, dancers can turn for longer periods before becoming dizzy. In turns with the torso off the vertical, as in modern dance and figure skating, the focus portion of spotting is included, but the fast rotation of the head is not. In these turns,

Dancers enhance the vestibular and proprioceptive systems when the head is not upright and vision is compromised.

dancers initially become dizzy, but they eventually acclimate to the sensation. To assist this process, teachers can have dancers start with a small number of turns with the body off the vertical and gradually increase the number of turns.

Enhancing Use of the Somatosensory System

Dancers must learn to deal with changing somatosensory inputs in the dance environment. If a dancer is always practicing on a smooth wooden floor and suddenly has to dance on a sticky or uneven surface, it can be devastating. The teacher should try to provide varying surfaces so that dancers can prepare for varied input from the feet. Going outside and dancing on the lawn is useful and fun, and reserving the theater stage on certain days to adjust to a new surface can be beneficial. Similarly, if dancers will be performing a dance in running shoes or slippers, they should rehearse in this footwear at least some of the time. Danc-

ers who like to dance in bare feet will resist, but the teacher must insist and explain why it is necessary.

The muscle spindles and gamma efferent system have a major impact on several aspects of dance training. Factors influencing flexibility include structural components such as joint, ligament, and muscle range of motion, and also neurological components that control muscle tonus. **Hypotonia** is decreased muscle tone caused by decreased gamma motor activity to the intrafusal fibers in the muscles. **Hypertonia** is increased muscle tone caused by increased gamma motor activity to the intrafusal fibers in the muscles, and it can lead to resistance to stretching. For flexibility training it can be useful to induce a degree of hypotonia to enhance stretching. Practices such as yoga emphasize breath, mental awareness, and a calming, nonjudgmental environment to enhance hypotonia. These same tools and environment can be used at the end of class both as a cool-down and to aid in flexibility training. In addition, the gamma efferent system assists in determining relative muscle balance in antagonist muscles that affect dynamic alignment. Dance teachers can use imagery, quiet awareness work, focus on breathing, and somatic practices to assist the process of reprogramming the brain's messages to these muscles so that the key alignment muscles are reorganized and adjusted. Attentional focus can be key in first recognizing and then addressing alignment issues such as rib/pelvis organization in forming new habits. For a detailed explanation of the gamma efferent system, review the discussion in chapter 6.

Conscious Perception

Dance is particularly well suited for the conscious perception of kinesthetic information as part of the training. Dancers are concerned with specific body postures as well as guiding limbs into particular positions and relationships to the external environment. Dance terminology includes the idea of a body hold, in which a limb maintains a set relationship to the body as the body rotates or travels in space. Examples include a turn done in arabesque or a flamenco dancer moving in space with the arms held overhead. Dance also includes the idea of a space hold, in which a limb stays in a fixed position in the space although the body is turning. Examples include a fouetté sauté, where the leg stays in one place as the body turns, and a movement of the arm from front to side by leaving the arm where it is in space and rotating the body away from the lifted arm, as might be seen in popping and locking in street dance. Both of these terms suggest the importance for dancers of the relationship of body parts to each other and to the environment. Teachers can use instructions, cues, imagery, and feedback to assist dancers in heightening their conscious perception of body positioning.

Similarly, because dancers can consciously perceive muscle tension, teachers can cue them to enhance their abilities in expressing a wide range of dynamics. From heavy to light, bound to free, gentle to aggressive, dabbing to thrusting, and floating to restrained, dancers need the widest possible palette in terms of muscle effort. Whether teachers use sensation-based descriptions or metaphorical imagery, dancers can develop their movement qualities with training.

Balance

Working with the eyes closed is an excellent way to improve the proprioceptive system to be more responsive to perturbations (challenges to balance). Dancers can try standing with the eyes closed on different surfaces such as foam pads, rugs, sand, grass, balance beams, or wobble boards. They can try standing with different bases of support, such as parallel feet, turned-

Dancers can use various apparatus, such as wobble boards, to enhance the proprioceptive system.

out positions, relevé, plié, en pointe, and on two feet or one foot.

In addition to varying the standing surface, many movement variations can assist in developing improved balance. Each of these balances can be done for 10 to 30 seconds:

- With the eyes closed and the feet parallel, slowly relevé. At first, the rise can be done taking the heels just off the floor. When this balance becomes easier, attempt the full rise.

- Standing on both feet and with the eyes closed, shift the weight to the right foot. Lift the left foot off the floor, bend the knee, point the foot, and place it at the side of the right ankle. Do both sides. When this version becomes easy, bring the gesture leg up to passé.

- Demi-plié on both feet, and do the same shift to one foot as described in the previous exercise. While on the right foot in plié, slowly straighten the right leg. Do both sides.

- Reverse the actions so that first the weight is shifted to one foot, and then demi-plié. Do both sides.

- Start balanced on the right foot with the left foot at the ankle. With the eyes closed, take a large step forward onto the left foot, and balance. Repeat the step onto the right foot, and balance. Do the same movements stepping to the side and back. The steps can also be done to plié on the supporting leg.

- Try any of the previous balances with the legs turned out. Arm gestures can be added. The tempo of these movements can begin very slowly and accelerate over time.

The sensory systems provide a wealth of information to the dancer about both the interior landscape of the body and the environment in which the dancer lives. At times these data are absorbed and processed nonconsciously, and at other times dancers are acutely aware of what they are seeing, hearing, touching, and feeling. The brain is miraculous in its ability to rapidly take in all of this information, sort it, and determine how best to use what the dancer needs at a given moment in time. Dancers and dance educators can optimize the process of actively using the senses to enhance dance abilities and the enjoyment of the art form.

Summary

Motor control depends on both open-loop and closed-loop systems. Control mechanisms must be closed-loop systems in order for the brain to use sensory information as feedback. The visual system comprises optical receptors and visual processing areas in the brain. Dancers use both central and peripheral vision in their practice. Dancers also use other aspects of the visual system, such as eye–hand coordination and integration of vision with locomotion. Timing issues include the time needed to make corrections and time to contact moving objects or other dancers. The auditory system comprises hearing receptors and processing in the brain, and it is crucial to most dance forms in terms of music and hearing other dancers. The vestibular system is located in the inner ears, and it sends continual information about the head and the body's relationship to gravity or other accelerations, such as being lifted. The vestibular system is critical for postural control in situations in which dancers have limited or distorted vision and proprioception. The somatosensory system includes cutaneous receptors and proprioceptors, and it sends information to the brain about touch, pain, pressure, and body position and movement. The brain can use all of this sensory information consciously or nonconsciously. Dance training can actively improve dancers' abilities to use the sensory systems in their dancing.

Chapter 9

Motor Control and Central Organization

*I*magine that a dancer named Jesse decides to go for a walk outdoors along a straight, uncluttered path. Jesse makes a conscious choice to begin walking and enjoy his surroundings. Jesse can take in the view of the landscape, the smell of the flowers, and the warmth of the sunshine. Fortunately, because he is walking on a simple path and not doing complex choreography or interacting with other dancers in complicated spatial designs, Jesse can pay very little attention to his walking actions. Movement patterns such as walking are controlled centrally; that is, they are organized in advance and accomplished without much consideration of the environment. Unless some person or object or event interferes with Jesse's journey, he can continue walking without changing his locomotor pattern until he decides to complete his walk. **Central control mechanisms** refer to the processes occurring in the central nervous system (the brain and the spinal cord) that organize movement. Central organization is one of the primary ways that motor control is determined.

Two basic models of motor control provide a foundation for describing how movement is initiated and executed: closed-loop and open-loop systems. Chapter 8 focused on closed-loop systems, which use **sensory feedback** (incoming information from the senses) during the movement to change the motor plan while it is being executed, such as the slow jazz layout. These movements are typically slower, and sensory feedback is compared to the initial plan during movement to make any necessary adjustments in order to complete the task. In this chapter the focus is on open-loop systems, which initiate and execute movement through central control mechanisms.

Open-Loop Systems

The term *open-loop system* is used in broader fields than motor control, and it applies to many mechanical devices, such older heating systems that do not respond to temperature change. In this text, the terminology relates only to motor control. An **open-loop system** does not use feedback during the movement to change

the motor plan while it is being executed. In doing skills that use open-loop processes, central control mechanisms—not instructions responding to sensory information—determine the movement. In the case of open-loop control systems, everything needed to initiate and continue the action exists in the initial commands to the muscles. In the case of a series of fast and repetitive open-loop movements, such as tapping the same step over and over or repeating the same jump many times, incoming feedback during the early attempts can be used to correct later attempts, which is important for long-term learning.

An example of an open-loop system from daily life is an MP3 player that has been pre-programmed. The memory holds all of the songs that are recorded. The MP3 player is programmed to play a given set of songs in a given order, called the playlist. Once this task is completed and the MP3 player is started, the microprocessor sends the signal through the decompressor, and eventually it comes out of the amplifier as sound or music. It continues the process through the entire playlist in its predetermined order. Once the MP3 player is started, no input from outside the system is needed in order to continue executing the playlist.

The street dancer can use the MP3 player for musical accompaniment on the street.

Human Movement as Open-Loop Processes

Human movement that follows an open-loop process is similar in structure to the MP3 player. Movements in this category do not rely on feedback during execution to complete the task. For example, teachers realize that once the students are in the air during a leap, they cannot use instructions from their teacher to change or correct their movement. They must complete that leap and use the feedback in the next attempt. The open-loop system is illustrated in figure 9.1.

The first item at the top of figure 9.1 is the input, which is what the dancer is trying to achieve, such as a fast leap. The **reference mechanism** is the standard or iconic representation that the system needs or desires to achieve. While the reference mechanism of the leap exists and feedback is occurring during the movement, they cannot be used during the movement execution in cases of open-loop control, and therefore they are not represented in the diagram in figure 9.1. The reference mechanism, the ideal model of the leap, is used in creating the executive instructions, which are the commands from the executive level or brain. It can be developed through observing the teacher or other dance students, from pictures

seen in books or magazines, dancers seen on stage, or even imagined goals. The dancer can use this reference afterward to compare the ideal to feedback about what occurred for subsequent trials. The dancer cannot use it during the initial movement, because the leap is too fast for using feedback to make mid-movement corrections.

The movement goal is sent directly to the **executive level**, which is the place where decisions are made; in other words, it goes to the brain. In this case the executive is programmed to send its instructions to the **effector level**, where the motor plan is determined. The effector level sends messages, called *output*, which would be messages to the muscles in the case of the leap. These messages go to the environment, sometimes called the *plant*, which would be the body in the case of the leap. The muscle contractions then cause the leap, which occurs in accordance with the initial instructions. In the open-loop system, mechanisms to modify the instructions cannot be used, even if problems arise with the plan. In the example of the leap, if dancers use too much force, they go higher than time allows, causing them to be late in relation to the music. This error cannot be corrected in mid-leap, and the step is completed as it was initiated; that is, the landing occurs after the designated beat in the music. It can, however, be corrected in the next leap.

Movement in the Absence of Sensory Feedback

It may seem that dancers rely on sensory information to achieve their movement tasks. However, dancers can achieve considerable movement without sensory feedback. Many of the fast dance movements are initiated and completed without responding to feedback, such as fast leaps and jumps; quick footwork in tap dance, flamenco, and classical Indian dance; and fast falls to the floor in contemporary and street dance. Much of the early understanding about central control mechanisms was theoretical, followed by studies done with animals. It is only in recent times that research has used human subjects, and very little of this research has

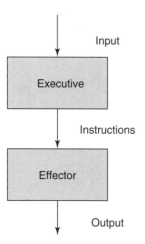

Figure 9.1 Elements of the typical open-loop control system.

Reprinted, by permission, from R.A. Schmidt and T.D. Lee, 2011, *Motor control and learning: A behavioral emphasis*, 5th ed. (Champaign, IL: Human Kinetics), 177.

Various stages of falls to the floor in contemporary dance.

involved dancers. In order to provide a better understanding of central control mechanisms, some of this early research is described.

Response-Chaining Hypothesis

The prominent experimental psychologist William James developed the **response-chaining hypothesis**, which states that movement begins with a muscle action caused by a stimulus. This action creates sensory information, called **response-produced feedback**, which triggers the next muscle contraction, and so on, creating a chain of actions and stimuli. The series of movements and resulting sensory feedback are shown in figure 9.2. James suggested that skilled movements do not seem to need much conscious control. Using his hypothesis, attention is only necessary in order to initiate the movement, and then the remaining actions happen as a nonconscious chain. In this model, the sensory feedback serves merely as a trigger for the next action. It is not used for error correction the way the reference mechanism uses sensory information in the closed-loop system.

Once a dance skill has been learned, a sequence of events happens automatically. For example, when a dancer thinks "jump," the deep core muscles engage, the muscles of the legs and hips fire, the legs extend, the feet push off the floor and fully point, the trunk muscles fire for additional spinal stabilization, and the arms are either moved in specific patterns or stabilized to remain still. Each part of the sequence triggers the next action in the chain.

Movement Control With Sensory Pathways Removed

Conditions exist in which animals or humans have the sensory pathways to the brain interrupted, but they still have intact pathways from the brain to the muscles. These conditions can result from injury or illness or from research techniques designed to reduce sensory input to the brain. While some of the early studies were contradictory, later research indicated that many species of animals, including humans, are capable of movement within normal limits in spite of losing sensory input. Larger move-

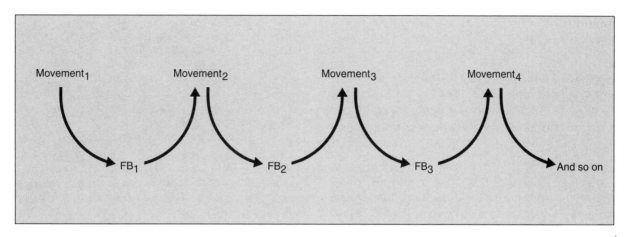

Figure 9.2 The response-chaining hypothesis suggests that response-produced feedback (FB) from earlier portions of the action serve as a trigger for later portions. A feedback series (FB_1, FB_2, FB_3, and so on) can continue to develop the movement sequence.

Reprinted, by permission, from R.A. Schmidt and T.D. Lee, 2011, *Motor control and learning: A behavioral emphasis*, 5th ed. (Champaign, IL: Human Kinetics), 178.

ments, such as climbing, swinging, and eating were affected in only minor ways. However, fine motor control was much more problematic. Hence, the absence of somatosensory feedback does not prevent movement, but it is needed for greatest precision and accuracy. These findings apparently contradict the response-chaining hypothesis, which may be too simplistic to cover the range of human activity.

Three methods have been devised that block sensory feedback in humans: anesthetic block, cuff technique, and tendon vibration technique. The purpose of these methods is to study the effects of loss of sensory information on motor control. **Anesthetic block** injects anesthesia into areas of the body such as the joint capsule to block sensation. **Cuff technique** blocks blood flow to the muscles, thereby temporarily shutting down feedback sensations. **Tendon vibration technique** involves high-speed vibration of a tendon connected to the agonist muscle, distorting proprioceptive feedback. Research using these methods demonstrated that movements could be performed without sensory feedback, but they were less accurate, and performance tended to deteriorate with continued repetition. In addition, sometimes vision was substituted for lacking tactile or proprioceptive information.

It would be highly unusual for someone to pursue the serious study of dance with a lack or detriment in sensory feedback mechanisms.

Dancers are dependent on visual, auditory, and somatosensory feedback to achieve the complexity of their art form. The **somatosensory system** includes discriminative touch, pressure, pain, temperature, and proprioception. Although dancers are dependent on somatosensory feedback, knowledge of motor control in the absence of sensory feedback gives insight into movement that can and cannot be executed through central organization alone.

Central Control

Imagine trying to dance in the dark with no sensation from the feet and no sound. Imagine further that proprioception and vestibular input (described in chapter 8) are disrupted, and no information about body position or relationship to gravity is present. Dancing would be impossible. Simply finding the door out of the room would be an amazing accomplishment. Although the following section deals with central control, keep in mind that these mechanisms do not exist in a vacuum. Their role in initiating and regulating movement is important, but the sensory contributions cannot ever be ignored.

Central Pattern Generators

When Jesse (see the first paragraph of this chapter) was outdoors for his walk, he was able to continue walking without any attention to his movement as long as the surface was clear of obstacles and no other people interrupted his path. The reason that walking is easeful in terms of attention is because of central pattern generators. **Central pattern generators (CPGs)** are groups of neurons that create rhythmic patterns without sensory feedback. These neurons are interneurons; that is, they lie completely within the spinal cord and act as connectors to other neurons. The CPGs do not need messages from the brain in order to cause the rhythmic movements. Regarding locomotion, they alternately fire on flexor and extensor motor neurons to the muscles in the legs. This alternating pattern (called *oscillation*) causes actions such as walking. Because the movement instructions originate in the spinal cord, CPGs are considered part of central control mechanisms. Both starting and ending CPGs are conscious choices, but they do not require conscious attention to continue. The same is true for shortening or lengthening stride length in order to turn or navigate obstacles. Jesse's walking will continue until he has to stop at a red light. CPGs can be modified by higher centers in the brain to increase speed or force. Jesse will need to make a decision to speed up if he realizes he is late and wants to walk faster. CPGs can respond to the environment, such as changes to the terrain. Jesse's leg muscles will apply more force when he reaches a hill and has to climb up the hill. Some CPGs, such as the one that controls running, do require conscious awareness unless no changes occur to conditions, such as on a treadmill or a completely flat surface. Debate continues about whether or not learned repetitive, cyclic movements are controlled by CPGs or another mechanism. It may be that CPGs must be genetically predetermined and naturally emerge. While walking and running are used in dance movement, they are controlled by CPGs that are learned by everyone as part of normal motor development. Some research suggests that if CPGs can be developed through practice, they are extensions or modifications of predetermined CPGs. Dance-specific examples of possibly learned CPGs include ones controlling continuous petit jetés in ballet or modern dance, or continuous golpes in flamenco dance.

The fast series of heel strikes created by the flamenco dancer is a possible learned central pattern generator.

Locomotion and Reflex Actions

Imagine that Jesse is in the studio practicing a dance work that he will perform next week. If someone left a hair clip on the floor and Jesse's bare foot comes into contact with it, the foot will reflexively retract. A **reflex** is an involuntary movement that occurs because of a particular stimulus. In this case, the stimulus that creates the response is the irritant of the uneven surface of the hair clip. In early ideas about locomotion, people theorized that gait (walking) consists of a series of reflexes. Motor control scientists now know that this is not the case. Gait is determined by CPGs, but reflexes guarantee that the pattern of action dictated by the CPGs is effectively carried out when unexpected environmental changes occur. In particular, the muscle spindles and GTOs assist in this role. For example, the gamma system (described in detail in chapter 6) helps determine muscle stiffness (resistance to stretch). If Jesse is texting on his phone during his outdoor walk and steps onto higher ground that he does not see, his leg will not collapse, but rather his muscles will react to the change in environment and yield in a smooth, coordinated fashion to allow for the change.

An interesting aspect of reflex integration into CPGs is reflex-reversal phenomenon. **Reflex-reversal phenomenon** means that based on the phase of the stepping cycle, two different reactive patterns can occur with the same stimulus. Consider the phases of walking seen in figure 9.3. In the swing phase, if the top of the foot comes into contact with an object, such as the cord to a lighting instrument in the theater, an increase in the flexion response occurs as a result of cutaneous reflexes. However, in the stance phase, the reaction would be the opposite. If Jesse has already placed his weight on the standing leg and is balancing when the cord touches his foot, his muscle reflexes will dominate, and he will remain in stance or, if anything, increase leg extension to secure the balance. In other words, the response to the same stimulus is opposite, given two different phases of the gait cycle. In the swing and swing-to-stance phases seen in figure 9.3, cutaneous reflexes determine the response. In the stance and stance-to-swing phases, muscle reflexes determine the response. Hence, reflexes in relation to CPGs are dependent on the task, the phase of the task, and the environmental context.

Finally, sensory information in relation to movement can be processed at the spinal cord level. While much of the sensory information does go to the brain for processing, the spinal cord can integrate substantial sensory and motor data. Given the considerable quantity of sensory information that is entering the periphery continuously, it is opportune that the entire CNS—both the brain and the spinal cord—participate in managing it.

Generalized Motor Programs

When Jesse was 6 years old, he took his first creative movement class. One of the exercises he did in class was to write his name in the air with various body parts. He used his dominant hand, his nondominant hand, his elbows, his knees, his head, and even his nose. All of this activity was possible because Jesse already had a generalized motor program for writing his name, even though he had never done it with all of these body parts before that day. It is noteworthy that the shapes remained remarkably invariant for Jesse, even recognizable as *his* writing even though he was using completely different muscles to accomplish each different version of his name. This ability forms the basis for much of what is called theme and variation in choreographic form—taking a given movement and varying it by doing it with different body parts, different dynamics, different facings, translating it to a different pathway, and different speeds.

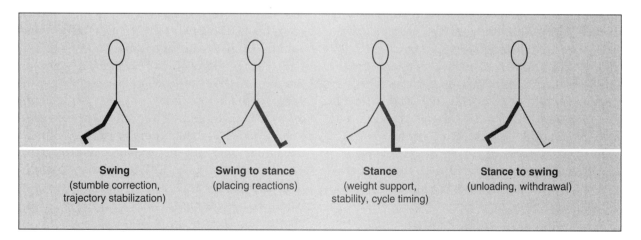

Swing
(stumble correction, trajectory stabilization)

Swing to stance
(placing reactions)

Stance
(weight support, stability, cycle timing)

Stance to swing
(unloading, withdrawal)

Figure 9.3 The phase-dependent role of reflexes in locomotion. Cutaneous reflexes dominate the swing and swing-to-stance phases, and muscle reflexes dominate in the stance and stance-to-swing phases.

Progress in Neurobiology, Vol. 58, E.P. Zehr and R.B. Stein, "What functions do reflexes serve during human locomotion?" pp. 185-205, Copyright 1999, with permission from Elsevier.

Richard Schmidt, one of the leaders in motor behavior research, first proposed the idea that generalized motor programs control motor actions. A **generalized motor program (GMP)** is a program that allows the motor system to execute an entire class of similar actions. It is stored in the memory, and it requires that various parameters be added preceding execution. It permits the motor system to be adaptable and flexible in doing variations of the motor program. **Parameters** are the aspects that can be varied from one execution of the GMP to another, such as speed, force, and body parts. Just as Jesse could write his name (the GMP) with various body parts or muscles (the parameter), he can also walk (the GMP) at different speeds (the parameter), or he can use varying amounts of muscle force (another parameter) when the terrain is flat or hilly. **Invariant features** are called the *signature* of the GMP; that is, they are the aspects that do not change from one action within the same class as another. In the case of writing, the invariant feature is the spatial pattern—the shapes of the letters.

Invariant Features and Parameters in Dance and Music

Music and dance provide excellent examples of invariant features and parameters. The rhythm of a piece of music or a dance step indicates the number of beats in a measure, occurring in a repeated pattern. For example, a waltz is designated as 3/4 time, meaning that the length of each beat is a quarter note, and each measure has 3 beats. This structure would be counted *1, 2, 3; 1, 2, 3; 1, 2, 3;* and so on. The tempo of the music piece or dance step is the speed of the music. A waltz can be slow, such as the Grand Pas de Deux from *Don Quixote*, or it can be fast, such as the Garland Waltz from *Sleeping Beauty*. Regardless of the speed of the waltz, it is always in 3 beats, and this aspect is the invariant feature. The tempo can change, and this aspect is the parameter.

Another example of an invariant feature is relative time. **Relative time** refers to the proportion of time each component or section requires within an overall movement task. A dance phrase can be choreographed so that the

The waltz is always done in 3/4 time, regardless of the tempo.

first movement takes 3 counts, the next movement takes 2 counts, the third movement takes 4 counts, and the last movement takes 1 count. Regardless of how slow or fast the dancers do the phrase, the relative time of each movement remains the same; that is, the first movement uses 30% of the total time, the second movement uses 20% of the time, the third movement uses 40%, and the last movement uses 10%. This relationship of the components is the invariant feature, but the speed is the parameter. Notice that the duration of the entire phrase also changes, so the faster the tempo, the shorter the duration. While these examples are specific to dance and music, common movements such as walking also shed light on generalized motor programs, invariant features, and parameters.

Walking and Running as GMPs

Relative time is such a common invariant feature that it has been a central focus in studies about gait for decades. Walking has these four phases, shown in figure 9.3: swing, swing-to-stance, stance, and stance-to-swing. Each phase takes up a certain percentage of the time, regardless of the speed of walking. Swing takes approximately 10% of the time, the swing-to-stance phase takes approximately 25% of the time, stance uses approximately 15% of the time, and the stance-to-swing phase takes about 50% of the time. While some variation in speed exists, the relative time of these four phases falls within limits of the given percentages.

While it may seem that running is very fast walking, running is a different GMP, even though the same four phases occur. Figure 9.4 illustrates the four phases of walking and running and their relative times. In the figure, F represents swing, E_1 is the swing-to-stance phase, E_2 is stance, and E_3 is the stance-to-swing phase. These pie charts clearly show the differences between walking and running. For example, in walking, the stance-to-swing phase uses 50% of the time, but in running it uses less than 25% of the time. Similarly, each of the other three phases has differences when walking and running. The phase that is the most similar between walking and running is the stance phase. The phase that shows the greatest difference is the stance-to-swing phase. Dancers can do both slow and fast walks, and they can also do slower and faster runs as part of dance training and choreography. The GMPs for walking and running are distinctly different, although each one can vary with the parameter of speed.

Force and Muscle Use as Parameters

Another possible parameter is force, which is related to muscle contraction. **Muscle force** is the amount of force a muscle produces. It depends on several factors, including the size of muscle, the number of fibers activated, the initial length of the muscle when activated, and the angle of the joint at the time of muscle activation. Dancers can take a movement and use a little or a lot of force in the execution. When Jesse is in a contemporary dance class performing soft curves of the spine (flexion) releasing to gravity, the muscle force necessary is minimal. However, when Jesse is in a Graham technique class, he is asked to create the same spinal movement, but he needs considerably more muscle force because of the dynamic and qualitative aspects of the Graham technique. Dancers are often asked to perform movement phrases with differing levels of muscle force to create variations of the same material.

Finally, dancers are expected to learn combinations on the first side and then reverse them

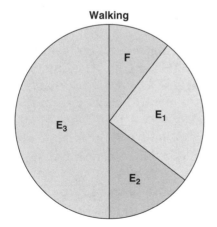
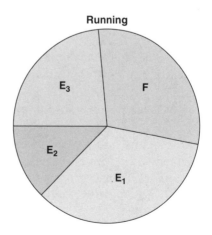

Figure 9.4 The four phases of walking and running have different amounts of time in the two locomotor patterns. E_1 is swing-to-stance phase, E_2 is stance phase, E_3 is stance-to-swing phase, and F is swing phase. Note how much more time is spent in E_3 while walking, whereas in running more time is spent in F.

In the Graham technique, the spinal curve (the *contraction*) requires far more muscle force than in other modern dance techniques.

- Walking and running at various speeds
- Walking or rolling across the space and imagining changing textures in the environment, such as moving through mud, honey, water, wind
- Drawing a particular shape (circles, lines, squares) with various body parts

For the Older Adolescent or Adult Dancer

- Changing the tempo of any dance step or combination—that is, trying it slower or faster than the way it was taught
- Changing the weight of a dance step— that is, exploring light to heavy qualities of the same movement
- Varying the leg positioning of the gesture leg in a particular elevation step, such as hops with the gesture leg front or side or back
- Varying the shape of the legs in a particular elevation step, such as leaps with both legs straight, one leg bent, or both legs bent
- Taking a combination and exploring different amounts of muscle force to change the dynamics of the phrase
- Any of the improvisations listed for children, adapted in complexity for an older population

on the second side in far less time than the original learning period. This skill, sometimes called *bilateral transfer*, can be examined in the context of generalized motor programs. **Bilateral transfer** is the transfer of learning from one limb to its counterpart on the other side of the body. Once the combination is embedded in memory, the GMP can initiate execution with the same muscles on the opposite side of the body. The invariant features would be the spatial and temporal aspects of the phrase. The particular muscle selection is the parameter.

Teachers and dancers can use a variety of strategies to encourage the development of the GMPs and their generalizability. Some ideas for the dance class are listed next. In each of these cases, parameters such as speed, muscle selection, or force are changing:

For the Child or Young Adolescent

- Writing one's name with various body parts

Central control mechanisms are highly important in the overview of how dancers plan, initiate, and execute complex dance skills. They allow dancers to generate movement from a literal library of possibilities living in the brain and the spinal cord. Because of the ongoing partnership between central control mechanisms and responsiveness to the body and the environment, dancers explore an ever-expanding vocabulary and skill set as they go through their years of training. From early experiences in creative dance playing with body part variations, to elite training that involves experimenting with nuances in timing and dynamics, dancers rely on central control mechanisms for the basis of movement instructions from higher centers and the spinal cord. Dance educators can more effectively teach the broad range of

Children can experiment with the generalized motor program for writing various letters by using different body parts.

essential skills by introducing variations in practice once central control motor patterns become crystalized in the dancers. In this way, teachers can encourage adaptable and versatile dancers as well as introduce a wide range of compositional structures in dance training.

Summary

Central control mechanisms are the processes occurring in the central nervous system (the brain and the spinal cord) that organize movement. When control is an open-loop system, no sensory feedback is necessary to execute the movement. When control is a closed-loop system, the movement instructions initiate the movement, but feedback is needed to continue and complete the execution. Early theories about motor control emphasized the response-chaining hypothesis, which states that movement begins with a muscle action caused by a stimulus. This action creates sensory information, which triggers the next muscle contraction, and so on, creating a chain of actions and stimuli. Central pattern generators (CPGs) are groups of neurons that create rhythmic patterns without sensory feedback. CPGs do not need messages from the brain to cause the rhythmic movements. They alternately fire on flexor and extensor motor neurons to the muscles in the legs and the arms, causing actions such as walking and swimming. Generalized motor programs (GMPs) are programs that allow the motor system to execute an entire class of similar actions. The GMP is stored in the memory and permits the motor system to be adaptable and flexible. GMPs have parameters that can be varied from one execution to another, such as speed, force, and body parts. They have invariant features—aspects that do not change from one action to another within the same class, such as relative time. GMPs are responsive to sensory information and reflexive action, and they allow for adaptability in motor skills.

Chapter 10
Speed, Accuracy, and Coordination

For centuries, audiences have marveled at seeing large groups of dancers performing in perfect musical unison while maintaining precision in the shape of the body and spatial design. It is particularly breathtaking when the movement is very fast and demands extreme accuracy, such as the work of Lord of the Dance or the Rockettes. Dancers know of the many hours of practice it takes to achieve this type of precision. Similarly, most dance forms demand a high level of coordination. Even audience members who have never danced realize the difficulty of moving the arms, legs, and torso in multiple ways while presenting the appearance of ease and fluidity. The demands on today's dancers require that they can simultaneously achieve speed, accuracy, and coordination in complex body and spatial patterns while following intricate musical scores. And they combine all of these aspects of motor control under stage lighting, changing performance spaces, and even with varying casts of dancers. For the purposes of this chapter, the terms *accuracy* and *precision* are considered interchangeable; it would be peculiar to train dancers to be accurate in term of arriving at a specific point in space without also being precise in terms of movement clarity.

While motor control of many dance movements requires specialized skill acquisition and considerable practice, movements involving speed, accuracy, and complex coordination present unique challenges. One of the complications of very fast movement is that it allows no time to use sensory information, particularly vision, to make adjustments to the movement once it is under way. Therefore, the initial messages from the motor control system must incorporate a high degree of accuracy at the start. Coordination in dance is equally challenging because of the necessity to organize multiple body parts in unusual combinations and musical timing. The demands of speed, accuracy, and coordination to the motor control system are so extraordinary that an entire chapter has been devoted to these aspects of motor control in dance performance.

Much of what is known about speed, accuracy, and coordination is derived from sports. The earliest studies date back to the late 1800s.

The Rockettes demonstrate incredible speed, accuracy, and coordination with their high kicks in unison.

These studies were concerned with what happens to accuracy as speed increases, often examining speed in relation to reaching a target. Because many sports involve objects, the goal of this research has focused on object-oriented activities, such as contacting, pushing, touching, gripping, capturing, or displacing an object. In dance, the goal in spatial terms is often for the limbs to arrive at exact places in space. Consider a single assemblé in ballet. At the height of the jump, the legs must arrive in fifth position in a very brief amount of time. The arms must also arrive at a specific position, often asymmetrical with the leading arm higher. The head is turned at a particular angle toward the leading arm.

The assemblé is executed with precision and speed, and it also demands accuracy in the placement of limbs in mid-flight.

The accuracy demand is so high that the point in space for each body part can be compared to an imaginary target. To succeed at an entire series of complex steps demands heightened coordination. Most teachers train these concepts based on their own personal background and educated guesses. Therefore, the information from sports serves as a foundation for this material, and conclusions for dance based on sports knowledge are suggested.

Speed and Accuracy

While dancers tend to focus on the problems of speed and accuracy relative to dance accomplishments, daily life provides its own pitfalls. Everyone has experienced knocking an elbow or knee on a piece of furniture while rushing to leave the house. The task of pouring a liquid into a bottle or bowl can result in spills if attempted too quickly. And running up a flight of stairs can end in trips and falls. The term for this effect is called the **speed–accuracy trade-off**. In other words, when a person selects speed, accuracy is diminished; when a person selects accuracy, speed is diminished. At the end of the 19th century, the influential psychologist Robert Woodworth did some of the earliest research and made the following observations:

- Error increases as movement speed increases.
- The dominant hand is more accurate than the nondominant hand.
- At slower speeds, accuracy is greater with eyes open than eyes closed, but at very fast speeds, little difference exists because of the lack of time to integrate visual feedback.

A half century later, the psychologist and motor behavior educator Paul Fitts developed a mathematical law explaining these conditions. It is beyond the scope of this book to detail the mathematics behind Fitts' law and the subsequent research. However, the conclusions and applications are of great interest to dancers, and they are explored in this chapter.

Fitts' Law

Fitts' 1954 article on speed and accuracy is considered one of the landmark publications in the field of motor control. In Fitts' task, the subject uses a pencil-shaped object to move between two targets, tapping them as quickly as possible for a set amount of time (figure 10.1). In dance, an equivalent might be moving the arms rapidly from fifth position to second position repeatedly during a series of piqué turns, or a series of leg kicks performed by a line of Rockettes. The difficulty of the activity changes according to how much distance is between the two targets (called **amplitude**) and how wide the targets are. In the case of the Rockettes, because the kicks are so high relative to the starting point of the leg, and the arrival point is so specific, this movement has a high level of difficulty. Fitts named this relationship the **index of difficulty**, a mathematical formula using the amplitude and width of the targets. In general, the higher

the index of difficulty, the more time it takes to complete the task. Fortunately this time can be reduced with practice. It is clear from the research that practice is essential for improving accuracy with movement speed, especially in movements with a high level of difficulty.

It is not uncommon for teachers and choreographers to practice fast phrases at a slower tempo, then gradually increase tempo as the dancers become more adept at the steps. Sometimes the faster version of a movement is actually a completely different **generalized motor program (GMP)**, a program that allows the motor system to execute an entire class of similar actions. As discussed in chapter 9, walking and running are different GMPs. Similarly, doing a very fast series of pliés and relevés is not the same as jumping. However, the slower practice can teach important aspects that both GMPs share. In the case of jump preparations, while doing slow pliés and relevés, dancers can practice alignment, arm organization, and

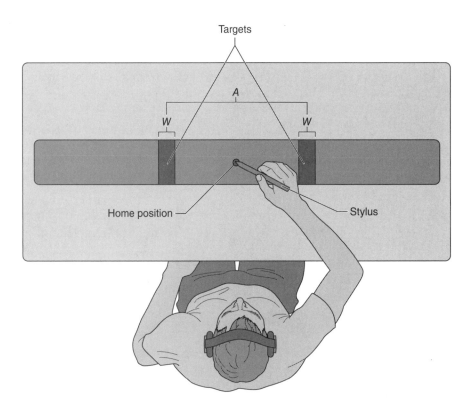

Figure 10.1 In Fitts' task, the subject taps with a stylus between two targets of varying width (*W*) and with varying amplitude between them (*A*), attempting to move as rapidly as possible while minimizing the number of target misses.

Reprinted, by permission, from R.A. Schmidt and T.D. Lee, 2011, *Motor control and learning: A behavioral emphasis*, 5th ed. (Champaign, IL: Human Kinetics), 125.

eccentric use of the plié. The ballistic attack to achieve the flight phase will still need to be taught as a new idea. Note the resemblance of this discussion to the use of the barre. While many components of dance skills can be taught at the barre, research has demonstrated that balance is not being trained during this phase of class. Hence, dancers can bring certain components of a skill to center practice, but then balance must be addressed anew.

Three reasons explain why Fitts' law is so important in the understanding of motor control. First, in spite of the complexity of motor behavior, Fitts' law is one of the motor control concepts that follow precise mathematical formulas and one of few that are simple and clear. Second, the law generalizes to a broad range of motor skills and circumstances. Third, in all of the time that has passed since the original publication, it still stands as an accurate model of the relationship between speed and accuracy, although subsequent researchers have refined and added to the mathematics.

Discrete Tasks

Unlike the repetitive tapping task in the original Fitts' task research, a **discrete task** is a single event having a definitive beginning and end, such as the arrival of a slashing arm movement from the front to the side. Although variations do exist as a result of the complexity of the range of movements, the speed–accuracy trade-off in these discrete tasks is similar to cyclical, repetitive movements. The faster the dancer does the arm slash, the less accurate the point of arrival will be. In fact, when practicing new, fast material, accuracy should be emphasized first, then speed added later. If dancers begin at high speed with little accuracy, it is unlikely that accurate movement will develop.

For discrete tasks, three phases exist to achieve the movement, and they are described in terms of how vision is used during the speed–accuracy trade-off. As examples, consider Bob Fosse's choreography involving placement of hats and canes in the musical *All That Jazz*, Jackie Chan jumping through a small window in the film *Rush Hour 2*, or Matt Damon leaping across a large space and through a glass window in the film *The*

Bourne Ultimatum. In the case of Fosse's work, objects must be placed in specific locations at high speed. In the case of Jackie Chan or Matt Damon (or their stunt doubles), they must aim their entire bodies into a small target area at high speed. Phase 1, called the **movement preparation phase**, begins with the decision to do the movement. Vision is needed to clarify the environmental setting affecting the movement. In phase 2, called the **initial flight phase**, the limb or body movement is set in action toward the target. The role of vision in this phase is still being debated, and vision during this phase may be more important than was initially thought. For the Fosse movement, once the target location for the hat or cane has been determined in phase 1, visual information might be needed to reassess the hat or cane

Dancers working with props, such as hats and canes, must work with accuracy and precision to accomplish complex prop manipulation.

position while the dancer is in motion. In the case of Jackie Chan or Matt Damon, once they have determined the exact distance to the window and its location in space, they may need additional visual information to set their bodies flying. Phase 3, called the **termination phase**, is the moment just before and when the target is hit. In phase 3 vision is necessary so that movements can be corrected if needed to achieve the goal. For Fosse's dancers, this phase would be the point of contact with the hat or cane at its target, or Jackie Chan and Matt Damon flying through the window and arriving at the other side. For anyone who has viewed outtakes of Jackie Chan films, the precision and practice necessary are obvious.

Broader Examples of Fitts' Law

Some educators might argue that a repetitive, tapping task or a discrete aiming task might not be indicative of more general types of fast and accurate movement skills. However, studies have shown that Fitts' law extends to many other skills and populations. For example, children exhibit the same speed–accuracy trade-off as adults. Also, studies with feet, arms, hands, and fingers follow the same principle, so one can generalize it to include dance movements involving multiple body parts. Fitts' law even applies underwater, in outer space, and when movements are so small that they must be magnified in order to be seen. An astonishing point is that Fitts' law applies when movements are being imagined and are not actually being executed. This result might suggest that when dancers mentally practice fast movement, it may be beneficial to visualize the skills slowly in the beginning stages of learning. Note that in the research being described, as in most sports, the target is visible to the participant. When the visible target is removed and the participant continues the aiming task, Fitts' law still applies. Therefore, one can assume that the law holds up in all of the dance examples stated with unseen or imaginary targets, such as the assemblé, the Rockette kick, and the arm slash. Finally, over the years, Fitts' law has been confirmed in a wide variety of everyday activities, such as typing on a computer and reaching for objects. These examples from everyday life are applicable to artistic endeavors such as playing a piano or partner work in dance.

Linear Speed–Accuracy Trade-Off

Dancers are rarely asked to move as fast as they possibly can. Usually, the tempo is set, often using music, and dancers aim for accuracy within that restriction. Certainly this set tempo might be exceedingly fast; nevertheless, the obligation is to stay in time with the music. Fitts' law has been tested in similar conditions. The **linear speed–accuracy trade-off** is a variant of Fitts' law in which the goal is not to move as quickly as possible between two targets or at a given single target; the goal is to achieve the task with accuracy at a given predetermined speed. In these situations, the same trade-off applies, and increases in preset movement speeds result in decreased spatial accuracy. Dancers know how much more difficult it is to be clear in body design (i.e., precise in body shape) when the teacher changes the music to a faster piece.

Temporal Speed–Accuracy Trade-Off

So far, the discussion has centered on the idea of speed and accuracy with regard to spatial concepts including body and spatial design, or arriving at a particular point in space with the whole body or a body part. The next variation of Fitts' law looks at temporal accuracy. The **temporal speed–accuracy trade-off** states that as movement goes faster, timing accuracy actually improves! This result is the exact opposite of the linear speed–accuracy trade-off. One explanation for this interesting outcome is called **temporal stability**, which describes how variable the timing of a given movement is from one trial to the next. Imagine asking a dancer to execute a series of similar jumps, such as 16 jumps in first position, without music. If each jump were timed, the variation from one jump to the next would be quite small. However, if the dancer were asked to do a series of slow développés without music, more variation would exist in the timing from one to the next. Hence, because the travel time in a jump is so much smaller than the travel time in a développé, it is easier for the dancer to be consistent in repeated movements of the jump. This result is the same whether the dancer is doing a discrete task or a repetitive series.

In many sports studies, timing is not set by an external audible source. However, dancers often must set their timing with a sound score. **Synchronization** refers to producing a movement corresponding to an external event, such as music, a metronome, or a vocal score. Many studies have also examined synchronization in a variety of circumstances. The most interesting result for dancers is known as **negative asynchrony**, a term meaning that two systems are not synchronized. In the case of the studies on dancers, their movement slightly preceded the sound. Even more fascinating is the fact that negative asynchrony is greater in musically untrained people when compared to people with musical backgrounds. This finding suggests that with musical training, novice dancers learn to be more accurate in their ability to stay on the music. Teachers can do this musical training in separate classes or incorporate it directly into dance classes. One of the advantages of incorporating musical training into dance class is that it can be accomplished with movement as a basis for the information.

Three variations of speed–accuracy trade-offs in dance have been considered—two spatial and one temporal. Spatial variations include movement done as rapidly as possible, or movement done to a predetermined speed. They involve both repetitive movements that cycle between two targets and linear, discrete movements that arrive at a single target. The temporal case involves speed and accuracy related to the timing of movements. While the research and the discussion separate these three models, it is not uncommon in dance for spatial and temporal speed and accuracy to occur simultaneously. Consider the well-known ballet landmark dance step, the 32-fouetté pirouette combination en pointe, which all prima ballerinas must accomplish. The foot of the gesture leg must arrive accurately at the same point in space in second position on each turn and at a precise beat in the music. The arms must also arrive exactly in front of the centerline of the body as each turn begins. Spatially, the standing foot must remain at a particular spot on the

Because of the speed of their movement, the dancers jumping in first position demonstrate little variation in timing from one jump to the next.

floor. Even if the turns are executed with precision to the music, if the dancer's standing foot travels around in the space during the 32 turns, it is considered poor technique. The combination of speed, accuracy, and musicality of this sequence is a highlight in many ballet concerts.

Coordination

Most dance forms involve intricate and complicated coordination. In classical Indian dance the detail work of the hands, fingers, and face—coupled with complex rhythms in the footwork—is astonishing, and it takes years to perfect. Street dancers are remarkable in their ability to move many body parts in seemingly random directions and timing simultaneously. Limón modern dancers and flamenco dancers achieve polyrhythms in the legs, arms, and torso while traveling in various spatial designs. And ballet dancers can accomplish extremely fast and complicated percussive footwork and beats while changing the arm and head positions in fluid phrasing. In addition, dancers are continuously coping with environmental changes. The Nicholas Brothers in *Stormy Weather* and Shirley MacLaine in *Sweet Charity* had to negotiate leaping on and off structures while maintaining dance steps, rhythms, and even handling props. All of these aspects of dance fall under the concept of coordination.

Defining Coordination

Coordination involves two crucial aspects of motor control: the patterning of the movements of the head, body, arms, and legs, and how the body parts relate to the environment, including objects and circumstances. In common usage, the word *coordination* often suggests elite or advanced achievement of a skill. However, the term is used in motor control to define a person's skill level at any point in time, whether novice or elite. This idea refers to the body organization and also to the ability to adapt to the context. For example, dancers might be able to execute a dance combination well in the studio, but then discover that under stage lighting, balance and turns are negatively affected. They would be less coordinated in

this context. Another example is practicing a dance in a small space, then moving it to a larger space. Adjusting the steps to cover this larger area can result in a compromised performance until the dancers adapt. One other aspect worth mentioning is the relationship of each dancer to other dancers. Additional dancers can be considered part of the environmental context, and staying in the correct spatial and musical connection is part of coordination.

Degrees of Freedom

The Russian neurophysiologist Nikolai Bernstein wrote his landmark book *The Co-ordination and Regulation of Movement* in 1957, but it was not translated into English until 1967 (see Bernstein, 1967). He is known for defining the concept of degrees of freedom. The **degrees of freedom** describe the number of independent components in a moving system, such as a machine or a human body. For the human body, degrees of freedom are defined depending on various levels of motor control. The individual motor units (neurons and muscle fibers) can each be considered an independent component, but this approach is not very useful for examining motor control, because humans do not consciously control this level of activity. It is more common to consider the joints of the body and the directions of movement. Considering directions of motion, the elbow and the knee have two degrees of freedom (flexion and extension), and the hip has six degrees of freedom (flexion, extension, abduction, adduction, external rotation, and internal rotation). The multiple degrees of freedom in the human body provide an infinite number of solutions for any movement task. Redundancy in ways to achieve a particular goal is highly advantageous, because it allows for varying solutions when one or more options are restricted. For example, if a person has a cast on a leg, walking is still possible, because the system finds an alternative way to accomplish the task.

The **degrees of freedom problem** examines the dilemma of selecting a particular strategy for achieving the movement goal from the infinite possibilities. The motor system must find a solution based on the organization of the body in reference to the environment and the movement goals. In life and in many sports, this choice is driven by the notion of achieving the task with optimal control and efficiency. The act of stepping illustrates the way that the motor system solves the degrees of freedom problem. Given the number of joints involved (lumbosacral, hip joint, knee joint, ankle, and foot joints) and the number of degrees of freedom at each joint, infinite solutions exist for placing the foot in a given location. And yet, stepping kinematics are remarkably consistent, restricting rotation (outward and inward) and abduction/adduction in the hip (sideways movement of the leg) and inversion/eversion in the foot (sideways movement) so that the movement is almost entirely constrained to the sagittal plane—that is, movement going forward and back—principally using only two degrees of freedom at each joint even when more are available. The system will choose the most direct path because it is economical and energy efficient.

The act of reaching is another example of how the motor system manages to solve the degrees of freedom problem. Given the number of joints involved (shoulder girdle, shoulder joint, elbow, wrist, hand), and the number of degrees of freedom at each joint, there are infinite solutions to reaching for an object. However, the system typically exhibits only one degree of freedom when the direction of reach is constant and two degrees of freedom when the direction of reach is varied, regardless of the object's distance and location in space. Once again, the system chooses the most direct path because it is economical and energy efficient. If an obstacle is present during stepping or reaching, or if the person has alternative reasons for using another path (e.g., choreographic choice), the system can still rely on the redundancy of solutions and choose a different, more indirect path. For example, consider the dance walk in which the gesture leg does a rond de jambe à terre instead of the standard swing phase. In this instance, the hip joint takes a major excursion out of the sagittal plane, using considerably more abduction/adduction and external rotation than common walking would use. Despite the motor system's tendency to achieve the task in the most efficient way, dancers still

have a myriad of possibilities for movement selection. The flexibility of the system in solving the degrees of freedom problem is one of the magnificent aspects of our motor control mechanisms.

In addition to the motor control theories discussed in chapter 2 in the context of motor development theories (such as reflex theory, hierarchical theory, maturational perspective, information processing perspective, ecological perspective, dynamic systems approach, and perception–action approach), additional theories of motor control have emerged. These later theories have included discussion of the degrees of freedom problem as part of their model of motor control. Two such historically influential theories are equilibrium point theory and uncontrolled manifold hypothesis, although both theories have been replaced by newer theories that develop their ideas. Probably the most recent, optimal feedback control theory attempts to reconcile the best strategies for goal achievement and the immense motor variability that the degrees of freedom provide. In this view, feedback is used selectively by correcting only those errors that interfere with the movement goals, and ignoring irrelevant feedback. Optimal feedback control theory includes the idea that some motor parameters are predicted by the system based on perceived environmental conditions and previous experience, and these conditions and experiences also contribute to the regulation of degrees of freedom. This theory shows promise in revising thinking about motor control issues, and ongoing research is exploring its usefulness.

In most instances, when novices start to learn a new skill, they unconsciously reduce the available degrees of freedom to make the learning of the skill manageable. This reduction is called **freezing the degrees of freedom**. This phase results in stiff, rigid, and poorly timed movement. As the learner progresses, degrees of freedom that were frozen are gradually released. This release is called **freeing the degrees of freedom**. They are reorganized into new patterns that are smoother, more fluid, and closer to the ideal of the movement. For example, when new dancers begin learning the various arm positions in ballet or modern dance, they often exhibit arms that move in one piece and carry excess tension. With time and practice, dancers learn to free the various joints of the arms and move fluidly and gracefully.

Some researchers have suggested that moving from freezing to freeing degrees of freedom depends on the task. Certain studies in sports and music have demonstrated that novices may show large degrees of freedom at the beginning of training, and then freeze degrees of freedom due to practice, or a trade-off might occur with some degrees of freedom decreasing and others increasing. A study examining violinists showed that as novices improved at the skill, they reduced degrees of freedom at the shoulder joint in flexion/extension but maintained degrees of freedom in other movements of the shoulder and at the elbow, with neither an increase or decrease in these joint movements. This result was demonstrated in both children and adults learning the skill, implying that the learning strategy is task-specific, not dependent on age. In a ball-kicking task, range of motion of the knees and ankles decreased with practice as range of motion at the hip increased. Hence, the general principle of initially freezing, and later freeing degrees of freedom may vary with high-level task acquisition.

Similarly, dance may contain tasks that do not always follow the usual pattern of going from freezing to freeing degrees of freedom. Dance presents an unusual set of conditions for two reasons. First, in terms of artistic choices, dancers deliberately find indirect ways to accomplish a movement goal for choreographic purposes. Second, in terms of aesthetics, dancers consciously restrict certain movements that could make the task easier to control but are not considered appropriate within the form. For example, beginning dancers often flex the knee as well as the hip as they initiate a tendu to the front, which is an easier strategy in terms of shifting weight off the gesture leg. With training and practice, dancers learn to maintain an extended knee throughout the entire tendu movement, so the system must find an alternate way to solve the degrees of freedom problem. Teachers often emphasize the increased pressure into the floor with the bottom of the foot to accomplish this strategy.

Another example is the execution of dégagés to the side in many dance forms. Research has demonstrated that nondancers incline (tilt) the pelvis when shifting weight to the supporting leg so that the pelvis is higher on the side of the gesture leg. Trained dancers translate the pelvis (i.e., the pelvic bones remain level to the floor). When the pelvis tilts, the spine laterally flexes to keep the upper torso vertical. Choosing to keep the pelvis level is considered a superior tactic, because it is believed to enhance stability and is also thought to be more aesthetically pleasing in some dance forms. In the translation strategy, the motor system chooses to solve the degrees of freedom problem differently; it uses increased hip flexion and abduction of the gesture leg with less pelvic inclination and less spinal curvature. This variability of the dancer's motor system at higher levels of skill allows for contextual flexibility and the completion of complex movement goals with changing conditions and demands.

Coordinative Structures

The previous examples of the kick, the tendu, and the dégagé all have one attribute in common. In each case, groups of muscles, called **coordinative structures** or **muscle synergies**, work together. These functionally linked activations help to solve some of the degrees of freedom problems. Sometimes synergies develop naturally, such as the pattern of arms and legs in walking and running. In other circumstances, synergies develop through practice and training, such as the tendu and dégagé in ballet and modern dance, or the hand and foot coordination in classical Indian dance. One aspect of coordinative structures is that they compensate to perform that task even when one or more joints are constricted in some way. If a brace is placed on an ankle recovering from sprain, the body compensates; it finds a way to walk without ankle movement. If a dancer has a hamstring injury, grand battement is accomplished with increased posterior pelvic tilt (tucking under) and even bending of the standing knee.

Long-term dependence on compensations can be problematic to dancers, because they change efficient motor patterns or encourage other injuries. The process of rehabilitation for dance injuries should include work that repatterns these compensatory movement habits to discourage reinjury. For example, when dancers sustain knee or ankle injuries, they often compensate by putting more weight on the noninjured leg. Rehabilitation procedures should examine alignment patterns to encourage returning to a more symmetrical organization after healing.

Coordination and Applications to Dance

Dancers face several issues in developing coordination in dance practice. **Timing coordination** includes moving each arm and each leg in different directions at the same time, and the use of **polyrhythms** (the simultaneous use of contrasting or conflicting rhythms). **Spatial coordination** includes attempting two different spatial designs or locations with various body parts at the same time, such as patting the head and rubbing the abdomen or performing a dance phrase involving a leg pattern in one direction with a different arm pattern in another direction (figure 10.2). Dancers share the challenges of **social coordination** (working with others) with synchronized swimmers and divers. Each of these aspects of coordination is explored separately.

Timing Coordination

When observing a pianist playing a complex piece, it is obvious that the hands are executing entirely different motor patterns from each other. This coordination is typical of playing many musical instruments. In dance, not only the arms but also the feet and legs are often asked to do different tasks. No dance form escapes these demands. The term for using both hands is *bimanual*, and the term for using both feet is *bipedal*. Bimanual coordination has been studied much more than bipedal actions. Some research indicates that when the two hands are doing different tasks, the brain develops one motor pattern to control both actions rather than coordinate two separate sets of directions to the muscles. Other research suggests two parallel processes rather than a single plan, but that each plan influences the other. In both points

Figure 10.2 This image of José Limón in his choreography *Concerto Grosso* demonstrates the ability of dancers to coordinate arms, legs, and torso in varying spatial directions and rhythms.

of view, the two hands do not remain entirely independent, and they have effects on each other. If this idea is generalized to the feet and legs, it may explain why it can be so difficult to do an elevation step and point one foot while flexing the other foot.

The next research question would be to examine what occurs with upper- and lower-limb simultaneous actions. Three options exist for this type of coordination. **Homologous movement** involves pairs of limbs—left and right arms or left and right legs. **Ipsilateral movement** involves movement on the same side—left arm and leg, or right arm and leg. **Contralateral movement** involves movement across the diagonal—left arm with right leg, or right arm with left leg. For example, with homologous movement, if moving both arms in the sagittal plane, dancers can take both arms up and both arms down at the same time, or move one arm up while the other arm is going down. For ipsilateral movement, dancers can kick the left leg and lift the left arm overhead, or kick the left leg up while bringing the left arm down. Finally, for contralateral movement, in low runs, dancers can bring the right arm forward as the left leg steps forward (what dancers call *opposition*) or take the right arm back as the left leg goes forward. Dancers often coordinate the four limbs in ways that are unnatural in terms of everyday motor coordination, such as placing the right arm forward while standing on the right leg in first position arabesque. Each of the three types of limb coordination—homologous, ipsilateral, and contralateral—requires different motor pattern organization. Dancers must practice many variations of arm and leg timing and coordination in order to achieve ease in execution. The skills must become sufficiently automatic that the dancers can focus on other aspects of the skill, such as attending to the space and other dancers.

The issue of polyrhythms presents its own complexities for dancers, because the rhythms are independent or conflicting. Imagine a relatively simple task of walking to the beat of one rhythm and clapping in double time. While the feet and hands are doing different phrasing, this exercise is not polyrhythmic, because the underlying beat is the same for both body parts. In this case, it is called **harmonic**. Now imagine beating out a rhythm with the hands on a table or drum in which the right hand is sounding out three beats during the same time period that the left hand sounds out two beats, termed a 3/2 rhythm. This example is one of many polyrhythmic expressions. Flamenco dancers often use a 4/3 rhythm, and musicians are capable of even more complex combinations. In general, harmonic rhythms are relatively simple to coordinate, while polyrhythms are difficult. When teaching dancers polyrhythms, teachers should make sure that the movement and spatial components remain fairly simple in the early stages of learning, allowing the dancers to focus on the rhythmic complexity.

Spatial Coordination

Try drawing circles with both hands, as if waxing a table. Next, try taking the hands linearly from the shoulders straight out in front of the body and back in repeatedly. Each of these tasks is fairly simple. Now try doing the circles with the left hand, and the lines with the right hand. This composite movement is far more difficult because of the spatial coordination required of the two limbs. Sometimes when two tasks are attempted at once, the limbs tend to do one or the other task, or they invent a new combination of the two. In the previous example, both arms might want to draw circles, or they might end up creating rectangular shapes (figure 10.3).

Studies have demonstrated that if the two tasks can be conceptualized in such a way that they integrate into one idea or metaphor, it is easier to achieve the bimanual coordination. For example, try this exercise: Draw a rainbow with your right hand while your left draws a smile underneath the rainbow at the same time. The composite shape created by the two hands is a full circle. Now try reversing the spacing of the hands so that the smile is on top. Because this shape created by the two hands is not a familiar pattern, the task is more difficult. Dancers often create metaphors or spatial constructs with complicated movement patterns to convert them into recognizable or unified shapes. This technique reduces the difficulty level of the spatial coordination.

Social Coordination

Some researchers refer to social coordination as **behavioral synchrony**, doing movement activities in unison or simultaneously. In most choreography that is not for the solo dancer, performers must work together to achieve a mutual goal. This challenge incorporates the ideas of timing and spatial coordination, and it adds the third component of synchronizing one's actions to other dancers. This concept may or may not imply unison movement. Even when dancers are executing individual choreography, they may still be required to be aware and in harmony with the movements of the dancers around them. Try this simple experiment: First, ask a group of dancers to execute 16 jumps in first position to music with a steady beat, landing on the downbeat (the beat you would usually count) of the music. Then ask the dancers to execute 16 jumps in first position, landing on the upbeat (the "and" beat of the music). Finally,

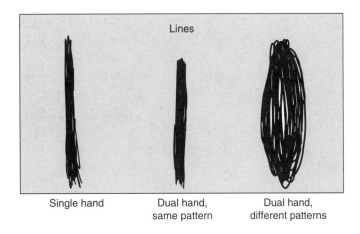

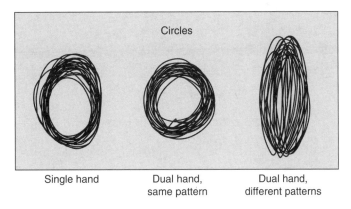

Figure 10.3 Drawing lines (upper) and circles (lower) under unimanual and bimanual conditions.

Reprinted from *Acta Psychologica*, Vol. 76(2), E.A. Franz, H.N. Zelaznik, and G. McCabe, 1991, "Spatial topological constraints in a bimanual task," pp. 137-151. Copyright 1991, with permission from Elsevier.

place the dancers in pairs facing each other, and have one dancer land on the downbeat while the other dancer lands on the upbeat. This simple task of jumping in first position suddenly becomes far more difficult than the original assignment. This example highlights the added level of complexity of social coordination.

The idea of social coordination deals with a concept called *entrainment.* In simple terms, entrainment is the coordination of organisms to an external rhythm or two or more organisms to each other. It is not uncommon for people walking together or sitting in side-by-side rocking chairs to end up in the same rhythm. Entrainment aids in group task performance in which synchronization is the goal, which is often the case in choreography. In addition, it encourages group cohesion on a social level. Researchers hypothesize that entrainment in the context of people practicing together aids in learning individual tasks demanding precision in timing. This aspect of entrainment suggests that dancers learn individual skills more effectively if they practice in unison with other dancers. Teachers should consider encouraging dancers in class to be aware of the process of entrainment instead of having the dancers focus entirely on themselves and their own movement execution. Finally, entrainment offers a means for physical mirroring as in dance, or for metaphorical mirroring as in empathy. Mirror neurons and the mirror system are examined in more detail in chapter 12.

Many sensory variables can contribute to the ability to coordinate as a group. Both vision and sound are important aspects for groups of dancers. Dancers listen to the music while they take in visual cues from their partners. Notice that in the previous jumping example, the music was assisting in the task, but vision was

Figure 10.4 Dancers in William (Bill) Evans' choreography *Velorio* rely on the sensation of weight transfer to assist in unison timing.

actually intruding. If the pairs are placed back to back, they are much better at achieving the task. A far more subtle sense that contributes to social coordination is the sense of touch, both tactile and haptic. In circular and weight sharing dance formations where dancers are in physical contact, such as the dance *Velorio* by William (Bill) Evans (figure 10.4), the dancers use the sensation of weight shift of the dancers on either side of them to stay in unison. Many novice dancers are under the illusion that if they know the musical counts, they will be in unison with the other dancers. However, they must learn to be receptive to *all* available feedback.

Speed, accuracy, and coordination are three aspects of high-level motor control for dancers, and it is breathtaking when all three converge. Lord of the Dance, Stomp, Twyla Tharp, New York City Ballet, Theta Nu Theta, the Nicholas Brothers, La La Human Steps, and the Rockettes are just a few of the dazzling professional dancers and companies that excel at integrating speed, accuracy, and coordination. The best dancers spend hours practicing material at slow speed and gradually increasing speed to achieve accuracy. They break down multi-limb coordination one limb at a time and build the phrase slowly. They spend days working alone on material in order to come together with other dancers to

perfect spatial and musical clarity. Only through determination and patience can these aspects of high-level dance performance be achieved.

Summary

Speed and accuracy follow Fitts' law, which describes the speed–accuracy trade-off. This chapter explored three conditions: two spatial and one temporal. The two spatial conditions look at cyclic, repetitive tasks and single-movement discrete aiming tasks. For these tasks, as speed increases, accuracy decreases. On the other hand, for the temporal condition, as speed increases, accuracy also increases. Coordination involves the patterning of the movements of the head, body, arms, and legs, as well as how the body parts relate to the environment, including objects and circumstances. Two concerns in the area of coordination are the degrees of freedom problem and the development of coordinative structures. Coordination can be explored in terms of timing, spatial, and social coordination. Each of these areas demands a different aspect of integrating coordinative patterns into complex activity. Finally, the merger of these three facets of dance performance creates the elite dancer that audiences love to watch.

Part III

Motor Learning

Chapter 11

Theories and Concepts of Motor Learning

otor learning is present in all facets of human experience. It is a major part of every person's life, including the recreational tennis player, the professional chef, a couple of girls braiding each other's hair, and the elite athlete or dancer. In dance, motor learning is the means by which dancers learn both basic and complex skills. These skills are not attained through the motor development that all children experience, such as walking, skipping, and grasping objects. They may include pirouettes, large jumps, tap dance sequences, and balances that are not part of everyday movement. Further, the dance teacher's goal is to teach skills so that they are executed with smoothness, expressivity, coordination, and accuracy, and so that they are retained in the dancer's memory. The dancer's objective is not simply to learn the skills but to achieve a level of proficiency that enhances movement quality.

Throughout the history of motor learning, several theories have emerged, and they now fall under two general classifications. These categories relate to the two broad types of motor control described in chapters 8 and 9, namely, centrally controlled (brain and spinal cord) and environmentally driven (responding to input from the senses) mechanisms. Some theories are interested in stages of learning (how beginner and advanced learners differ in their processes and how learners progress from one stage to the next). In addition, theories of motor learning include descriptions of various forms of learning and whether learners are consciously aware of their procedures in the learning experience or learn through repetition without any awareness. For example, children learn how to write through intentional methods, but they learn how to get to their school simply by observing the trip every day without making any attempts to memorize the route. Finally, researchers have been interested in differences between procedural learning (which takes place when a movement skill is automat-

The continuous turns done with the leg held to the side in second position is a complex skill traditionally taught to male ballet dancers.

ically repeated over and over and requires no attention to the mechanisms of the movement) and declarative learning (which occurs when what is learned can be expressed in declared sentences, and involves attention and reflection). For example, when dancers learn a how to do series of steps by following the teacher, it is procedural; when they learn the names of steps and can recall them, it is declarative. Dancers and dance teachers are involved in motor learning every day as part of the training experience, and a better understanding of the theoretical underpinnings of motor learning can enhance the process.

Theories of Motor Learning

Motor learning describes the relatively permanent changes associated with practice or experience that govern a person's capability for generating a motor skill. Although the outcome of motor learning is comparatively permanent, the motor system remains capable of change throughout the life span. Most people relate motor learning to the acquisition of skills. Motor learning also refers to changing aspects of motor control, such as how to use core support during turns or how to improve the aesthetic appearance of a balance. Motor learning of higher-level skills can be based in **motor program–based theory**, which emphasizes rules or structures existing in the brain that can direct a general group or class of movements. For example, if dancers are taught how to do pliés in first position, they can apply the rules to pliés in other leg positions. Motor learning of higher-level skills can also be based on **systems theory**, which emphasizes interaction with the environment. For example, young children in dance classes can learn how to jump by jumping over real or imaginary objects.

This chapter explores both theoretical constructs in developing an understanding of motor learning as it applies to dance. In addition, this broad theoretical base will provide a variety of possible teaching and learning strategies to increase effectiveness in dance training. Examining the history of the field fosters an appreciation for the evolution and breadth of current ideas about motor learning.

Adams' Closed-Loop Theory

Jack Adams, a psychologist in the 1970s, was the first researcher to put together a motor learning theory. Although this theory is now viewed as limited, its basic principles help to form the basis for some of the later, more developed theories.

In Adams' theory, people need sensory feedback (information from senses such as vision and touch) to monitor movement and movement outcomes. This feedback is particularly necessary in the early stages of learning in order to direct efforts to achieve the movement, and to detect and correct errors for improved performance. To learn a movement, two states of memory are necessary, the memory trace and the perceptual trace. The **memory trace** is theorized to select and to initiate the movement in the appropriate direction. Practice and feedback can strengthen the memory trace. The **perceptual trace**, also known as *internal reference of correctness*, serves to compare the movement in progress with the correct version of the movement in the memory. Through repeated practice and correction of errors, attempts at movements become more accurate, and the perceptual trace becomes increasingly useful. According to Adams' theory, the way to create a strong perceptual trace is to practice doing the identical movement over and over with ongoing error correction. Practice does not make perfect; practice makes permanent. Both the memory trace and the perceptual trace are necessary, because one trace cannot be both initiator and comparator.

For example, when dancers are learning to turn, their initial introduction to the turn starts to create a memory trace. The next time they attempt the turn, this memory trace initiates the turn with the patterns first learned. The perceptual trace compares what the dancers are doing with the model or reference of the turn as the teacher demonstrated it. Through the comparison, the dancers can accomplish the turn better in the next attempt. Each time the turn is executed, it becomes closer to the ideal version, and the perceptual memory is more clearly and more firmly embedded for future use.

It is now known that humans can make purposeful movements in a total absence of

Difficult leaps such as this one require extended practice in order to perform with ease.

sensory feedback. Further, the brain can compare knowledge of results of motor actions with stored memories in the absence of sensory information during the movement. Adams' theory does not account for these situations, and therefore it is limited in its scope.

Schmidt's Schema Theory

Cognitive psychologist Richard Schmidt developed a theory emphasizing the open-loop process, which is the most widely known of the motor program–based theories of motor control. An **open-loop process** (also called an *open-loop system*) does not use sensory feedback about the movement itself during the movement in order to change the motor plan, such as the calypso leap in jazz dance. However, incoming information about the environment is still needed in order to accomplish the task. These movements are typically rapid, the necessary information for movement execution is included in the instructions, and once they are triggered, they proceed to completion.

Schmidt proposed that when people explore new actions, rather than learn movement spe-

cifics, they learn generalized rules for groups of movements. These rules can be used in a wide variety of situations. A similar construct exists in language. Consider a child seeing an automobile for the first time and being taught the word *car*. At first the child thinks *car* is the name of that one vehicle. However, after seeing several varieties of cars, the child forms a general picture of cars and can then identify a car even if it is a model that the child has never seen. In dance, a similar example might be turns on one leg that remain in one place. Dancers might first be taught a turn en dehors (turning in the direction of the lifted leg). They might first learn it with the lifted leg at the ankle of the supporting leg, then try it with the lifted leg at the knee of the supporting leg. Next they might be asked to try different arm positions. In more advanced classes, they might learn how to change arm and lifted-leg positions while doing multiple turns. Each of these possibilities is a variation on the generalized rule for turns en dehors.

Schmidt's theory deals with some of the expressed limitations of Adams' theory, such as the ability to create movement without sensory information. In Schmidt's theory, movement can be achieved using a representational model of the movement, following through to completion without the aid of sensory input about the movement itself, although considerable sensory information regulating posture and balance may well be needed. An example of an open-loop process would be dancers executing a fast drop to the floor. Another problem with Adams' theory is that it would be impossible to store every single variation of every movement learned, which could exceed the human brain's memory capacity. With Schmidt's theory, many movements fall under one general rule, and the memory can handle the models for various classes of movements.

The central theme of this theory is the concept of schema, which Schmidt applied to motor learning. The notion of a **schema** states that one can store in memory an abstract classification of an object; in other words, it can store a set of rules that is representational. Figure 11.1 demonstrates the concept of schema as it relates to the dance movement sissonne. During the training process, dancers learn to recognize all of the variations as the sissonne step, even when learning a new variation that they have not seen before. The general schema of the sissonne (jumping from two feet to one foot) makes it easier to learn the variations.

Schmidt claimed that each time a movement is made, these four elements are stored:

1. Conditions at the start of the movement (such as weight or position of the body)

2. Parameters that can be varied (such as force, tempo, and velocity)

3. Sensory consequences (such as how the movement felt and appeared)

4. Knowledge of results (the outcome)

These four elements are eventually abstracted to a schema in two sections, and the motor program contains both. The first is the **recall schema**, the motor portion, which is used for selecting the specific response desired. Each time variations of a particular movement are attempted, the recall schema develops an association between specific parameters and the result of the movement. Each attempt adds more information to the recall schema and broadens the generalized rule for this class of movements. The specifics may alter with new attempts and variations, but the rule of the recall schema applies.

The second is the **recognition schema**, the sensory portion, which is used to evaluate the response and update the motor program to correct for error. The recognition schema contains sensory consequences and outcomes of previous movements. These factors are compared to the current attempt, and a model of the movement is developed. Therefore, the more variety that exists in practice, the stronger the schema once a model of the movement has been established. In this theory, learning is dependent on constantly updating the recognition schema by adding the results of new attempts that are understood through knowledge of results. In addition to predicting that variability of practice improves learning, Schmidt's theory also suggests that a movement

Figure 11.1 Sissonne in an open position, moving forward with legs externally rotated. Sissonne is a jump from both feet to one foot, landing with the gesture leg in an open position or with the second foot quickly closing into first position or fifth position with the landing foot. The sissonne can be done moving forward, side, or back, with the gesture leg at different heights, and with the hip of the gesture leg in external rotation or both hips in parallel.

never before attempted can be done effectively if it is based on a previously developed rule. In the example of dancers learning turns, once they have practiced a sufficient variety of turns en dehors, they can achieve a new leg or arm configuration in a turn at a high level of skill. While the concept of variability of practice seems reasonable, it has not yet been indisputably supported in research, and it seems to be dependent on the type of task and the type of learner. For example, research on children seems more supportive of the use of variable practice for motor learning than research on adults. This difference may occur because adults are generally experienced in a broad range of movement skills, whereas children are totally naive to many new movements and have not yet formed schemas.

In addition to the recall and recognition schemas, a central idea in Schmidt's theory is the generalized motor program (GMP), which is described in detail in chapter 9. A **generalized motor program (GMP)** is a program that allows the motor system to execute an entire class of similar actions. It is stored in the memory, and it requires that various parameters be added preceding execution. It permits the motor system to be adaptable in doing variations of the motor program. **Parameters** are aspects such as speed, force, and body parts that can vary from one execution of the GMP to another. **Invariant features** are called the *signature* of the GMP. They are the aspects that do not change from one action within the same class as another. The GMP theory is particularly relevant for ballistic and fast movements, in which lack of time restricts the ability to use feedback.

One of the limitations of Schmidt's theory posed by other researchers is the problem of how a person can initiate the first trial of a movement before any schema exists—how new types of coordination develop. For example, on the television series *So You Think You Can Dance*, classically trained ballet dancers immediately learn krumping or Bollywood dancing when learning new choreography without any previous coordination patterns resembling these styles.

Male dancer executing the dance form known as krumping.

Ecological Theory

Newer theories of motor learning began to emerge in the late 1970s. These theories were generated by ideas from ecological theory or ecological perspective, detailed in chapter 2. This approach emphasizes the interactions between the individual, the environment, and the task. In this view, actions need information from the environment (perceptual information) that is specific to the desired motor action.

Karl Newell is a well-known ecological motor theorist, writing his seminal work in 1991. Newell's theory draws on ideas from both the dynamic systems theory and the ecological perspective. The dynamic systems theory considers the body as a mechanical system, and it views behavior as emerging from the interaction of the physical/nervous system and the environment. This concept combined with the idea that perceptual information is necessary to learn movement skills, creating Newell's theory. According to Newell, learning is done through search strategies, and one must search through the perceptual-motor workspace to solve a new motor problem. The **perceptual-motor workspace** is part of the thinking processes that consider both relevant sensory cues and the best possible motor strategies to achieve the goal. This theory emphasizes exploration and active problem solving in order to develop new movement skills. Through this process, the person eventually develops optimal abilities in motor skills. Newell suggests these three ways that teachers can assist their students in motor learning:

1. Help the learner understand the perceptual-motor workspace.

2. Appreciate the intuitive search strategies used by people learning movement.

3. Provide additional information to enable the exploration.

Teaching leaps is one example that elucidates these three methods. If a teacher is teaching leaps to a group of dancers, first the teacher might encourage the dancers to sense the floor and how its surface and resilience will affect the jumping technique. They might also explore what motor strategy, such as push-off with the feet, might create the best height. Second, the teacher can acknowledge and support how dancers experiment with timing and use of arms and legs to get good elevation. Third, the teacher can provide feedback about ways the dancers can improve these strategies to enhance jump height.

In addition, teachers can encourage exploration and active problem solving by posing questions rather than offering solutions. For example, if dancers are losing their balance during a particular portion of a combination, the teacher might ask, "Why do you think you are struggling with your balance? Have you considered your strategy for the weight transfer to one foot at that point? Are you engaging your core support? What is happening with your visual focus? Are your arms assisting in counterbalance? How might you time them differently

for a different result?" Then the teacher would need to give the dancers time to experiment with each of these ideas.

Ecological theory addresses the limitations of previous theories in dealing with the acquisition of novel movements and new coordination. Because movement is learned through exploration and experimentation, it is not necessary to have a model or schema of the movement in order to attempt it. One concept advanced by this theory is that a skill will most likely be useful in a new context if it is learned initially in a context that is similar.

In this text both schema theory and ecological theory are presented as the bases for motor learning. Dancers rely on representational models of movement (or schema) to organize classes of movement and make learning and executing new variations of skills easier. These schemas can be useful in both daily training as well as in working with a new choreographer. Schema theory allows dancers to be increasingly versatile and efficient at learning dance skills as the demands on dancers continue to escalate. In addition, exploration of the environment has importance in the context of motor learning. Dancers who explore the environment and are active problem solvers are more effective in the training and performance settings. As choreographers incorporate improvisation and technique fusions into their work, dancers are required to rely on recognizing relevant sensory cues and determining the best possible motor strategies. Teachers and choreographers should aim to acknowledge and integrate all of the methods that the various motor learning theories provide.

Stages of Motor Learning

Another theoretical approach to understanding motor learning looks at stages that people pass through over time. Consider walking into a club where people are engaged in Argentine tango. It is almost immediately apparent who the beginners are and who the experts are. In addition to the clear differences in coordination, the experts seem easeful in their execution and appear to have ample time to attend to the

The Argentine tango is a complex partner dance. It takes years to achieve an advanced level.

relationship with their partners. In contrast, the beginners seem to struggle more with the steps and need to spend most of their concentration on executing the dance form.

Two main theories examine stages of learning and explain what occurs over time as people become more proficient at a skill. Fitts and Posner proposed a three-stage model, and Gentile proposed a two-stage model. The following sections describe these theories and provide examples from dance to clarify the learning phases.

Fitts and Posner's Three-Stage Model

Psychologists and researchers Paul Fitts and Michael Posner proposed a model for stages of learning in 1967, and it is still considered useful today. Their theory proposes that learning a skill occurs in these three stages: the cognitive stage, the associative stage, and the autonomous stage. This theory's simplicity and practicality are among many reasons it is attractive for coaches and dance teachers to apply in training.

Defining the Stages

During the first stage (the **cognitive stage**), the student learns to understand the nature of the task, develops new strategies for solving the task, and learns to determine how best to evaluate which strategy to apply. This stage requires much attention, and the student experiments with many different strategies. In addition, the student listens to substantial feedback and relies on assistance from the teacher. Performance tends to be variable with many errors, and improvements are large. In this stage, learners are often aware when something is wrong, but they do not know how to improve it. They begin to learn how to assess their own abilities and to develop the selective attention necessary for the various aspects of the task. The primary goal of this stage is learning what to do.

During the second stage (the **associative stage**), the skill is being refined, meaning that spatial and temporal components of the skill become better organized. The movement shows less variability from one trial to the next, and subsequently improvement is slower. No specific amount of practice or level of improvement determines when the student enters this stage. The verbal and cognitive aspects are less important in this second stage, because the student has learned to associate the appropriate environmental conditions with what is required. Errors are less frequent and less extreme, and the student is learning to identify and correct errors without the teacher's assistance. The weight of feedback begins to shift from visual to proprioceptive. The primary goal of this stage is to improve the motor pattern organization.

The final stage (the **autonomous stage**) requires little or no attention, and it only occurs after ample practice and experience with the task. Action is fairly automatic (habitual), and the person can do the task and attend to other tasks simultaneously. In fact, in this stage paying too much attention to components of the skill can actually decrease performance. Variability in this stage is small; in other words, repeated executions have excellent consistency. It is critical to practice the task in different environments and conditions. In the autonomous stage, students can detect and correct their own errors. Fitts and Posner believed that it is not possible for everyone to reach the autonomous stage of a given task. Factors that determine whether or not this phase can be achieved include the quality of instruction and the quality and amount of practice. The primary goal of this stage is developing a high level of skill and performing at that level consistently.

Learning Strategies

Teachers and dancers can utilize awareness of the three stages in determining the best methods for working on a new skill. Consider a group of dancers learning a stag leap, in which the front leg is bent and the back leg is straight, or both legs are bent. In the cognitive stage, the dancers need to concentrate intensely on organizing the leg actions and possibly arm movement coordi-nation at the same time. The teacher can begin by highlighting the purpose and form of the leap and demonstrating accurately. The teacher can also use other students as models, which can help dancers solve problems and learn to differentiate discrepancies in execution. Errors are frequent, and the dancers demonstrate considerable variation from one attempt to the next. If the teacher or another student distracts the dancer who is attempting the stag leap, it will most likely be poorly executed. For slower skills, the teacher can use hands-on (tactile) guidance, such as using light touch to direct the shape of the arms while the dancers slowly practice the upper extremities. Breaking up complex movements into component parts is useful in the cognitive stage.

In the associative stage, the dancers are beginning to refine the movement. They are more consistent in the relationship, timing, and shape design of the two legs, and fewer errors occur in terms of the articulation of the legs and their shape. In addition, the dancers begin to understand how to correct their own errors. Teachers should encourage and guide dancers in their abilities to self-correct, perhaps by asking questions such as why the dancers thought their bodies bucked during the leap, or why the landing was very abrupt. This may be a better teaching strategy in the associative stage than telling the dancers what they did incorrectly each time. In the associative stage, variability with practice expands the motor pattern (schema) and encourages versatility.

In the autonomous stage, dancers can execute the stag leap with little attention. They can concentrate on other aspects, such as staying in unison with other dancers, and their use of the space, and even less variability occurs from one leap to the next. It is increasingly important for teachers to challenge dancers with speed and accuracy demands as well as with appropriate distracters such as changing the music or the spatial pattern regularly. In the autonomous stage, the teacher should place increasing emphasis on letting the dancers self-correct, even with new and untried variations of a skill. During this stage, many learners are unable to verbally express how all of the elements of the movement are performed. In fact, they exhibit a

The stag leap demands coordination, using the lower limbs in differing shapes and using all of the limbs to assist in elevation.

loss of immediate conscious recall of the more specialized elements of the skill. This change is why so many highly skilled athletes and dancers are not necessarily the best coaches and teachers. At this point, the learner who wishes to teach must cognitively analyze the movement, using declarative learning to understand the components of the skill execution in order to share these components with others.

When teachers are able to recognize the signs of progression from one stage to the next, they are more effective in pacing the learning process. Teachers can recognize the students moving from one phase to the next by observing the amount of variability, aptitude in rapidly learning new variations, and whether or not conscious attention to detail is necessary. Each of the stages of learning in the Fitts and Posner's three-stage model has different activities and focus, and these variations require flexibility in teaching strategies. When they understand their students and acknowledge what their learning process needs to be, teachers can be successful guides in the practice.

Gentile's Two-Stage Model

In the 1970s, professor of psychology and education Antoinette Gentile developed a two-stage model of motor learning that emphasized the goal of the learner. The two stages are called the *initial stage* and the *later stages*. The plural name of the second category suggests more than one stage; it is actually a collection of stages. Gentile's model places a large emphasis on the type of skill and how it influences goals and subsequent approaches to learning new skills.

Defining the Stages

In the **initial stage**, the learner has these two goals: acquiring movement coordination patterns and learning to discriminate between regulatory and nonregulatory conditions. The first goal in the initial stage, **movement coordination patterns**, allows for the correct organization of the body parts in order to achieve the movement goal in the context of the appropriate environmental conditions. For dancers, these conditions might be the amount of space each dancer needs to use or the timing of the music that will determine the temporal structure. Environmental conditions that affect the success of the movement goal are called **regulatory conditions**. In addition to space and timing, regulatory conditions might include props, set pieces, and other dancers, especially in partnering and improvisational work.

The second goal in the initial stage is learning to discriminate between regulatory and nonregulatory conditions, or those conditions that do and do not affect movement execution. Dancers need to focus on the skills and combinations they are executing, the music accompanying their work, the space and any possible obstacles, and other dancers involved in what they are doing. If dancers attend to unnecessary conditions while dancing, their attention is compromised. For example, dancers must learn to ignore sounds occurring in or around the space that do not affect the dancing, such as noise coming from outside the dance space. If this discriminating ability is not developed, dancers can be very distracted in performance when audience members cough or babies cry. Another possible nonregulatory condition would be movement in the wings that catch the dancer's eye. If technicians or other dancers need to move around backstage, the onstage performers need to ignore these distracters.

Gentile describes strategies for the movement learner in the initial stage. First, the learner uses trial and error (experimentation), and both successful and unsuccessful attempts inform the learner about progress. Second, the learner engages in problem-solving activities, and a high level of cognitive involvement is necessary. By the end of the initial stage, the learner has a good general concept of the skill and how to approach it, but the learner is not yet consistent or efficient in execution.

In the **later stages**, these three characteristics must be achieved: adaptability, consistency, and economy of effort. **Adaptability** means that the learner must develop the ability to use the skill in any context or environment required. If dancers can do excellent pirouettes in a simple exercise but cannot execute them in a longer combination or at a different speed, they are not adaptable in the skill. **Consistency** means that

the dancer can execute the skill in the same way each time, and that variation from one trial to the next is small. When tap dancers execute a series of complex steps in a combination, they must be able to repeat it with the same speed, precision, and musicality each time. **Economy of effort** (also called *efficiency*) means that the dancer does not use more effort than is necessary in order to achieve the task. This idea can be a bit confusing for dancers. It does not mean that the minimum muscular effort is always the goal. It means that the minimum effort for that particular skill or event must be exerted. If dancers are in a class or a dance work requiring very bound (effortful) muscle use in order to achieve a certain dynamic or aesthetic effect, high exertion would be appropriate economy of effort in that context. This quality is apparent

The tap dancer demonstrates speed, precision, and musicality in the later stages of learning.

in Graham technique and in certain forms of street dance. In the instances described, more experienced dancers use far more muscular effort than dancers who are in the initial stages of learning these styles.

Learning Strategies

One aspect that differentiates Gentile's model from Fitts and Posner's model is that the goal for the learner differs depending on the type of skill, closed or open. This concept is different from open-loop *processes* (or systems) and closed-loop *processes* (or systems), which deal with movement instructions preceding movement execution and the use of movement feedback during the movement. **Closed skills** are skills that are done precisely the same way each time, such as the 32-fouetté pirouette combination en pointe in classical ballet. In terms of processes, however, the fouetté is an open-loop process, because once the movement is initiated, it cannot be easily altered in mid-turn. Another aspect of closed skills is that they place little demand on the performer from changing environmental conditions, such as whether or not the dancer tries to move through space doing the fouettés or whether other dancers will interfere with the execution. With repeated practice the skill becomes more consistent and efficient, which is known as **fixation**. Dancers spend many hours over several months practicing the same skill in the identical pattern in order to enhance consistent execution. They work toward the goal of eventually executing the skill with little conscious thought.

Open skills are skills that need to be done in many variations of timing, gestures, and spacing, such as leaps. They usually involve conditions that are frequently changing, such as a wide range of tempos and use of space. Introducing increasing variations of an open skill encourages **diversification**, the ability to modify the skill to multiple conditions and requirements and to adapt quickly. The dancers can attempt different arm gestures during the leap and change facings in a series of leaps. Dancers can work in different tempos and rhythmic structures, such as 2/4 or 3/4 time. In a modern or contemporary dance class, teachers can introduce the use of torso movements during various leaps. With varied practice the skill becomes more diversified, and dancers can adapt rapidly to changes in music and spacing. Figure 11.2 shows the difference in development between closed and open skills.

Finally, how movement is modified between varying trials differs between closed and open skills. For closed skills, parameters such as movement force or speed may need to vary, but the invariant features (the basic pattern or coordination) of the skill do not. In the case of the dancer doing the 32-fouetté pirouette combination en pointe, she may need to accelerate if the

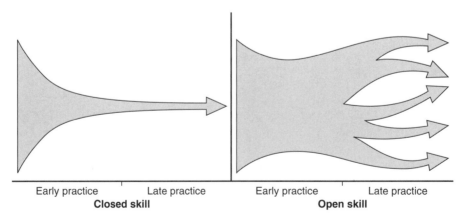

Early practice   Late practice
Closed skill

Early practice   Late practice
Open skill

Figure 11.2 Schematic representation of movement patterns associated with open versus closed motor skills. Closed skills require refinement of a single or limited number of movement patterns (movement consistency); in contrast, open skills require a diversity of movement patterns (movement diversity).

© 1979 From *Quest*, 17(1), 61-69, "Relationship between consistency of movement and environmental conditions" by J.R. Higgins and R.A. Spaeth. Reproduced by permission of Taylor & Francis LLC (http://www.tandfonline.com).

orchestra plays faster one evening or use more effort if the floor is sticky. In these situations, however, the basic coordination pattern of the turn does not vary. For open skills, either the parameters or the invariant features may need to be modified. For leaps, in addition to potential changes in force or speed, doing a brush or straight-leg initiation is a different coordination than doing a développé initiation, as is using arms in opposition or using the same arm and leg forward. Doing choreography with improvisational elements demands an even higher degree of adaptability and ongoing monitoring of the environment.

Changes Across Learning Stages

In both Fitts and Posner's model and Gentile's model of motor learning, learners show certain characteristics as they pass through the various stages. Examining these characteristics can explain why a variety of instructional strategies need to be created for the various learning stages. These characteristics include changes in the following:

- *Improvement rate.* Rate of improvement decreases as learners become more advanced. Big improvements occur in early stages, and improvements slow down in later stages. This relationship is called the **power law of practice**. Although improvement is rapid in the early stages, it is fragile and can easily be lost. On the other hand, learning is much slower in the later stages, but it is robust and much more likely to sustain over time.

- *Coordination.* In the early stages of learning, performers must solve the **degrees of freedom problem**, which is a control problem for the motor system to determine how to limit the many degrees of freedom in order to achieve coordinated movement and accomplish a task. At first, the motor systems of learners freeze degrees of freedom (restrict movement), and later the rigid joints are released (freed) for better coordination. Neither phase is a conscious choice of the learner but happens through the practice stages.

- *Adjustments to familiar movement patterns or habits.* When learners are attempting

a skill that resembles a skill already known, they show movement biases. Later, they learn to adopt new and more useful strategies.

- *Muscle selection during a skill.* In early learning stages, more muscles are used than are needed, and timing of activation is often incorrect. Later, the number of muscles used decreases, and timing of muscle activation improves.

- *Use of energy (movement economy).* In early stages of learning, performers use excessive amounts of energy, and in later stages, economy of movement or efficiency is the goal, with the added benefit of delayed fatigue.

- *Attention to meaningful visual cues.* As learning progresses from early to later stages, performers become more effective at visually focusing on what is needed in order to accomplish the task.

- *Demands on conscious attention.* The beginner needs to think about almost every aspect of a new skill, but the experienced learner can diminish conscious attention to the task until it becomes automatic.

- *Ability to detect and correct errors.* In the early stages, even when learners know that they have made an error, they are incapable of knowing how to correct it. In the later stages, learners can both detect and correct their own errors.

- *Activity in the brain.* Brain areas active in early stages of learning are different from the areas of the brain active in later stages.

Regardless of the theoretical construct of the stages of motor learning, the theories support the idea that all learners pass through various stages to move from a beginner to an advanced mover in a particular skill. Returning to the Argentine tango example, it is now clear why the beginners are attending consciously to their movements, seem to use far more tension than necessary, fail to time their movements well, and could definitely benefit from feedback from an instructor. The advanced dancers seem effortless in their skills, are attending to their partners and the music, and have clearly invested many hours of practice in attaining both consistency and adaptability. The theories and stages of learning can assist dance teachers in being sensitive to the needs of their students at the various stages in their training.

Forms of Motor Learning

Aside from theories and stages of motor learning, several forms of learning affect dancers. Through the process of training, dancers experience various types of learning. For example, some forms of dance are learned in group settings without consciously breaking down or analyzing the movement. Other forms are analyzed and taught in component parts with the teacher expecting attention and reflection from the students. Basically, forms of motor learning can be divided into nondeclarative and declarative learning.

Nondeclarative Learning

Nondeclarative learning (also called *implicit learning*) refers to learning without conscious effort, and it is acquired simply through repeated exposure. Children often learn basic dance skills such as jumps and turns by copying the teacher and absorbing the motor patterns unconsciously. Nondeclarative learning can be further divided into nonassociative, associative, and procedural learning.

Nonassociative Learning

Nonassociative learning occurs when one stimulus is given repeatedly and the nervous system learns the characteristics of that stimulus. The two main forms of nonassociative learning are habituation and sensitization. **Habituation** occurs when frequent exposure to a nonpainful stimulus causes decreased receptiveness. It is neurologically the simplest form of learning. A common example might be that if dancers hear children yelling and playing in the next studio during a dance rehearsal, eventually they will no longer notice the noise and can concentrate easily on the rehearsal. **Sensitization** occurs when frequent exposure to a possibly threatening stimulus causes increased receptiveness. For example, if a dancer receives a painful grab by her partner in a lift attempt, then the next time

that the partner grasps her gently to do the lift, her response will be much stronger than usual, even to light touch.

Associative Learning

Associative learning occurs when two ideas or stimuli are associated together. For example, dancers become so conditioned when hearing music in their practice that they often unconsciously move in their seats when they see a dance concert. Movement and music become associated together. Sometimes associative learning can establish a cause and effect scenario. A dancer might think, *During my weight transfer from two feet to one foot, I lifted one hip, causing me to lose balance.* The two most common forms of associative learning are classical conditioning and operant conditioning.

Classical conditioning helps a person to predict relationships between two stimuli in the environment. The most famous example of classical conditioning was Pavlov and his experiments with dogs. He took a strong stimulus (food), which had an unconditioned response (the dogs salivated), and he associated it with a weak stimulus (the ringing of a bell), which had no response. Eventually the bell, called the unconditioned stimulus, became effective in soliciting the response, even without the presence of food, the conditioned stimulus. Because the bell and the food were associated together, the dogs responded to the bell as if food were present. This form of conditioning is reflexive, not voluntary.

Operant conditioning is trial-and-error learning, and it is voluntary. Eventually a person learns to associate a certain response among many with a particular desired consequence. This form of learning follows the **law of effect**, which states that rewarded behaviors are selected at the cost of other behaviors, and the reverse is also true; that is, aversive or noxious stimuli can cause behavior to decrease with respect to other behaviors. Skinner performed the classic experiments in this form of learning with rats. The rats were put in cages and received food by touching a certain lever. As the rats learned that touching the lever gave them food, lever pressing increased while other behaviors decreased.

Dancers can learn movement skills involving shape or body design by associating body formations of groups of dancers with known forms.

Another form of associative learning that dancers experience is sometimes referred to as **sensory learning**, which refers to gaining knowledge simply by what is taken in through the senses. Experienced touring performers might walk into the performing space, look around once, and then go directly to the dressing room to prepare for the show. They can absorb through visual information everything they will need in order to space the choreography without having to physically mark the pieces in the new space. Dancers' abilities to adapt to this new stage in order to do a good performance is dependent on how well they remember the sensory experiences of the stage's specific dimensions, how center and quarter stage are marked, what obstacles are present in the wings, where the stage lights are focused, how large the audience area is and how it is distributed, where the offstage changing areas are located, how the floor surface will affect turns, and a multitude of other facts about the space, taken in on the sensory (visual) level.

Procedural Learning

Procedural learning refers to acquiring a movement skill by automatically repeating it over and over, and it requires no conscious attention to the mechanisms of the movement. Learning develops slowly through high repetition, and it is expressed through improved performance. If the practice involves varied forms of the task, it may facilitate formulating a schema, which was discussed in the section titled Schmidt's Schema Theory. An example of procedural learning is learning to tie shoelaces. Dancers use extensive repetition of skills in the learning process, often without analysis or extensive verbal instructions. This form of learning is controlled by the cerebellum.

Declarative Learning

Declarative learning, also called *explicit learning*, results in knowledge that can consciously be recalled, and it requires attention and reflection. It is not actually a form of motor learning, but it may assist in learning motor skills, such as learning the names of steps or skills in dance class. What is learned can be expressed in declarative sentences, and the process involves actually thinking or saying the rules while doing the action. Often declarative learning requires remembering factual knowledge, such as learning the names of the various ballet positions, or learning the sequence of exercises in a codified technique. It also includes learning facts and events, because dancers might be in an anatomy or dance history class. This form of learning is controlled by the cortex.

In some dance settings, particularly in the public school system, dance classes are expected to cover a wide array of dance-related topics, including composition, dance history, dancer health, anatomy, ethnology, and dance criticism, to name a few. The students in these programs may only have a physical dance practice a few days a week, for an hour or two at most. The teachers in these programs can assist their students' development by using declarative learning to reinforce the physical practice. For example, alignment issues the dancers are addressing in technique class can be discussed in the context of anatomy and learning terminology. Dance history discussions can overlap with technique. Teachers can have students verbally name and describe dance steps, and they have them present their own projects on the historical foundations of these steps. Dancers can discuss a performance they have seen from a critical perspective, but they can also reflect on their own physical practice and the comparisons they observe. Declarative learning can play a role in broadening and accelerating physical training if the students are conscious of the connections between their various studies.

Many forms of motor learning exist, and dancers can use the wide variety to enhance their dance training. When they begin learning dance, many dancers have a bias. Some dancers prefer to model after the teacher or other dancers and do not consciously try to learn new skills. Other dancers are more comfortable breaking down the movements and attending to the rules and structures of the material. Teachers can best address the whole class if they encourage and allow for a variety of learning forms and techniques in their classes. And dancers will make optimal gains in the learning environment if they challenge themselves to use various forms in their daily practice.

Learning Styles

So far the focus of this chapter has been on the theoretical models that address how dancers learn. Most dancers realize that they have preferences about how they learn. Some dancers prefer to see the material and learn it through visual means. Other dancers need to analyze or break down the material and reflect on it. Some dancers cannot learn a phrase of movement unless the rhythmic structure is clearly delineated. And still other dancers learn best if the teacher or another student uses tactile cueing. **Learning styles** can be defined simply as the way people approach learning something new. In order to help dancers understand their learning preferences and to assist teachers in broadening their strategies for relaying information to dancers, the following text discusses two theoretical models for differences in learning styles.

Gardner's Theory of Multiple Intelligences

Developmental psychologist Howard Gardner created his theory of multiple intelligences in the 1980s. Gardner theorized that humans do not have a general intelligence factor that operates for several abilities; they have multiple intelligences that operate independently in guiding learning. He describes eight intelligences that act as determinants of learning:

1. Linguistic: the use of words, written or spoken
2. Logical/mathematical: ability to reason, consider abstractions, use numerical skills
3. Spatial: awareness of space and how objects and the self occupy space
4. Musical: a sense of rhythm, pitch, and musical composition
5. Bodily/kinesthetic: a sense of the body and movement ability
6. Interpersonal: interactions with others
7. Intrapersonal: awareness of self and personal goals and standards
8. Naturalistic: relating to the laws of nature and the natural surroundings

Two main criticisms exist regarding this theory. First, in testing humans, some studies indicate a high correlation between different aspects of intelligence. Generally people who learn well in one area do well in others, which is not what Gardner predicted. This research supports general intelligence, not multiple intelligences. On the other hand, studies also exist that refute this point of view, and they demonstrate that people can excel in some areas of intelligence while being very poor at others. This issue is still to be resolved. Second, no empirical evidence or research outcomes support this theory. At this time it is only supported by subjective observations. Therefore, for the purposes of this text, the theory is considered as a model for examining various learning styles. Dance teachers can enhance their teaching methods by incorporating explanations and exercises that allow for a range of learning preferences, and dancers can become aware of their biases and broaden how they approach new material. Gardner's work serves to aid teachers in identifying areas of strength and areas where growth is needed in their students.

McCarthy and Kolb: Combining Two Theories

Educator and author Bernice McCarthy described four learning styles in her educational system, which she named 4MAT:

- Dynamic: experimentation and trial-and-error, risk takers, intuitive

- Innovative: social interactions and discussion, cooperative

- Common sense: hands-on and practical, more cautious

- Analytic: logical, seek facts in systematic ways

David Kolb, another educational theorist, focused his work on experiential learning, and he described a cycle of learning. This cycle includes the following:

- Concrete experience
- Reflective observation

- Abstract conceptualizing based on observing and reflecting

- Testing the new ideas through experimentation

Authors Debra Rose and Robert Christina merged these two constructs into a single model for learning preferences, shown in figure 11.3. This combined model situates learners by both personal style and activity preferences for learning. In this construct, a particular dancer might learn best through experimentation (dynamic) with concrete movement experiences. Another dancer might prefer logical, analytic descriptions (analytic) and reflecting on what is observed in demonstrations.

The common thread through all of the various theories and systems of learning styles is that each student is unique and has varying methods and preferences in the learning process. If teachers are only capable or willing to use one teaching strategy, such as demonstration, they will only reach a portion of the class. Teachers can thoughtfully design lessons

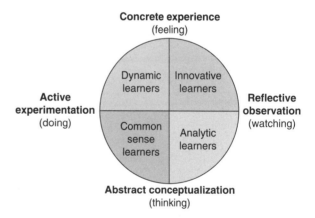

Figure 11.3 McCarthy's (1987) four styles of learning combined with Kolb's (1985) cycle of learning. Both dynamic and common sense learners tend to rely on active experimentation, but dynamic learners prefer concrete experiences, whereas common sense learners prefer abstract conceptualization. Both innovative and analytic learners tend to use reflective observation, but innovative learners prefer concrete experience, whereas analytic learners prefer abstract conceptualization.

to incorporate a variety of learning styles and nurture each student.

Training Dancers to Execute a Dance Task

Dancers can gain a deeper understanding of the theories, stages, and forms of motor learning by exploring the process of learning one specific movement skill. A common task involving balance in dance is passé relevé (balancing on the metatarsals of one foot while the other foot is placed at the knee of the supporting legs. It is a position universally used in every Western theatrical dance form, and in classes much time is devoted to achieving this balance in both static and locomotor tasks.

Consider learning this skill from the perspective of Adams' closed-loop theory. Certainly many repeated attempts of this task in a nonlocomotor situation would be a good starting point. With beginners, it is appropriate to simplify the task even more by lowering the gesture leg, which diminishes the tendency to tilt the pelvis, and trying the balance on the whole foot rather than the rise. While many teachers train this task at the barre, holding on to a support for balance means that this approach may not be training the correct anticipatory responses necessary for the weight shift. **Anticipatory responses** occur when the muscles activate preceding the weight shift from two feet to one foot to stabilize the body for balance. According to Adams' theory, it may be more appropriate to attempt the task without assistance immediately, and continue repeating the task until it is accomplished. Possible errors in this task are illustrated in figure 11.4.

Considering Schmidt's schema theory, it would be appropriate to give many versions of

The dancer is executing the passé relevé skill en pointe.

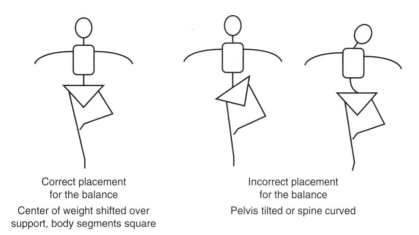

Correct placement
for the balance
Center of weight shifted over
support, body segments square

Incorrect placement
for the balance
Pelvis tilted or spine curved

Figure 11.4 Learning to align the body correctly for passé relevé takes awareness and control. Common errors include tilting the pelvis and curving the spine.
Created by Donna Krasnow.

a one-legged balance to create the schema of the skill. Examples include having the gesture leg in parallel as well as externally rotated, and varying the arm positions in multiple ways. Once the dancer develops a schema for passé balances, the correct postural adjustments will be made in variations of the position and not just in the initial one that is learned. Given the wide range of positions and movement demands that teachers and choreographers make on dancers, it is beneficial for dancers to develop schema for common types of balances and movements in the dance vocabulary, and variability in practice is the key in this theory.

According to Newell's ecological theory, which emphasizes active problem solving, the student should be encouraged to search and explore different solutions to problems with the task. Suppose a student can achieve the balance slowly, but as soon as speed is required, the dancer falls over. Rather than telling the student what to do, advising the student to try a wide range of solutions is an effective learning tool. Asking the dancer these questions can facilitate active problem solving: *Have you looked at what your ankles are doing? What about hip strategy? Is your head losing its vertical placement as you make the shift? Are you trying different images to engage trunk support? Are your arms delayed in the movement, creating a negative momentum factor?* While students often want quick answers, this exploratory process is a better learning strategy for them in the long run, because it assists in developing internal error detection and correction mechanisms.

The three stages of learning in Fitts and Posner's three-stage model can be a useful guide for the teacher and student when the student is ready to advance the material. If the student is still in the cognitive stage, he or she will be exploring many strategies with high variability of success. At this point the task should remain simple. In addition, the student can benefit from the teacher's feedback and guidance. When the student is refining the strategy during the associative stage, more challenges can then be added to the task. By the time the balance mechanisms are automatic, the student is able to achieve the balance while the attention is focused on other aspects, such as a complicated rhythmic demand or a partner. If the balance deteriorates when these other layers are added, then the student has probably not reached the autonomous stage and needs continued practice.

Similarly with Gentile's two-stage model, it is important to start with the goals for the early stage and focus on teaching the movement coordination for the passé balance. Dancers need to learn the basic pattern of shaping the gesture leg while correctly transferring the weight to the standing leg, simultaneously using arm positions. While the various parts can be practiced in isolation at first, the coordination of all of the components must be integrated early in the process. And because dance is so involved with musicality, dancers need to learn the precise timing of the coordinative patterns. Music is one of the key regulatory conditions. It is of little value to dancers to learn the task at such a slow tempo that it can never be incorporated into dynamic combinations. As dancers enter the later stages, the focus can shift to adaptability, consistency, and economy of effort. Adaptability can be enhanced in the same manner as with Schmidt's theory, by attempting many variations of the passé balance in shape, body parts, and timing. Turns and jumps in the passé position can be added. Doing repeated practice of the basic form develops consistency. Economy of effort is achieved through practice but also through instruction that encourages letting go of unnecessary muscle tension.

Many teachers approach this and many dance tasks as procedural learning, simply doing the task repeatedly with no conscious attention to the mechanisms. Dancers—especially very young ones—can learn the passé balance to a certain degree this way. However,

other methods can give a deeper understanding of the skill. In a declarative learning style, the dancers might think about weight shift and balance while doing a passé as follows: *I need to initiate the balance by shifting the pelvis over to the supporting leg, keeping the hip bones level. I should be aware of my arms and shoulders staying level as well. As my gesture leg rises up to the passé position, I need to feel that hip dropping downward against the upward pull of the leg, keeping both hips level to the ground. I can imagine the trunk becoming longer and narrower, which helps to engage abdominal support for the trunk, improving my balance.* As an additional part of the declarative process, dancers can be asked to visualize themselves in the position on balance, and then image themselves jumping or turning in the position.

To guarantee long-term changes to the neural system and not just a short-term accomplishment of the task, dancers must repeat the task often enough over time. Unfortunately, the nec-

The dancers are improvising with eyes closed to enhance sensory awareness of what their bodies are doing.

essary amount of repetition can be difficult to motivate. Using operant conditioning by praising dancers when they achieve a good balance is one way to approach this form of learning. In this way, they associate the balance with positive feedback. However, it is even better to find an intrinsic positive association, such as making dancers aware of desired goals that can be achieved if the balance is regularly practiced. For example, dancers may be motivated to know that after the simple balance becomes automatic, the likelihood of success at multiple turns in the passé position will increase.

One area of learning not specifically covered in the theories and stages discussed in this chapter relates to earlier chapters on postural control. Consider both **proactive mechanisms** (muscular responses that precede a disturbance) and **reactive mechanisms** (muscular responses that occur after a disturbance) when teaching balance control for this skill. Often what is practiced in class is proactive control; dancers know ahead of time that they are going to be shifting their weight and disturbing balance. Emphasizing the anticipation of a shift of weight preceding the lifting of the gesture leg facilitates development of proactive control. Research suggests that dancers demonstrate different anticipatory (proactive) mechanisms for one-legged balances than nondancers, because of this emphasis on anticipation in the training. Images can assist in developing these proactive responses. For example, dancers can imagine seeing a line from the foot that will be the support and moving the torso in one unit onto that line (figure 11.5). However, dancers also need to realize that unplanned events can cause unexpected disturbances to balance, such as another dancer running by and accidentally bumping into them. These situations call for reactive balance control. Dance teachers can implement interesting improvisational games to explore situations that heighten reactive control. One example is having dancers work in pairs. One dancer stands with eyes closed while the other lightly disturbs that person's balance with small, unexpected pushes in various directions.

Finally, dancers need to learn to integrate balance mechanisms into locomotor patterns and

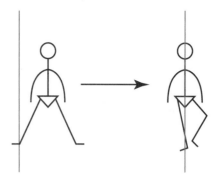

Figure 11.5 The dancer can imagine the vertical line (plumb line) to facilitate good trunk alignment during weight shift.

Created by Donna Krasnow.

more complex voluntary actions such as turning and jumping. At the most complex level, the balance must be integrated and adapted for movements where the upper torso is taken off the vertical while the lower base maintains the same support (figure 11.6). This variation is one of the most difficult to achieve, because visual and vestibular contributions to balance are limited, and the dancer must rely heavily on proprioception. Therefore, it is best to wait for the associative or later stages of learning to attempt this material.

Throughout all of these procedures, teachers and dancers can address the wide variety of learning styles using demonstration, analytic description, exploration, and social interactions, to name a few. The dance class can act not as a factory, producing high-level technicians, but as a laboratory, nurturing dancers who are skilled but also proactive, thoughtful,

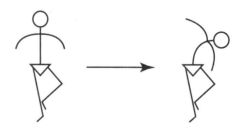

Figure 11.6 Balance becomes more complicated as the torso in taken off the vertical alignment. The dancer can imagine that the plumb line comes out of the side of the body instead of the top of the head.

Created by Donna Krasnow.

and experimental, eventually becoming their own teachers.

It is clear looking at this one dance task of the passé balance that each motor learning theory can make a contribution to enhancing the learning situation. If dancers think about their classes and the methods of their teachers, they will realize that the concepts of many of these theoretical models are present in their training. Dancers can also have a better understanding of their stage of learning for various tasks and how they should approach the task over time given this perspective. Keep in mind that dancers can be at different stages for different skills and dance forms. A highly skilled modern dancer might be one of the beginners at the Argentine tango club, and an expert ballroom dancer might feel very unskilled at hip-hop. Each new challenge calls upon the dancer to experiment with a variety of methods to make the greatest gains in skill acquisition.

Summary

Motor learning describes the relatively permanent changes associated with practice or experience that govern a person's capability for generating a motor skill. Theories of motor learning give a conceptual construct for understanding the process, and each theory has a different emphasis. Adams' closed-loop theory focuses on the need for sensory feedback, Schmidt's schema theory describes the development of schemas and generalized motor programs that control classes of movement, and ecological theory emphasizes exploration and the perceptual-motor workspace. Two theories consider the stages of learning as learners change from beginner to advanced movers. Fitts' and Posner's three-stage model describes the cognitive, associative, and autonomous stages, while Gentile's two-stage model considers the initial and later stages. Gentile's model stresses the type of skill in determining the learner's goals. Forms of learning include nondeclarative and declarative learning. Nondeclarative breaks down further into nonassociative, associative, and procedural learning. One major differentiation in the forms of learning describes how much conscious or cognitive thought is involved in the learning process. Finally, learners have a variety of individual learning styles and preferences that yield insight into both how comfortable a learner is in a particular context and how effective that context will be. Dancers and dance teachers are involved in motor learning every day as part of the training experience, and a better understanding of the theoretical underpinnings of motor learning can enhance the process.

Chapter 12
Instructional Strategies

The dance class is about to begin, and the teacher enters the studio. The teacher begins by demonstrating the first combination for the start of class. After a few demonstrations, the teacher provides instructions about the movement. For example, the teacher says, "Make sure that your pelvis shifts from two feet to one foot and back to two feet between each change of direction." As the dancers are executing the phrase of movement, the teacher calls out cues, possibly reminding the dancers about the counts or about changes of facing in the space. After this first attempt, the teacher immediately divides the class into two groups, and each group watches the other as they attempt the phrase again. After both groups are finished, the teacher gives corrections and asks the groups to try the phrase one more time. This time, the teacher gives corrections while the dancers are performing. During each of these attempts, the dancers are also receiving information from their own sensory systems (such as losing balance or noticing that they are off the music) and information from the mirror (such as the proper positioning of the arms). All of these types of information are **instructional strategies**, methods of relaying information about correct execution of a skill.

While instructional strategies are not always essential in order for motor learning to occur, they can be useful in a variety of contexts. With any type of skill acquisition, people require information about how to do the skill, which can come from a wide array of sources. Even a baby learning how to pick up a spoon watches a demonstration by a parent and is cued through physical touch how to grasp the object. Elite skills are far more complex, but the same idea applies; instructional strategies are among the main components in teaching motor skills. In order for teachers to be effective in their strategies, they need to understand what type of instruction is best for varying skills, how often strategies should be applied, and how much information should be transmitted, among other things. The focus of this chapter is on these two areas of instructional strategies: demonstration and verbal instructions, which give general knowledge about the skill, and various forms of feedback, which give specific commentary or insight on observed or experienced performance.

Demonstration and Verbal Instructions

Before learners even attempt a new skill, they can receive important information in two main ways. One way is to observe a physical demonstration of the skill, and the other is to receive verbal instructions about how to do the skill. Each of these methods focuses on various aspects of the skill. For example, dancers can see the body shapes and the timing of a dance phrase by watching the teacher, but they can learn about how to maintain their core support by listening to the teacher describe this facet of the skill. Because vision is such an important means of motor learning, demonstration is a primary tool in the dance class.

Demonstration

Demonstration is also known as **modeling**. Because the information is being transmitted to learners through having them observe the performance, this method of learning is called **observational learning**. A common myth in dance and athletic circles is that demonstration is always effective in teaching a skill. Although research has suggested that demonstration is better in some situations than others, educators must determine whether demonstration would be effective in a given circumstance or for a particular aspect of a skill. In addition, young children (ages 4-7) do not use demonstration in the same way as older dancers. First, they do not label or organize what they are seeing in a way that they can easily recall later when they are doing the movement. Second, they do not mentally rehearse the demonstration while they are watching. Hence, the teacher should either encourage the young dancers to mentally practice as they watch or to mark along with the teacher.

Teachers must decide whether or not demonstration would be beneficial for dancers given their age, level, and abilities. Further, they need to know whether the skill being taught is one that is accessible through observational learning. In order to determine when demonstration is the best approach, it is imperative to understand what learners visually perceive when they are observing a demonstration.

The child can use observational learning while marking or following the teacher as she demonstrates.

Visual Perception of Motion

What learners perceive when they observe movement is related directly to the coordination pattern of the skill. Another way of saying this idea is that **invariant relative motions** exist in a particular movement, and they are the relationships between joints and body parts in a given action. For example, whether a développé is done at 45° or at hip level, or whether it is done quickly or slowly, the coordination pattern of the hip, knee, and foot remains constant. Similarly, dancers can recognize a développé regardless of the height, sex, age, or weight of the person executing it. However, those relative motions of the joints change if the leg does a straight-legged brush, even if it is to the same height or timing. The perception of coordination patterns can be either conscious or nonconscious as people observe movement. Elite dancers in a dance class can often pick up many aspects of a movement phrase without being aware of seeing or learning these components, which is one reason they have the ability to absorb large quantities of material at one time.

Most people are familiar with the method of creating animated characters in films such as *Avatar.* Reflective markers or balls are placed on joints and bones of the body, and then the person is filmed (figure 12.1). The fantasy character is then computerized using these moving balls. In this way, movement of the avatar appears realistic because it is modeled after actual movement. This same technique has been used to research what people observe when they watch movement. This research procedure is called **point-light technique**. It allows an observer to see only the motion of the light-reflective markers placed on the joints of the body as white dots when observing videos of humans performing activities or skills. This research suggests that people do not recognize changeable aspects (parameters) of the movement, such as the speed of the action;

rather they recognize the coordination pattern (relationships between the joints). People can distinguish a wide variety of motor skills, such as walking, running, biking, jumping jacks, and elite sports, simply by viewing the videos of reflective markers and the changing patterns of the markers. They can even identify the sex of the person doing the movement, and they can recognize people they know just from the points of light.

In studies examining the usefulness of demonstration for learning skills, researchers have wanted to clarify what characteristics of the movement are critical to the learning process. Some studies have suggested that learning how to change parameters of a skill, such as speed or force, can be aided through observa-

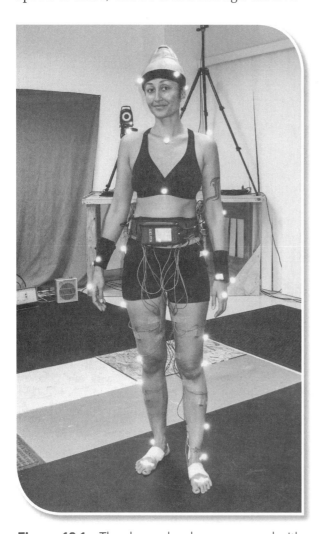

Figure 12.1 The dancer has been prepared with light-reflecting markers for a dance biomechanics study.

tion. However, probably the most important aspect that determines whether demonstration will be useful is whether the learner needs to develop a new pattern of coordination in order to achieve the skill. Very recent research about the brain has revealed how and why demonstration can be so successful in these learning situations.

Mirror Neurons

Mirror neurons were accidentally discovered in studies done on monkeys in the early 1990s. Areas of monkeys' brains would respond whether the monkeys were picking up a peanut themselves or they were observing a human or another monkey picking up a peanut. **Mirror neurons** are special neurons in the premotor cortex, supplementary motor area, parietal cortex, and other areas of the brain that fire when primates and humans are doing an action or observing someone else doing the same action. The **premotor area** organizes movement before initiation and handles rhythmic coordination. The **supplementary motor area** plays an important role in sequential movements and in preparing and organizing movement. The **parietal cortex** deals with integrating visual and motor information, and it assists in the planning stages of movement. Each of these areas of the brain is important in planning movement. Although the research on mirror neurons in humans is relatively new, it suggests that the mirror system does exist in humans and that it is an important aspect of how people learn through observation and relate to each other socially.

Viewing Expert Versus Novice Demonstrations

Beginners develop different abilities when they observe expert and novice demonstrations. In order to develop the most accurate model of the task, the demonstration should be as clear and specific as possible. Observing an expert execute a skill in the most precise form gives beginners a high-quality example to use as their model. They can glean accurate information about the coordination patterns from this demonstration. On the other hand, when observing their peers, learners develop problem-solving abilities. They can compare what they are seeing with the expert demonstration seen previously, and they can determine the discrepancy between the two examples. The observers can also hear any comments that the instructor is giving to the practicing novices and then observe the strategies and changes that they make. In this way, the observers develop error detection and correction mechanisms as well as a more refined way to analyze movement skills. Research has shown that beginners who have observed other beginners execute a particular task will perform better at the task than the original beginners they were observing. This result suggests that beginners derive benefits from watching each other perform.

One excellent strategy that can be implemented in the dance class is to have students work in pairs and observe each other performing a dance phrase or exercise. Each pair has an active dancer and an observer. When the dancers are beginners, the teacher should provide specific aspects of the activity that the observer is to critique and suggest how to do the critique. For example, the teacher might suggest that the observer establish what the most important elements are to describe, and to limit critiques to two or three main points. After the first group does the phrase, the observers give comments to their partners. Then the pairs switch roles. This process has three benefits for the dancers. First, they develop problem-solving and analytic skills as they observe and prepare to give comments. Second, their understanding of the sequence, timing, and positioning of the phrase is reinforced. Third, they develop communication skills, which will be important in later roles as teachers and choreographers. With more advanced dancers, the observers can self-select what and how to do their critiques; they will be more knowledgeable about what is involved in learning the skill, and they will have more experience observing teachers giving critiques.

Timing and Frequency of Demonstrations

One of the common strategies that teachers use in introducing new material is to begin with a detailed and lengthy explanation of either the purpose of the new exercise or how the students should approach it. However, this strategy can be less effective than an initial demonstration, because the dancers have no image or context for using this information. Dancers should see a demonstration of the new material or phrase before attempting it. Too much verbal instruction at this stage can overload their attention, which needs to be directed to the basic content. This issue is particularly pertinent for beginners. They need to see the material and attempt it; more information can be added later.

A second issue concerning demonstration is frequency. The general rule with demonstration is that more is better, and research supports this perspective. The teacher should be willing to demonstrate, or ask a student to demonstrate, as often as the dancers need to see the material. Further, demonstrations should be interspersed with practice attempts, not simply done several times at the beginning. Both form and accuracy are enhanced through this instructional strategy. The concern that students will become dependent on teacher demonstration is unsupported in the literature, and as dancers develop their visual perceptual skills, they will need fewer demonstrations to learn new material.

It may seem that these recommendations present unique challenges for teachers who are not able to demonstrate often or full out, perhaps because of injury or age. In these instances it is even more important to accustom students to demonstrating for each other, either in pairs or for the entire class. These demonstrations can act simply as models of the material, or they can be vehicles for stimulating problem-solving discussions.

Aural Perception of Motion

Because dance is so inherently connected to music, dancers can also benefit from creation of sound as a form of demonstration. Timing, rhythm, phrasing, and emphasis can be addressed with certain instructional techniques. If a movement sequence is complex, it can be helpful to the dancers to put aside the physical movement phrase temporarily and focus on learning the timing through auditory means, which might include clapping, foot stepping, or singing the rhythm. After the dancers feel secure in the timing aspects of the

Clapping adds to aural perception of rhythm; therefore, it can serve as a valuable tool in motor learning.

phrase, they can return to the physical practice and focus on other aspects of the material.

It is clear from these considerations that demonstration is a powerful and necessary tool for learning certain aspects of motor skills, particularly when new coordination patterns are being acquired. Two theories are proposed for how demonstration affects motor learning. The first, called **cognitive mediation theory**, suggests that as a person observes a skill, the brain forms a model (also called *representation* or *code*) of the movement that it stores in the memory, and it uses this model on future attempts and as a criterion for error detection and correction. In essence, the model is a mediator, an additional stage between seeing the demonstration and actively executing the task. The development of error detection and correction is a highly important component of motor learning in elite skills. The second

view, called **dynamic view of modeling**, suggests that learners can see a demonstration and automatically process the information in a way that allows them to do the movement without cognitive mediation. In fact, research has indicated that seeing a movement in a point-light technique video is as useful as seeing an actual person doing a demonstration of the movement. At this time, both theories are regarded as valid explanations for the value of demonstration in the learning process.

Verbal Instructions and Cues

As a means of teaching movement skills, verbal instructions are as popular as demonstrations. Verbal instructions are explanations of how a skill is accomplished, and often they can educate the learner about aspects of the skill that cannot be observed through demonstration. Instructions are usually general; that is, they do not give feedback about a particular person's performance, and they do not necessarily refer to any incorrect execution that the teacher has observed. In effect, they lay down a general blueprint for the skill. Various factors influence what constitutes good verbal instruction.

Factors Influencing Instructions

Attention and memory are major factors that affect verbal instructions. People have a limited capacity for attention (discussed in chapter 7), and this limitation places restrictions on both the quantity and content of verbal instructions. Dance teachers need to be sensitive to these aspects in designing their instructions.

Dancers, especially beginners, can easily be inundated with too much information. Generally, one or two main ideas are sufficient, because the dancers are already concentrating on all of the material they saw in the demonstration. If the teacher offers too many additional points of focus, the dancers will be unable to attend to everything involved and also will not be able to retain all of the information during

movement execution. While it is tempting to tell dancers everything at once that they will need to know to achieve a new skill or dance phrase, it is more effective to distribute the information over time. In order to avoid information overload, initial instructions should be limited, concise, and straightforward.

Instructions should also be age appropriate. For example, when teaching body swings sitting on the floor to children, the teacher can say, "Keep the sitz bones attached to the floor; with a pencil sticking out the top of the head, draw a circle on the floor." With older dancers, the teacher can describe ideas about core support, and making sure that the torso pathway encompasses all of the directions of the swing from side, to diagonal, to forward, to diagonal, to the other side. This description would be too complex for children, and therefore it would not be age appropriate. Finally, instructions should include information not only about what the new material is, but also about why the material is important. For example, the teacher might emphasize keeping the heels on the floor

The teacher is overloading the dancer with information while she is trying to learn a new movement.

in first position demi-plié, explaining that it is important to lengthen the calf in the plié and reduce undue stress on the calf muscles.

Verbal instructions should also be precise in terms of directing the learner's attention to the most important features of the skill or the environment. Research consistently demonstrates that when performers at any skill level direct their attention to movement outcomes rather than specific components, they will achieve greater success, a view called the **action effect hypothesis** (discussed in chapter 7). In other words, dancers should be encouraged to think in terms of movement outcomes and not focus on the particular single movements or muscles they are using. For example, in doing a body roll in a modern or jazz dance class, dancers can be instructed to think about the circle that the head is creating in the space rather than concentrate on how they are using the back and abdominal muscles. Another way of expressing this idea is that dancers should be encouraged to use external rather than internal focus of attention when learning new skills.

This strategy of using external focus can be accomplished in these two ways: creating a discovery learning situation and using metaphoric imagery. In a **discovery learning situation**, the teacher gives instructions that describe the intended action of the skill, and through practice the learner discovers how to move in order to achieve the intended action. For example, in doing a series of runs across the floor, students might be encouraged to get across the floor in as few steps as possible. In trying to achieve this goal, dancers might explore shifting their weight further forward or using more push with the propelling leg. **Metaphoric imagery** is the representation of the desired movement with a figure or likeness. With metaphoric imagery, the dancer concentrates on the image or idea of the movement, and the movements and muscles are determined on a nonconscious level. For example, to encourage keeping the torso forward in low runs, dancers can imagine that they are the figurehead on the front of a Viking ship leading the way through the water.

Using verbal analogies is another form of verbal instruction. **Verbal analogies** are used to emphasize how two actions are similar or related in some way. When dancers relate something new with a skill or activity they have previously experienced, it assists them in understanding the new activity. For example, one metaphor that teachers use to teach leaps to children is to imagine that they are deer in the woods jumping over logs or streams. In addition to this image being a delightful metaphor, it also gives them a context for a new movement (a dance leap) with something they have previously encountered in their children's stories. Verbal analogies encourage **implicit learning** (learning without conscious effort or awareness of what is being learned). Implicit learning reduces the stress and pressure of having to do something correctly in terms of conscious or detailed instructions, and therefore it can be a beneficial tool in motor learning.

Verbal instructions can also draw attention to the environmental conditions that are necessary in achieving the task. For example, a teacher can describe the angle of the head by directing the line of focus and the face to a particular point or object in the space. Also, a teacher can describe the amount of distance that leaps or traveling steps must cover in terms of landmarks in the space. An additional advantage to giving instructions that relate to the larger space is that it can prepare dancers for choreography that deals with set pieces as well as for touring that involves changing environments.

Verbal Cues

Verbal cues are brief, succinct phrases that act as prompts for main ideas or components of the movement, or direct the attention to vital environmental circumstances. For example, the teacher might say, "Reach the arm" or "Look for the wing" to direct attention to movement components or to the space. Teachers can introduce verbal cues during demonstration, during instructions, or while dancers are in motion. In each case, they provide a short reminder of essential elements of the task. Verbal cues are as useful for elite dancers as for beginners. In both cases, as dancers use cues, an association forms between the cue and the prompted action, allowing the dancer to focus on fewer movement elements and direct attention to other aspects of the work, such as the music or interacting with other dancers.

In addition, teachers can consider the use of the voice in giving verbal cues. They can sing counts in musical phrasing, which can give dancers important information about not only which movements arrive on certain counts but also about the phrasing, accents, and effort in the movement. Words can be accented with various dynamics, use long, lingering sounds for lyrical movement, and use sharp, abrupt sounds for percussive movement. The sound of the cues can be as critical for the learning process as the actual words being spoken.

Demonstration and verbal instructions are the two most common methods of introducing new skills to dancers. How they are executed or described can be critical to their effectiveness in the motor learning process. The first introduction of a skill leaves a lasting impression in the mind of the dancer, and teachers should make every effort to guarantee a clear and valuable image of the task and accompanying directions. Once the dancers have seen the new dance skill demonstrated and have heard the concise instructions about the purpose and task elements, they are prepared to try the skill. The next stage of their learning process involves receiving information about their execution in the form of feedback.

Augmented Feedback

Once dancers have seen a demonstration and heard instructions for a skill, they attempt it for the first time. Most likely, they will make several errors in execution. The next stage in the motor learning process involves feedback. **Feedback** is a response to a movement trial that

The dancer is doing a relevé with the feet supinating (called *rolling out* in dance). The teacher can give feedback to assist in correcting this poor lower-limb alignment.

gives information about the result of the trial or about what caused that result, to be used as a basis for improvement. The two main types of feedback are task-intrinsic feedback and augmented feedback. **Task-intrinsic feedback**, or simply intrinsic feedback, is sensory information—such as visual, auditory, proprioceptive, and tactile—provided innately while performing a skill. For example, when doing grand battement devant, a dancer receives visual feedback if the leg veers out to the diagonal and does not stay in direct line with the body. A dancer receives proprioceptive feedback when the ankle rolls out (inverts) on relevé. While dancers cannot change the amount or type of task-intrinsic feedback, they can learn to become more attentive to various forms of sensory information, which has been described in other chapters. **Augmented feedback** (also called *extrinsic feedback*) adds to or enhances the intrinsic feedback and comes from a source external to the performer, such as a teacher, choreographer, or video. For example, a teacher might say, "Your standing leg is bent when you are doing your turn" or, "You need to lift your focus at the top of the leap." Figure 12.2 shows both types of feedback. Because this chapter is looking at instructional strategies, the focus of the next section is on augmented feedback.

Describing Augmented Feedback

Every dance teacher uses augmented feedback in the dance class. Usually, teachers refer to this process as *corrections*, and they try to give information to students, either as a group or to individuals, to improve performance. This feedback can also describe the causes of errors and why the changes are being suggested. Sometimes augmented feedback is used as a motivational tool, and it can also be used to inspire dancers to work more cooperatively. Feedback can be given during or after a performance of a task. Two types of augmented feedback are knowledge of results (KR) and knowledge of performance (KP). Each of these types provides different information for various desired effects.

Defining Types of Augmented Feedback

Knowledge of results (KR) is augmented feedback that gives information about the outcome of executing a movement task or about whether or not the goal was successfully accomplished. Examples include statements such as "During the traveling turns, you got ahead of the music" or "You accomplished 10 head spins in your break-dance routine." Sometimes dancers can determine outcome results through task-intrinsic feedback, which would make the KR feedback redundant. At other times, they cannot determine the outcome, and the KR feedback would be essential. For example, when doing an arabesque, some dancers are able to determine that their gesture leg is not straight from proprioceptive (task-intrinsic) feedback. However, other dancers may not yet have developed sophisticated kinesthetic awareness, and they would need to hear from the teacher that the gesture leg was bent. Figure 12.3 shows a lighthearted example of redundant and essential feedback.

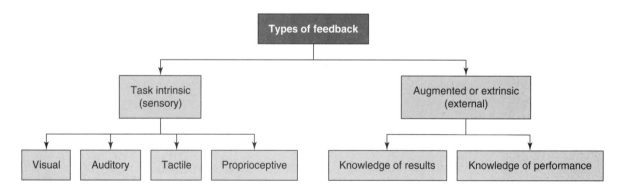

Figure 12.2 The various types of feedback in the feedback family that are related to learning and performing motor skills.

Adapted from R.A. Magill, 2011, *Motor learning and control*, 9th ed. (New York, NY: McGraw-Hill Education).

Figure 12.3 Knowledge of results is mainly helpful when it provides information that performers are not able to obtain from their own intrinsic feedback.

Knowledge of performance (KP) is augmented feedback that gives information about the movement features that determine the result (outcome) of the movement trial. KP can be given in both verbal and nonverbal forms. In the previous example, the teacher might say, "Reach further into the space behind you with the foot of your gesture leg." In a nonverbal case, the teacher might go to the student and gently pull the gesture leg until the knee is fully extended. Table 12.1 shows several examples of KR and KP.

Another form of nonverbal KP is video. Dancers can be recorded on video while executing movement skills or phrases, and then observe their performance. The effectiveness of viewing videos as a learning tool is partly dependent on the level of the learner. When using video with beginners, the instructor must be present in order to point out the essential information and direct the learners' attention accordingly. Further, certain aspects of movement can be improved by self-observation in video, while others cannot. In a study with adolescent gymnasts,

Table 12.1 Examples of Augmented Feedback

Action	Knowledge of results	Knowledge of performance
Pirouette turn	"You did not complete your triple turn."	"When you initiate the triple turn, bring the arms in faster."
Body roll in standing second position	"You lost your balance during the arch."	"When you arch during the body roll, increase your core support."
Jazz layout	"You fell backward at the final shape."	"Keep your body weight forward as the body arches back."
Ballroom salsa	"You lost contact with your partner on the turning step."	"As you initiate the turning section, make your steps smaller."
Partner lift	"You did not get your partner all the way to the intended top of the lift."	"Use more plié at the onset of the lift, and keep your partner closer to your body on the way up."

observing video enhanced these four aspects of the material: precision, execution, size of movement, and spatial orientation. These four aspects were not improved by the use of video: rhythm, elegance, coordination, and lightness in jumps and tumbling. This result suggests that not all aspects of movement are easily understood through video observation, and it should be used sparingly.

Although its use is less common in dance, equipment is available that can show dancers computer-generated kinematics of their skills. **Kinematics** is the branch of mechanics that describes the motion of bodies and body systems; in particular, it describes the motion of systems composed of joined parts (also termed *multilink systems*), such as the skeleton of the human body. Figure 12.4 shows a computer-generated view of an elite dancer executing grand battement devant. In physical therapy for an injury, dancers might be asked to use biofeedback devices, which give dancers a signal, such as a sound or sensation, when they are using the muscle or muscles needing rehabilitation. Another form of biofeedback is the use of **electromyography** (described in chapter 3),

a research tool that measures electrical activity created by muscles during action, then gives information about when muscles contract and how much force is being used. Dancers can view graphs of their muscle use during rehabilitation, then apply this knowledge to enhance muscle activity. While dancers do not use kinematics, biofeedback devices, or electromyography in the dance class, these tools are being used more frequently in research settings involving dancers. In this way, they are enhancing the teaching of motor skills.

Roles of Augmented Feedback

Augmented feedback has two primary roles in teaching motor skills. The first is to enable the person to acquire the necessary skills in order to accomplish the task—to execute the movement accurately. Because the task is new to the learner, augmented feedback provides information that can allow the learner to improve more easily than using only task-intrinsic feedback. For example, if dancers are learning salsa for the first time, they may be putting weight on the foot during the count that is done as a touch step. This incorrect action will cause them to be

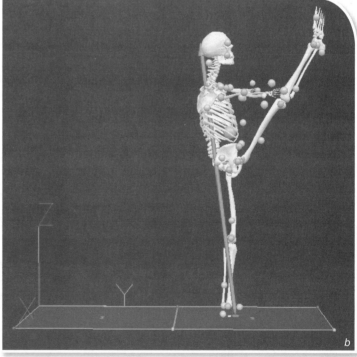

Figure 12.4 Grand battement devant in (a) real time and (b) kinematic representation.

on the wrong foot for the next count. Watching the teacher, it might take the dancers considerable time to figure out how to make the correction. With augmented feedback, the teacher can simply say, "On count 2, touch the floor lightly with the foot, but don't put the weight on that foot until count 3." This feedback will quickly correct the error.

The second role of augmented feedback is to motivate the learner to continue practicing and attain the goal. Augmented feedback can give dancers an objective view of how close they are to achieving the skill, even if their own perceptions suggest otherwise. For example, when dancers are learning turns with the body off the vertical for the first time, they lose balance quite dramatically. However, the teacher can give the feedback that they are closer to achieving the goal than it may seem, and just a few small adjustments will result in success. This information can motivate the dancers to

continue trying. The teacher must use a positive tone of voice, or the students could interpret this feedback as negative criticism.

Feedback can be given in both positive reinforcement and negative reinforcement. **Positive reinforcement** is feedback that increases the possibility that given similar conditions, the desired performance will be repeated, and the result is reliable and favorable change. **Negative reinforcement** occurs when the teacher eliminates an unpleasant circumstance, thereby increasing the possibility that the desired performance will be repeated. Note that negative reinforcement is not the same as punishment, which actually decreases the possibility that the performance will be repeated or continued.

Imagine a rehearsal setting with a choreographer in the final stages of cleaning a dance. Positive reinforcement would include the choreographer saying, "That was a much better run-through; you did all of my corrections!"

Catching dancers in tossed lifts requires not only concentration but also confidence, which can be diminished through negative reinforcement.

However, imagine that every time the dancers made errors, they had to stop and start over from the beginning. Then, in a particular run, the choreographer allowed the piece to continue to the end and said, "We do not need to rerun the dance." This example represents negative reinforcement, because the negative of having to start over again has been removed, and the chances of the dancers repeating the excellent performance are increased. Now imagine that one of the dancers makes several errors, and the choreographer removes this dancer from the choreography. This action is punishment, which can make the other dancers so tense that their performance deteriorates. Research suggests that positive reinforcement results in advancements that are superior to results of negative reinforcement and punishment.

Necessity of Augmented Feedback

Dance educators sometimes wonder whether augmented feedback is necessary for learning skills. The answer to this question is complex, and one answer does not settle the issue. Here are four possible answers: (1) Sometimes augmented feedback is necessary, (2) sometimes it is not needed, (3) sometimes it can enhance the skill, and (4) at other times it can actually obstruct the learning of a skill.

First, for some skills, augmented feedback is absolutely necessary, especially in situations in which the task-intrinsic feedback does not supply sufficient information. Cases include the following:

- When sensory feedback is insufficient
- When injury does not permit sensory information to be readily available
- When the person cannot use the sensory feedback even though it is available

An example of the first case (when sensory feedback is insufficient) is when teachers have dancers move backward across the floor in a dance class. Because the students cannot see where they are going, the teacher will ask other students to use tactile feedback by placing their hands on the moving dancers' backs to stop them when they arrive at the end of the space. Eventually dancers learn to use peripheral vision and spatial cues to know when to stop moving, but initially they need this additional feedback. An example of the second case (when injury does not permit sensory information to be readily available) is when dancers have repeatedly sprained an ankle, they may no longer be receiving proprioceptive feedback about foot position, therefore they may need verbal or tactile information from the teacher to align the foot properly. An example of the third case (when the person cannot use the sensory feedback even though it is available) is when dancers are learning how to work with hyperextended knees. They usually receive the proprioceptive and visual information to make the correction, but they do not know how to use this sensory feedback, and they may need directions or images provided by the teacher to realign the leg.

Second, for other skills, augmented feedback may not be needed at all. For example, children learn skipping rope and hopscotch simply by watching other children. They improve by practicing. Augmented feedback is entirely unnecessary for these skills. In dance situations, some skills are simple enough that dancers can learn them by observing the teacher initially and then by observing each other learning the skill. Children can learn to jump by seeing others jumping. Feedback may be necessary to in order refine the aesthetics of the skill, but the action is learned through observation. Observation is not only helpful for learning fundamental movement skills. For example, the social dance Macarena is simple enough that most people learn it by watching and following along.

Third, dancers can learn movement through observation, but augmented feedback enhances skill acquisition, either by speeding the process or enabling a higher skill level. Examples of this condition in dance and sports include movements that require very fast speed. Often dancers get to a certain point in the learning process, but they cannot improve beyond this point. While many reasons exist for this plateau of learning at various stages, it may be that feedback can support the dancer's process. Appropriate feedback might assist the dancers in increasing the speed of a movement skill, such as feedback that changes arm timing to enhance the speed of turns. Other movements that are enhanced by feedback are movements requiring multi-limb coordination. Because of the complexity and unusual nature of some of these multi-limb dance skills, they cannot be learned at a high level without some assistance through feedback.

Fourth and finally, augmented feedback can actually obstruct learning. This situation can occur if the feedback is flawed, given while the learner is executing the task in a way that distracts the learner, or given too frequently. In all three of these conditions, the feedback interferes with the attention of the learner to the necessary cognitive processes, causing poor learning. An example of flawed feedback is the instruction to maintain full external rotation in the push-off leg for a leap. In fact, the leg must move toward parallel position to be able to use the gastrocnemius and soleus (calf muscles) to full advantage, and the research on elite dancers demonstrates that this use of parallel is the best strategy. Giving feedback to remain fully turned out hinders learning good elevation execution techniques.

Content of Augmented Feedback

Teachers generally give two types of corrections. One type tells dancers what they have done correctly (KR), and the other type gives information about what can be improved (KP). The question arises as to which type is better for motor learning. The research strongly indicates that information about errors is better for enabling acquisition of skills. Without information about errors, learners do not have tools to alter or correct movement characteristics that are inhibiting high-level skills. On the other hand, feedback about what has been done correctly encourages the learner to continue engaging in the practice, and it is highly important for motivation.

Knowledge of Results Versus Knowledge of Performance

In examining whether teachers use KR or KP more often, research suggests that teachers overwhelmingly use KP up to 94% of the time. While the studies in the literature do not include dance classes, it is likely that the same result would be observed in that setting. In addition, KP is more effective than KR for enhancing motor skill learning, although both forms of augmented feedback can be useful. KP is beneficial in the following circumstances:

- When the features of the skill are extremely specific and precise
- When the skill includes complex coordination
- When specific muscles or joint activity are part of the skill organization
- When KR would not be useful because it would be redundant with the task-intrinsic feedback

KR is beneficial for these reasons:

- Learners use KR as reinforcement of their own evaluation of their performance.

Skills that are complex and fast can benefit from receiving knowledge of performance (KP) from an expert.

- Learners may need KR in cases where the task-intrinsic information is not sufficient to determine progress.
- KR can be used as motivation.
- Teachers can give KR with the goal of encouraging learners to self-discover how to improve the skill.

Quantitative and Qualitative Augmented Feedback

Content of augmented feedback can be quantitative, qualitative, or both. **Quantitative augmented feedback** contains a numerical value relating to the measure of the skill, such as the number of turns or the height of a jump. **Qualitative augmented feedback** describes the quality or some essential property of the movement, such as stating that the turn has good fluidity or the jump has explosive power. Augmented feedback can be both quantitative and qualitative at the same time, and both types of feedback can be verbal or nonverbal. The previous examples about turns and jumps would be verbal. An example of nonverbal quantitative feedback is clapping out the number of turns or jumps in a sequence. An example of nonverbal qualitative feedback is to make a gesture of approval when a correction has been accomplished. In the early stages of learning, dancers are trying to achieve a rough estimation of the movement; refinement occurs later. For this reason, qualitative feedback is more valuable than quantitative feedback, and in fact beginners will select the qualitative feedback even if quantitative feedback is provided.

Program Feedback and Parameter Feedback

Movement skills of a similar class have two basic characteristics: the general concept or motor pattern of the skill, and the parameters. **Parameters** are the aspects that can be varied from one execution of the skill to another, such as speed, force, and direction. When a beginner is first learning a skill, the teacher should give **program feedback**, which focuses on the general or fundamental pattern of the movement. Later, when the concept is clear, the teacher can give **parameter feedback**, which focuses on the changeable features of the movement, such as speed, force, and size. Until dancers are clear about the basic movement pattern, it is not useful to give feedback about variable features. For example, beginners can learn the sequence *step, ball–change* in a jazz class. In the early stages, the teacher would need to emphasize the fundamental coordination regarding when the weight is transferred from one foot to the other and which part of the foot contacts the floor. Later, the teacher can give feedback about speed changes, direction changes in mid-step, and adding arm and focus variations. Figure 12.5 shows a clear plan of determining when it is beneficial to give varying forms of feedback.

Withholding Feedback

Dance teachers make intuitive decisions about how much error to allow during the learning of new movement skills. Few teachers would correct a new skill or phrase repeatedly, expecting perfection. In sports, teachers and coaches use a concept called **performance bandwidth**, which provides a range of tolerable error. Feedback is only given when the learner's performance falls outside this range. In the case of the 32-fouetté pirouette combination en pointe, one of the goals is to remain precisely on the same spot on the floor for all 32 turns. However, if the dancer drifts a few inches in any direction, it would still be considered an acceptable execution and would not be criticized. With beginners, teachers are even more generous with the acceptable range. Even with concepts such as positioning of arms and legs, teachers should allow a bit more leeway while dancers explore and experiment in the learning process.

Previously, this text described the impact of flawed or erroneous feedback on learning and how it can obstruct the learning process. Even in situations in which learners start off doing well with a new skill, when using their task-intrinsic feedback, performance deteriorates if they are given erroneous feedback. Sadly, although they are aware that performance has worsened, they continue to try to apply the erroneous feedback. This problem is especially true for beginners who rely on their teachers and choreographers for information and who may be uncertain about their perceptions of

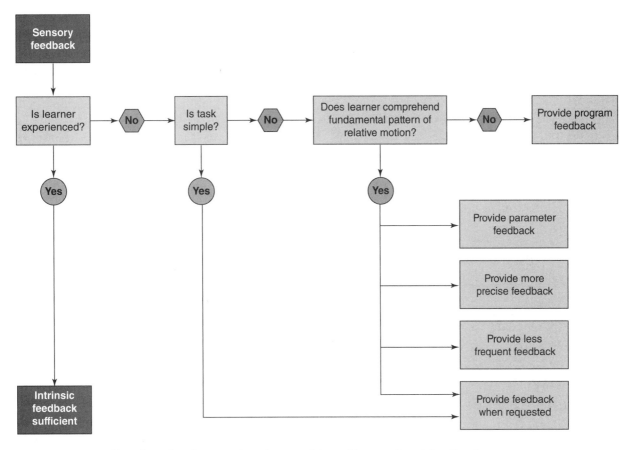

Figure 12.5   A flowchart for determining the provision of instructional feedback.

Reprinted, by permission, from R.A. Schmidt and C.A. Wrisberg, 2008, *Motor learning and performance: A situation-based learning approach*, 4th ed. (Champaign, IL: Human Kinetics), 297.

task-intrinsic feedback. Therefore, it is essential that teachers are sure they are communicating the correct feedback.

Timing of Augmented Feedback

Another concern for educators is the timing of feedback, and whether it should be given during movement execution (called **concurrent augmented feedback**) or after the movement execution (called **terminal augmented feedback**). While teachers often use concurrent augmented feedback, it can have a negative effect on learning. The learner might direct attention away from task-intrinsic feedback and toward the augmented feedback, which then becomes an essential aspect of what is learned. It becomes necessary in future attempts at the skill. Evidence in both retention and transfer tests suggests the possibility of this result. **Transfer tests** have the learners changing to different tasks or

conditions. **Retention tests** occur after a period of time but usually test the learner on the same task or conditions. Concurrent feedback can be useful in skill learning if it enhances task-intrinsic feedback rather than distracts from it. For example, encouraging dancers to extend their lines further in space during an adagio adds to the proprioceptive experience of their limbs. In other words, concurrent augmented feedback can be effective if it supports the understanding of the main features of the movement task, consistent with the relevant task-intrinsic feedback.

Regarding terminal augmented feedback, often dancers must wait between receiving feedback and having another chance at executing the skill or the phrase. This delay may be because of other dancers receiving feedback or another group doing the phrase in the next time interval. In the case of rehearsal, the choreographer may give feedback, work on another section of the piece, and then do another run-through. In these intervals between execution, feedback, and another attempt, regardless of how long they are, dancers need to be planning their strategies for improvement. Other activities, such as practicing an entirely different skill, will hinder learning, making the terminal feedback less valuable. Sometimes choreographers give notes at the very end of rehearsal. This strategy is probably not the most effective, unless the choreographer specifically asks the dancers to practice certain sections or movements before the next rehearsal. It might be a better solution to hold the last notes of the evening and give them at the beginning of the next rehearsal. The same approach could be used for giving corrections about a dance combination in class. Unless the dancers will have another opportunity to try the phrase, it may be best to save that information for the next day.

Frequency of Augmented Feedback

Research indicates that constant feedback is not useful for motor skill acquisition. However, no absolute way exists to determine the optimal frequency of feedback, as it is dependent on the type of skill. Because so little research has been done with dancers, it is difficult at this time to recommend specifics regarding frequency of feedback. What can be stated is that it is important to provide dancers with opportunities to repeat material without receiving feedback so that they can develop their own problem-solving strategies. In addition, if feedback is given 100% of the time, dancers can become dependent on receiving feedback and may not do well in terms of retaining information. This idea is called the **guidance hypothesis**, which states that feedback should be used to improve or guide correct performance, but it should not be offered constantly; otherwise, a dependency can develop, impeding performance. Beginners require more feedback, but more skilled dancers need less feedback. As teachers see dancers gaining in skill level, they can gradually reduce the frequency of feedback. This process is known as the **fading procedure**.

Ways that frequency can be reduced to allow dancers to develop problem-solving strategies include using performance bandwidths and giving summaries of feedback only after a certain number of trials. Using performance bandwidths in dance simply means allowing a certain amount of error and not giving feedback, such as in the drift permitted for the 32-fouetté pirouette combination en pointe (figure 12.6). Using summaries of feedback, dancers might attempt six tries of a jump combination, and then they are told that overall their arms were late in going to the lifted position, which diminished the jump height. These methods would be more effective than giving the feedback after every attempt.

The dance class is an experimental laboratory for learning the skills and artistry required of the dancer. It is almost impossible for dancers to see a new movement skill for the first time and immediately execute it with accurate and exacting form. Learning is a process of trial and error, persistence, and gradual improvement. Mistakes are a vital part of the class atmosphere, and all of the various types of guidelines, cues, and feedback are essential. Dancers need and desire the expertise and encouragement of their teachers in guiding their learning experience.

Summary

Using instructional strategies is a foundation of the teaching and learning experience. Demonstration and verbal instructions are the first stage of learning a new skill. To determine when demonstration can be most effective, one must understand that what the learner sees is the coordination pattern of the movement. Mirror neurons may play an important role in how the brain perceives movement demonstrations. Learners can benefit from seeing both expert and novice demonstrations. Demonstrations should be done often, and they should be interspersed between attempts at execution. Learning movements involving complex rhythms can benefit from aural demonstrations. Verbal instructions should be limited to one or two main ideas, and they should be concise and

Figure 12.6 The 32-fouetté pirouette combination is judged not only by the movement but also by remaining in one place in space.

straightforward to avoid information overload. Instructions should direct the learner's attention to external focus rather than internal focus. Instructions that are beneficial include creating discovery learning situations, metaphoric imagery, and verbal analogies. Verbal cues are brief, succinct phrases that act as prompts for main ideas or components of the movement or direct the attention to vital environmental circumstances. Feedback can be task-intrinsic or augmented (provided by an external source). Augmented feedback can be used to enhance skill acquisition or as motivation. Augmented feedback should not be given constantly, because this strategy can create a reliance on the feedback. Forms of augmented feedback include knowledge of results (KR) and knowledge of performance (KP), quantitative and qualitative augmented feedback, and program and parameter feedback. In general, novices need more augmented feedback than skilled performers. Demonstrations, instructions, and augmented feedback are vital components of teaching that secure motor learning efforts of dance students.

Chapter 13
Motivation

*I*magine attending a dance class as an observer. Even if the class is a certain level—perhaps an intermediate class—a range of skills and abilities is apparent. However, another difference between the dancers is noticeable. Regardless of skill level, some dancers seem to be trying harder than others. Their concentration is visible, they are practicing between exercises, they are listening to every correction with intensity, and they may even stay after class to continue working. These dancers are the highly motivated dancers. Other dancers seem less focused, pay less attention to the comments of the teacher, and may even appear to give up quickly if they cannot accomplish something easily. These dancers have low motivation, and their learning will probably suffer as a result. Like arousal, motivation is on a continuum, and people can have a range of motivational states. While motivation is inherent in some people through personality and background, others need to be inspired. This chapter is designed to assist dancers and teachers in understanding the components of motivation and how to stimulate it.

Defining Motivation

Motivation can be viewed from different points in time. Initially people must be motivated in order to start a new activity. Then, motivation must be the driving factor in why people persist in the activity. Finally, motivation engages people so that they are willing to expend time and energy toward improvement. Several factors interact to determine a person's motivation, including attitudes, goals, context, and self-image. Motivation both stimulates the person to perform and also helps to focus activity toward accomplishing a goal. Two reasons people might be motivated include the satisfaction of personal success in mastering a skill and showing higher competence than others at a skill. Highly motivated people exert more effort, are more focused and determined during practice, and are willing to practice for extended amounts of time.

Motivation and performance results are not the same. A person can be highly motivated but still struggle for a long time to acquire a skill. Reasons for this difference include limits to abilities, poor comprehension of the skill, the skill not being age-appropriate, or the person simply needing additional time to acquire the skill. The experience of being motivated is a psychological state, triggered by the person's personal desires and interests. A component of this psychology is the need for self-satisfaction, the desire to do an activity that enhances self-esteem and self-efficacy. **Self-esteem** is a dancer's feelings of worth or value, and it is specific to domains of activity. For example, a dancer can have high self-esteem in dance classes but low self-esteem in science classes. Further, self-esteem is related to the belief in ability, whether or not the dancer's perception of personal talents and skills is accurate. **Self-efficacy** is a dancer's belief that a specific task can be performed successfully, and it is one of the best predictors of successful achievement. If dancers are convinced that they cannot do a particular skill, it will have a negative impact on their ability to accomplish the task. Motivation can be instrumental in affecting both self-esteem and self-efficacy.

Intrinsic and Extrinsic Motivation

Motivation can come from within an individual or can be stimulated by an outside source. **Intrinsic motivation** is generated by internal factors such as a person's curiosity, and it drives the person to continue exploring the task. For example, suppose dancers arrive before class or stay after class to ask questions about a skill and how they can improve it. If their reasons are exclusively because they have a desire to learn and improve, it represents intrinsic motivation, because the motive lies within them. **Extrinsic motivation** comes from factors that lie outside the person, such as praise and criticism. In the case of the dancers arriving early or staying late, if their reasons are because of fear of receiving a poor grade in the class, it represents extrinsic motivation. Some motivators, such as receiving a big part in a new choreography, can be seen as rewards or positive reinforcement. In the end, teachers should strive for all of their dance students to reach a point of being intrinsically motivated. Research on motivation concludes that intrinsic motivation drives people much better and further than does extrinsic motivation.

Persistence

In order to understand how to motivate dancers, it is useful to consider the factors that encourage dancers to persist (continue) with dance activity. These factors include the following:

- The drive to be capable at a skill through perceived improvement, and to be in competitions and performances with an audience
- The need to be a part of a social community (make friends) and to join a performing group or company
- The desire for pleasure and enjoyment, and to be in good physical condition
- The drive to be artistic, to feel a sense of accomplishment, and to feel important and a part of something larger than the self
- The need to please family, friends, and teachers
- The desire to attain **states of flow**, which involve deep immersion in the activity, loss of the sense of time, and a feeling of the activity being effortless

The psychoanalyst and social theorist Erik Erikson developed a model of stages of psychosocial development that describe changes across the life span that affect how motivational factors shift in different age groups. Children have the need to show that they are capable and can achieve skill competence. Therefore, they look for chances to learn and exhibit new skills. Children who perceive that they are successful develop intrinsic motivation. It may be that the levels of intrinsic motivation in adults relate to their experiences in childhood with perceived accomplishment. Research suggests that younger children are more motivated by external reasons, such as family, friends, and teachers, while teenagers are more motivated by internal reasons, such as feelings of success and enjoyment.

Young dancers enjoy opportunities to learn and exhibit new skills.

On the other side of the issue is the question of why people leave an activity. Probably the most common reason is that they lose interest and switch to another activity. As people become aware of new activities, they may simply decide that the newer activity is more suited to their personality and physical attributes than the older activity. Sometimes people are forced to quit because of injuries or because lack of funds compels them to spend more time working and less time doing activities. In addition, negative experiences can cause dancers to drop out of dancing, including the following:

- Conflict with the dance teacher or school director
- The pressures of the activity or the time demands
- Overemphasis on winning awards at competitions
- A decrease in the enjoyment derived from dance

- A failure to see progress or improvement and a lack of opportunities to perform
- Chronic pain
- Disdain from peers, especially for male dancers
- A lack of skill or inability to continue to the next level

Although negative experiences are not the primary reason that people leave an activity, teachers should understand these factors in order to create a positive motivational environment. Many of the negative factors described are avoidable. How teachers and learners jointly create a motivational climate requires knowledge of a variety of methods designed to keep dancers enthusiastic and involved.

Motivational Methods

Motivational methods are strategies designed by the teacher or the learner that engage the learner in approaching a task with energy and enthusiasm. When dancers practice skills with no motivation, the chances for improvement or progress are low. Adding motivating comments during instruction and demonstration can stimulate both interest and enthusiasm for learning the new skill. Additional motivating ideas can be added right before and during practice. For example, while students are doing a traveling combination a teacher might say, "That's it! Move a little farther, and get across the floor by the end of the phrase!" Sometimes it is necessary to explain why the skill or task is important to the learner. The teacher can achieve this goal in several ways. First, the teacher can compare the task at hand to a more desirable long-range goal. For example, practicing balances in passé relevé can be compared to doing pirouettes; when the students realize that the balance practice can improve their turns, they will be more motivated. Second, seeing videos or live performances of elite and professional dancers doing the same or similar skills can be motivating. Third, letting students know that when they succeed at a particular task, the class will move on to new material can also encourage them to work harder at learning a skill. Once dancers have been excited by the

awareness of why learning a particular new skill is important, they are ready to begin their practice. Factors that affect motivation include setting goals, praise and criticism, success and failure, cooperation and competition, and feedback.

Setting Goals

Goals serve to motivate people to do their best. **Goal setting** is the process of determining challenging yet attainable goals before practice begins. American psychologists and pioneers in goal setting theory Edwin Locke and Gary Latham have done extensive research over decades on the subject of goal setting and motivation. Based on their research, they developed these principles of goal setting, which have much to offer dancers and dance teachers in thinking about the learning environment:

- Direct or precise goals are better than vague goals. Simply encouraging learners to do their best does not lead to progress; it is not specific enough to be helpful. General encouragement without exacting goals may show benefit during the initial learning of the new skill, but in the long run, specific goals result in better skill acquisition and retention.
- Goals that present challenges are better motivators than easy goals, assuming the task is not too far beyond the abilities of the learners. If goals are too easy, they do not stimulate the best learning efforts.
- Short-term goals can lead to the accomplishment of long-term goals, and the best strategy is setting a combination of short-term and long-term goals. For a dancer, if the long-term goal aims to achieve speed at a certain fast combination, a short-term goal would be to increase the speed a bit each day.
- In order for goals to be effective, learners need feedback about progress. If learners have no feedback about how they are doing, they have no way to measure changes in their performance or to assess their work.
- Learners must accept the goals. If learners do not accept the goals as valid, they will not commit themselves to achieving them and will not accomplish them. At times, dancers need discussion of the value of a goal, such as

making a change in alignment, to understand its importance. In addition, they need support during the process of working on a new or difficult goal.

- In order to achieve goals, a plan of action must be in place. Teachers without clear curricular plans over time, outlining specific goals in a reasonable sequence, will have a difficult time getting learners to sustain the motivation to progress.

- In many sports, competition is a type of goal setting. In dance, competition can also be used, but it should not be encouraged to such an extent that it creates a hostile learning environment. Dance is a form that requires both cooperation and competition in the learning environment.

- Goals alter performance by influencing effort, persistence, and attention. Both the clarity of the goals and the encouragement provided by ongoing success will continue to motivate learners to achieve their goals.

In addition, the researchers propose four characteristics that explain why goal setting works. First, goals focus on the specifics of the activity, and they direct the learner's attention and energy. Second, goals assist the learner in controlling and determining the effort needed for the activity. Third, goals assist the learner in sustaining the attention and persistence needed in order to achieve the goal. Fourth, goals can encourage the development of new approaches to enhancing skill learning.

Goals act in the capacity of a reference or standard that learners can use to compare their current activity to what they desire to achieve. Each time learners assess their performance in relation to their goal, they can see if they are

When dancers construct group shapes together, cooperation is needed.

getting closer to the goal and use this observation as a measure of success, even if they have not yet achieved the goal. For dancers who tend to be highly self-critical and place high expectations on themselves, this aspect of goal setting can be an important positive reassurance, as long as the teacher makes sure that the goals are not unrealistic or unattainable.

Depending on the level and age of the learners, it can be useful at times to have them participate in the development of goals. Suppose a teacher asks a group of dancers why they are struggling with balance in their adagio work. The dancers might say that they think their core support is insufficient. At this point, the dancers might decide that their goal over the next month is to do exercises outside class time to improve their core support. The teacher can then assist them by cueing them in class about their core in balancing work and praising them when changes are observed.

Finally, goals can be developed with the specific purpose of improving self-confidence. One

When corrections are given in a positive manner, dancers can improve in both skills and self-confidence.

aspect of this approach is to allow learners to see in small stages that they are indeed improving. Another aspect is to keep the attention on the goal, which might act to diminish tension, nervousness, or self-critical thoughts. In this way, goals can provide a kind of mental training that works to enhance both self-confidence and skill acquisition.

Praise and Criticism

As described in chapter 12, feedback can be delivered in the form of praise or criticism. Feedback can be used as a form of motivation to help people learn a new skill. At this point it is not clear from the research whether praise contributes to skill acquisition, but it is known that it functions as a motivational tool. Criticism (relating errors to the learner) is useful for improving skills, and psychologically it can be better for motivation than giving no commentary at all. Both praise and criticism are most effective in certain conditions. First, the learner must understand that praise and criticism are not given routinely and unconditionally. Second, learners cannot expect praise and criticism on a constant basis. Third, learners must realize that the teacher often designs praise and criticism to be specific to each learner. **Constructive criticism** involves comments given in a supportive, positive tone and with the intention of being helpful to the learner. **Destructive criticism** involves insults that are often given in a tone of annoyance or frustration. Constructive criticism is highly effective in giving learners information that they can use to improve performance, while destructive criticism tends to lower self-esteem and impede learning. Content of the criticism is as important as the tone. After constructive criticism is given, dancers are able to change something based on what the teacher says. Destructive criticism is generally vague, and it focuses on the dancer rather than the skill, leaving the dancer with nothing concrete to change.

Sometimes teachers become frustrated because they have been giving dancers the same corrections repeatedly without seeing any change. Strategies exist to help teachers and learners deal with this situation. First, both need to remember that change can take a long time, and lack of progress does not indicate a lack of effort or concentration. Second, they need to acknowledge that dancers learn at very different rates and that some dancers will not acquire a skill when others do. Third, teachers can ensure that they are delivering material in a variety of methods so that different learning styles are recognized. It is always beneficial for teachers to continue to assess their methods and word choice in delivering corrections to ensure the most positive results. Fourth, it may be beneficial to discontinue work on a particular skill temporarily and return to it at a later date, which can psychologically be a boost for both the teachers and the dancers. Finally, times do occur in the training of dancers when they need a discussion regarding work ethic and concentration. It can also be noted that as discussed in part I, regression of motor skills can occur at various stages of motor development, such as the adolescent growth spurts. Both teachers and dancers need to acknowledge these phases and not become discouraged.

Success and Failure

Success and failure in learning motor skills has a powerful effect on the psychology of learners. Learners who are often successful tend to feel competent and self-assured, while learners who deal regularly with failure tend to be anxious, be less self-assured, and have difficulty setting appropriate goals. Recurring failure also diminishes motivation. Teachers can offer opportunities for a combination of success and failure to students who are highly motivated, but it is best with those who have low motivation to focus primarily on opportunities for success. This difference can be achieved through differing feedback and demands, giving praise to those learners with low motivation to boost their self-confidence. However, it is essential that the praise be deserved. For example, effort can be complimented, and a skill can be praised even if only a small portion of the skill was successfully executed. Finally, the exercises or combinations can be adapted in class for dancers at different levels of experience and training. For example, some dancers can do a traveling combination with turns while others do it without the turns. At the barre, some dancers

can execute a combination relevé while others execute it on flatfoot. Finally, dancers should be made aware that errors do not imply failure; errors are required in order for learning to take place. The system must know what is wrong so that it has a basis of comparison, and trial and error is a proven method of effective learning.

Cooperation and Competition

Dance training requires both cooperation and competition, and both can act as motivators to encourage learning. **Cooperation** is the process of working together or acting in harmony. Usually when people think of dancers working cooperatively, it is in the choreographic setting. However, dancers should learn cooperation in the training setting as well. **Competition** is a challenge between two or more people, and it can occur for a variety of goals, such as being the best at a skill, prestige, recognition by the teacher or audience, awards, and placement in a company or choreography. It is seen as the opposite of cooperation. It occurs when people are striving for the same goal, but it cannot be shared. Note that cooperation and competition are not necessarily mutually exclusive. A dance class can be structured to provide the best of both approaches, and how the teacher balances the two depends on a variety of factors, including age, skill level, and material being presented. For example, with younger children, the balance should be weighted toward cooperation. Also, if a class has dancers of widely varying levels, favoring competition would not foster self-esteem in each dancer. Dancers have different preferences; some respond better in a competitive atmosphere, and others respond better to a cooperative environment. In dealing with competition, two guidelines are useful. First, even if dancers are trying to outshine each other, the dancers should keep in mind that their primary goal is to achieve their best individual effort—their personal best. Second, the environment must allow for everyone involved to have the opportunity for success in some way and be recognized for outstanding effort. Dancers do not learn well in an environment where they think that only some of the dancers present are going to succeed. Teachers should be cognizant of giving praise to all of dancers, asking different dancers to stand in the front of the class, and having different dancers go across the floor first.

Extensive research exists on the theory and value of cooperative learning. However, it is not sufficient to place students in groups and give them no structure for how to work together. All cooperative learning methods emphasize the notion that students are not only working together, they are responsible for each other's learning. Cooperative learning has certain specific parameters. **Positive interdependence** suggests that members of the group have common goals and understand that working together benefits both the individuals and the group. Also, in order to achieve success, everyone must participate. **Individual accountability** takes this idea a step further. It means that groups will receive rewards based on the learning of everyone in the group. **Equal participation and equal opportunities for success** means that no individual is singled out, but everyone has chances to get involved and succeed. **Explicit teaching of social and collaborative skills** means that the teacher is clear in the instructions that a primary goal of group work is related to fostering collaboration. **Simultaneous engagement or interaction** suggests that everyone is participating actively in the process. These parameters help to ensure that group work in class has clear goals and will lead to enhanced learning for every member of the group in addition to fostering the much-needed ability in dancers to work together.

Feedback

Feedback in its many forms (introduced in chapter 12) can have a powerful effect on motivation. As stated previously, praise influences self-confidence, which in turn affects motivation. Motivation has two components. The

Dancers can assist each other in developing new skills and cooperate in the learning process.

directive function of motivation aids people in directing their energy to achieve goals and choose certain courses of action. The arousal function of motivation determines how much energy people employ on future attempts at the skill. Teachers and learners can more effectively stimulate motivation when they know which component of motivation needs attention at a given time. Teachers can select to give feedback that encourages a particular strategy (directive function), or they can select feedback that suggests more effort is needed (arousal function). Dance and sports training involve the extensive repetition of many simple exercises and skills, and it is crucial to provide motivational feedback to keep learners interested and energetic in the process.

Generally, praise is best for motivation, and criticism (information about errors) serves to enhance skills. Recent research indicates that praise may in fact have a learning effect. Learners demonstrated improved performance after receiving information about successful attempts, seen in a sport skill and in a balance test. In addition, learners preferred receiving feedback telling them when they had done a task correctly. While the research is sparse in this area, teachers should not dismiss the potential strength of positive feedback and praise for both motivation and skill enhancement.

Motivation plays an important role in skill acquisition. Most dancers have experienced phases of boredom, complacency, or frustration in their practice. Both dancers and teachers can aid in overcoming these periods through effective motivational methods. Even when dancers are doing well and are enthusiastic, motivation can give them incentive to strive for higher achievement. Goal setting, feedback, and a healthy balance of cooperation and competition can all serve to excite and direct dancers in the challenges of dance training.

Special Considerations for Children

Motivation is not a constant across the life span. Children and adults have differing needs and respond to different motivational strategies. Children may participate in an activity simply because their parents want them to try it or because their friends are doing it, while adults need some internal or personal motivation for engaging in a new activity.

Children who attend dance classes may be enrolled because they asked to take a class or because the parents made the decision. Generally, children who self-select to take dance classes are intrinsically motivated to participate. Unless the experience is disappointing or they become interested in a different activity, they will continue to be active learners. On the other hand, children who are placed in classes by parents or by the school system may need additional encouragement to engage. In the early years, the class should avoid excessive repetition, and it should include creative play as a foundation of the material. Children respond well to praise, and they need reassurance that they are accepted and recognized. The occasional opportunity to display their work for family and friends is a benchmark of achievement, but the competitive atmosphere should be downplayed. Finally, boys who want to dance should be placed in classes with other boys whenever possible, even if it means being less rigid about age groupings.

Recently, discussion in childhood educational circles has been generated around the topic of teacher-centered versus student-centered learning. These concepts are not new; for example, they can be seen in the structure of Montessori Education, founded in the late 1800s by physician and educator Maria Montessori. However, with an increasing interest in divergent learning styles, a renewed discussion of these ideas has occurred in both academic and motor learning circles. In teacher-centered learning, the teacher designs the activities and decides when the students are ready to move to the next level. In student-centered learning, students can make autonomous decisions about the content and timing of learning. Studies involving motor skills have demonstrated that student-centered learning can be highly successful. Designing a student-centered program involves allowing children to make choices on activities, letting children be involved in decision making and self-evaluation, and providing children with exploration time. Teachers still act as the primary authority and in monitoring activity and progress. More research is needed to determine if a teacher-centered or a student-centered approach yields better results in motor learning.

Guidelines for Teaching

Dance educators have pondered the dilemma of wanting to create a positive, supportive atmosphere in class that encourages the development of high self-esteem but also wanting an atmosphere that impels dancers to reach their optimal levels of skill mastery. Many teachers think that the class can do one or the other, but both cannot be realized at the same time. Psychologist Lynda Mainwaring and dance researcher Donna Krasnow proposed an alternative perspective that presents a series of guidelines for the dance class embracing the best values of each approach; it is outlined in figure 13.1. These guidelines combine aspects of dance pedagogy, education, physical education and sport pedagogy, and psychology. The guidelines are divided into three sections: clarifying the process and goals of the class, discussing various influences that affect the dancer's progress, and clearly defining the class structure and content. Three areas and the content outlined in figure 13.1 are discussed in detail in the next three sections.

Process and Goals

SMART planning states that teachers should encourage students to set SMART—**s**pecific, **m**easureable, **a**ge-appropriate, **r**ealistic, and **t**ime-targeted—goals. Most of these categories were described in the section titled Setting Goals. If goals are well defined and follow these guiding principles, a context is established that determines how dancers can perceive their progress and achieve realistic success.

Decision making by objective implies providing variety in decision-making aspects of class and identifying the objectives to be met by each task. One of the practical approaches is for dancers to write their goals in a journal that can emphasize defining personal directives

with clarity, insight, and a progressive plan. In addition, the teacher can allow both individual and group decision making. For example, the teacher might ask the class whether they would like to try an elevation phrase across the floor at a slower tempo, which increases difficulty. Some students may choose to try it slower, and others may wish to continue working at the same tempo.

Optimizing the self within community means to recognize individual differences and optimize individual potential, while encouraging students to work in collaboration with peers. Dancers can be taught to appreciate differences in anatomical build, movement qualities, and expressive characteristics. In recognizing these differences, dancers can be encouraged to take different approaches to personal development. Flexible dancers can address strength and core support issues, and stronger dancers can work on their flexibility. As dancers learn to rely more on themselves and each other, they can be less dependent on the teacher for approval. Finally, allowing time for work in pairs and small groups develops self-confidence, an exploratory approach to learning, and an experience in collaborative work process.

Ritualizing respect means fostering an environment of mutual, reciprocal, and self-respect in and out of the classroom. All teachers design rules or class etiquette for their dance classes that establish protocols for class behavior. It is useful to explain these rules in terms of creating an environment that supports concentration and respect rather than an autocratic structure. Students can learn to balance their needs with sensitivity for the whole class. For example, asking students not to talk during class is not so that the teacher can control them, it is so that the environment is concentrated. This focus encourages an ideal learning atmosphere, and it creates a sense of cooperation rather than competition. Class ritual creates a motivational climate and simultaneously allows for open discussion.

Influences Affecting the Dancer

Mentoring involves embodying the qualities of a positive leader and role model. The teacher offers a variety of perspectives to the dancers: personal background and views, the informa-

Process and Goals

- *SMART planning:* Encourage students to set **s**pecific, **m**easureable, **a**ge-appropriate, **r**ealistic, and **t**ime-targeted goals.
- *Decision making by objective:* Provide variety in decision-making aspects of class, and identify the objectives to be met by each task.
- *Optimizing the self within community:* Recognize individual differences, and optimize individual potential; encourage students to work in collaboration with peers.
- *Ritualizing respect:* Foster an environment of mutual self-respect in and out of the classroom.

Influences Affecting the Dancer

- *Mentoring:* Embody the qualities of a positive leader and role model.
- *Nurturing the learner:* Provide positive reinforcement and constructive criticism in such ways that the student can develop skill mastery and comprehension of principles.
- *Creating fun and challenges for all:* Foster an enjoyable, challenging atmosphere for learning and experience.
- *Empowering the self:* Recognize and positively reinforce the dancer for personal qualities and contributions to the class; empower students to feel good about their bodies and their self-development.
- *Focusing on the task:* Encourage students to focus on the task at hand and not the outcome or social or interpersonal comparisons.
- *Thinking about learning:* Provide opportunities for students to explore personal metacognitive strategies ("How do I learn?" activities and discussion).

Structure and Content of the Class

- *Building foundations:* Build foundations of domain-specific knowledge in progressive sequence and with complementary background information.
- *Mixing and matching:* Provide opportunities to learn or process information in various ways across learning tasks and situations, including somatic and analytic strategies, and contextual variety.
- *Developing body awareness:* Provide somatic experiences, information, and opportunities.
- *Enhancing body image:* Provide opportunities to discuss and reinforce healthy body image and supportive strategies in terms of nutrition and conditioning.
- *Embracing the safe and sound:* Ensure that safe practices are established and based on sound scientific, medical, and empirical evidence regarding alignment work and prevention and management of injuries.
- *Creating enlightened practice:* Provide constructive feedback and incorporate appropriate repetition.

Figure 13.1 A summary of the guidelines for teaching and learning dance.
Based on Mainwaring and Krasnow 2010.

tion from the teachers with whom they studied, and a broad knowledge of the dance world. Teachers should acknowledge that they have tremendous influence and embrace this role without abusing it. They can be positive role models in terms of their respect for each person's desires and differences and in terms of their own behavior and attitudes.

Nurturing the learner means providing positive reinforcement and constructive criticism

It is important for dancers to understand the focus and attention needed right from the start of class.

in ways the students can develop skill mastery and comprehension of principles. This aspect of influences was described in the section Praise and Criticism. In addition to the tone and content of feedback, dancers exhibit more progress if the material is presented in terms of concepts and principles. Another way of nurturing the learner is to recognize different learning styles, such as visual, analytic, and kinesthetic. Finally, teachers can include procedures that enrich self-esteem and self-efficacy. Teachers should remember that their attitude toward the dancer is communicated not only by the words they use but also by their body language and tone.

Creating fun and challenges for all suggests fostering an enjoyable, challenging atmosphere for learning and experience. It is easy for class to become so serious and demanding that stress, tension, and anxiety become the dominant psychological states. Some practical strategies for fostering enjoyment include using humor, embracing the positive gains learned from mistakes, adding occasional improvisation, using joyful music, and giving praise for good work. The tasks must be sufficiently challenging that dancers do not become bored, but they cannot be so difficult that everyone is constantly frustrated. Finding the balance is key.

Empowering the self includes recognizing and positively reinforcing the dancer for personal qualities and contributions to the class, and empowering students to feel good about their bodies and their self-development. Teachers and dancers can engage in a dialogue about the dance culture's definition of what determines a great dancer. In some dance circles, this definition is only about the dancer's body, such as excessive flexibility, excellent proportions, perfect turnout, or extreme thinness. Dancers can become depressed and disheartened, thinking that they have no control over their advancement. The definition of a great dancer can include performance skills, energy, musicality, and artistry. Further, another influence to discuss is negative self-talk—thoughts that reflect on destructive ideas about the self and skill level. While dancers do want the ability to self-correct, which requires a certain amount of self-criticism, they cannot be constantly consumed with negativity that disrupts concentration. Finally, teachers and dancers can discuss external aspects: media such as images of hyper-thin dancers, common perspectives from the dance culture such as continuing to dance in pain and injury, and previous negative dance experiences.

Arabesque is a difficult skill that can overwhelm dancers psychologically because of the emphasis that is sometimes placed on perfection.

Focusing on the task means to encourage students to focus on the task at hand and not the outcome or social or interpersonal comparisons. Self-assessment in relation to the dancing of others can create a pressure to compete rather than concentrate on the task. It can also lead to obsession with body image and being overly concerned with teacher approval. When teachers respect each dancer's attributes and they give criticism and praise to all, it creates an environment that encourages dancers to remain focused on personal accomplishment.

Thinking about learning involves providing opportunities for students to explore personal metacognitive strategies—that is, "How do I learn?" activities and discussion. The teacher can ask the dancers to discern their learning preferences, whether it is visual or kinesthetic, melodic or rhythmic, or body or space orientation. Dancers are inspired and empowered by understanding their personal learning styles.

Structure and Content of the Class

Building foundations should be of domain-specific knowledge in progressive sequence and with complementary background information. Class should be more than a series of warm-up exercises followed by choreographic material. If not teaching a specific traditional technique, the class should have a certain approach or set of unifying principles. Classes should progress from basic skills to complex skills, which means that teachers need to understand what the foundation is for their particular area, whether it is ballet, modern, jazz, tap, contemporary, African, flamenco, classical Indian, or urban dance. In addition, the foundation should include general body skills such as alignment, balance, awareness of space and music, and coordination.

Mixing and matching involves providing opportunities to learn or process information in various ways across learning tasks and situations, including somatic and analytic strategies, and contextual variety. Teachers can emphasize different methods of introducing material at different times, such as one day with a focus on verbal instructions, another day on demonstration. On another day, the teacher might focus on a somatic approach. Each of these approaches highlights a different learning style: analytic, visual, and kinesthetic. Another strategy for varying class is the occasional elimination of familiar aspects, such as use of the barre, floor work, mirrors, and music. The class can change facings in the room, and students can even work with the eyes closed or in silence. Variety can serve to prevent boredom as well as enhance learning.

Developing body awareness means providing somatic experiences, information, and opportunities. Somatic approaches and imagery are both excellent tools to enhance awareness of the body and to develop mind–body connections. Somatic practice and imagery can enhance alignment, improve coordination, and encourage expressivity. Suggesting to dancers that they develop and communicate their own created images has three purposes. First, it expands their tools for working on body awareness. Second, it builds confidence by letting dancers know that their ideas are appreciated by the teacher and the other students. Third, it assists dancers in developing their ability to communicate with others about the body, preparing them to be choreographers and teachers.

Enhancing body image suggests providing opportunities to discuss and reinforce healthy body image and supportive strategies in terms of nutrition and conditioning. The dance literature suggests that many dancers have poor self-image and as a result suffer from eating disorders. The teacher can encourage discussions of proper nutrition and healthy means of sustaining an appropriate body weight for dance. Subtle messages, such as only allowing very thin dancers to perform in shows, send the wrong message. In many ways the teacher sets the tone for weight management, positive body image, and acceptance of a wide range of body types.

Embracing the safe and sound suggests ensuring that safe practices are established based on sound scientific, medical and empirical evidence regarding alignment work and prevention and management of injuries. Teachers can take several approaches to give dancers a better basis for safe practice. One is introducing supplementary conditioning so that the dancers have better levels of strength, flexibility, proprioception, and overall fitness for dance practice. Second, teachers can incorporate knowledge about injury prevention and management. Third, teachers can make dancers aware of organizations devoted to healthy artistic practice such as the International Association for Dance Medicine & Science, the Performing Arts Medicine Association, and Healthy Dancer Canada. Third, teachers need to understand the pacing or timing of the dance class in order to build stamina but avoid excessive fatigue. Both complexity and repetitions need to be increased progressively. Fourth, teachers can allow dancers to modify material to suit individual and timely needs, such as during growth

spurts or injury rehabilitation. Modifications might include lowering the height of legs or the number of jumps or reduced range of motion in the spine. As dancers gain both knowledge and physical attributes that contribute to safe practice, fear and apprehension will diminish, and motivation can increase.

Creating enlightened practice means providing constructive feedback and incorporating appropriate repetition. The value of constructive feedback was described at length in the section titled Praise and Criticism. It is advantageous for dancers to repeat a combination after hearing the feedback, in order to have the chance to improve their efforts. In addition to consolidating the information, it enhances self-confidence through perceptions of success. How teachers discuss mistakes is crucial to the long-term success of dancers. The myth that dancers should aim to make no mistakes during class is destructive. Mistakes are an essential part of the learning process. For example, the balancing mechanisms actually need disturbance and loss of balance to learn new balancing strategies. As dancers embrace the positive aspects of making mistakes, experimentation and risk taking become part of their class approach and attitude. While it may seem that this method is asking teachers to be less demanding, the opposite is true, because error and experimentation achieve better gains. As a result, teachers can accelerate the class progression, and over time they can demand a higher level of achievement.

Every dancer is in pursuit of excellence. Whether active as a recreational dancer or aspiring to be a professional dancer, all dancers want to do their best. The single most important factor in achieving personal goals is motivation. Motivation is what drives people to start a new activity, to strive for improvement, to persist through difficulty, and to excel in the end. The love of dance is important, but without the drive to confront obstacles and keep going, success is impossible. Film director and producer George Lucas said, "You have to find something that you love enough to be able to take risks, jump over the hurdles and break through the brick walls that are always going to be placed in front of you. If you don't have that kind of feeling for what it is you are doing, you'll stop at the first giant hurdle." Dancers need to bring their love of dance to the process and then find the ongoing motivation to keep going, despite obstacles and setbacks. Both are essential to success.

Summary

Motivation brings people to begin a new activity, is the driving factor in why people persist in the activity, and engages people so that they are willing to expend time and energy toward improvement. Motivational methods are strategies designed by the teacher or the learner that engage the learner in approaching a task with energy and enthusiasm. Both intrinsic and extrinsic motivation encourage dancers to succeed in their goals. The persistence to continue dancing includes many factors, such as the drive to be capable at the skills, the need to be artistic and to feel a sense of accomplishment, and the desire to feel important and a part of something larger than the self. Motivational methods include goal setting, praise and constructive criticism, creating a balance of cooperation and competition, and feedback. Children have special needs in terms of motivational climate, and they start out extrinsically motivated. Teacher guidelines for all ages include methods for establishing and positively affecting process and goals, influences affecting the dancer, and structure and content of the class. Teachers have the responsibility and knowledge to establish the best possible motivational environments for their dancers.

Chapter 14
Conditions of Practice

All dancers understand that improving at dance demands practice. In both myth and reality, many ideas revolve around practice. Some sayings about practice include the following:

- "Practice makes perfect."
- "Practice is everything."
- "Practice does not make perfect; only perfect practice makes perfect."
- "If practice makes perfect, and no one's perfect, then why practice?"
- "They say that nobody is perfect. Then they tell you practice makes perfect. I wish they'd make up their minds."
- "They say that practice makes perfect. Of course, it doesn't. For the vast majority of athletes it merely consolidates imperfection."
- "Practice makes permanent."
- "Nobody likes practice, but what's worse—practicing, or sucking at something?"
- "Excellence is a habit, not an act. It takes practice and perseverance."
- "Expertise in any field is the result of intense practice for a minimum of 10 years. It takes about 10,000 hours or 10 years of dedicated practice to truly master a skill, be it playing the violin, computer programming, skateboarding, or dancing."

The need for practice is so widely recognized that it is actually referred to as the *law* of practice. The **law of practice** has mathematical formulas connected to it, but simply stated, it says that only practice improves performance, and that after a certain point, improvement slows as skill increases. However, most teachers and dancers realize that skill does not improve with just any practice. Activities must be carefully constructed with the intent of improving skill execution, called **deliberate practice**. In order to design effective and deliberate practice, several aspects must be clear. One is how much constancy or variety of a skill should be included in its practice. A second is how much practice should be encouraged and how

this practice time should be allocated. A third aspect is whether to practice parts of the skill or the entire skill. All of these aspects fall under the category of conditions of practice. This chapter describes conditions of practice, including how to implement and organize variability, which involves changes to practice. It also explores how specific to make practice, how the environment affects practice, and mass and distributed practice. Both whole and part practice are explained, as well as various forms of part practice, including use of attention. The chapter explores the benefits of improvisation and the use of mirrors in dance training in light of recent research. To aid in understanding the effects of practice on performance, the chapter begins with a description of two methods for assessment of learning.

Variability in Practice

Teachers and dancers are always seeking to understand how to design practice conditions that will be successful in teaching and learning new skills. As with feedback, sometimes performance of a skill improves immediately during a practice session, but the skill has not necessarily been learned. Two ways that can determine learning are transfer tests and retention tests. **Transfer of learning** is the effect or influence that skill or knowledge acquired in one circumstance has on skill acquisition and problem-solving ability in another circumstance; **transfer of training** is transfer of learning applied to motor skills. **Retention** is the ability to recall or recognize what has been learned or experienced. Researchers have developed both transfer and retention tests to determine if a skill has been learned or if it simply exhibits improvement in a given practice session. Transfer tests and retention tests are similar in that they both assess the persistence of the acquired ability for performance. **Transfer tests** have the learners changing to different tasks or conditions. **Retention tests** occur after a period of time but usually test the learner on the same task or conditions. Teachers can use transfer and retention assessments in order to determine the best practice conditions for what they are teaching. These assessments give teachers information about whether or not their methods are successful in helping their students learn dance skills.

When incorporating skill practice into the dance class, teachers make decisions about whether to use variable or constant practice. **Variable practice** includes varying both the movement and the environment that the learner experiences while practicing. For example, dancers can practice ballroom dances at various speeds and add turns, which varies the movement, and they can practice with different partners and shoes, which varies the environment. Figure 14.1 shows variable practice in a dance triplet. **Constant practice** refers to keeping the movement and environmental elements the same each time the skill is practiced. The majority of research studies involving motor skills suggest that variable practice is superior to constant practice in both transfer and retention. Variable practice increases the **generalizability** of a skill, which is learning a specific skill or process and applying it broadly to many skills or skill variations. It might seem that variability would be problematic, because it is associated with an increase in errors during practice. However, it is not necessarily the case that increased errors lead to detriments in skill learning. Errors during practice can lead to better transfer of the learned skill to novel contexts or skill variations, especially during the early stages of learning. This result has been demonstrated in research involving transfer tests, but it is thought to be dependent on the type of the skill and the type of errors. These

parameters have not yet been clearly defined in the literature.

Implementing Variability in Practice

In order to determine how to create variability in practice, two aspects of the skill need to be analyzed: the features of the physical environment and the skill characteristics. Aspects of the physical environment for dancers that directly affect movement are floor surfacing, the size of the performance space, mirrors, music tempo, costumes, and props. For example, if the floor of the performance space is made of a different material than the floor of the practice space, time should be reserved in the performance space for some of the practice sessions. Research shows that learners associate dynamics of movements with particular spaces. For example, a sprung floor in one space causes dancers to use their muscles in one way, and a floor in another room that is not sprung causes them to use their muscles in another way. The main consideration is that while some generalization exists across the spaces, one must allow for a period of learning and adjustment to the dynamics of each space.

If live music will be used, dancers should have the opportunity to practice with the musicians or at least practice at varying tempos. In addition, dancers should have opportunities to work in the costumes if they will have an impact on the movement. Other aspects of the environment do not directly affect the movement but can have an influence. For example,

Weight stays where it is on step preceding the 1, and the gesture (left) leg brushes forward

Weight is shifted forward so the weight lands between the two legs on the 1

Weight shifts more forward so the weight lands completely on the leading (left) leg on the 1

Figure 14.1   Three variations of the low (plié) step in various dance triplets.

Created by Donna Krasnow.

the height of the ceiling can psychologically alter how dancers move in elevation work. Adding a large group scene behind a solo or duet can affect the dancer's experience of the choreography.

The second aspect, the movement characteristics, depends on whether the skill is closed or open. **Closed skills** are skills that are done the same way each time; they follow the same general motor plan, and little demand is on the performer because of changing environmental conditions. If the closed skill involves changes to parameters outside the general motor plan (GMP), then practice should be varied regarding only the specific aspects that can change from one trial to the next. Variety is not needed regarding aspects that will not change. For example, if dancers are learning a particular leap that will be done at different tempos or covering different distances, practice should include variations of time and distance, but it should not include variations of aspects such as the arm and torso movements. **Open skills** are skills that need to be done in many variations of timing, gestures, and spacing, and they usually involve conditions that are frequently changing. These skills require even more variability of practice, providing experiences that alter every aspect of the skill, including gestures, timing variations, multi-limb coordination, spatial patterns, organization of body parts, and differing ways to share weight with a partner.

Dance is a mixture of closed and open skills, and different forms emphasize one or the other. In ballet classes and choreography, many skills are repeated in the same way, with perhaps some slight timing variations. Practice with little variation would benefit learning of many of these skills. An example would be the large circling coupé jeté sequence done by male ballet dancers. At the other extreme, contact improvisation comprises open skills with constant variation, variability, and unexpected changes occurring for the dancers. While contact impro-

Weight sharing between dancers can build confidence and connection to others as well as movement skills.

visation classes do include some repetition of certain lifting skills, the classes and performances in this form are always changing.

Organizing Variability in Practice

The benefits of variability in practice have been established, and therefore the next factor to consider is how to organize practice. The best approach to this challenge is to involve contextual interference. **Contextual interference**, also called **contextual variety**, is the disturbance of performance and memory caused by practicing multiple skills or variations of a skill within one practice situation. The **contextual interference effect** refers to the benefits to learning caused by performing multiple skills or variations of a skill in a practice context with high contextual interference. For example, doing a leg exercise in a modern or jazz class could combine développés front, side, and back with rond de jambes, interrupted by body cambrés (curves in all directions) in between leg actions. This combination includes variations of the développé along with other skills, all mixed together.

Other terms that are used to describe this concept are random practice and blocked practice. **Random practice** is practice that involves high contextual interference, or practicing many variations of a skill mixed together with other skills, within a given practice session. The structure of most dance classes encourages random practice. Dancers move from one skill to the next in all phases of the class, and they even mix skills within the same combinations. **Blocked practice** is practice that involves low contextual interference (practicing a skill the same way with many repetitions) within a given practice session. Examples of blocked practice include doing an excessively long exercise of the same skill repeatedly, such as executing pirouettes in a ballet class from fourth position demi-plié with the same arms and timing, or practicing step, ball–change across the floor in jazz class over and over with no variation in arms or timing. Therefore, in order to benefit from the contextual interference effect, it is essential to include random practice.

Results of research suggest that variable and random practice show better results on both transfer and retention tests than constant and blocked practice. Two points should be emphasized. The first point is that during many of the studies, groups doing constant or blocked practice often appeared to have better skill acquisition during the practice sessions. However, they had worse results than the variable or random practice group in the later testing for learning effects. The second point is that random practice yields an even higher learning effect on transfer tests for more complex skills. Researchers suggest that when learners practice the same skill repeatedly for extended periods (constant/blocked practice), they become less adaptable, and they cannot execute the skill in novel ways. These principles of practice apply to both beginners and skilled learners. Teachers sometimes think that beginners need to practice a new skill repeatedly with no variation. This may be true for a very brief time when they are first learning it, but the research suggests that even beginners need variable practice in the learning environment. One way to achieve variable practice with children and beginners while avoiding overloading them is to intersperse improvisations between practice of a given skill. This technique breaks up blocked practice and also prevents mental fatigue. It is noteworthy that while some methods of randomizing practice would be beneficial, they are too impractical to implement. For example, skills that dancers need to do in both bare feet and en pointe must be practiced in different practice sessions. It is not feasible in a given session to go back and forth between the two.

One reason proposed for the efficacy of random practice is known as the forgetting hypothesis. The **forgetting hypothesis** states that random practice avoids repeating the same task over and over, allowing short-term forgetting, which necessitates the learner to produce the movement plan on every trial. In this way, the method of producing the plan is learned, aiding in effective skill retention. Blocked practice does not accomplish this result.

An additional observation about contextual interference is that people who participate in blocked practice do not judge their progress accurately, and they tend to overestimate what they have learned. When they are given and learning style of the learner can have an impact on how much or how little variability should be involved. For example, elite performers can clearly handle more variation in practice than beginners. Some skills benefit more from higher levels of variation than other skills. More research would be needed to determine the specifics of these factors, but based on what is now known, teachers should use variation in training. They should also follow their instincts about balancing constant with variable practice and blocked with random practice.

Specificity of Practice

Imagine two ballroom dancers practicing a partner dance in preparation for a competition. Sheila practices in jeans and comfortable character shoes. Colin practices in baggy pants and a t-shirt. They are practicing in a gymnasium with a wood floor, and they use the same music every day and play it on an MP3 player. They never practice with anyone watching. In the competition, they wear standard clothing for their dance: a fitted dress and high heels for Sheila, and a fitted suit for Colin. The performance space is smaller than the gymnasium, with a vinyl floor. The judges have asked for a change in music, coming from loudspeakers. A large and noisy crowd has arrived to see the competition. Sheila and Colin are quite disoriented by all of these changes, and they do poorly in their first competition. They realize that they would have been better prepared if their practice conditions had more closely resembled their competition or test conditions. The **specificity of practice hypothesis** states that when two situations have physical and mental components in common, greater transfer between the two situations will occur. This hypothesis is supported by research in three areas of motor learning: sensory–perceptual elements, performance environment, and cognitive skills.

Sensory–Perceptual Elements

Sensory–perceptual elements refer to vision, hearing, and proprioception, and how these senses add to motor skill learning. The sensory information available during practice must specifically be present during later executions of

This dancer is trying to vary her practice by performing both in bare feet and en pointe at the same time!

retention and transfer tests later, they do worse than anticipated. On the other hand, people trained with random practice are much better at ascertaining their level of improvement. This phenomenon can occur with children who study only ballet syllabus. They think that they have acquired a certain skill, but they can only accomplish it in the context of the learned exercise and have difficulty transferring it to a new combination. Therefore, teachers who usually instruct in syllabus for exams should give nonsyllabus classes during the year.

A final point regarding contextual interference and variability of practice is that the type of skill and the level, age, intellectual capacity, the skill. For example, if dancers only practice in a well-lit studio and use what they see on the walls and floor to set their spacing, they can have great difficulty transferring the dance piece to a stage where they see open and dark space in front of them, the floor landmarks gone, and altered lighting. These visual changes may cause a decrease in ability. Further, the longer dancers practice with set conditions involving visual, auditory, and proprioceptive input, the more their dependence on this input in the future actually increases. Hence, varying these parameters during practice will lead to flexibility in the integration of this information in later situations and conditions.

Performance Environment

The performance environment is also an important part of what people learn when performing a new skill. Even aspects of the environment that are not a definitive part of the skill can be embedded in the learning process, and sometimes these aspects are learned nonconsciously. All of the components of the environment can serve as cues later in transfer and retention of the skill, and when they are missing in the test environment, ability can diminish. One example of this effect is the use of mirrors, described later in this chapter.

Another example is learning choreography with the teacher or choreographer always clapping the beat. When this part of the auditory context is removed, dancers can struggle to follow the music. They have learned the timing dependent on the sound of the clapping, and when this cue is removed, the dancers' ability to stay with the music can diminish. While cueing of this kind can be useful in the early stages of learning, it should be removed as soon as possible so that the dancers can learn to depend on the music alone for their sound cues.

Cognitive Skills

Even when people are learning and executing two skills that share no physical components, transfer of skills can occur if they share cognitive processes. **Cognitive skills** involve processes such as problem solving, decision making, spatial organization, and musical analysis. For example, regarding spatial organization, the ability to make rapid adjustments to spacing by seeing and adapting to other dancers can transfer from a ballet class to an urban dance environment or even walking through a crowded mall. The negative is also true; if the cognitive processes are very different, skills may not transfer. For example, practicing a wide variety of set choreography will not necessarily

For dancers to be versatile in partnering skills, they need to practice a variety of types of lifts.

help dancers in contact improvisation settings, because the cognitive element of spontaneous and rapid decision making is missing. The type of practice that yields the best learning is practice of skills with similar cognitive aspects, as well as similar performance environments and sensory–perceptual elements.

Variability and Specificity Principles Compared

It would seem that practice variability (supported by the contextual interference effect) and specificity (supported by the specificity of practice hypothesis) contradict each other. One says to vary the skill as much as possible, and the other says to make the skill specific to what you want to perform. However, these two principles relate to different aspects of the skill. *Practice variability* refers to the skill's movement characteristics, such as speed, coordination, force, and all the possible variations of the skill. *Practice specificity* refers to characteristics of practice and test conditions or contexts, such as sensory–perceptual elements, performance environment, and cognitive skills. In addition, the two approaches have different goals. Practice variability will develop dancers who are more resilient and versatile. Practice specificity will prepare dancers to do well in a clearly defined and specific context. Both principles can be accommodated in the practice setting if the elements are understood and practice is well designed.

It is easy for dancers and teachers to fall into a pattern of practicing a skill repeatedly and in the same manner. Dancers can be seen going into a studio and doing the same skill for an hour or more with little or no variation. This process is not the best approach to learning. For both beginners and elite dancers, variation in practice is a far more effective strategy. Mixing skills together, trying many variations of the same skill, and changing the environmental aspects all yield better learning. Teachers need to express to their students that constancy of repetition may yield short-term results in practice, but variation with trial and error will provide a more successful long-term experience.

Amount and Distribution of Practice

All dancers realize that any dance skill requires considerable practice in order to reach high levels of achievement or even competence. Few guidelines exist in the dance pedagogy literature to help teachers understand how much practice is needed and how to extend or design practice over time. Often choreographers dramatically increase hours of rehearsal right before performances, and they place the rehearsals close together. However, research suggests that this strategy is not the best approach to help dancers learn material. In addition, from a physiological standpoint, the prevailing wisdom is to taper practice in order to increase readiness, and to avoid potential fatigue and injury.

Overlearning

It is rare that dancers cease to practice a skill at the moment that they can execute it successfully. **Overlearning** is continuing practice after dancers have accomplished or acquired a particular skill; it is sometimes called *post-mastery learning.* This term should not be confused with **overtraining**, which is training or practicing to the point of fatigue and burnout. Both motor program and dynamic systems theories of motor learning support overlearning as an appropriate tool. Chapter 11 provides a detailed description of these theories of motor learning. Overlearning has a beneficial impact on skill retention, although the amount of overlearning and the type of skill affect how much influence it will have. Two cases with a direct relationship to dance training have demonstrated positive results. The first is procedural learning, and second is dynamic balance skills.

First, overlearning benefits procedural skills. **Procedural learning** is acquiring a movement skill by automatically repeating it over and over. Learning develops slowly, and it is expressed through improved performance. **Procedural skills** are skills that involve a series of simple movements that must be done in a particular sequence in order to accomplish the larger task. For this reason, procedural learning is usually the process used in teaching procedural skills.

For example, fouetté turns have a particular sequence of events. They begin from either a fourth position demi-plié or from another preceding turn. The leg preparation includes a demi-plié on the supporting leg and an extension of the gesture leg devant (to the front). The next event is a rond de jambe en l'air of the gesture leg from front to side, followed by movement from the side to passé. At the same time, the standing leg goes from demi-plié to relevé, and the turn is initiated from the momentum of the gesture leg and arms. The arms also have a particular sequence, usually beginning with one arm front and one arm side, followed by both arms meeting in front. As the body is turning, the next part of the sequence is the spotting (quick turning of the head during the turn). A series of turns is completed, and the end of the sequence is usually a pirouette or series of pirouettes ending in a lunge in fourth position. As with all procedural skills, each component part is relatively simple to execute, but coordinating and sequencing the events is difficult. Overlearning is necessary because once people have learned a skill, they tend to forget how to execute the full sequence in the proper order. Overlearning can consolidate the skill sequence for the learner.

Second, dynamic balance skills can also benefit from overlearning. Practicing a dynamic balance repeatedly after the balance has been done successfully can improve ability at this skill. However, the **point of diminishing returns**, defined in the context of balance studies, demonstrates that overlearning only has benefits up to a certain amount of practice. After that point, extra practice will not have any additional benefit, or any additional benefit will take a long time to become evident. In some situations, teachers may notice an actual decrease in ability from excessive overlearning. Possible reasons for the decrease are physical fatigue, boredom, reduced attention, and a drop in motivation from seeing no improvement. This aspect of overlearning reinforces the need for variability in practice. Further, the amount of practice is not the sole factor in determining the permanence or retention of a skill. How the practice is distributed plays a vital role.

In most dance forms, including street dance, dancers' skills benefit from overlearning.

Massed and Distributed Practice

Distribution of practice is the spacing or frequency of practice sessions and the length of the sessions. Distribution of practice can be divided into massed or distributed practice, which are two ways of determining frequency and session length. Dance teachers want their students to take class daily, and many choreographers would prefer to rehearse as often as their dancers are available. The traditional idea in dance is that more training, more rehearsal, and more practice lead to better results. In motor learning, the concept of practice distribution is not only concerned with the frequency of practice, it is also defined by the amount of rest for the learner between sessions. At the two ends of the continuum are massed practice and distributed practice.

Massed practice is a timing that involves little rest between sessions. **Distributed practice** is a timing that involves relatively longer rest between practice sessions; the rest periods are as long as or longer than the active practice. Suppose a group of dancers is preparing for a street dance competition. One of the dancers wants to practice the routine repeatedly for 4 hours on the day before the competition—a massed practice schedule, which involves fewer but longer practice sessions. Another dancer wants to practice for only 1 hour a day for the 4 days before the competition—a distributed practice schedule, with more but shorter practice sessions. Note that the same overall amount of practice (4 hours) is achieved in these two example schedules. However, the first case has no rest in the one extended session, while the second has 23 hours of rest between each of the four sessions. Further, if the street dancers' routine is 5 minutes long and they take a break between runs of 1 to 5 minutes, it is still considered massed practice. The rest time must be longer than the skill being practiced to qualify as distributed.

Even if rest is provided between sessions, the optimal length of practice sessions (how much time is allocated) must still be determined. In general, shorter sessions for practice yield better improvement in retention than do longer sessions. Often learners prefer longer sessions, but they have better results with shorter and more

frequent practice. In addition, learners who participate in less frequent, shorter sessions (distributed practice) are better at predicting their retention than those who participate in frequent, longer sessions (massed practice). In the case of the street dancers, both the shorter practice times and the extended rest between sessions of the 4-day schedule will yield better results that the one 4-hour session.

Including rest as part of the training process has several benefits. First, periods of rest help to consolidate memory. **Memory consolidation** is a category of processes that stabilize changes in the nervous system after the initial acquisition and exposure to a new skill. It refers to two types of processes. **Synaptic consolidation** has to do with changes to the neural connections in the brain and occurs in the first minutes to hours after learning. **System consolidation** takes much longer—weeks or more—and refers to shifts in brain areas responsible for the memories. It aids in transferring information from the working memory to long-term memory and stabilizing the memories in long-term memory. Without consolidation, the brain would have no way to store information, which is a necessary stage in forming, storing, and retrieving memories for later use.

Second, rest improves the recall of motor skills. Dancers may learn phrases or skills in class or rehearsal, then have a difficult time remembering the material the next day if they are very tired and have had little rest. Sleep, particularly dream sleep, is especially important in memory consolidation for nondeclarative tasks—those tasks often acquired simply through repeated exposure, which includes many motor skills. Studies have demonstrated that it is not simply the time delay in hours that improves recall of the motor task; periods of sleep are essential for some types of motor skill learning. Further, additional nights of sleep seem to increase learning benefits.

Finally, rest and sleep improve performance of motor skills. When dancers lack rest or sleep, execution of known skills can suffer. Research has also supported the idea that sleep can enhance certain aspects of motor skills beyond what rest can provide. In one study, a night of sleep improved speed without loss of accuracy by 20% beyond what rest provided. In addition, with sleep, improvements in accuracy of motor skills can occur that are not seen in hours of wakefulness during the day. Dance educators should be cognizant of the need for rest periods during the day's activities, and dancers should maintain a sound schedule of regular sleep for optimal motor learning and performance. Both periods of rest during activity and periods of sleep benefit learning and are essential to the dancer's training process.

One way of looking at distributed practice in the dance education context is the use of somatic education. Interest in somatic practice has been growing in dance education as a way of accomplishing changes to motor patterns, particularly involving alignment and injury-provoking habits. In somatic classes, far more rest is interspersed with movement than in a dance class. During rest periods in a somatic class, teachers use guided visual or kinesthetic imagery or small, slow movements with guided attention. It is theorized that these periods of thoughtful rest allow dancers to become aware of novel sensations and permit the motor control system to reorganize. Research into this theoretical model is just beginning to surface.

The value of rest and sleep in motor learning has not been sufficiently recognized in dance training. While dance teachers are beginning to appreciate the issues of physical fatigue and its relationship to injury, the connection of rest to motor learning in dance is less understood. Glenna Batson—internationally known dance artist, educator, physical therapist, and Alexander Technique teacher—has described rest from the perspectives of dance training, somatic practice, and neural anatomy. She observes that traditional dance training is built on a work ethic of rigorous and persistent physical activity, and rest has a negative connotation of a lack of commitment and seriousness. Batson's approach is working with somatic practice and introspection to enable dancers to reflect on the experience and benefits of rest as an essential part of their training process.

In summary, both number and length of practice sessions are factors in learning, and research supports distributed practice. Dancers and dance teachers should consider practicing skills in short time periods that are separated by periods of rest. Research has identified several benefits of distributed practice. The first is avoiding fatigue, which has a negative impact during massed practice. Second, dancers actually use less cognitive or mental effort during the repetitiveness of massed practice, and they can become bored, resulting in less learning. Third, it has been demonstrated that during periods of rest and periods of sleep, ideas or skills become consolidated or strengthened in the memory. Distributed practice allows for this effect, but massed practice does not.

Whole and Part Practice

One of the most common strategies that dance instructors use to teach new material in dance class is to present one section of a combination at a time. If teachers show a full combination of several phrases of dance all at once, students become overwhelmed. This technique of introducing a longer combination by teaching its parts or sections first is one of the forms of part practice. **Whole practice** is practicing a skill or dance phrase in its entirety. **Part practice** is practicing one section, or one component, or one body part of a skill or phrase before practicing the entire skill. This technique has been used in dance and sports for decades, and all dancers and athletes recognize its value in the learning process. The issue is determining when to use whole or part practice and how to divide the skill if part practice is the selected method. The answer to this question lies in the complexity and organization of the skill.

Complexity and Organization of Skills

Complexity of a skill depends on these two factors: the number of sections, parts, or components of the skill, and how much attention the skill requires. Clearly skills such as bike riding and running are simple (low in complexity), but high dives with flips and fast footwork in flamenco dance are complicated (high in complexity). Note that complexity does not necessarily describe the level of difficulty. Threading a needle with a fine eye is simple because it has one step, but it can be a difficult to accomplish. For many dancers, balancing on one foot en pointe without support is difficult but not complex. **Organization** of a skill is about the components or parts of the skill and how they relate to each other in time and space. When the parts are interdependent or interrelated, the skill is considered to have a high level of organization. For example, the elevation portion of a turning jump combination in dance is entirely dependent on the plié before it and after it, and the rotary component is dependent on the push-off action and possibly the arm movements preceding the turn. In contrast, when the parts of a skill are independent, the skill is considered to have a low level of organization. For example, a balance followed by three walking steps followed by a leg gesture are not interdependent parts and could actually be done in any order. Also, a dancer could practice any one of the three parts by itself.

It is better to practice a skill in its entirety (whole practice) when the skill is low in complexity but high in organization. This description refers to simple skills with parts that interrelate. Tossing a Frisbee and doing a leap are examples of skills that should use whole practice. Part practice is effective when the reverse is true—the skill is high in complexity and low in organization. Shifting gears on a bicycle and développé into grand rond de jambe en l'air are examples of skills that should use part practice. Note that most skills fall along the continuum of high to low complexity and the continuum of high to low organization. Where a skill falls on these two continua determines the type of practice needed. In addition, many skills have components that are **natural units**, groupings or parts within a larger skill that have interdependent components but are independent of each other. Each natural unit must be practiced as a whole, but the larger skill can be practiced in parts defined by the natural units. If a dance combination is composed of a pas de bourrée followed by a glissade, followed by a fall to the floor and a recovery, followed by a grand battement into exiting runs, each of these sections can be practiced in isolation. However, each section is a natural unit, because each has components that are interdependent and must be done together.

With some simple analysis, teachers can determine the level of complexity and organization of a skill, thereby deciding if whole or part practice is more beneficial. Many skills in dance can profit from part practice. Note that if part practice does not result in transfer to the whole skill, it is not useful, even if the dancers improve at each of the parts. The next level of analysis is to decide which form of part practice is best for the task at hand.

Part Practice

Dance teachers intuitively use different approaches to part practice. Sometimes they teach a longer combination by teaching each section one at a time, and other times they introduce the whole combination but first try it without embellishments such as the arms or adding turns. Three part-practice strategies that are regularly used are fractionization, segmentation, and simplification. The choice of which strategy to use depends on the various components, natural units, rhythmic structure, complexity, and organization of the skill.

Fractionization

Fractionization is a method used for a skill or a phrase with asymmetric leg and arm coordination, and it involves practice of individual limbs before trying the whole skill. Choosing to use this method requires that the two arms or two legs are doing different spatial or timing organization. This method is commonly used in practicing musical instruments, such as the piano or drum, that involve asymmetric multi-limb coordination. Figure 14.2 shows a common jazz step that benefits from fractionization. In this phrase the arms do the following asymmetric pattern; note that the right arm is in a 3-count pattern, and the left arm is in a 2-count pattern.

a. Both arms are up.

b. Right arm is to the side; left arm is down.

c. Right arm is down; left arm is up.

d. Right arm is up; left arm is down.

e. Right arm is to the side; left arm is up.

f. Both arms are down.

It is beneficial to practice one arm at a time before putting the two arms together. Later, a

Figure 14.2 The jazz combination involving bimanual coordination of the upper extremities.

traveling foot rhythm can be added and, for advanced dancers, pelvis motions can be added. It is best to practice the more difficult coordination first. So, in the case of the jazz step, the right arm (the arm doing the 3-count phrase) should be practiced first. Note that if the two arms and the two legs are doing symmetrical tasks, then practicing just the arms or just the legs is not considered fractionization. This case will be covered in another method of part practice. The asymmetric nature of the limbs is the critical component in fractionization. Dance forms that regularly use asymmetric coordinations are classical Indian dance, flamenco, street dance, and jazz dance.

Segmentation

Segmentation, also called the **progressive part method**, involves skills that have a series or sequence of components. The learner begins by practicing the first part, then practicing the second part, then adding it to the first part, and so on, until the entire sequence is learned. In other words, for a combination that is represented by A + B + C + D, practice would look like the following sequence:

- Practice A
- Practice B
- Practice A + B
- Practice C

- Practice A + B + C
- Practice D
- Practice A + B + C + D, or the whole skill

This method is one of the most common techniques for teaching dance phrases, especially as the phrases become longer. When the segments have varying levels of difficulty, it is more effective to go from the easiest to the most difficult in terms of the order of practice, even if this is not the order that the segments are arranged in the phrase. One of the interesting features of the progressive part method is that the learner gains the advantages of both part and whole practice. By learning one part at a time, the learner can focus on specific aspects of that segment. By gradually putting the parts together, the learner acquires the spacing and timing of the whole phrase. There is an additional idea called **overlap** in which learners practice the transition from one movement to another, which also demonstrates learning benefits.

Another approach that also falls into the segmentation category is practicing arms and legs separately in a multi-limb skill. For example, a fast jump combination in any dance form can involve all four limbs. It is not unusual for teachers to ask dancers to practice the leg action first, then practice the arm coordination, and then put the two together. In the first phase the dancers are learning the specific coordination and timing patterns of just the upper or lower extremities. Then, by putting them together, the dancers can concentrate on the timing organization of all four limbs simultaneously.

Simplification

Simplification involves a method that lowers the difficulty level of either various portions of the skill or different characteristics of the skill. Simplification can be applied in a variety of ways, including limiting the demands of attention, diminishing speed, using auditory cues, sequencing the order of the skills, and reducing difficulty in work with props. Each of these strategies entails practicing the skill in its entirety, but it is used with various kinds of skills.

Limiting attention demands can alter the complexity of the skill. A main tactic for achieving this method is the use of physical devices, such as harnesses that are used in physical therapy to help improve locomotor skills in rehabilitation settings, and in research on enhancing athletic abilities. In gymnastics, learners use training belts or spotters for new high-level skills for safety and to reduce fear. In dance, the use of the barre achieves the goal of simplifying the tasks by removing instability. Dancers can attend to various aspects of the skills they are learning—such as body design, timing, and coordination—without any attention or concern for balance. In some ways, use of floor work in modern, contemporary, and jazz classes accomplishes the same result. Dancers can practice torso and arm movements and work on core support without the distraction of loss of balance. Balancing skills are not enhanced when working at the barre or on the floor, and they must be trained in unsupported stance and locomotion.

Diminishing speed is probably one of the most common simplification techniques used in dance classes. Slower speeds allow learners to attend to more aspects of the skill, and in particular allow for accuracy to develop. When slowing down material in order to teach it, two factors must be considered. First, the relative time of the various segments must remain constant. In other words, assume a three-part skill is being taught. If part A takes 4 counts, part B takes 1 count, and part C takes 3 counts, this ratio of segments must be maintained, no matter how slow or fast the skill is done. Second, it is problematic to slow down a skill to the point that a different motor pattern is required. For example, it is not very useful to practice jump combinations at such a slow tempo that elevation is impossible. In this case, the slow version and the fast jumping version are two different generalized motor patterns. Similarly, slowing running to the point of walking is also not useful for the same reason. (For a detailed review of this concept, see chapter 9.) Finally, reducing speed also benefits the learning of asymmetrical multi-limb coordination, such as the jazz phrase described in the section titled Fractionization.

Using auditory cues is useful with skills that have a rhythmic or musical component. Because dance is almost always connected to music, this technique is highly beneficial.

Teachers often clap, speak in rhythm, sing, and even play a variety of small musical instruments to emphasize the rhythmic structure of a skill. Another tactic is to call out a verbal cue on a particularly important moment within a skill. For example, teachers will call out "Spot!" at a certain count in a turn combination. However, the auditory cues should be dropped as early as possible in the learning process, as discussed in the section Sensory–Perceptual Elements. Using too many cues can overload the dancers and draw attention away from other essential elements of the skill.

Sequencing the order of the skills determines an order that starts with less complex variations of the skill leads to more complex variations, sometimes called a **task progression strategy**. It is effective for beginners as well as advanced dancers. For example, most turns on one leg are taught first as a balance without the turn, and with simple gesture leg and arm configurations. Later, turns are added, and dancers attempt more difficult body designs. In ballet, jumps with beats are not incorporated until the dancer can accomplish jumps without the beats. In modern and contemporary dance, balances with the torso off the vertical are not given until dancers can achieve balances in vertical alignment. In tap dance, generally steps with one sound are taught before the two-, three-, and four-sound variations. Even the progression throughout a class can follow the sequencing principle, with simpler exercises at the start of class leading to complex work toward the middle and end of class.

Reducing difficulty in work with props and sets is not as common in dance as it is in athletics, which use objects and equipment in most activities. In dance, if a prop is very heavy or difficult to hold, dancers might initially use a substitute prop that is easier to manipulate. If the movement using the prop is complicated, the movement can be practiced first without the prop, and then the prop can be added later. An example of this process is choreographer Charles Moulton's *Precision Ball Passing*. If dancers are struggling with the movement execution while passing the balls, they can work on the timing and shape of the movement phrase without the balls first.

Charles Moulton's dance piece *Precision Ball Passing* involves intricate and rhythmic use of props.

Use of Attention as Part Practice

As mentioned previously, some skills should be practiced as whole skills because they are low in complexity but high in organization. However, in such cases attention can be used as a way to achieve a form of part practice. The teacher can direct the dancers' attention to a specific feature of the skill. For example, dancers might be learning a complex leap involving legs and arms changing positions while in the air. The teacher could suggest that the dancers focus their attention on the leg transitions only, even though they are doing the whole skill. After they have achieved the leg transitions, the teacher could suggest attention to a different aspect of the skill. In this way, the dancers are focusing on parts of the skill even though they are executing it in its entirety.

Whole and part practice are both essential strategies in learning dance. Once teachers and dancers understand the complexity and organization of skills, they can determine the best possible methods for learning. Dance teachers are highly accomplished at many of the successful part practice strategies, such as breaking dance phrases into parts, diminishing speed, and auditory cues. When they have a clear awareness of how to match strategies with skill types, teachers can optimize class time.

Dance-Specific Conditions of Practice

Two conditions of practice that are specific to dance or have dance-related concerns are improvisation and the use of mirrors. These tools are used in other fields, particularly in the arts and in athletics. For example, musicians regularly use improvisation in both composition and performance. Weightlifters often work with mirrors to examine their lower limb alignment. How improvisation and mirrors influence or affect dancers requires special focus. Improvisation is widely used as a creative tool in dance, but its potential use in motor learning has not been investigated. More thoroughly studied is the use of play in animal models, and the evidence is clear that playing leads to greater flexibility and resilience in unexpected circumstances as well as better problem-solving skills. The use of mirrors is widespread in dance training, although little knowledge exists of their effect on skill acquisition or of some of the negative consequences on self-esteem and motivation. Dancers and teachers can enrich dance training by addressing these two conditions of practice and assimilating them more effectively into dance classes.

Improvisation

Improvisation offers another way for dancers to explore variability of practice. **Dance improvisation** is the process of creating movement in a spontaneous and experimental manner, and it is facilitated through a variety of sensory explorations. Different approaches to improvisation include systems such as Laban Movement Analysis (LMA), based on the work of one of the pioneers of European modern dance, Rudolf von Laban; Body-Mind Centering, founded by artist and therapist Bonnie Bainbridge Cohen; and contact improvisation, founded by experimental choreographer Steve Paxton. Historically, improvisation has been regarded as a tool for early childhood development, creativity in choreographic processes, group sensitivity work, and as a means of employing nontraditional elements in the dance context, such as voice work. Voice work in dance can involve audible text or singing or random sounds as part of the score for a dance. To date, little has been done to examine the potential for motor learning through the use of improvisation as a complement to traditional dance training. However, several aspects of improvisation may contribute to the acquisition of motor skills for dancers.

How Improvisation Can Aid Various Facets of Dance Training

One facet of dance training that is particularly difficult for beginners is the multitude of elements to consider simultaneously, including counts, phrasing, directions, level changes, shape design, dynamics, and technical challenges such as balance and multi-limb coordination. In the midst of this array of elements to process, dancers must comprehend fundamental concepts, such as use of space and levels or use of weight, which can be considered movement principles. Improvisation can provide a context in which dancers self-select the various components while maintaining a primary focus on a singular concept of the movement. For example, a teacher may wish to focus on the use of weight in a combination going to the floor and returning to stance. Allowing the dancers to determine their own timing, method of descent, and body shaping enables them to concentrate on the concept of release of weight without multiple elements to achieve.

Improvisation also changes the main focus of the work by means of attentional mechanisms.

When performing the skills within set choreography, a dancer might only attend to an ideal prescribed by the teacher or the dancer (top–down attention), with arousal being a determining factor (the fear of doing the movement incorrectly). Improvisation allows the student to notice or observe features of the movement or environment (bottom–up attention), which allows for a student-based (discovery) learning situation. In the previous example of the use of weight, after the improvisation the teacher can ask the students to describe something that they noticed about releasing their weight to the floor.

Another facet of dance training that is critical to success in movement skills involves balance and postural control. Both anticipatory (preceding a disturbance to balance) and compensatory (following a disturbance to balance) muscle responses are important in dance practice. In the traditional dance class, most disturbances to balance are known in advance, such as a transfer of weight from one leg to another or the body moving off the vertical. While dancers need to practice these important transitions, it is also important that dancers experience unplanned disturbances to balance in order to prepare for new choreographic experiences and

possible mishaps on stage. Improvisation provides unplanned, surprising challenges to the balancing mechanisms. Balance can be tested and developed in conditions that have not been predetermined by set material. It is particularly apparent in contact improvisation, where dancers are continually reacting to surprising and unplanned changes of spatial orientation and a shifting relationship to gravity.

A third facet of dance training that is fundamental to every dance form is the use of focus and vision. Use of focus in the traditional class can be limited, often involving verticality of the head and straightforward focus, and it is usually predetermined by the form or the instructor. Improvisation provides an opportunity to disrupt the habitual use of focus, possibly allowing the motor system to establish new mechanisms of integrating visual stimuli and challenging the vestibular and proprioceptive systems. It also demands the use of peripheral vision to maintain an awareness of the other dancers in the surrounding space.

A fourth facet of dance training that improvisation can enhance is the process of changing poor alignment habits. Alignment is a component of motor skill acquisition that is the focus

Dancers can explore balancing through the use of improvisation.

of a great deal of time in many dance classes. While teachers may have disagreements about what constitutes good alignment for dance, or what strategies dancers should use to make corrections to alignment, all would probably agree that how the body organizes is critical to success in dance. In known or previously experienced movement phrases or skills, each person has nonconscious neuromuscular patterns (motor neural maps) that support alignment and motor strategies. Improvisation can disrupt the habitual use of muscle recruitment supporting alignment and preset strategies by introducing unplanned movements, possibly allowing new recruitment patterns to develop. This disruption to habitual patterns can provide an ideal opportunity to use imagery and exploration to find new ways to organize the body, and attend to new sensory experiences in the body.

A fifth facet of dance training that improvisation can influence is the way dancers interact with each other in the learning process. Dance is a communal art form. While dancers with solo careers exist in the field, most dancers spend much of their artistic time dancing, training, rehearsing, and performing with other dancers. In the traditional technique class, few opportunities are provided for dancers to interact with each other in novel movement sequences and settings. Improvisation can provide an environment in which unplanned interactions can occur with other dancers—including spatial conflicts, movement dialogues, and tasks such as copying and mirroring—and in which spontaneous visual and kinesthetic responses to external stimuli are explored. All of these interactions can prepare dancers for choreographic and performance experiences, and they can broaden their abilities to concentrate beyond their own bodies in the dance environment.

Improvisation facilitates associative learning (particularly operant learning, discussed in chapter 11) by pairing images, movement provocations, and novel ideas with movement exploration. **Associative learning** occurs when two ideas or stimuli are associated together. **Operant conditioning** is trial-and-error learning, and it is voluntary. Eventually a person learns to associate a certain response among many with a particular desired consequence.

Improvisation allows dancers to associate images and structures offered by the teacher with their own movement explorations and solutions.

Finally, improvisation changes the locus of control from the teacher to the students, and it provides students with the opportunity to take risks and play at the edge of their abilities, thereby improving motor learning. Dancers are often willing to try movement ideas that they might be fearful or insecure attempting in the context of a technical phrase, thereby accomplishing new levels of unanticipated achievement.

The Brain and Movement Organization

In recent years, interest in how the brain organizes and perceives movement has been growing. Modern technology is now capable of mapping parts of the brain that for centuries were little understood or even misunderstood, including areas of the brain involved in movement planning, initiation, and execution. **Positron emission tomography (PET)**, **functional magnetic resonance imaging (fMRI)**, and **electroencephalography (EEG)** are three methods of differentiating brain areas and seeing the functional processes that are occurring in the brain. Through these methods, scientists are learning how the brain organizes movement and how experiences create changes in the brain. Traditional dance class by its nature involves repetition of known movements, skill sets, and even phrases and combinations. Improvisation can provide an opportunity for the brain to create new neural pathways and potentially use different areas of the brain in order to organize previously untried and experimental movement sequences.

Two recent studies involving the brain shed some light on the value of improvisation for motor learning, creativity, and the brain. Because so little research exists in the area of the brain and creativity, some detail is provided about these two studies. Both studies suggest that areas of the brain involved in creative thinking, spatial planning, decision making, and artistic creation are used in improvisation, but they are not used in practicing or thinking about set artistic expressions.

The first study by researchers Andreas Fink, Barbara Graif, and Aljoscha Neubauer examined what occurs in the brain during creative thinking and dance. In their 2009 study, they looked at EEG activity, which is the recording of electrical activity along the scalp, resulting from current flows in the neurons in the brain. The study compared 15 professional ballet dancers with a group of 17 novices who had only basic experience in dancing and no comprehensive training. The EEG was recorded during the following visualization activities:

- Participants were asked to imagine dancing the waltz, a standard dance that involves a sequence of repetitive steps (lower creative demands).
- Participants were instructed to mentally perform a dance that should be as unique and original as possible (improvisational dance).

- Brain activity was also measured during performance of the Alternative Uses test. In the Alternative Uses test, people are asked to imagine all possible, unusual uses for common objects such as a brick, a newspaper, an umbrella, a vase, or a paper clip.

The researchers observed that during the generation of alternative uses, professional dancers show stronger alpha synchronization in posterior parietal brain regions than novice dancers. Alpha synchronization is indicative of creative thinking, and the posterior parietal brain regions integrate sensory information (visual, auditory, and somatosensory) into the planning of movement and visual-spatial processing. During improvisational dance, professional dancers exhibited more right-hemispheric alpha synchronization than the group of novices did, suggesting higher creative activity

Children can take known objects and explore imaginative or alternative uses for these objects.

in the brain for the dancers. However, during imagining dancing the waltz, no significant group differences emerged, and the brain areas active in the other two conditions were quiet. Imagining a set dance step stimulated little brain activity related to creativity in the professional dancers and in the novices.

A second study involved musicians, but it offers interesting results in terms of improvisation and brain activity that may be applicable to dance. In 2008, researchers Aaron Berkowitz and Daniel Ansari examined improvising musicians using fMRI. The goal was to study brain activity during musical improvisation in both rhythmic and melodic motor sequence creation. Brain scans were collected while 12 classically trained pianists performed four activities:

- Prelearned melody pattern with a metronome setting the rhythm
- Improvised melody with a metronome setting the rhythm
- Prelearned melody pattern without the metronome, improvising their own rhythms
- Improvised melody without the metronome, improvising their own rhythms

In this way, the researchers could examine both rhythmic and melodic improvisation and the intersection of the two. The researchers discovered an overlap between melodic improvisation and rhythmic improvisation in three areas of the brain: the dorsal premotor cortex (PMd), the anterior cingulate (ACC), and the inferior frontal gyrus/ventral premotor cortex (IFG/PMv). The PMd uses information about where the body is in space, creates a motor plan, and sends it to the motor cortex for execution. The ACC is involved in conflict monitoring and hence decision making. The IFG/PMv is involved when people speak and understand language, and when people hear and understand music. This study suggests that music improvisation stimulates areas of the brain involved in spatial planning, decision making, and creation of music. While these results cannot generalize to all disciplines, if the dancers are also improvising with rhythmic ideas, it

is possible that this research would extend to that type of improvisation as well.

Additional Benefits of Improvisation

Finally, added benefits to motor learning may occur with explorations in improvisational dance techniques. Improvisation may enhance motivation by adding an element of pleasure and novelty. It might provide breaks in the traditional class and may avoid fatigue and fatigue-related injury. Improvisation could enhance the range of dancers' expressive and dynamic capabilities as well as assist in developing body awareness. In addition, it may boost self-esteem, which can in turn assist dancers in accelerated acquisition of motor skills.

Several dance forms have improvisation built into the study of the practice. In Argentine tango and flamenco, improvisation is encouraged as a means of reaching high skill levels. Middle Eastern or belly dance includes improvisation as part of the performance event, especially when working with live music. Breakdance and tap dance are heavily influenced by improvisation, particularly the solo work. Improvisation is often part of contemporary or modern dance training, but short periods of improvisation can easily be incorporated into any traditional dance class. Teachers might ask dancers in a ballet class to improvise their own timing in an exercise, and simple contact improvisation exercises can be added to the beginning of partnering classes. Teachers in a ballroom class might explore how partner dances change if dancers work on solos with the material, and how this experiment affects their partner work. Teachers in a jazz class can have dancers improvise on body part isolations. Some dancers easily move into improvisation, and others are initially intimidated and shy. However, with encouragement and a playful environment, all dancers can benefit from the addition of improvisation to their training. Seeing improvisation as play can assist dancers in accepting and enjoying the experience in the dance class. Creative play begins in early childhood, and it is an important part of children's development. Creative play can involve using familiar objects in a new way, engaging in role playing, and spontaneously using the imagination. In young children it encourages the development of sensory exploration, motor skills, problem solving, awareness of shape and spatial relationships, social interactive skills, and decision-making abilities. Similarly, older dancers can make progress in all of these areas by using improvisation as creative play.

Use of Mirrors

When dancers enter the studio, the common experience is the sight of mirrors along one or more of the walls in the space. Some studios have curtains or covering that can be used to mask the mirrors so that the teacher has the option of using the mirrors or not. Other teachers turn the dancers some or all of the time to face a wall that has no mirrors. Mirrors have been part of the dance environment for so long that many teachers and dancers do not even question their presence as a learning tool. However, the use of mirrors can have an impact on how dancers learn, and much of the research in dance and athletics suggests that some of this impact is negative. Two aspects of motor learning that are affected by the use of mirrors are skill acquisition and self-esteem, which can in turn influence motivation.

Skill Acquisition

Recently, teachers and researchers have been asking questions about the value of learning dance skills looking at oneself in the mirror. The debate in the dance community revolves around the question of whether using the mirror accelerates learning or serves as a distraction in terms of attention and a detriment to improving kinesthetic awareness. Research in dance on this topic is sparse, and it has offered mixed results. In some instances, dancers using mirrors had better retention of dance movements than the dancers learning without mirrors. In other cases, the dancers without the mirrors had better retention and stronger technical execution. It may be that the results are dependent on the type of skill and the level and experience of the dancers. For very slow skills, such as adagios, the mirror seems to act more as a distraction than a learning tool, but this result has not been demonstrated for very fast movement. Beginners seem to benefit less

in terms of movement retention than advanced dancers when using mirrors. Advanced dancers are most likely equipped with the cognitive skills to learn valuable information from the mirror without being affected by some of the distracters that influence beginners. In addition, advanced dancers may already have the requisite kinesthetic awareness and do not need to focus consciously on the sensations of new movements in order to learn the skills.

One study from the sports literature provides valuable insight for dancers. Kinesiology professors and researchers Luc Tremblay and Luc Proteau studied weightlifters who were using the mirror to ensure keeping the knees aligned over the feet during a squat lift. This task would be similar to dancers maintaining alignment of the knees over the feet in grand pliés. When the mirrors were taken away, a significant increase in error occurred—up to a 50% deviation in knee alignment. In this instance, use of the mirrors led to poorer movement execution rather than serving to enhance it. This result may relate to a characteristic in motor learning that does not change across the stages of learning, reliance on sensory feedback, which relates to specificity of training. Various characteristics do change across stages of learning, such as rate of improvement, coordination, use of energy or economy of movement, attention to visual cues, and demands on conscious attention (as described in chapter 11). However, reliance on sensory information that is present during learning does not diminish across stages of learning. In other words, if sensory feedback such as visual cueing from the mirror is present in the early stages of learning, the learner's need for that feedback does not diminish as the learner becomes more advanced. This characteristic is known as **feedback dependency**, and it has been demonstrated in several studies in sports. Further, the longer the skill is practiced with the sensory information present, the more difficult it is to accomplish the task once the feedback is taken away.

Another issue with use of the mirror is that some feedback provided by the mirror is excellent, and other feedback is nearly useless. Imagine a dancer standing with arms in second position and looking in the mirror. The ideal

Looking in the mirror may not provide the information dancers need in order to correct their body positioning.

position has the shoulder girdles depressed (the shoulders down), the elbows sloping gently from the shoulders, the wrists extending softly below the elbows, and the elbows slightly flexed and in front of the shoulders. The mirror provides very good information about the slope of the arms from shoulders to hands, and very poor information about the position and curve of the elbow, because of the view of the arms that the dancer has.

Despite some of the dance research suggesting that mirrors are useful for skill acquisition, it may be wise to limit use of the mirrors some of the time in dance training to ensure the development of kinesthetic awareness and to reduce the chances of feedback dependency. Working both with and without the mirror would provide the broadest range of experiences for dancers and potentially optimize skill learning.

Self-Esteem

The impact of mirrors on self-esteem presents a different dilemma. Mirrors heighten dancers' self-consciousness and in general increase feelings of body objectification and negative competitiveness with other dancers. Research suggests that dancers of higher skill levels feel better about themselves and have better body image when not using mirrors, and they feel worse about their appearance when they work with mirrors. In fact, the higher the level of skill, the more self-critical dancers become. On the other hand, nondancers in recreational dance classes and lower-level dance students have improved self-esteem when using mirrors—the opposite effect. As with skill acquisition, the best approach regarding building self-esteem is to limit mirror use some of the time and encourage dancers to focus on the sensory experience of movement, not only on how the movement looks. In addition, it would be helpful to give specific instructions on how to use the mirror, emphasizing observation of line, alignment, and form. Giving dancers clear directives may prevent them from using the time looking in the mirror to be self-critical and negative.

Mirrors have been used for a long time in dance training, and their presence in dance studios probably will continue. Teachers can make the most of this condition of practice by guaranteeing variability (working both with and without mirrors) and helping dancers understand the best use of the mirror. Teachers should make sure that any new material learned using mirrors is retained over time and that the new skills can be done when the mirrors are removed. In this way dancers can be aided in developing kinesthetic awareness and better self-esteem while on the path to high-level skill acquisition.

Summary

All over the world, millions of children dance each day, eager and energetic to do their best dancing and succeed at learning dance skills. Some of their success will depend on their individual motivation, intelligence, innate coordination, persistence, and artistic and musical abilities. Added to the mix is what the teacher brings to the studio, and conditions of practice are a large component of the teacher's contribution. Teachers who understand variability, challenge, changing environments, altering sensory elements, and stimulating attention provide the best atmosphere for their students' accomplishments.

Several aspects of conditions of practice affect skill acquisition and attitudes about learning. Variability of practice is essential, and both implementation and organization of variability can affect the efficacy of practice. Practice can be either constant or variable, or random or blocked. The best approach involves adding contextual interference to develop variable and random practice within sessions. Certain aspects of practice are enhanced by specificity, including sensory–perceptual elements, performance environment, and cognitive skills. Overlearning is continued practice after acquiring a skill, and it can be beneficial up to the point of diminishing returns. Amount and distribution of practice are other crucial features that must be considered in designing practice schedules. Mass and distributed practice are concerned with the length and timing of practice as well as the amount of rest between sessions. In general, distributed practice is better for learning than massed practice. *Whole practice* and *part practice* refer to practicing a skill in its entirety or in portions, determined by the complexity and organization of the skill. Forms of part practice include fractionization, segmentation, and simplification. With whole practice, attention can be used to function as part practice. Two dance-specific areas of consideration for conditions of practice are the use of improvisation and the use of mirrors. If conditions of practice are thoughtfully designed, dancers will have the greatest benefit from practice in class and rehearsal.

Chapter 15
Retention and Transfer

Cyndi has arrived at the audition for a major televised dance competition. She makes it through the first round and has been sent forward to the choreography segment. She is thrilled to work with one of the major jazz choreographers on the show, and she spends a short but intense period of time learning a jazz pas de deux with dancer Tony. By the end of this session, Cyndi can execute the phrase beautifully, and she and Tony feel confident. Afterward, they are unable to continue practicing because so many dancers are competing for space. Two hours later, it is time for her group to go before the panel. At the last minute the panel switches her to a different partner. To her dismay, Cyndi does a terrible job. She forgets some of the steps, she works awkwardly with her new partner, and she is sent home. What accounts for this deterioration in the 2-hour interval is not a skill deficit but rather a problem of retention and transfer, which are influenced by complicating factors of arousal and emotional states. Retention and transfer are two of the major signposts of learning. Several features of learning indicate whether the skill in practice has been permanently learned or accomplishments in practice sessions can only be temporarily achieved.

Five Features of Learning

Motor learning describes the relatively permanent changes associated with practice or experience that govern a person's capability for generating a motor skill. Five features are indicators that learning has occurred. The first is *improvement* of skill execution over time. It is not necessary that the skill improves with each successive attempt, but rather that over time the general development is higher levels of the skill. The second is *consistency*. As with improvement, repeated executions of the skill become increasingly similar over time. In other words, in early attempts variability is high, but later attempts have a more predictable outcome with less variation. The third feature is *stability*, which suggests that disturbances have less effect on skill execution. These disturbances can be internal, such as stress, fear, or fatigue, or they can be external or environmental, such as changes

to lighting, partners, costumes, or music. The fourth feature is *persistence*. Persistence relates to retention and suggests that skill improvements last over longer time periods. In the definition of motor learning, persistence relates to the idea of change being relatively permanent. The fifth and final feature is *adaptability*, which is sometimes called *generalizability*. This feature means that improvements of a skill can be demonstrated in a variety of individual, task, and environmental circumstances. Adaptability relates to transfer of learning. While each of these five features can be assessed to determine learning, this chapter will focus on retention (persistence) and transfer (adaptability).

Retention and Memory

Retention of motor skills implies that the skills have somehow been stored in the memory. In an article in *American Psychologist*, memory researcher Endel Tulving defines memory as the "capacity that permits organisms to benefit from their past experiences." Memory serves a variety of functions in both everyday life and elite skill acquisition. The three that are the most important to motor learning are storage of information (putting learned material into the memory), retrieval of information (getting material out of the memory), and functions that are particular to various memory systems. Through the course of elite dance training, dancers are inundated with a massive amount of dance material and skills. Only a portion of this information is retained and retrievable over time. In order to understand how this process is accomplished, one must examine the functions of the various aspects of memory and how it is structured. Memory has both a working memory component and a long-term memory component, and each of these components has further functional factors. The following section describes how these factors interact and serve to aid in learning and recalling movement.

Structures of Memory

Memory has two functional aspects (systems), which are commonly known as short-term memory and long-term memory. The philosopher and psychologist William James first identified these two components of memory in 1890. James referred to them as "elementary," or "just past," and "secondary," or "properly recollected." The term *working memory* is used in place of *short-term memory* to more closely represent its various roles. The working memory and long-term memory interact, but each has its separate functions in the process of allowing dancers to assimilate and retain dance material over time.

A third early stage in the memory processes is the short-term sensory stage that precedes information entering the working and long-term memory systems. Two features of memory, duration and capacity, are important in differentiating the three memory systems. **Duration** is the interval of time that material can remain in the memory. **Capacity** is the amount of material that can reside in memory at a given point in time. These two features differ markedly between the short-term sensory stage, working memory, and long-term memory.

Short-Term Sensory Stage

The **short-term sensory stage** takes in all of the environmental features through the sensory systems, such as visual, auditory, tactile, and haptic. It has a large, possibly even limitless capacity, but it can hold the information for only a short period of time (less that 1 second). The information either moves to the working memory or disappears and is replaced by new incoming sensory information. This stage allows people to drive down the highway seeing everything in the environment, but then immediately see the next part of the journey moment by moment. Similarly, dancers can sit in the theater, seeing the other audience members coming, hearing all of the conversations, and feeling the sensation of the program as they turn the pages; moments later, all of that sensory information is forgotten as the lights go down and the first dance begins.

Working Memory

The **working memory** is a system of limited capacity that temporarily stores recently

The teacher is overloading the dancer with information while she is trying to remember the movement sequence learned the day before. The information clearly did not transfer from working memory to long-term memory!

acquired information. Its temporary storage feature gave this structure its traditional name, *short-term memory*. In addition, the working memory provides an interactive workspace to integrate this new information with material retrieved from long-term memory in order to solve problems and make decisions about future actions. Further, working memory assists with producing and evaluating movement. The working memory has three subsystems: a central executive and two storage systems—the phonological loop and the visuospatial sketchpad (figure 15.1). The **central executive** is the controller that coordinates the new information and the retrieved information from long-term memory. The **phonological loop** is the temporary storage of verbal material, while the **visuospatial sketchpad** is the temporary storage of spatial material that has been perceived visually. The sketchpad also has a kinesthetic component.

It is surprising to learn that the duration of retaining information in the working memory is only 20 to 30 seconds. After that, the brain begins to forget the newly acquired information, because it is overwritten by new incoming information. This 20- to 30-second time interval is valid whether the information is in the form of words or movements. Unless movements are rehearsed or mentally processed in some way beyond the 20 to 30 seconds, they will be lost. The capacity of the working memory is approximately seven items, plus or minus two items. One way to increase this amount is a process called chunking, which will be described in detail in the section titled Improving Memory Performance. Elite athletes have what is called a *long-term working memory*, which means that they have capacity in the working memory that is larger than normal, and it is a skill-specific memory. In other words, elite dancers can store more than the five to nine items in working

memory in their dance practice but not necessarily in everyday life.

The working memory has a processing function with two components. First, it helps learners remember what they have just seen or heard in order to reproduce it. Second, they may use this recently absorbed information to solve problems in organizing the new dance material. Ideally these two components will assist learners in future situations. If the material can be directly associated with retrieved material from long-term memory, both current and future attempts will be more successful. For example, when dancers are learning a new dance skill, if they can associate it with a skill that they already know or with a meaningful image, they will learn the skill more successfully and remember it more easily in the future.

Long-Term Memory

The **long-term memory** is responsible for permanently accumulating or storing information. In particular, it stores what can be recalled about how to do activities including motor skills, personal past events, and universal or general knowledge. Long-term memory houses three systems; they are procedural, semantic, and episodic memory. They are defined by the method of obtaining the information, the type of information, the representation and expression of the information, and the type of awareness needed in order to use the information. The structures of both the working memory and the long-term memory are illustrated in figure 15.2.

Procedural memory is the memory system that facilitates understanding how to do an action rather than what is needed in order to do the action. Sometimes, such as when putting on pointe shoes or driving a car, people can execute a skill (the *how*) but cannot describe it (the *what*). Procedural memories are accessed and used even if people cannot consciously describe

Figure 15.1 The central executive (controller) both sends and receives information to the phonological loop (verbal information) and the visuospatial sketchpad (spatial information).

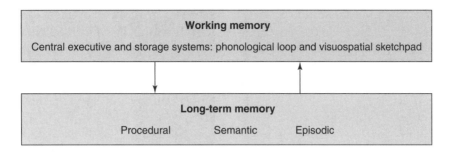

Figure 15.2 The subsystems of the working memory (phonological loop, visuospatial sketchpad, and central executive) interact with the subsystems of the long-term memory (procedural memory, semantic memory, and episodic memory).

Adapted from Magill and Anderson 2014.

what they are doing. This system is extremely important for motor skills, because it is essential that they can be executed, whether or not they can be verbalized. Procedural skills require enough practice to reach the habitual stage.

Semantic memory is the memory system that stores general information about the world, particularly understanding ideas or facts that are not present at that moment. Examples include the names of all the oceans on the planet, when the Titanic sank, the names of the famous Alvin Ailey dancers who have danced *Cry*, concepts such as excellence and love, or the generic representation of objects such as *horse* and *bridge*. It is not known at this time whether information in semantic memory includes personal experiences representing these ideas or only the abstractions and schemas (generic representations).

Episodic memory is the memory system storing personal experiences and the time period with which they are associated. It is considered the only memory system that allows humans to reexperience their past consciously. Examples include the first birthday party, being bullied in grammar school, the first dance recital, graduating from high school, and auditioning for an important dance company. Episodic memories are susceptible to breaking down and are the most vulnerable. This system is important for motor skill execution in dance, because it lets dancers compare a previous skillful execution with a current problem they are having with a skill or performance.

Declarative knowledge is knowledge that can be described or stated verbally (the *what*), and it is the type of knowledge in the episodic and semantic memory systems. **Procedural knowledge** is knowledge that cannot be stated verbally but rather facilitates the performance of the skill (the *how*), and it is the type of knowledge in the procedural memory system.

The image of a ballerina dancing *Giselle* can be stored in episodic memory if a dancer has personally seen a performance of this work.

The other major difference between working memory and long-term memory relates to duration and capacity. Unlike the 20- to 30-second duration for the working memory, information in the long-term memory is permanent. When information is forgotten, it is probably because the person cannot locate and retrieve it, even though it is still there. And unlike the capacity in working memory (seven, give or take two items), no known limits exist in the long-term memory capacity. The demand of unlimited capacity is that it must be well organized.

Evaluating Remembering and Forgetting

In their practice, dancers need to remember large amounts of both cognitive and physical information. Ballet dancers need to know all of the accepted classical vocabulary and how to physically execute those skills. Modern and contemporary dancers must understand the difference between tilting and curving the spine in order to differentiate between various techniques, and how to maintain balance physically in movements that are off the vertical. Jazz dancers need to know the concept of stabilization in relation to mobilizing body parts for isolations, and how to perform the necessary techniques. Classical Indian dancers are required to understand all of the stories and translations of movement into ideas to perform their work, and how to execute all of the complex gestures. Sometimes dancers learn these skills through observation without conscious analysis or awareness, a process called **implicit learning**. At other times they must make a conscious concerted effort to learn the material and are aware of their learning process, called **explicit learning**. In dance, as in other motor skills, explicit learning can sometimes interfere with effective learning if the dancer is given too many detailed instructions or is overanalyzing the process. In order to evaluate what has been remembered and what has been forgotten for each of these ways of learning, people have developed various procedures for testing retention.

Explicit and Implicit Memory Tests

Explicit memory tests evaluate what is consciously remembered. The two types are recall and recognition. **Recall tests** require responses without cues or suggested answers to help the person remember the information. Typically, in written form, these are tests in which learners fill in the blanks. For motor skills, the learners must demonstrate a skill that they are asked to produce. For example, the street dance teacher might ask a dancer to show a krump dance movement and a robot dance movement, without demonstration or any cues, to see if the dancers can remember these steps and how they differ. **Recognition tests** give cues or suggested answers to help the person remember the information. Usually several choices are given and the person must recognize or select the correct choice from the options. For example, the street dance teacher might show several movements and ask the dancer to identify the robot move. Table 15.1 shows examples of written recall and recognition tests.

Sometimes a circumstance requires both recall and recognition in one situation. In a contact improvisation, first a dancer must recognize from visual cues that another dancer is about to share weight, and then that first dancer must recall what techniques to use to manage the weight effectively and safely. Each of the two types of test gives the teacher different information about what has been learned. Recognition tests let the teacher know whether information has been stored in the memory, but the dancers need cues or aids in order to retrieve it.

Implicit memory tests are not structured like the recall and recognition tests for explicit memory. For motor skills, the teacher would simply ask dancers first to try to verbally describe or explain the skill, and then ask them to execute the skill. If they cannot describe it but can perform it, the skill is in implicit memory; in other words, it is procedural knowledge. This kind of evaluation would help the teacher understand what aspect of a skill the dancers were able to comprehend and what needed additional work is needed in order to execute it successfully. Conversely, sometimes dancers can describe a skill but cannot actually perform it; they have declarative knowledge of the skill. For example, a modern dancer might be able to describe the 32-fouetté pirouette combination en pointe in classical ballet but not have sufficient skills to execute it. Similarly, a ballet

Table 15.1   Comparison of Recall and Recognition Tests in Dance

Information being tested	Recall test	Recognition test
Definition of classical movements	What is the name of the movement in which the foot rapidly strikes the floor?	Select the name of the movement in which the foot rapidly strikes the floor. a. dégagé b. grand battement c. tendu d. frappé Answer: d
Names of historical dance figures	Who is the modern dance pioneer who designed a technique based on contract and release?	Select the name of the modern dance pioneer who designed a technique based on contract and release. a. Isadora Duncan b. Martha Graham c. Ted Shawn d. Hanya Holm Answer: b
Skill understanding	What are two important components of flamenco footwork?	Select two important components of flamenco footwork: a. golpe b. floreo c. compas d. punto e. alegrias Answers: a and d

dancer might be able to describe a series of turns with the body off the vertical but not have the training to execute it as the male dancer is doing in the photo. And a flamenco dancer may be able to articulate the rhythmic pattern of a tap dance but not be able to achieve it in tap shoes.

Reasons for Forgetting

In the early example, Cyndi forgot some of the choreography for her major televised dance competition audition when it came time to perform. Understanding how and why this occurs can help dancers be more successful in retaining dance material in both immediate and distant experiences. The three causes of forgetting are trace decay, proactive interference, and retroactive interference.

Trace decay is forgetting that occurs as time passes because of the deterioration of the memory trace (representation of the movement in the memory). Trace decay on working memory can be tested, but the effect of trace decay on long-term memory is unclear. The reason for forgetting in terms of long-term memory has more than one possibility. For example, suppose a group of dancers learns choreography for a performance. Over the next few months, they learn two more pieces without rehearsing the first piece. Then, they come into the studio and try to run the first piece, but they have forgotten many of the sequences. The memory of the first dance is still there, but the dancers cannot locate it. This forgetting might be caused by trace decay, but it might also be from the learning of later pieces interfering with the memory of the first piece. No way to confirm it currently exists, but most experts think the cause is the learning of the second activities or

The dancer has developed the skill through modern dance training to execute turns with the body off the vertical.

a failure to be able to retrieve the first dance, and not trace decay.

Proactive interference refers to forgetting because of something that happens before attempting to learn the target skill, activity, or information, which hinders acquisition of the new endeavor. For example, assume that a choreographer wishes to audition dancers for a new dance. The choreographer enters the audition space while the dancers are warming up. Some of them appear highly skilled, and others are uninteresting to the choreographer. Twenty minutes later, the choreographer teaches the dancers a phrase from the new dance and then observes them executing it. The dancers leave, the choreographer speaks with her assistant, and then she sits down to select dancers. At this point, what the choreographer saw during the warm-up before observing the dance phrase

might interfere with her memory of their dancing. Her selection could then be influenced by this previous experience. Proactive interference is most likely to occur when the material to be remembered is similar to the previously seen material.

Retroactive interference refers to forgetting because something occurs just after the event or activity that should be remembered, during the interval between learning the target skill and executing it, and it hinders acquisition of the target skill or activity. For example, four dancers were chosen for the choreographer's dance piece. The choreographer teaches two of the four dancers an extended section of the dance. Then, she teaches the other two dancers a different section of the dance with similar material that has variations. The first two dancers watch the choreographer teaching the other dancers. When it is time for them to show their section, they cannot remember all of it. Retroactive interference has occurred, because what they observed during the waiting interval interfered with remembering what they learned previously.

Note that in both cases of proactive and retroactive interference, the similarity of the target material and intervening material is important. If the material seen before or after the target skill is very different, it is much less likely to create problems with remembering. Also, some types of skills are remembered better than others in long-term memory. Skills known as continuous motor skills—such as bike riding, swimming, and jumping rope—remain in the memory over long periods of time.

Movement and Memory

Much of what has been described deals with memory of many types of information, including verbal, mathematical, and motor. Certain issues involving memory are specific to retention of motor skills. Two of these issues are spatial features and meaningfulness.

Spatial Features

The two critical spatial features in remembering movement are location and distance. The endpoint location is easier to remember than distance, especially when the endpoint is within a person's body space. For example, if the teacher tells the dancers to lift their gesture leg level to the mid-thigh of the standing leg, the dancers can more easily recall this position than if the teacher says to lift it 2 feet (60 cm) off the floor. Body-part cueing can be highly successful in assisting dancers to remember particular placement of limbs. With children, it is common to teach the arm position of high fifth by suggesting that the hands are placed above the forehead. However, the teacher should not have the dancers look to the location where the limb is moving. Kinesthetically learned locations and visually learned locations for limb actions are different, and dancers need to develop kinesthetically sensed locations.

Meaningfulness

Movements are more easily remembered if they are related to something that the learner already knows. For example, if a teacher tells dancers to make a spatial configuration that is a half circle followed by a direct line, recalling this spacing is easier than if the teacher had simply demonstrated it without describing the shape. Also, if movements can be associated with known objects, remembering is enhanced. For example, locations of body parts can be related to the face of a clock, or arms in second position can be compared to holding a large beach ball. An experiment for dancers is to take dancers who have never heard the Village People's song "YMCA" or seen the video, and see how long it takes for them to learn the four-movement arm sequence with only drumming or humming the tune. The four movements spell the letters *Y*, *M*, *C*, and *A* with the arms. If the dancers hear voices singing "YMCA," it is easy to learn the movements. With the song and video, it takes people only one or two observations to learn the phrase, but without the words, it would take much longer to learn four seemingly abstract movements. The association of the dance phrase with the four letters of the alphabet increases the meaningfulness of the movements. From this discussion it might seem

Children can be cued with spatial features to learn various arm positions in dance.

The dancers are creating the letters *Y, M, C,* and *A* using their bodies and limbs.

that dancers would have an easier time remembering choreography that has some narrative or emotional dialogue than purely abstract dances. In fact, anecdotally, some professional dancers maintain that they create their own narrative or dramatic content when learning abstract dances in order to make the process easier. However, more research would be needed to validate this idea.

Improving Memory Performance

Given what is known about movement and memory, teachers and dancers can use various strategies to improve memory performance. If memory performance is enhanced, dancers have better and faster skill acquisition. Research has supported these three strategies for improving memory performance: meaningfulness of movement, strengthening the intention to remember the movement, and structuring the organization of the movement.

Heightening Meaningfulness

Teachers can create or heighten the meaningfulness of new movements by using visual imagery and by attaching verbal labels. When dancers form a visual picture of the movement in their minds, called **visual metaphoric imagery**, and the picture is something very familiar to the dancers, complex coordinations are simplified. Comparing certain arm gestures in dance to life activities can be helpful, such as throwing a dagger or gathering balloons. The imagery helps the dancers in both learning and remembering the material. Research suggests that when people are affectively or emotionally engaged, retention is considerably enhanced.

A second strategy is connecting a **verbal label** to the movement, or using a short verbal cue that relates to some aspect of the movement. This technique is so effective that when verbal labels related to position are used with children, movement retention for children in elementary school is the same as for adults. Reasons for the effectiveness of verbal labels include the following:

- Verbal instructions are simplified.
- Abstract and complicated movements are translated into concrete, meaningful movements.
- The learner is encouraged to focus on movement outcome rather than specific movement components.
- Movement processing is accelerated, because retrieval of related movements in the memory is enhanced.

For example, the verbal label "pick the apple" could describe a hand and arm movement of reaching up, seizing an imaginary globe with the hand, and bringing it down to waist level. The verbal label "lean over a barrel" can encourage a large side bend that creates space between the torso and pelvis. Verbal labels are often metaphoric, but they are brief, simple, and can create complex movement from just a few words.

Strengthening Intention

Teachers can aid dancers in retaining dance skills and material by explaining to them in advance the goal or purpose of the movement and encouraging their concentration. **Intentional memory** refers to learning and remembering information with a conscious awareness and goal toward learning, also known as explicit learning. **Incidental memory** refers to learning and remembering that happen without conscious awareness simply by being subjected to the information, also known as implicit learning. In general, dancers learn better if they are using intention to remember. Incidental memory can be effective if the learner has previous experience with the material being learned, although even in this instance, incidental memory is not as good as intentional memory.

Advanced dancers can learn more material without conscious attention than beginners. This attribute may explain why they can learn many aspects of a combination even though they may only be concentrating on one or two aspects, such as rhythm or spacing. Another aspect of intentional memory is that learners have more success in remembering material if they know in advance that they will be tested or required to perform at a later time.

Structuring Organization

Teachers and dancers can accelerate learning and thereby enhance memory if they organize the material into units or groupings, sometimes called **chunking** or **clustering**. **Subjective organization** is organizing the material in a manner that is meaningful to each dancer. Dancers will find personal ways to learn long sequences by dividing them into smaller chunks. The size of the chunks gradually increases until the entire sequence is learned. Some dancers automatically develop an organizational structure when learning dance sequences even without the teacher's encouragement or instruction. One of the differences noted between beginning and elite athletes is that the beginners tend to see long sequences as series of individual movements, whereas the elite athletes instinctively divide the sequence into clusters. This effect may contribute to the skill-specific increased capacity in working memory for elite athletes and dancers. Researchers studying young novice and expert dancers reported that the novices were only able to recall half of the sequences in a ballet routine that they were trying to learn, while the experts recalled the routine perfectly. And while doing this study, the researchers observed a principal dancer in the elite dance company who performed a sequence of 96 steps after seeing the combination demonstrated only once. These reports all indicate that subjective organization in a given skill is a useful way to enhance memory, and seems to increase as dancers become more skilled.

Encoding Specificity Principle

The **specificity of practice hypothesis** states that when two situations have physical and mental components in common, greater transfer between the two situations will occur. The **encoding specificity principle** applies the specificity of practice hypothesis to the context of memory, suggesting that retention of material is better when practice and performance situations have physical and mental components in common. The principle is supported by the fact that environmental and sensory components of a skill are stored with the movement components. This concept emphasizes the importance of giving dancers opportunities with performance setting conditions such as lighting, size of space, floor surface, and costuming in rehearsal settings.

It is clear that memory has different stages and systems, and teachers and dancers can work in varying ways regarding retention. In an environment where many elite dancers work in established companies and dance students spend months working toward exams or recitals, the dancers who can retain repertory over time are valued. In a more recent environment where many elite dancers work in short-term contracts (called *pick-up companies*) and televised dance events, the time to learn material is brief, but they are not expected to have long-term retention. Similarly, company directors have moved from selecting dancers for the company who they know through classes and workshops to having large auditions and selecting dancers who have learned material rapidly for a single showing. Perhaps what people value in dancers regarding retention is shifting, and the daily training needs to reflect this process. The dancer valued in the dance culture of the future may not necessarily be the one who can come to company rehearsal after not seeing the choreography for a year yet still remember it.

Transfer

Dance teachers and dancers often make the assumption that transfer of learning is occurring in the training process. Dancers in many dance forms practice pliés and relevés and assume that these exercises will transfer to jumps. They practice long balances at the barre and expect balance to improve in dynamic dancing. Dancers work on their core support in conditioning classes and assume that this work will have an impact on their dancing. Evidence from sports and dance suggests that certain conditions must be present in order for transfer to occur.

Defining Transfer of Learning

Transfer of learning is defined as the effect or influence that skill or knowledge acquired in one circumstance has on skill acquisition and problem-solving ability in another circumstance. When describing this effect in motor learning, it is sometimes called **transfer of training**. As with retention tests, **transfer tests** assess the persistence of the acquired ability for performance, but they have the learners changing to different tasks or conditions rather than being tested after a time interval of no practice. For example, a teacher of jazz dance may initially teach a series of isolations in the rib cage and pelvis during center practice with the legs in parallel position. Then, to assess them on

The dancer working at the barre assumes that the learned skills and balance will transfer to working in the center without support.

transfer, the teacher can have the dancers do the isolation series while traveling across the room.

Three Types of Transfer

These three variations of transfer have been identified: positive transfer, negative transfer, and zero transfer. **Positive transfer** is the beneficial effect that skill or knowledge acquired in one circumstance has on skill acquisition and problem-solving ability in another circumstance. For example, practicing body swings in first position turned out will have a positive influence on executing this torso action in second position turned out. **Negative transfer** is the detrimental effect that skill or knowledge acquired in one circumstance has on skill acquisition and problem-solving ability in another circumstance. For example, the study of ballet for many years can have a negative effect on in-line skating leg coordination because of the necessity to remain in parallel position in the legs. Just a few decades ago, some ballet companies did not allow their dancers to take modern and jazz dance classes because they believed that it would have a negative training effect on their ballet skills, but today many ballet dancers take classes in other forms with no detriment to their classical technique. **Zero transfer** means that no effect or influence exists in the learning of two skills. For example, learning krump dancing probably has no effect on learning classical Indian dance.

Applications of Transfer

Understanding transfer of learning is essential in designing effective training practices. Three applications of transfer of learning have been established in various environments. The first is skill sequencing. It is most commonly acknowledged in the educational setting, and its effectiveness has been tested over time. Writing provides an excellent example. Students first learn to print individual letters, then learn to print words, and finally they can print entire sentences. In dance, teachers begin with basic skills such as hopping, galloping, and skipping for children, then they move on to more complex skills, such as chassés and leaps. In ballet training for adolescents, skills are taught on flatfoot, then on relevé, and finally en pointe. For motor skills, a logical progression from foundational skills to complex skills yields better skill learning. If teachers try to teach advanced material before dancers have the basics, at some point the dancers will need to return to the fundamental skills. Some researchers have referred to this form of transfer as **far transfer**, which suggests that learning basic skills will be applicable for long periods of time and over a wide variety of more complex skills. These basics are essential for achieving the complex skills in later motor learning.

The second application deals with designing instructional strategies other than sequencing. Examples include advancing the environmental context, using part practice, and reducing dangerous experiences. If musical theater or tap dancers are learning choreography going up and down stairs, the steps and sequences can be learned on a flat surface first. Part practice (described in detail in chapter 14) would involve teaching a long sequence by either simplifying it or breaking it into segments. If two dancers are going to execute a lift with both of them running into the lift, they can practice first from static stance to reduce the potential danger of an accident.

The third application is using the principle of transfer to evaluate the efficacy or success of teaching strategies. Transfer tests can provide the best information to dance teachers about the success of their teaching methods. Exams and performances provide excellent opportunities for teachers to evaluate their teaching. Teachers can also observe their dance students in other teachers' classes, whether in the same technique or a different technique, to assess what skills are transferring. The efficacy of dance practice can only be verified based on how well the learners do in a testing condition, whether it is a formal exam or an informal observed practice.

Causes for Positive Transfer

While the concept of transfer has generated considerable discussion in motor learning circles, few definitive conclusions have been universally accepted as causes for positive transfer. The reason accepted by most experts is the similarity between the two tasks. First, the skills can be similar in terms of the physical movement and performance components. For example, when considering movement components, turns using similar gesture and direction such as en dedans pirouettes and traveling piqué turns would have a positive transfer effect. Second, the skills can be similar in terms of the cognitive processes needed during learning. For example, two skills may both require rapid decision making, even if they are very different physically, such as choosing a wing for an exit or dodging a dancer in the wrong place on stage.

Similarity of Skills

Edward Thorndike, who is considered the father of educational psychology, developed the identical elements theory. The **identical**

elements theory states that elements are defined as the general features of skills, such as movement components and mental or cognitive processes, and performance context, such as the individual's mental state or the goal of the task. He went on to say that high similarity of elements leads to transfer between two skills, and low similarity means learning one will have no benefit in learning the other.

Currently, the most commonly accepted premise for the success of transfer is the similarity of the movement components or performance context. In order for this premise to be useful to dance teachers and dancers, first they must understand what the components of a given skill are. Two skills may seem similar, but when the kinematic properties are examined, they can be quite different. **Kinematics** is the branch of mechanics that describes the motion of bodies and body systems—in particular, to describe the motion of systems composed of joined parts (multilink systems), such as the skeleton of the human body. Two dance skills that may seem similar but have different kinematic properties are grand battement devant and développé devant. While they can seem similar in terms of beginning and endpoints, their kinematic properties are entirely different. The flexing of the gesture knee in the développé creates an entirely different kinematic pattern than that of the battement, in which the knee remains straight. Another component that skills can share is similarity of dynamic coordination patterns, where **dynamics** refers to the energy, force, emphasis, or accents in the movement. For example, grand battement devant is more related to grand jeté in dynamic accent than to a slow straight-leg raise.

While these two dancers may appear to be doing two very different skills, grand battement and grand jeté share the dynamic coordination of the kick of the leading leg.

Similarity of Cognition

The second premise for the success of transfer is based on the idea of **transfer-appropriate processing**, which suggests that if the necessary cognitive processing of two skills is similar, it will enhance transfer. This concept suggests that even if the kinematic properties are not alike, transfer can occur if cognitive skills are similar. Examples of cognitive processes needed to learn and execute a motor skill are problem solving, rapid decision making, applying rules or forms, focus of attention, and performing tasks at the same time. An example of a problem-solving similarity is figuring out whether a foot closes in front or in back of the other foot in legwork. In addition, once the dancer understands the rules, this knowledge can be transferred from a learned skill to a new skill. For example the idea of *dessus* (over) from an assemblé will help to learn a glissade dessus.

Negative Transfer

While negative transfer also defines influences of the learning of one skill upon the learning of another skill, the effect is detrimental rather than positive. Negative transfer occurs when a new skill resembles a known skill, but the needed response is different. The two most common situations that cause negative transfer are changes in the location in space of the movement, and changes in the timing of the movement.

Causes for Negative Transfer

An example of this effect in dance for spatial location is the use of arms in arabesque. If young dancers are usually asked to do first arabesque (with the same arm and leg forward) and practice it repeatedly in this form, first arabesque becomes their habitual choice. If they are then asked to do fourth arabesque (with the opposite arm forward), they automatically do first arabesque. In other words, the previous learning

The dancer on the left is doing first arabesque, and the dancer on the right is doing fourth arabesque. Dancers need to practice variations in order to be versatile with their technique.

of first arabesque negatively transfers to the learning of fourth arabesque. The result suggests a sound reason for contextual interference (performing multiple skills or variations of a skill in a practice context). This strategy may help reduce the effects of negative transfer.

An example of negative transfer for timing in dance is the situation in which dancers learn choreography to one piece of music or rhythmic structure such as music in 4/4 time, and then they are asked to change to a different timing structure, such as 3/4 time. Dancers usually stay with the original timing for a certain period of time. Once again, the previous learning of the first timing negatively transfers to the learning of the second timing. Note that this effect is not about slowing down or speeding up movement. As long as the relative timing of the various segments is maintained, dancers have little problem changing the timing. When they are asked to execute an entirely different rhythmic structure or relative timing, negative transfer occurs.

Research has suggested an overall view regarding sequencing and timing relationships between two skills and the learning process. When two dance skills or phrases have relative timing and sequencing that is similar, positive transfer occurs. When the two skills have similar sequencing but different timing, negative transfer occurs. If both sequencing and timing are different, zero transfer occurs.

Changing Habitual Patterns

In general, conditions that create negative transfer are those situations in which learners are trying to cease using a method of doing a skill and learn a new way to execute the skill, or change old habits and create new habits. An example in dance practice is the execution of turned-out leg positions to the side, including tendu, dégagé, passé, développé à la seconde, and grand battement à la seconde. These movements are common in ballet, modern, contemporary, jazz, and musical theater. They are sometimes taught with the leg moving directly to the side of the body. For most dancers this placement is not anatomically possible unless the pelvis rotates around the vertical axis in the

The dancer has the gesture leg in front of the body as determined by her anatomy; therefore, she can maintain good alignment of the pelvis.

direction of the gesture leg or tilts anteriorly to allow it. The correct placement for the execution of these skills is with the gesture leg forward of the pelvis; the amount differs for each dancer's individual anatomical structure. If the leg is correctly placed relative to the dancer's pelvis and hip joints, the various side gestures can be achieved without pelvic rotation or anterior tilt. However, when dancers practice the spatial location of the leg directly side and the accompanying pelvic movement for long periods of their training, it takes considerable time to cease using this pattern and replace it with a more efficient one. Learning and repeatedly practicing the old habit can negatively affect achieving the correct anatomical position.

Changing habitual patterns is a complex process, and different approaches work for different dancers. Probably the common element across all dancers who succeed at this task is motivation. If dancers are committed to the old approach and do not see a strong purpose to make changes, it is unlikely that the habit will be altered. For some students, a discussion of the anatomical basis for changing what they are doing and the potential injuries that the old habit might cause is a successful method of motivating change. Applying this idea to the previous example, students can be told about the stresses placed on the lumbar spine and the standing knee by taking the leg too far back in second position. Other students need to discuss and rethink their aesthetics and determine why they think one approach is more beautiful in their value system than another. Sometimes seeing professional dancers in live performance or on video with different work values can shift ideas about aesthetics, especially if the professionals are dancers that the students hold in high esteem. Other students may need physical practice that involves repatterning work. This work can take the form of somatic practices or any of the current dance-related systems that focus on alignment and patterning issues, such as C-I Training, Pilates, and Floor-Barre Technique. These systems work mainly on the floor or on a mat. Like many of the somatic practices, they allow the body to reorganize with the assistance of support and with a framework of exploration and attending to the sensory experience. Also, some students

are highly responsive to images, light touch (discussed later, in the section titled Guidance), and verbal suggestions or cues in the context of an active dance class, and they are able to make habitual changes without work done in another context.

Teachers should let students know that habits are slow to change; it takes vigilance and patience to change them. They may experience frustration and even see skills diminish during the transition period between habitual ways of working. During this extended phase, students need encouragement and ongoing reminders. One more point needs to be emphasized in this discussion. It is not uncommon for students to see corrections about their habitual patterns as an attack on their previous teachers. Students may have worked with these original teachers for a long time during their formative years. It is essential to be delicate in the presentation of this information, avoiding harsh criticisms or judgments about students' previous experiences. It is helpful to talk about different approaches, try a new way of working, and explore the differences. In time, students become more receptive. Finally, teachers should understand that not all students are capable of changing habitual ways of working, regardless of the method used, and others are simply not ready and may need to be approached again at a later date.

The common understanding of negative transfer in the sports literature is that the effects are only found in the early learning of a new skill, and they are temporary. With time, people can supersede negative transfer and learn the new approach. Athletes are highly motivated to change old habits once they understand that the new habit either produces a better result in the goal of the skill, or it is more efficient and healthier for the body. However, dance practice is multifaceted, and it is concerned with aesthetics, as well as skill achievement; sometimes these aspects are in contradiction. As discussed previously, even when dancers are given the anatomical knowledge about leg placement, enhanced balance, or reduced injury with better placement, those who are committed to the visual appearance of the leg in the flat side position may not be motivated to change. Sometimes it takes more than knowledge and consistent reminders to affect this change in body organization. It may be necessary for the teacher to initiate a discussion about the difference between achieving a particular look and what is anatomically sound for the body, and the subsequent responsibility for choices the dancers will need to make during the span of their careers.

Balancing Positive and Negative Transfer

Finally, highly complex skills have several elements. Given two skills, a previously learned and a new skill, they may have some elements that are similar and create positive transfer, and other elements that differ and create negative transfer. While it is not fully understood what occurs in these instances, it can be viewed as a balance, in which the positive and negative effects are weighed, and the overall transfer depends on which is greater.

Bilateral Transfer

Bilateral transfer is the transfer of learning from one limb to its counterpart on the other side of the body. While most dance teachers and dancers are aware of this phenomenon, the best method of testing for bilateral transfer comes from the sports literature, because most athletes are heavily biased to their dominant hand or side. In the typical testing design,

the first step is to teach the skill to both the preferred and nonpreferred limb. After initial learning, both sides are tested; this test is called the pretest. The second step is to practice the skill repeatedly with one limb, for example, the preferred limb. The third step is to retest both the preferred and nonpreferred limbs; this test is called the posttest.

If the preferred or practiced limb improves in the posttest but the nonpreferred limb does not, no bilateral transfer has occurred. However, if the nonpreferred limb improves even though it is the other limb that has practiced, bilateral transfer has occurred. Note that the test can also be done with the nonpreferred limb as the one that practices. In this way, it can be determined whether bilateral transfer is better from preferred to nonpreferred limb or from nonpreferred to preferred limb. Table 15.2 shows a summary of this testing method.

It is generally acknowledged that bilateral transfer does occur. It is also agreed that bilateral transfer is **asymmetric** (transfer is not the same in both directions). A controversial point is which direction has better transfer. The common recommendation, and what is supported by the sports literature, is that it is best to start practice with the preferred limb, because transfer is better from preferred to nonpreferred limb. This choice is not only about motor learning; it also involves motivation.

Table 15.2 Testing Bilateral Transfer

Testing transfer from preferred to nonpreferred limb			
	Pretest	Practice trials	Posttest
Preferred limb	Test the preferred limb before any practice	**Practice only with the preferred limb**	Test the preferred limb after the practice sessions
Nonpreferred limb	Test the nonpreferred limb before any practice		Test the non-preferred limb after the practice sessions of the preferred limb
Testing transfer from nonpreferred to preferred limb			
	Pretest	Practice trials	Posttest
Preferred limb	Test the preferred limb before any practice		Test the preferred limb after the practice sessions of the nonpreferred limb
Nonpreferred limb	Test the nonpreferred limb before any practice	**Practice only with the nonpreferred limb**	Test the non-preferred limb after the practice sessions

Adapted from Magill and Anderson 2014.

Because people have greater success when initially learning with the preferred limb, they have greater motivation to continue practice.

Unlike the sports literature, the dance studies are few, the study designs are unorthodox, and the conclusions are contradictory. First, most of the writings are theoretical, and only a limited number have any original research. Many of the theoretical comments are based on one study from 1983. Second, none of the studies used the standard design illustrated in table 15.2, and the research designs used are untested for validity and reliability. Third, much of the dance research has been done on ballet dancers. This is true not only on the subject of bilateral transfer, but in almost every aspect of dance inquiry. Hence, it is not known whether results can generalize to other dance forms.

Some of the conclusions regarding bilateral transfer recommend starting on the preferred side, some recommend starting on the non-preferred side, and some indicate that it is of no consequence. Perhaps one of the issues is that the dance researchers use long, complex phrases for testing rather than a single skill. Hence the issue of preferred and nonpreferred

becomes clouded, because the phrase switches back and forth, and too many variables are included.

Perhaps the more important issue for dance practice is numbers of repetitions on each side. When teachers introduce a new skill or phrase on the right side, the dancers learn it, mark it, practice it, review it, and then execute it all on that side. Then they perform on the left side, and ultimately they complete far fewer repetitions. In this way, an imbalance occurs in the training, not because of the initial side of learning, but due to the imbalance in practice conditions. Teachers should either start on the left side for some of the work or be conscious of giving equal time to both sides.

Two Types of Transfer in Dance

In addition to the transfer conditions described, dancers use the principles of transfer in two general ways. **In-context transfer** is transfer that occurs within the dance class or practice from one phase to another. For example, ballet teachers assume that practicing dégagés at the barre will transfer and improve skills in petit allégro.

Dance research subject in a study comparing (a) work at the barre with (b) work in the center.

Modern teachers assume that torso material practiced sitting on the floor will transfer and improve skills in standing and traveling material. **Between-context transfer** is transfer that occurs from a dance-related practice to dance class and performance. For example, dancers attend Pilates and yoga classes assuming that the learned skills and material will transfer to enhanced dance skills, such as core support in turns and greater flexibility in extensions. Dancers do balancing tasks on Bosu balls and exercise balls assuming that it will transfer and improve balance in dance tasks. To date, little evidence exists to support some of these underlying assumptions within the dance context, as demonstrated in an extensive review of the dance research.

While the studies have examined many areas of dance practice, four topics stand out in their relationship to the discussion of transfer of learning: alignment, applications of barre to center and traveling, movement transitions, and supplementary training for dancers.

Alignment

While it may seem that alignment is a constant across various conditions and dance styles, this assumption is not the case. Alignment for individual dancers can vary from one position to the next, such as parallel first, turned-out first, third, and fifth. Within one practice session the same dancer can exhibit different ways of aligning the body in these positions. Alignment and muscle use can vary between techniques, such as ballet and modern. When executing the same movement, such as demi- and grand pliés, ballet and modern dancers use their muscles differently. However, different ballet and modern dancers were assessed in dance studies, so the issue of whether the training for pliés does not transfer from ballet to modern or modern to ballet is unanswered. The differences may be because of the different anatomical types in these forms. Finally, static alignment can differ considerably from dynamic alignment. Dancers who are organized beautifully in static stance can become poorly aligned in dynamic and traveling material.

Use of the Barre

An ongoing discussion among dance teachers is the use of the barre. Currently, more con-temporary dance teachers are using barre work at the start of classes as well. The question arises as to whether or not skills done at the barre transfer to center and traveling work. Because barre exercises are complex in that they contain several elements, probably some elements transfer and some do not. In particular, strategies that dancers use to shift their weight from two feet to one foot and back to two feet do not transfer from barre to other conditions. Dancers shift the weight toward the standing leg less at the barre than what is needed when doing the same skill without a barre, in both développé and grand battement assessments. Dance teachers and dancers often claim that advanced dancers do not rely on the barre as beginners do, but the studies demonstrate that advanced and beginner dancers rely equally on the support of the barre. In addition, muscle use varies between barre, center, and traveling. In particular, the supporting leg muscles are not as active at the barre as they are in the other conditions. Barre work does train for strength and endurance of the supporting leg and can allow the dancer to focus on alignment of the foot and ankle. Certainly the strength will have benefit elsewhere, and possibly the foot and ankle alignment. Teachers may need to reconsider what they think the benefits will be and avoid making assumptions about other nontransferrable aspects.

Movement Transitions

Teachers and dancers assume that certain simple skills are transitional or contained as a component part of complex skills, and practice in the simpler skill will therefore transfer to the complex skill. For example, in modern dance, a side bend of the torso is a transition between front and back in a body roll. The action of dégagé is contained in the elevation step assemblé, and grand battement devant is a component of grand jeté. The question arises as to whether the execution of these transitions or component parts is the same movement when it occurs in the more complex skill. Studies have demonstrated that demi-plié is a different motor pattern than the transitional moment of demi-plié during a grand plié. Stopping in the demi-plié during a grand plié does not improve this skill. The same is true for demi-pointe and full pointe. Probably the best strategy is to move fluidly through these transitional phases, and consider the demi-plié and demi-pointe as separate movements from grand plié and full pointe.

Supplementary Training

Supplementary training has become increasingly popular for dancers in the last few decades. These training methods range from dance-specific systems such as Pilates, Floor-Barre Technique, Gyrotonic and Gyrokinesis, and C-I Training to populist systems such as yoga, resistance training with weights, Bosu and other exercise ball work, and exercise band work. To date, little research exists to support the claims that these methods transfer to dance practice. In general, studies with dance-specific systems have not supported the idea of transfer in the areas of jump height and alignment. One study did show a change in alignment, but it was only in the condition of dynamic movement involving torso work with grand pliés, not static alignment. Work with jumping apparatus does not necessarily improve jump height, but the researchers suggest that this result is because dancers choose aesthetics over height.

Much of the dance research looks at highly complex skills. Based on the idea of similarity of components, it may be that in each of the movements studied, some elements are similar, but others are not. For example, with barre work, the components that did not transfer were strategies for shifting weight and muscle use for the standing leg. However, elements such as line of the body, dynamics or effort, and body-part coordination such as movements of the head and arms may in fact transfer from barre to center to traveling. With supplementary training, factors that might assist transfer such as cueing and imagery have not yet been fully explored. Teachers and dancers can continue to explore strategies to optimize both in-context and between-context transfer.

Guidance

A method used to assist athletes and dancers in skill learning is called **guidance**, in which the learner is assisted through hands-on work (physical touch). Techniques range from very light touch that suggests movement corrections to manually pushing and pulling the learner into the correct actions. Aggressive techniques in which the learner is forced into correct action have positive effects on performance during the practice session but not on learning. Guidance that is interspersed with unguided practice and guidance that is less restrictive have better results on retention and learning. One effective technique is using a fading feedback approach. For example, if the skill to be learned is placement of second position arms, the teacher can begin by actively guiding the student's arms the first time. Next, the student moves the arms to second position until the arms comes into contact with the teacher's guide, and finally, the teacher reduces the guidance until the student can find the destination shape proprioceptively. Guidance is also more effective when used in the early stages of learning and for movements that are slow. These principles from sports training are entirely consistent with the approaches of somatic practice and somatic-based teaching methods. The early somatic practitioners emphasized that aggressive guidance may create alignment and movement that looks correct but is inefficient in muscle use and has long-term negative consequences. In order to achieve the best results in learning dance skills, dance training can employ techniques of light touch and suggestion, paired with appropriate feedback.

Looking back to Cyndi and Tony, their experience could have been enhanced by following some basic ideas about retention and transfer. While learning the duet, they could mentally create a narrative and verbal labels that make a stronger memory representation of the dance. Afterward, they might verbally describe the dance to each other to assist declarative learning. In a cooperative spirit, because the space was limited, they could join with other couples and take turns practicing. They could observe each other and give feedback. They might even switch partners to have more variability of the duet experience. They should avoid other distracting activities, such as reading unrelated material, texting their friends, and practicing other dances. They could even sit quietly, think about the music, and mentally practice the dance. Each of these techniques would enhance their retention and assist in their adaptability or transfer to the conditions presented by the judges in the performance experience.

Summary

Retention and transfer are two of the most powerful reflections of learning. The five features of learning are improvement, consistency, stability, persistence, and adaptability. Persistence relates to memory, which has three stages: short-term sensory stage, working (short-term) memory, and long-term memory. Capacity and duration differentiate the three stages. Explicit and implicit memory tests are used to assess working memory. Memory of movement relates to spatial features and meaningfulness of the movement. Three strategies that can assist in improving memory are heightening the meaningfulness of movement, strengthening the intention to remember the movement, and structuring the organization of the movement. Adaptability relates to the transfer of learning, which has three types: positive, negative, and zero. The most common reasons for positive transfer are similarity of skills and cognitive processes. Bilateral transfer is asymmetric and is best from preferred to nonpreferred limb. Issues specific to dance transfer include alignment, use of the barre, movement transitions, and supplementary training. Guidance, if too forceful and too frequent, can fail to enhance retention, but lighter and less frequent guidance can successfully aid learning.

Chapter 16
Mental Practice and Imagery

*I*magine that it is a few days before a major dance performance. The dancers are in a late-night rehearsal and have been working for many hours. The choreographer realizes that the dancers are becoming fatigued, but she wants to run the piece at least one more time. She asks the dancers to lie on the floor, close their eyes, listen to the music, and visualize performing the choreography. In addition to giving the dancers a rest period to avoid fatigue-related injuries, this experience, known as mental practice, will also enhance their learning of the material. After the dancers finish this process, the choreographer adds imagery to the choreography. She goes through the dance, incorporating metaphors and poetic descriptions of various phrases to enhance the artistic expression of the dancers. Although the choreographer's intention is related to issues of fatigue and artistry, mental practice and imagery are two techniques that can make major contributions to motor learning. In dance, several uses of mental practice and imagery exist, and the field continues to develop. Because the large majority of studies in this area have been done in sports, the chapter begins by addressing the general knowledge about mental practice and imagery, then moves to the applications for dance.

Mental Practice

Every dancer has observed advanced dancers learning new material and marking the steps with slight movements of the hands. In their minds, they are actually executing the whole phrase. This strategy is known as mental practice, which the dancers are using for the acquisition of new skills or new movement sequences. **Mental practice** is rehearsing a skill or sequence of movements cognitively (using thought) without physical execution. Mental practice can involve reviewing the procedural parts of the movement or visualizing specific movement details. It can occur with no actual visual activity, such as the dancers in the opening example with their eyes closed, or it can occur while watching other dancers or a video of the dance. In the example of the dancers learning a phrase while marking it with their hands, they are using mental practice for learning new skills or sequences. In addition to skill acquisition, mental practice can be used for preparing to execute a skill that has already been learned, such as thinking through the steps of a known turn combination just before executing it, or reviewing an entire choreography before going onstage.

Uses of Mental Practice

In sports, mental practice has two main benefits, skill acquisition and preparation for skill execution and performance. These uses are also seen in dance practice. The two can be combined; dancers might be observing the teacher demonstrating a new skill, and the dancers might use mental practice to aid both the learning of the skill and to prepare them for executing the skill. Skill acquisition can refer to learning a skill for the first time, or it can mean relearning a skill in various situations, such as postinjury or **movement reeducation**, a term used to describe the process of changing habits and forming new ways of working. The needed change might be an alignment issue that could cause strain to the body, or it may be a poor habit that could lead to a sudden injury, such as improper use of the feet in jump landings. Overwhelming research evidence exists in the sports literature that mental practice is successful for both skill acquisition and preparation for skill execution.

Skill Acquisition

Dancers might wonder whether it is indeed possible to mentally practice a skill and get better at its execution. In fact, it partly depends on the type of skill. Mental practice affects skills with cognitive components, not simply motor components. For example, doing a series of continuous leaps would probably not benefit from mental practice, but a piece of complex choreography with many difficult transitions to solve would benefit.

Mental practice has been tested in relation to physical practice. Studies show that physical practice is superior to mental practice, but mental practice is superior to no practice at all. Further, when physical practice is mixed

The skill of using various arm coordinations with back attitude can benefit from mental practice.

When dancers are recovering from injuries, mental practice is an effective tool for learning and maintaining skills. It can provide dancers with the opportunity to review known skills and choreography when they cannot physically practice during the recovery phase. It can allow them to observe classes and mentally practice new skills. Finally, it can assist dancers in the movement reeducation process of changing habits that may have led to the injury in the first place. One of the issues for injured dancers is the psychological impact of being injured and the fear of losing time. Mental practice provides a positive opportunity during this stressful period.

Mental practice is also beneficial in improving both power and speed. Physical educators and researchers Geraldine Van Gyn, Howard Wenger, and Catherine Gaul studied both power and speed training, using mental practice during the training. Two points are of interest for dancers in their study. First, they used between-context training; the training the athletes used to improve power and speed was not the target activity, similar to dancers training flexibility in a yoga class to improve their flexibility in dance class. Second, the best results for speed were demonstrated by the athletes who combined mental and physical training at the same time. For dancers, this information suggests that mentally practicing fast dance skills while doing supplementary speed and power training could support the improvement of these dance skills.

Preparing for Skill Execution and Performance

Mental practice is used when preparing for skill execution and performance in two main respects. First, it is used as a motivational tool in three ways. One motivational goal is to focus on specific objectives, such as accomplishing a difficult skill in a dance combination or succeeding at an audition. Another motivational goal is to improve confidence and attention when facing challenges, such as learning new difficult choreography. The final motivational goal is to reduce stress and anxiety in tense situations, such as dance performances. The second use of mental practice relates to cognitive processes in two ways. One goal is

with mental practice, the two combined are almost as effective as physical practice alone. For example, if dancers practice a skill 15 times physically and 5 times mentally, it is almost as effective as physically practicing the skill 20 times. The benefits of this combined approach are that it can avoid physical overuse and fatigue, and some of the practice can be done in a small space. In fact, studies showing this effect suggest that the benefit would be as great as if the dancers were doing 10 physical and 10 mental practices. Mental practice is most likely effective in skill acquisition because it enhances problem-solving abilities. However, if the dancer is capable of dancing, then mental practice should be a supplement to physical practice and not a substitute.

in accomplishing specific movements, such as executing a series of coupé jetés in a circle or complex hand and foot coordinations in classical Indian dance. The second goal is more general and involves planning strategies, such as learning complicated spatial designs in a dance piece.

Reasons for Effectiveness of Mental Practice

Mental practice is successful for three possible reasons. First, when people are imaging a movement, the neural pathways from the brain to the target muscle are activated. The muscle activity is specific to the task or movement being imagined, but not great enough to cause the limbs to move. This activation of the pathways can assist in learning new skills by forming the appropriate coordination patterns. It can also help before the performance of a known skill by preparing the pathways for activation, thereby increasing the chance of a correct execution.

Second, activity occurs in specific areas of the brain, whether a person is doing a movement or mentally practicing the movement, especially if the person is also using imagery. Even when learning a new movement sequence, the same changes occur in the brain whether the person is mentally or physically practicing the sequence. The brain areas used in imagining movement are the same areas that are used in planning and executing movements.

Third, in the early stages of learning, a large amount of the thought process is involved in problem solving to figure out what to do in order to accomplish the task. This cognitive function is important whether learning a new skill or relearning and retraining an old skill. The advantage of this strategy is that the learner

The complicated hand and foot shapes and rhythms can be practiced mentally to enhance skill execution.

can solve problems without the distraction of the physical concerns and challenges.

Mental practice is a wonderful companion to physical practice in the learning of new skills, the relearning and reeducation of old skills, and in preparing to execute skills. Its benefits in enhancing physical practice and as a psychological tool are powerful reasons for dancers and dance teachers to consider adding mental practice as a regular part of dance training. Dancers are accustomed to using mental rehearsal, but usually while practicing choreography, whereas dancers commonly use imagery in both the training (dance class) and the choreographic (rehearsal) settings. Historically, this exploration of imagery is probably because of the strong effect that imagery can have on dramatic interpretation of choreography, and on movement quality in learning different dance techniques and styles. However, imagery has a wider range of uses than is generally understood by dancers. The next section on imagery describes the various forms and uses of imagery for dance training and practice.

Imagery

Mental imagery is a psychological activity that evokes the physical characteristics of an absent object or dynamic event. It can be external or internal, which relates to the perspective. **External imagery** suggests that the dancer is like an outside third person and sees the movement as if viewing a video of the self. **Internal imagery** suggests that the dancer uses the perspective of being inside the body and experiences the sensations and sights as if doing the movement. Three properties that give images usefulness are how vivid the image is, how easy it is for the person to use the image, and how precise or accurate the image is in relation to the movement. Several ways exist to categorize images. First, they can be defined by the strategies used to experience the image. **Visual imagery** is a representation of concrete objects, events, or movements as perceived through vision. **Kinesthetic imagery** is a representation of concrete objects, events, or movements as perceived through sensation.

Direct imagery is a nonverbal representation of the actual movement. **Indirect imagery**, also called **metaphoric imagery**, is a representation of the movement that is not literal, and it can be a representation of the desired movement with a figure or likeness. Second, images can be defined based on their spatial orientation. **Lines-of-movement imagery** designates a specific direction required in the relative positions of body parts. **Global imagery** involves images that create an overall state or feeling sense. Finally, **anatomical imagery** uses specific anatomical terminology, but it is presented in a metaphorical sense.

Examples for our dancers in the choreographer's rehearsal could include any of the following: "Imagine seeing an expansive ocean in front of you as you dance the third section" (visual). "Imagine feeling sand under your feet as you cross the space" (kinesthetic). "Imagine as you do the movement that you are an arrow flying through space" (direct). "Imagine moving as if you are being pushed by the wind" (indirect/ metaphoric). "Imagine a string that connects your pubic bone to your navel" (lines-of-movement). "Imagine you are in a sauna, and move in a relaxed, fluid way" (global). "Imagine the

Dancers can use metaphoric images to improve the quality or dynamics of the movements they are executing.

heads of the femurs or thigh bones as they float inside the hip sockets" (anatomical).

Imagery is not effective if the dancers have never actually executed the skill, unless it is combined with observational learning. In other words, dancers can use imagery if they are watching the teacher or another student demonstrate the material. And they can use imagery for a skill with which they are already familiar. However, it is not useful to ask dancers to use imagery with an untried skill that they are not observing at the moment of imaging.

Not all people have the same capacity to use imagery, nor respond to the same types of imagery. It is best to allow people to select the type of imagery that they wish to use. Further, some people can imagine movement with great vividness and can play with the image easily in the mind. Others have difficulty using images and are not successful in manipulating them. This skill is called imagery ability.

Personal Imagery Ability

Imagery ability is the ability to image a movement with precision and control. It differs with each person. In 1983, researchers Craig Hall and John Pongrac devised the Movement Imagery Questionnaire (MIQ), which was revised by Craig Hall and Kathleen Martin in 1997. The questionnaire is designed to assess individual imagery ability. Figure 16.1 shows an example of imagery scales from the MIQ. The MIQ contains a series of questions that ask a person to mentally perform certain movements. The person is asked to do this process in one of two ways, either to form exact and vivid images visually or attempt to feel the sensations of creating the movement. Then the person rates the difficulty level of the completed mental task. A person might be good at visual imagery, kinesthetic imagery, or both. The researchers proposed that people with high imagery ability would be better able to use imagery to enhance their physical practice. The MIQ has been tested successfully and is used commonly in imagery research. It has also been determined that imagery ability is not related to motivation and attention but rather to neurological properties of the person. Even if people have low imagery ability, they can still benefit from the use of imagery.

Dance-Specific Uses of Imagery

Imagery has been used in dance practice for centuries, and it has been documented since the early 1900s. Its traditional role has been to enhance movement quality and to inspire artistry and expressiveness. One major difference between the use of imagery in sports and its use in dance is that dancers use imagery both in stillness and while moving, whereas athletes only use mental imagery when not actually moving. The use of imagery in dance from a motor learning perspective is relatively new. It found its beginnings in the somatic practices. Much of the dance literature on imagery is the-

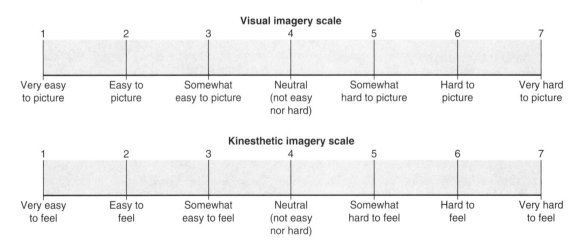

Figure 16.1 Movement Imagery Questionnaire (MIQ).

Reprinted, by permission, from Craig Hall, School of Kinesiology, Western University, Canada.

oretical. Research studies are limited, and the conclusions about the effectiveness of imagery for motor learning are not unanimous. Both theoretical and research-based aspects from the dance literature are discussed.

Theoretical Work in Dance Imagery

The theoretical work in dance imagery is not theory in the sense of being confined to writing and discussion. Use of imagery in dance has always been practical and studio based, even though it was not initially supported by research studies. The early theorists were interested in imagery as a way of exploring movement reeducation, particularly alignment and poor movement habits. Some of the early theorists whose work is still widely studied today include Irmgard Bartenieff, Mabel Todd, and Lulu Sweigard.

Irmgard Bartenieff developed her work based on the work of Rudolf Laban, founder of Laban Movement Analysis (LMA) and the effort/shape system. This method examines all movement in terms of its effort, space, shape, and action of body parts. Each of these areas describes a different continuum of a particular aspect of movement. For example, effort describes the dynamics of movement, concerning such components as flow (free/bound), weight (strong/light), time (sudden/sustained), and space (direct/indirect). Bartenieff claimed that dance artists can use Laban's conception of movement in the execution of their tasks by relating their own bodies to the qualities they perceive in images, and then transmitting those qualities through the dance medium.

Mabel Todd stated that the study of posture must be approached through application of neurological as well as mechanical principles. What Todd called *posture* is what is now generally called *alignment*. Todd discussed at length the importance of the balanced functioning of antagonist muscles around joints. In her view, establishing new alignment patterns requires these two facilities: the facility to form adequate mental concepts for stimulating activity in deep-lying muscles; and the kinesthetic sense, which gives rise to the perception of movement, position, and strain. This idea of forming mental concepts to facilitate muscle function, rather than thinking about voluntarily contracting the muscles, has formed the basis of current work in dance training, particularly in the areas of alignment and movement patterning. Todd's basic premise was that concentrating on the image resulted in the neuromuscular responses necessary to carry out the movements in the most efficient way. She named the process that supported her work *psychophysical* or *psychophysiological*, and she claimed that the location of movement and the direction of movement must both be incorporated into the images for appropriate muscle response.

Lulu Sweigard worked extensively with Mabel Todd, and they continued developing the theories and practices of Todd's work. In using the term *muscle balance*, Sweigard was referring to the balance of strength and flexibility of muscles, and the subsequent inefficient movement patterns that develop when imbalance exists. Sweigard believed that changes in alignment and movement patterns were only

The constructive rest position was developed by Lulu Sweigard, and it is used in conjunction with imagery to assist in changing poor alignment habits.

possible through the re-coordination of neuromuscular pathways responsible for habitual muscle balance and the resulting movement patterns. In addition, muscular components of a movement should not be voluntarily directed while the subject is learning new patterns; they must be organized at a nonconscious level of the nervous system. From 1929 to 1931, Sweigard analyzed 200 dance subjects, using her imagery system called Ideokinesis as a treatment method to alter alignment patterns. She concluded that there were unequivocal changes in the alignment of subjects as a result of the use of imagined movement in her system of Ideokinesis. By rigorous scientific standards, these conclusions are unsubstantiated, because the study had no control group and was not a blind study. (The person assessing the subjects knew the subjects and was the person who designed the protocol.) Nevertheless, Sweigard was a pioneer in attempting to observe and measure the effects of a system of somatic practice on alignment in dancers, and she paved the way for future researchers.

Sweigard discussed reasons for the use of visualization. Ideokinesis uses Sweigard's nine lines of movement, each with a clear location, direction and purpose. In addition, she applied the use of Ideokinesis, which entails imaging without any movement or muscular activity, to minimal tasks designed to encourage efficient muscular use in dance practice. For example, in an exercise involving slow hip flexion while lying on the back, the abdominal muscles must not be engaged voluntarily before or during the activity. In Sweigard's words, their use must be determined subcortically—not consciously—in response to the appropriate image, although it is now understood that muscle activation does not need to be subcortical to be nonconscious. Although her ideas about brain function were hypothetical, Sweigard's goal was to encourage dancers to avoid consciously engaging specific muscles, and instead rely on imagery and nonconscious motor patterns to achieve the desired results. According to Sweigard, all limits to movement range and vocabulary are products of imbalance, and the balance of strength and flexibility of muscles must be attained through visualization. Figure 16.2 shows an example of

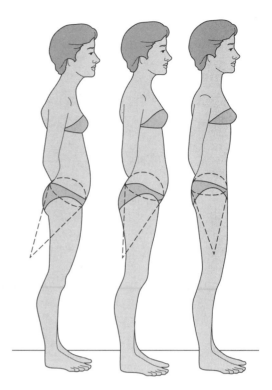

Figure 16.2 Sweigard image for pelvic alignment. The dancer can use the image of the ice cream cone in the pelvis to realign the spine and pelvis. When imagining that the bottom of the cone points directly down to the legs, and the rim of the cone is level inside the pelvis, the anterior pelvic tilt can diminish.

Reprinted from L.E. Sweigard, 1974, *Human movement potential: Its ideokinetic facilitation* (Lanham, MD: University Press of America), 247.

one of her images to create muscle balance in the muscles of the pelvis.

Irene Dowd, a student of Sweigard and currently a highly respected neuromuscular retrainer, has continued the evolution and practice of Ideokinesis. She has explored the uses of imaging during actual movement, both minimal and complex. Dowd reiterates the idea that joint and muscle pain, as well as limited movement range and vocabulary, are products of muscular imbalance, referring to strength/flexibility imbalances of antagonist muscles around joints. She emphasizes that the kinetic nature of dance means images must be dynamic, not static, and she presents suggestions for practical sessions using imagery designed to improve muscular efficiency and neurological coordination for a variety of anatomical areas.

Other dance and movement educators have been applying the principles and images of Ideokinesis to motion and dance practice. It has become increasingly common for dance teachers to use various types of images during dance classes, including visual, kinesthetic, direct, and indirect imagery. This use of imagery is thought to have several benefits, including enhancing learning skills and performance, improving memory of dance sequences, supplying creative inspirational sources, clarifying movement intention, and integrating the body and the mind.

Some dance teachers employ an extensive dance training system called body–mind dancing, which uses several forms of imagery and imparts knowledge in anatomy, kinesiology, and physiology. They believe that dance movement should balance attention to both the external and internal environments, thereby creating an awareness in the dancer that permits learning through a variety of perceptual channels, both voluntary and nonconscious. Other teachers claim that imagery is especially helpful in teaching good alignment to dancers. They state that the use of imagery works at a nonconscious level to facilitate muscular changes, which improves alignment through body reeducation. However, it has yet to be determined how effective the use of imagery in the dance studio is, either in producing more biomechanically efficient muscle patterns, or in improved dance performance and alignment.

Research Studies in Dance

Since the early theoretical work encouraging the use of imagery, several studies have been conducted specifically on dancers. Most of these studies were on small, specific populations, and few were longitudinal. One exception is a study by Donna Krasnow and colleagues, in which dancers did 8 weeks of training using various methods: imagery alone, conditioning alone, and the two combined. Combining the two was most effective in making changes to dynamic (in motion) alignment.

Not all of the conclusions of the various research studies are in agreement, but some general ideas have been established. First, imagery can be helpful in retention of move-ment, particularly involving spatial locations and timing. For example, using the image of a clock face in describing the location of limbs aids in remembering the limb position. Second, imagery can be effective in making changes to alignment and can be more successful than traditional conditioning work.

Because the brain's messages that regulate alignment during complex movement are on the nonconscious level, conscious directions to muscles are insufficient to accomplish the organization needed for movement tasks. The use of imagery is hypothesized to work on this nonconscious level of muscle activation. Imagery can improve skill level in specific dance movements in the technical aspects of movement, such as leg height, and may also reduce anxiety. It has been established that imagery is successful with children as young as 5 years old, and metaphoric imagery can be more effective than verbal instructions about the movement. Finally, as dancers become more advanced, they use imagery more frequently and tend to move from visual to kinesthetic images.

Reasons for Use of Imagery and Types of Images in Dance Practice

Dancers use imagery for a wide variety of reasons. Five categories have been identified:

- *Cognitive reasons* include using imagery to remember long sequences or complex timing.

- *Motivational reasons* include images that encourage higher skill attainment, such as thinking about leaping like a gazelle.

- *Artistic reasons* are perhaps the most common use of dance imagery. They are used in rehearsal and performance settings, and they imbue the movement with the specific artistic statement of the work, such as imaging a kick or a punch to the center of the torso to illicit a powerful and anguished response.

- *Healing reasons* include using images of clean air or cool water flowing through injured areas to heal them.

- *No-reason* images are perhaps the most curious. They seem to be spontaneous images that arise in the psyche while dancing or thinking about dancing, perhaps triggered or stimulated by the music or a sensory experience.

Dancers use a myriad of images to enhance their dance practice. Some dancers imagine environments of water or wind or fire to change the quality of movement. Other dancers imagine a string coming out the top of the head, or the rib cage like an accordion to influence alignment. Other dancers imagine light or energy coming out of the limbs to improve their lines. And many dancers visualize themselves executing skills both in the learning stage and as preparation. Regardless of the type of image, the purpose of the image, or whether using images in stillness or while moving, imaging is a necessary component in a dancer's training and leads to greater success and artistry.

Clearly, the mind has a powerful effect on both motor learning and movement execution. While most dancers understand how processes such as concentration, attention, and memory affect their dance training, mental practice and imagery can now be recognized for their influence on dance training. When they acknowledge all of the roles of mental practice and imagery and they understand their personal strengths in the uses of these tools, dancers can optimize their hours of practice and enhance their artistry for performance.

Summary

Mental practice has two main uses, to improve skill acquisition and to prepare for movement execution. One advantage of mental practice is that it can be used when dancers and athletes cannot do physical practice, such as during injury rehabilitation. Three reasons mental practice is effective include the stimulation of neural pathways, the similarity of brain areas used, and cognitive function. Imagery is a type of mental practice that occurs in the thought processes. Dancers use it both in stillness and during movement. People have different imaging abilities, but all dancers and athletes can benefit from the use of imagery. Dancers use several types of images, including visual imagery, kinesthetic imagery, direct imagery, indirect (metaphoric) imagery, lines-of-movement imagery, global imagery, and anatomical imagery. Early theorists in the use of imagery were somatic practitioners. More recently, research has supported their claims of the efficacy of imagery in affecting alignment and in learning and reeducating movement patterns.

acoustic flow field—The various sounds occurring in the observer's environment.

action effect hypothesis—The hypothesis that when performers at any skill level direct their attention to movement outcomes rather than specific components, they achieve greater success.

action selection theories—Theories suggesting that selection, not capacities that limit the thought process, is the basic system for determining attention.

adaptability—Ability to learn a skill, then use that skill in any context or environment required.

afferent neurons—*See* **sensory neurons**.

agonist—The muscle contracting and thus creating the action during a movement.

alignment—A particular linear organization of the body parts with respect to gravity and the dance aesthetic in both static and dynamic conditions.

allocation policy—The brain's decision maker, controlling how much attention will be given to each of several tasks.

ambient vision system—System that identifies location of objects and motion in the larger environment using peripheral vision.

amplitude—The distance between two targets.

anatomical imagery—Imagery that uses specific anatomical terminology presented in a metaphoric sense.

anesthetic block—Injection of anesthesia into an area of the body, such as the joint capsule, to block sensation.

antagonist—The muscle stretching and thus creating the opposite movement from the agonist during a movement.

anticipatory postural reflexes—Activity of the postural muscles that occurs before a disturbance. Also called *feedforward control.*

anticipatory responses—Responses preceding an action, such as muscles that activate preceding weight shift from two feet to one foot to stabilize the body for balance.

arousal—A person's general state of excitability, reflected by physiological responses such as heart rate and respiratory rate.

arousal function of motivation—Determines how much energy or effort people employ on future attempts at the skill.

articulate—A relationship between the head and trunk in which the neck muscles remain fluid and are not statically held on the trunk.

associative learning—Learning that occurs when two ideas or stimuli are associated together.

associative stage—The second stage in the three-stage model of Fitts and Posner; the skill is being refined; therefore, less variability exists and subsequently improvement is slower.

asymmetric bilateral transfer—Idea that transfer is not the same in both directions: preferred to nonpreferred limb or nonpreferred to preferred limb.

attention—Concentrated mental activity, including aspects of concentration, consciousness, and focus, requiring that some issues be set aside in order to deal with selected thoughts.

auditory system—The sense of hearing, using the ears as receptors and the temporal lobe of the brain for processing.

augmented feedback—Adds to or enhances the intrinsic feedback and comes from a source external to the performer, such as a teacher, choreographer, or video. Also called *extrinsic feedback.*

autogenic inhibition reflex—A reflex that functions to allow the muscle to adjust its level of contraction.

automatic actions—Actions requiring little or no attention.

automatic processing—Making an automatic rather than a volitional choice; it often cannot easily be prevented. It is relatively fast and does not require attention, and it is parallel, meaning that thoughts and processes can happen simultaneously.

autonomous stage—The third and final stage in the three-stage model of Fitts and Posner. It requires little or no attention, and it only occurs after much practice and experience with the task.

axons—Nerve cell processes responsible for sending messages to the next neuron or possibly on to muscle fibers. Also called *nerve fibers.*

balance—The ongoing loss and recovery of equilibrium during dynamic movement.

Glossary

ballistic skills—Skills in which a person provides impetus to an object or body part through forceful and rapid exertion, setting the object or body part into motion along a specific trajectory.

basal ganglia—Clusters of neurons buried deep in the cerebral hemispheres that are critical in the control of antagonist muscles during movement and the control of force.

behavioral synchrony—*See* **social coordination**.

behaviorism—Asserts that psychologists should focus on behavior that can be observed, rather than try to understand or interpret what is happening in the mind.

between-context transfer—Transfer that occurs from a dance-related practice to dance class and performance.

bilateral transfer—The transfer of learning from one limb to its counterpart on the other side of the body.

blocked practice—Practice that involves low contextual interference, which means practicing a skill the same way with many repetitions within a given practice session.

bottleneck theories—Theories suggesting that in the early part of processing information, many functions can occur because it is happening in the large part of the bottle. Further down the line, the bottleneck is reached, and information not needed at that time is filtered out. *See also* **filter theories**.

brain stem—Part of the brain that connects directly to the spinal cord and has three areas that are involved in movement.

broad focus—Directing attention to a large environmental area or on many components that need concentration.

capacity—The amount of material that can reside in memory at a given point in time.

capacity interference—What occurs when no structural interference arises, but rather the mental capacity to attend to multiple events does not exist.

center of mass—The central point in the body with equal mass in all directions. In women the center of mass lies in the pelvis, and in males it tends to be higher, toward the sternum. Also called *center of gravity*.

central control mechanisms—Processes occurring in the central nervous system (the brain and the spinal cord) that organize movement.

central executive—The system in working memory that is the controller coordinating the new information and the retrieved information from long-term memory.

central nervous system (CNS)—System that comprises the brain and the parts of the nervous system that reside in the spinal cord. This system has the capability to direct the muscles to organize and to engage in various locomotor behaviors.

central pattern generators (CPGs)—Neural pathways in the spinal cord that create rhythmic patterns such as walking, running, and other rhythmic behaviors without sensory feedback.

central resource capacity theories—Theories suggesting that all activities needing attention compete within one centralized base for attention resources.

central vision—A visual process that allows one to consciously perceive information in the middle 2° to 5° in the visual field. It requires contrast and adequate light, and it is needed for object identification and conscious awareness of the environment. Central vision is in color.

cephalocaudal—Head to tail; refers to a progression over time.

cerebellum—Part of the brain that fine-tunes motor control, giving smoothness of motion and exactness of positioning, and controls the force and range of movements. It acts as a movement error correction and detection system; therefore, it is sometimes called the *comparator*.

cerebral cortex—Layer of the brain that covers the hemispheres and is an undulating, gray-colored mass. Also called *gray matter*.

cerebrum—Part of the brain that consists of two halves, the right and left hemispheres, and is crucial in the both the planning of movement and the integration of sensory and motor functions.

chunking—A way of accelerating learning and enhancing memory by organizing the material into units or groupings. Also called *clustering*.

clamping—Muscular action that completes the intended action in a smooth, controlled manner.

classical conditioning—Process of behavior modification that helps a person to predict relationships between two stimuli in the environment. It is reflexive, not voluntary.

closed-loop process—System that uses feedback or incoming information during movement to change the motor plan while it is being executed. Movement is typically slower, and feedback is compared to the initial plan during movement to make any necessary adjustments in order to complete the task.

closed-loop system—*See* **closed-loop process**.

closed skills—Skills that are done precisely the same way each time (i.e., follow the same general motor plan) with little variation in timing, gestures, and spacing. Little demand is on the performer because of changing environmental conditions.

clustering—*See* **chunking**.

coactivation—Simultaneous contraction of the agonist and antagonist during a given movement.

codes of processing information—Ways of categorizing information, such as verbal codes and spatial codes.

cognitive development—Development of mental processes such as conscious thought, reasoning, abstract thought, and problem-solving abilities.

cognitive mediation theory—Theory suggesting that as a person observes a skill, the brain forms a model (code) of the movement that it stores in the memory, and it uses this model on future attempts and as a criterion for error detection and correction.

cognitive skills—Mental activities that include problem solving, attention, memory, learning reasoning, decision making, spatial organization, and musical analysis.

cognitive stage—The first stage in the three-stage model of Fitts and Posner; the student is learning to understand the nature of the task, developing new strategies for solving the task, and learning to determine how best to evaluate which strategy to apply.

cognitive tunneling—*See* **inattention blindness**.

compensatory (reactive) reflexes—Activity of the postural muscles that occurs after a disturbance. Also called *feedback control*.

competition—A challenge between two or more people that can occur for a variety of goals, such as being the best at a skill, prestige, recognition by the teacher or audience, awards, or placement in a company.

complexity—The measure of a skill based on (1) the number of sections, parts, or components of the skill, and (2) how much attention the skill requires.

concurrent augmented feedback—Feedback given during movement execution.

consistency—Ability to execute a skill in the same way each time, allowing for very little variation from one identical trial to the next.

constant practice—Keeping the movement and environmental elements the same each time a skill is practiced.

constrained action hypothesis—Hypothesis stating that using internal focus constrains the motor system because the learner is trying to assert conscious control, which disrupts the automatic processes of the motor control system.

constructive criticism—Criticism involving comments given in a supportive, positive tone and with the intention of being helpful to the learner.

contextual interference—The disturbance of performance and memory caused by practicing multiple skills or variations of a skill within one practice situation. Also called *contextual variety*.

contextual interference effect—The benefits to learning caused by performing multiple skills or variations of a skill in a practice context with high contextual interference.

contextual variety—*See* **contextual interference**.

contralateral—Opposite side. *Contralateral arm and leg use* means using the opposite-side arm and leg.

contralateral movement—Movement across the diagonal (left arm with right leg, or right arm with left leg).

controlled processing—A volitional choice that can be easily ceased or prevented. It is also relatively slow and requires attention, and it is serial.

cooperation—The process of working together or acting in harmony.

coordination—Involves two important aspects of motor control: the patterning of the movements of the head, body, arms, and legs; and how the body parts relate to the environment, including objects and circumstances.

coordinative structures—*See* **muscle synergies**.

corpus callosum—A fine sheet of nerve cells that connects the two hemispheres of the cerebrum.

crawling—A form of locomotion using both arms and legs with the chest and abdomen on the floor. Independent sitting occurs at 6 to 7 months.

creeping—Movement seen in children at 8 to 10 months that uses both arms and legs, but the torso is lifted off the floor.

cuff technique—Procedure that blocks blood flow to the muscles, thereby temporarily shutting down feedback sensations.

cutaneous receptors—Receptors located in the skin that serve to inform the brain about touch, pressure, pain, heat, cold, and chemical stimuli such as odors.

dance improvisation—The process of creating movement in a spontaneous and experimental manner; it is facilitated through a variety of sensory explorations.

declarative knowledge—Knowledge that can be described or stated verbally, it is the *what* and is the type of knowledge in the episodic and semantic memory systems.

declarative learning—Learning that requires attention and reflection and results in knowledge that can consciously be recalled. The learner can express learned material in declarative sentences; the process involves actually thinking or saying the rules while doing the action. Also called *explicit learning*.

degrees of freedom—The number of independent components in a moving system, such as a machine or a human body. For the human body, it is common to consider the joints of the body and the directions of movement.

degrees of freedom problem—A control problem for the motor system to determine how to limit the many degrees of freedom in order to achieve coordinated movement and accomplish a task.

deliberate practice—Practice that involves activities that are carefully constructed with the intent of improving skill execution.

dendrites—Branched extensions from the nucleus of the neuron that receive impulses or messages from other neurons.

destructive criticism—Criticism involving insults that are often given in a tone of annoyance or frustration.

diencephalon—Lying between the cerebrum and the brain stem, it contains the thalamus and hypothalamus.

direct imagery—A nonverbal representation of the actual movement.

directive function of motivation—Aids people in directing or focusing their energy to achieve goals and choose certain courses of action.

discontinuous—A plateau in behavior followed by a sudden change, such as the shift from supported walking to independent walking.

discovery learning situation—A context in which the teacher gives instructions that describe the intended action of the skill, and through practice the learner discovers how to move in order to achieve the intended action.

discrete task—A single event having a definitive beginning and end.

discriminative touch—Includes touch, pressure, and vibration perception.

distributed practice—A timing that involves relatively longer rest between practice sessions; rest periods are as long as or longer than the active practice.

distribution of practice—The spacing (frequency) of practice sessions and the length of the sessions.

diversification—A characteristic of motor skills that suggests the ability to modify a skill to multiple conditions and requirements and the ability to adapt quickly.

divisible attention—Suggests that attention can be separated among alternating sources of information.

double-knee lock—A movement pattern during walking with three phases: (1) an extended knee when the heel contacts the support surface, (2) a slight flexing of the knee as the weight transfers onto the foot, and (3) extension of the knee again during push-off.

duration—The interval of time that material can remain in the memory.

dynamic view of modeling—Idea that learners can see a demonstration and automatically process the information in a way that allows them to do the movement without cognitive mediation.

dynamics—The energy, force, emphasis, or accents in the movement.

dynamic systems approach—Suggests that the human body's physical structure constrains or restricts motor behavior in conjunction with the physical environment. Also called *spontaneous self-organization.*

ecological perspective—Emphasizes the interactions between the individual, the environment, and the task.

economy of effort—Efficiency; the dancer does not use more effort than is necessary in order to achieve the task.

effector level—The stage in the closed-loop system where the motor plan is determined and the actual changes to the motor plan can occur.

efference copy—A copy of the motor plan for a given movement sent to other areas of the brain, such as sensory areas.

efferent neurons—*See* **motor neurons**.

electroencephalography (EEG)—The recording of electrical activity along the scalp, resulting from current flows in the neurons in the brain.

electromyography—A research tool that measures electrical activity created by muscles during action, and gives information about when muscles contract and how much force is being used.

en bloc—A relationship between the head and the trunk in which the neck muscles are held stable relative to the trunk.

encoding specificity principle—Principle suggesting that retention of material is better when practice and performance situations have physical and mental components in common.

end-product assessments—Assessments used to measure results such as accuracy, distance, or velocity.

enduring dispositions—Those events that involuntarily and automatically draw dancers' attention and distract them from the focal task.

episodic memory—The memory system storing personal experiences and the time period with which they are associated.

equal participation and equal opportunities for success—Principle implying that no one person is singled out, but everyone has chances to get involved and succeed.

error—The difference between what the system wants to achieve and what the feedback relays about what is actually occurring.

evaluation of demands on capacity—An assessment of the requirements made on attention resources.

excitatory or facilitatory interneurons—Neurons that transmit impulses between other neurons and encourage muscle response, thereby causing muscles to contract.

executive level—The place in the closed-loop system where decisions are made to reduce error.

experiential anatomy—A creative and practice-based learning approach using movement, touch, and other art forms to embody the understanding of anatomical principles.

explicit learning—Learning that requires a conscious concerted effort to learn the material and an awareness of the learning process.

explicit teaching of social and collaborative skills—What occurs when the teacher's instructions make it clear that a primary goal of group work is related to fostering collaboration.

external focus—The effects of the movements (the general outcome).

external imagery—Idea that the dancer is like an outside third person and sees the movement as if viewing a video of the self.

extrafusal fibers—Skeletal muscle fibers that are striated throughout their entire length, which means that they have contractile proteins that interlock throughout the entire fiber and give it a striped appearance.

extrinsic motivation—Motivation resulting from factors that are external, such as praise and criticism from others.

fading procedure—A technique used by teachers to gradually reduce the frequency of feedback as dancers gain in skill level.

far transfer—Idea that learning basic skills will be applicable for long periods of time and over a wide variety of more complex skills.

feedback—A response to a movement trial that gives information about the result of the trial or about what caused that result, to be used as a basis for improvement.

feedback dependency—Idea that if sensory feedback such as visual cueing is present in the early stages of learning, the learner's need for that feedback does not diminish as the learner becomes more advanced.

feedforward information—Somatosensory information sent to parts of the brain before a movement plan is executed.

filter theories—Theories suggesting that in the early part of processing information, many functions can occur because it is happening in the large part of the bottle. Further down the line, the bottleneck is reached, and information not needed at that time is filtered out. *See also* **bottleneck theories**.

fixation—A characteristic of motor skills arising from repeated practice of the skill, which becomes more consistent and efficient.

focal vision system—Identifies the details of objects using central vision.

forebrain—The largest and most forward part of the brain, which can be further broken down into the cerebrum and the diencephalon.

forgetting hypothesis—Hypothesis stating that random practice avoids repeating the same task over and over, allowing short-term forgetting, thus necessitating the learner to produce the movement plan on every trial. In this way, the method of producing the plan is learned, which is then effective in skill retention.

fovea—Part of the eye, located in the center of the posterior retina.

fractionization—A method that takes a skill or a phrase with asymmetric leg and arm coordination, and involves practice of individual limbs before trying the whole skill.

freeing the degrees of freedom—Later stages of learning when degrees of freedom that were frozen are gradually released. They will be reorganized into new patterns that are smoother, more fluid, and closer to the ideal.

freezing the degrees of freedom—An early stage of learning when novices unconsciously reduce the available degrees of freedom to make the learning of the skill manageable. This phase results in stiff, rigid, and poorly timed movement.

frontal lobe—The most anterior portion of the brain, in front of the central sulcus, containing areas that are essential to the planning and control of voluntary movement, reasoning, and the inhibition of socially unacceptable behavior.

functional magnetic resonance imaging (fMRI)—A method of differentiating layers of the brain and seeing the functional processes that are occurring.

galloping—An asymmetrical traveling step consisting of a step on the leading foot, then an elevation step with the back foot as it chases the front foot.

generalizability—Ability to learn a specific skill or process and apply it broadly to many skills or skill variations.

generalized motor program (GMP)—A program that allows the motor system to execute an entire class of similar actions. It is stored in the memory, requires that various parameters be added preceding execution, and permits the motor system to be adaptable and flexible in doing variations of the motor program.

global imagery—Using images that create an overall state or feeling sense.

goal setting—The process of determining challenging yet attainable goals before practice begins.

Golgi tendon organs (GTOs)—Proprioceptors found in the tendons of the muscle that are responsive to stretch. They regulate muscle tension in coordination with the muscle spindles.

gray matter—Layer of the brain that covers the hemispheres and is an undulating, gray-colored mass. Also called *cerebral cortex.*

guidance—A teaching method in which the learner is assisted through physical touch (hands-on work).

guidance hypothesis—Hypothesis stating that feedback should be used to improve or guide correct performance, but it should not be offered constantly or a dependency can develop, which impedes performance.

gyrus—Ridges of the gray matter of the cerebrum.

habituation—Occurs when frequent exposure to a nonpainful stimulus causes decreased receptiveness.

haptic exploration—Intentionally exploring the environment through the sense of touch to gain greater coordination and understanding of changing circumstances.

harmonic—Rhythm with an underlying beat that is the same for both body parts, even if one is double or triple time the other.

hierarchical theory—States that as a baby develops, reflexes emerge in a certain order and that the nervous system is organized in a hierarchy. Also called *reflex/hierarchical theory.*

homolateral—Same side. *Homolateral arm and leg use* is using the same-side arm and leg.

homologous movement—Movement that involves pairs of limbs, such as left and right arms or left and right legs.

hopping—An elevation step pushing off one foot and landing on the same foot.

hypertonia—Increased muscle tone caused by increased gamma motor activity.

hypervigilance—A severe state or anxiety or stress, resulting in diminished performance skills.

hypothalamus—Part of the brain that controls regulation of body responses to temperature, hunger, thirst, and stress.

hypotonia—Decreased muscle tone caused by decreased gamma motor activity.

identical elements theory—Theory stating that elements are defined as the general features of skills, such as movement components and mental or cognitive processes, and performance context, such as the goal of the skill or the individual's mental state.

imagery ability—The ability to image a movement with precision and control.

implicit learning—Learning that is achieved through observation without conscious analysis or awareness of what is being learned.

inattention blindness—Condition of failing to see something in the environment because the focus is so engrossed in a selected event. Also called *cognitive tunneling.*

incidental memory—Learning and remembering that happen without conscious awareness, simply by being subjected to the information.

incidental selective attention—Occurs when events are considered regardless of intentions.

in-context transfer—Transfer that occurs within the dance class or practice from one phase to another.

index of difficulty—A mathematical formula using the amplitude and width of the targets.

indirect imagery—*See* **metaphoric imagery**.

individual accountability—Idea that the learning of each person in the group contributes to the rewards of the entire group.

information processing perspective—Looks at the brain like a computer, taking in information and processing it; the resulting output is movement.

inhibitory neurons—Neurons that reduce muscle response and thereby cause the muscle to stop contracting or reduce muscle contraction.

initial flight phase—The phase in which the limb or body movement is set in action toward the target.

initial stage—The first stage of Gentile's two-stage model in which the learner has two important goals: acquiring movement coordination patterns and learning to discriminate between regulatory and nonregulatory conditions.

input and output modalities—The receptors of incoming information (input) and the outgoing motor messages (output), such as vision, hearing, muscles of the limbs, and speech.

instructional strategies—Methods of relaying information about correction execution of a skill.

intentional memory—Learning and remembering information with a conscious awareness and goal toward learning.

intentional selective attention—Occurs when people choose between competing events.

internal focus—Concentrating on the specific movement components of the task.

internal imagery—Technique of using the perspective of being inside the body and experiencing the sensations and sights as if doing the movement.

interneurons—Neurons found only in the spinal cord that act as connectors between sensory neurons and the spinal neurons ascending to the brain, or between neurons descending from the brain and motor neurons.

intersensory integration—The processes in the brain that can take sensory information from more than one sensory modality and sum or organize the input to create an appropriate response by the muscles.

intrafusal fibers—Fibers in skeletal muscles that are striated only at the ends; they are part of the gamma efferent system.

intrinsic motivation—Motivation that is generated by internal factors, such as a person's curiosity, and drives the person to continue exploring the task.

invariant features—The *signature* of the GMP; in other words, the aspects that do not change from one action within the same class as another.

invariant relative motions—The relationships between joints and body parts in a given action.

ipsilateral movement—Movement on the same side—for example, left arm and leg, or right arm and leg.

ironic effect—Involves attentional focus that causes a motor action by mentally concentrating on avoiding it.

jumping—Movement consisting of pushing off the ground with both feet and landing on both feet.

kinematics—The branch of mechanics that describes the motion of bodies and body systems, in particular, to describe the motion of systems composed of joined parts (multilink systems) such as the skeleton of the human body.

kinesthesis (kinesthesia)—The conscious sensation of movement.

kinesthetic imagery—A representation of concrete objects, events, or movements as perceived through sensation.

knowledge of performance (KP)—Feedback that gives information about the movement features that determine the result or outcome of the movement trial.

knowledge of results (KR)—Feedback that gives information about the outcome of executing a movement task, or about whether or not the goal was successfully accomplished.

later stages—The second phase of Gentile's two-stage model, in which the learner must acquire three general characteristics or qualities: adaptability, consistency, and economy of effort.

law of developmental direction—A law stating that the direction of development is head to foot and proximal to distal in each developmental segment.

law of effect—In psychology, a law stating that rewarded behaviors are expressed at the cost of other behavior, and the reverse is also true; in other words, aversive or noxious stimuli can cause behavior to decrease with respect to other behaviors.

law of practice—Law stating that only practice improves performance and that, after a certain point, improvement slows as skill increases.

learning styles—The ways that people approach learning something new.

limbic system—The most primitive area of the cerebral cortex. It is crucial to the formation of memories and to the desire or motivation to act. In association with the hypothalamus, it is regarded to be the primary center of emotions.

limited attention—The finite capacity to pay attention; a person can effectively think only one thought at a time.

linear speed–accuracy tradeoff—A variant of Fitts' law in which the goal is not to move as quickly as possible between two targets or at a given single target; the goal is to achieve the task with accuracy at a given speed.

lines-of-movement imagery—Imagery that designates a specific direction required in the relative positions of body parts.

long-term memory—Memory that is responsible for permanently accumulating or storing information.

massed practice—Timing that involves fewer but longer practice sessions.

maturational perspective—Emphasizes the innate or genetic characteristics of the human system in motor development.

medulla (medulla oblongata)—Part of the brain that interacts with the pons and controls functions like breathing and heartbeat.

memory consolidation—A category of processes that stabilize changes in the nervous system after the initial acquisition and exposure to a new skill. It aids in transferring information from the working memory to long-term memory.

memory trace—Persistence of memory; used to select and to initiate the movement in the appropriate direction. Practice and feedback can strengthen the memory trace.

mental imagery—A psychological activity which evokes the physical characteristics of an absent object or dynamic event.

mental practice—Rehearsing a skill or sequence of movements cognitively (using thought) without physical execution.

metaphoric imagery—The representation of the desired movement with a figure or likeness. Also called *indirect imagery*.

mirror neurons—Special neurons in the premotor cortex, supplementary motor area, and possibly other areas of the brain that fire when a person is doing an action or observing someone else doing the same action. In humans, this concept is generally known as the *mirror system*.

miscellaneous determinants—Elements that can affect levels of arousal, such as amount of sleep and food before dancing.

miscellaneous manifestations of arousal—Blatant actions, such as fidgeting resulting from over-arousal, that generally have a negative effect on performance.

modeling—The demonstration of a skill in the learning environment.

momentary intentions—A conscious decision to focus on certain ideas or tasks and relate to specific goals at a given time; this is one of the components of Kahneman's model of attention.

motivation—What brings people to begin a new activity, is the driving factor in why people persist in the activity, and engages people so that they are willing to expend time and energy toward improvement.

motivational methods—Strategies designed by the teacher or the learner that engage the learner in approaching a task with energy and enthusiasm.

motor control—Field of study that explores how the nervous system organizes and directs all of the muscles and joints to produce coordinated movement and how sensory information from the body, such as vision and hearing, and from the environment surrounding it are used to accomplish this task.

motor development—Involves three characteristics: (1) it describes ongoing change in movement function and ability; (2) it examines these changes throughout stages of aging, from prenatal to senior years; and (3) developments are progressive and irreversible, and result from changes within the individual as well as environmental interactions.

motor homunculus—A graphic way to represent the anatomical segments of the brain directly responsible for movement and for the exchange of sensory and motor information.

motor learning—Examines changes in a person's skill capabilities that are caused by experience or practice rather than development; these changes cannot be measured directly, but rather are inferred by alterations in performance, and they are relatively permanent.

motor milestones—Certain stages or basic progressions that the child must achieve in order to be able to walk. Each of these stages allows the child to gain essential motor skills that lead to complex behaviors.

motor neurons—Neurons that send impulses or messages from the CNS to the skeletal muscles to create movement. Also called *efferent neurons*.

motor program–based theory—A theory of motor control and learning that emphasizes rules or structures existing in the brain that can direct a general group or class of movements.

movement coordination patterns—Patterns allowing for the correct organization of the body parts in order to achieve the movement goal in the context of the appropriate environmental conditions, such as the space the dancer needs to use or the timing of the music that will determine the temporal structure.

movement preparation phase—The phase in which the decision to do the movement is made.

movement reeducation—The process of changing habits and reforming new ways of working.

multiple resource theories—Theories stating that several resource capacities exist and each has its own limitations.

muscle force—Amount of force a muscle produces. It is dependent on several factors, including the size of muscle, the number of fibers activated, the initial length of the muscle when activated, and the angle of the joint at the time of muscle activation.

muscle spindles—Sensory receptors that are located in the belly of skeletal muscles and detect muscle length. They consist of special muscle fibers called intrafusal fibers, the gamma motor neuron, and the gamma sensory neuron. They are responsible for regulating stretch in the muscle, length of the muscle, speed, and rate of change in the muscle. They work in coordination with the Golgi tendon organs.

muscle synergies—Groups of muscles that work together. These functionally linked activations help to solve some of the degrees of freedom problems. Also called *coordinative structures*.

myelin—The insulating fatty sheath around the nerve cells responsible for the speed of neural transmission.

myelination—The growth of the insulating fatty sheath around the nerve cells responsible for the speed of neural transmission.

myotatic reflex—The simplest of the reflexes. It is strongly activated by rapid stretch of a muscle, such as a bouncing hamstring stretch or a twisted ankle. Also called *stretch reflex*.

narrow focus—Directing attention to a small environmental area or fewer cognitive components.

natural units—Groupings or parts within a larger skill that have interdependent components but are independent of each other.

negative asynchrony—Timing of systems that is not synchronous; for example, for dancers their movement slightly precedes the sound in a specific synchronization test.

negative reinforcement—Occurs when a teacher eliminates an unpleasant circumstance, thereby increasing the possibility that the desired performance will be repeated.

negative transfer—The detrimental effect that skill or knowledge acquired in one circumstance has on skill acquisition and problem-solving ability in another circumstance.

neurons—The most basic cells in the brain. Also called *nerve cells.*

nonassociative learning—Learning that occurs when one stimulus is given repeatedly, and the nervous system learns the characteristics of that stimulus. The two main forms of nonassociative learning are habituation and sensitization.

nondeclarative learning—Learning without conscious effort; it is acquired simply through repeated exposure. Also called *implicit learning.*

observational learning—A method of learning in which information is being transmitted to the learners by having them observe the execution of a skill.

occipital lobe—The most posterior section of the brain. It is crucial to visual perception, which is why it is sometimes called the *visual cortex.*

ontogeny—The developmental history of an individual organism.

open-loop process—Process that does not use feedback during the movement to change the motor plan while it is being executed. These movements are typically rapid; all necessary information is included in the instructions, and once the movements are triggered, they proceed to completion.

open-loop system—*See* **open-loop process**.

open skills—Skills that need to be performed in many variations of timing, gestures, and spacing; they usually involve conditions that are frequently changing.

operant conditioning—Learning that is voluntary and uses trial and error. Eventually a person learns to associate a certain response among many with a particular desired consequence.

optical flow field—The apparent motion of objects and surfaces that an observer sees in a specified visual area.

optical flow patterns—Patterns of light rays as they strike the eye; the word *flow* suggests that these patterns are dynamic.

organization—The components or parts of the skill and how they relate to each other in time and space.

orientation—The relationship of the body to the environment and of the parts of the body to each other.

otolith organs—Located in the inner ear and comprising the saccule and the utricle, they measure the change in velocity of linear movements caused by gravity or body movement. The otolith organs register how the head is oriented relative to gravity because of the constant linear force it exerts.

overlap—A practice strategy in which learners practice the transition from one movement to another, demonstrating learning benefits.

overlearning—Continuing practice after dancers have accomplished or acquired a particular skill. Also called *post-mastery learning.*

overtraining—Training or practicing to the point of fatigue and burnout.

parallel processing—Simultaneous occurrence of thoughts and processes.

parameter feedback—Augmented feedback that focuses on the changeable features of the movement such as speed, force, and size.

parameters—Aspects that can be varied from one execution of the GMP to another, such as speed, force, direction, and body parts.

parietal cortex—Part of the brain that deals with integrating visual and motor information, and assists in the planning stages of movement.

parietal lobe—Part of the brain posterior and adjacent to the frontal lobe. It is the key area for the perception and integration of sensory information, including heat, cold, pressure, pain, and the position of the body in space. It communicates closely with the primary motor area in the frontal lobe, and it is associated with attention and intention to movement.

part practice—Practicing one section, one component, or one body part of a skill or phrase before practicing the entire skill.

perception–action approach—States that the development of perception and the development of movement cannot be separated.

perceptual-action coupling—The spatial and temporal coordination of the eyes and hands or eyes and feet to achieve movements involving objects.

perceptual-motor workspace—Part of the thinking processes that consider both relevant sensory cues and best possible motor strategies to achieve the goal.

perceptual trace—Serves to compare the movement in progress with the correct version of the movement in the memory. Also called *internal reference of correctness.*

performance anxiety—Commonly called *stage fright,* it involves a conflict between the desire to publicly perform in one's art and the fear of being inadequate and experiencing public humiliation.

performance bandwidth—Provides a range of tolerable error, and feedback is only given when the learner's performance falls outside this range.

peripheral nervous system (PNS)—Comprises the parts of the nervous system that lie outside the spine and connect to the muscles and organs.

peripheral vision—Vision occurring outside the limits of central vision. It can range to 200 degrees horizontally and 160 degrees vertically. It does not need focus and can function in low light. Peripheral vision is poor at color recognition.

perturbation platform—A mechanical device used to test responses to disturbances. The platform moves quickly forward and backward, and it tilts up and down.

phonological loop—The system in working memory that is the temporary storage of verbal material.

physiology—The study of the human body and its systems. While anatomy focuses on form, physiology is concerned with function.

point-light technique—A research procedure that allows an observer to see only the motion of the light-reflective markers placed on joints of the body when observing humans in motion.

point of diminishing returns—Demonstrates that overlearning only has benefits up to a certain amount of practice. After that point, extra practice will not have any additional benefit.

polyrhythms—Contrasting or conflicting rhythms occurring simultaneously.

pons—Part of the brain that controls body functions such as chewing, swallowing, salivating, and breathing; it may be involved in balance control.

positive interdependence—Idea that members of the group have common goals and understand that working together benefits both the individuals and the group, and participation of everyone is needed to achieve success.

positive reinforcement—Feedback that increases the possibility that given similar conditions, the desired performance will be repeated, and the result is reliable and favorable change.

positive transfer—The beneficial effect that skill or knowledge acquired in one circumstance has on skill acquisition and problem-solving ability in another circumstance.

positron emission tomography (PET)—A method of differentiating brain areas and seeing the functional processes that are occurring.

possible activities—All of the possible choices regarding cognitive processes or tasks that dancers might address.

postural control—The ability to acquire, maintain, or regain a state of balance during activity.

postural reflexes—Responses that occur when groups of muscles (sometimes called *muscular synergies*) prepare for or react to disturbances using an automatic sequence in order to maintain equilibrium.

power law of practice—Law stating that the rate of improvement decreases as learners become more advanced; large amounts of improvement occur in early stages, and improvement slows down in later stages.

premotor area—Part of Brodmann's area 6, it organizes movement before initiation and handles rhythmic coordination. It is also involved in how learning can be accomplished by observing others.

primary motor cortex—Part of Brodmann's area 4, it sends messages to specific skeletal muscles in all parts of the body. This area is essential for initiating movement, for postural coordination, and for fine motor skills such as the finger movements for playing a piano.

proactive interference—Forgetting because of something that happens before attempting to learn the target skill, activity, or information, which hinders acquisition of the new endeavor.

proactive mechanisms—Muscular responses that occur preceding a disturbance to balance.

procedural knowledge—Knowledge that cannot be stated verbally but rather facilitates the performance of the skill. It is the *how*, and it is the type of knowledge in the procedural memory system.

procedural learning—Acquiring a movement skill by automatically repeating it over and over. It requires no conscious attention to the mechanisms of the movement. Learning develops slowly and is expressed through improved performance.

procedural memory—The memory system that facilitates understanding how to do an action rather than what is needed to do the action.

procedural skills—Skills that involve a series of simple movements that must be done in a particular sequence in order to accomplish the larger task.

program feedback—Augmented feedback that focuses on the general or fundamental pattern of the movement.

progressive part method—*See* **segmentation**.

proprioception—The sense using receptors below the body surface that give the brain information about muscle stretch, joint position, and tendon tension. These receptors are found in muscles, fascia, tendons, ligaments, joints, and (according to some scientists) even the skin.

proprioceptive neuromuscular facilitation (PNF)—A form of stretching using muscle reflexes and responses to aid in flexibility gains.

qualitative augmented feedback—Feedback that describes the quality or some essential property of the movement, such as stating that the turn has good fluidity or the jump has explosive power.

quantitative augmented feedback—Feedback that contains a numerical value relating to the measure of the skill, such as the number of turns or the height of a jump.

random practice—Practice that involves high contextual interference (practicing many variations of a skill mixed together with other skills) within a given practice session.

reactive mechanisms—Muscular responses that occur after a disturbance to balance.

recalibration of the sensorimotor system—What happens when the sensorimotor system learns new strategies for postural control.

recall schema—The motor portion in Schmidt's schema theory, which is used for selecting the specific response desired.

recall tests—Tests that require responses without cues or suggested answers to help the person remember the information.

reciprocal excitation—Occurs when both agonist and antagonist muscles respond simultaneously to reflex stimulation.

reciprocal inhibition reflex—The reflex used to inhibit or relax the antagonist of a muscle when the muscle is contracting.

recognition schema—The sensory portion in Schmidt's schema theory, which is used to evaluate the response and update the motor program to correct for error.

recognition tests—Tests that give some cues or suggested answers to help the person remember the information.

reference mechanism—The standard or iconic representation in closed-loop control that the system needs or desires to achieve.

reflex—An involuntary movement that occurs in response to a particular stimulus.

reflex arc—Comprises the neurological components that create a response to a stimulus consisting of a receptor, an interneuron, and a motor neuron.

reflex/hierarchical theory—*See* **hierarchical theory**.

reflex-reversal phenomenon—Based on the phase of the stepping cycle, two different reactive patterns can occur with the same stimulus.

reflex theory—Explains motor development based on the idea of behavior as reflex-based.

regulatory conditions—Environmental conditions that affect the success of the movement goal.

relative time—The proportion of time each component or section requires within an overall movement task.

response-chaining hypothesis—Hypothesis that movement begins with a muscle action caused by a stimulus. This action creates sensory information that triggers the next muscle contraction, and so on, creating a chain of actions and stimuli.

response-produced feedback—The sensory information caused by the initiating muscle contraction that triggers the next muscle contraction.

retention—The ability to recall or recognize what has been learned or experienced.

retention tests—Assessments that occur after a period of time but usually test the learner on the same task or conditions.

reticular formation—A link between sensory receptors in the body and motor control centers in the brain. It plays an important role in regulating CNS messages to the body, hence affecting skeletal muscle activity and tonus.

retroactive interference—Forgetting because something occurs just after the event or activity that should be remembered (during the interval between learning the target skill and executing it), hindering acquisition of the target skill or activity.

running—A locomotor pattern with the same timing pattern as walking, but including a period in which neither foot is in contact with the support surface (a period of flight).

schema—An abstract classification of an object stored in the memory; a representational set of rules.

segmentation—Involves skills that have a series or sequence of components. The learner begins by practicing the first part, then practicing the second part, then adding it to the first part, and so on, until the entire sequence is learned. Also called *progressive part method*.

selective attention—Idea that a person can choose to focus on one idea or source of information while ignoring another.

self-efficacy—The belief that a specific task can be performed successfully; it is one of the best predictors of successful achievement.

self-esteem—Feelings of worth that are specific to domains or areas of activity.

semantic memory—The memory system that stores general information about the world, and particularly understanding ideas or facts that are not present at that moment.

semicircular canals—Channels that measure the change in velocity of rotational movements of the head or body.

sensitization—Process that occurs when frequent exposure to a possibly threatening stimulus causes increased receptiveness.

sensory feedback—Incoming information from the senses during the movement that is used to change the motor plan while it is being executed.

sensory homunculus—A graphic way to represent the anatomical segments of the brain directly responsible for movement and for the exchange of sensory and motor information.

sensory learning—Gaining knowledge simply by what is taken in through the senses.

sensory neurons—Neurons that send impulses from the body to the CNS, giving the brain information about the environment through sight, sound, touch, smell, and taste. Also called *afferent neurons.*

sensory–perceptual elements—Vision, hearing, and proprioception, and how these senses add to motor skill learning. The sensory information available during practice must specifically be present during later executions of the skill.

serial processing—Idea that one thought or part of the process happens after another in a sequence.

shiftable attention—Idea that people can choose to move back and forth between two sources of information in the thought process.

short-term sensory stage—The stage of memory that takes in all of the environmental features through the sensory systems, such as visual, auditory, tactile, and haptic.

simplification—A method that lowers the difficulty of either various portions of the skill or different characteristics of the skill.

simultaneous engagement or interaction—Idea that everyone is participating actively in the process.

skipping—A continuous series of movements consisting of a step followed by a hop, alternating legs.

social coordination—Coordination relating to other people, such as working with other dancers in the coordination of movement or doing movement activities in unison. Also called *behavioral synchrony.*

somatosensory cortex—Area of the brain that plays a major role in visual and auditory attention and interacts with the three motor areas described previously by integrating sensory information into the planning stages of movement as well as during movement.

somatosensory system—Sensory system that is divided into three parts: discriminative touch, which includes light touch, pressure, and vibration perception; pain (nociception) and temperature, which includes the sensations of itch and tickle; and proprioception, which gives the brain information about muscle stretch, joint position, and tendon tension.

spatial coordination—Coordination related to spatial factors, such as attempting two different spatial designs or locations with various body parts at the same time.

specificity of practice hypothesis—Hypothesis stating that when two situations have physical and mental components in common, greater transfer between the two situations will occur.

speed–accuracy trade-off—Relationship between speed and accuracy such that when a person selects speed, accuracy is diminished, and when a person selects accuracy, speed is diminished.

stability—The ability to maintain the center of mass over the base of support.

stages of information processing—The various cognitive steps such as perception, memory, and response.

states of flow—Involve deep immersion in an activity, loss of the sense of time, and a feeling of the activity being effortless.

stepping reflex—Movements traveling forward that occur when an infant is held upright and inclined forward with the feet touching a flat surface. It is not independent walking.

stretch reflex—*See* **myotatic reflex.**

striated muscle fibers—Fibers in skeletal muscles with contractile tissues throughout the entire length of the fiber.

Stroop effect—Occurs when a stimulus suggests one response, but the actual event needs a different response.

structural interference—Occurs when physical or neurological interference causes a decrease in attention.

student-centered learning—Learning that occurs in settings in which students can make autonomous decisions about the content and timing of learning.

subjective organization—Organizing material in a manner that is meaningful to each learner.

sulcus—The grooves of the gray matter of the cerebrum.

supplementary motor area (SMA)—Part of Brodmann's area 6 that plays an important role in executing already-learned sequential movements, in preparing and organizing movement, and in bimanual coordination.

sustainable attention—Attention focused on just one source for a prolonged period of time.

synapses—The connections from axons to dendrites between neurons.

synaptic consolidation—Occurs in the first minutes to hours after learning and involves changes to the neural connections in the brain.

synchronization—Occurring at the same time and speed; producing a movement corresponding to an external event, such as music, a metronome, or a vocal score.

system consolidation—Shifts in brain areas responsible for memories. It aids in transferring information from the working memory to long-term memory and in stabilizing the memories in long-term memory. It takes longer than synaptic consolidation.

systems theory—A theory of motor control and learning that emphasizes interaction with the environment.

task interference—What occurs when one thought competes with another for attention.

task-intrinsic feedback—Sensory information that is provided innately while performing a skill, such as visual, auditory, proprioceptive, and tactile. Also known as *intrinsic feedback.*

task progression strategy—A simplification method involving sequencing the order of the skills, determining an order that starts with less complex variations of the skill and leading to more complex variations.

tau—A mathematical variable that determines a relationship between object size, its velocity and acceleration, and the distance between the object and the person.

teacher-centered learning—Learning that occurs in settings in which the teacher designs the activities and decides when the students are ready to move to the next level.

temporal lobe—Part of the brain that is located laterally and deals with memory, abstract thought, and judgment. It also contains the processing center for hearing.

temporal speed–accuracy trade-off—Relationship between speed and accuracy such that as movement goes faster, timing accuracy improves.

temporal stability—How variable the timing of a given movement is from one trial to the next.

tendon vibration technique—Technique that involves high-speed vibration of a tendon connected to the agonist muscle, distorting proprioceptive feedback.

terminal augmented feedback—Feedback given after the movement execution.

termination phase—The moment phase just before and when the target is hit.

thalamus—A complex computational relay station that sorts important information from insignificant information. Almost everything going into and out of the cerebral cortices passes through the thalamus.

It also plays a role in attention, mood, and the perception of pain.

threshold—The degree of stimulation needed to cause a neuron to fire.

timing coordination—Coordinating the timing of movement or sound, such as moving arms and legs in different directions at the same time, the use of polyrhythms, or the simultaneous use of contrasting or conflicting rhythms.

trace decay—Forgetting that occurs as time passes due to the deterioration of the memory trace or representation of the movement in the memory.

transfer-appropriate processing—Idea that if the necessary cognitive processing of two skills is similar, it will enhance transfer of learning.

transfer of learning—The effect or influence that skill or knowledge acquired in one circumstance has on skill acquisition and problem-solving ability in another circumstance.

transfer of training—Describes transfer of learning for motor skills.

transfer tests—Tests that assess the persistence of the acquired ability for performance. These tests have the learners change to different tasks or conditions rather than be tested after a time interval of no practice.

triple-burst (triphasic) EMG pattern—Three phases of agonist–antagonist–agonist activity that control ballistic movements.

variable practice—Practice that includes varying both the movement and the environment that the learner experiences while practicing.

verbal analogies—Instructions that are used to emphasize how two actions are similar or related in some way.

verbal cues—Brief, succinct phrases that act as prompts for main ideas or components of the movement, or direct the attention to vital environmental circumstances.

verbal label—A short verbal cue that relates to some aspect of the movement.

vestibular ocular reflex (VOR)—Used to stabilize the eyes during head movement.

vestibular system—Sensory system that has its receptors in the inner ear and is mainly concerned with providing information about the head's position in space and about quick changes in direction of movements of the head.

vision—Involves both seeing and processing what has been seen. It includes the eyes, which are the receptors that receive the visual information and transmit it to the brain, and the occipital or visual cortex in the brain, which interprets the information.

visual imagery—A representation of concrete objects, events, or movements as perceived through vision.

visual metaphoric imagery—Forming a visual picture of movement in the mind.

visuospatial sketchpad—The system in working memory that is the temporary storage of spatial material perceived visually.

white matter—Brain matter that lies underneath the cerebral cortex and transmits signals to coordinate communication between different brain regions.

whole practice—Practicing a skill or dance phrase in its entirety.

working memory—A system of limited capacity that temporarily stores recently acquired information and provides an interactive workspace to integrate this new information with material retrieved from long-term memory in order to solve problems and make decisions about future actions.

zero transfer—Idea that no effect or influence exists in the learning of two skills.

Bibliography

Chapter 1

Alexander, F.M. (1985). *The use of self: Its conscious direction in relation to diagnosis functioning and the control of reaction* (2nd ed.). London: Orion.

Bainbridge Cohen, B. (2008). *Sensing, feeling, and action: The experiential anatomy of Body-Mind Centering* (3rd ed.). Northampton, MA: Contact Collaborations.

Bartenieff, I., with Lewis, D. (1980). *Body movement: Coping with the environment.* New York: Gordon and Breach Science.

Batson, G. (2009). *Somatic studies and dance.* Resource Paper. International Association for Dance Medicine & Science. www.iadms.org/display common.cfm?an=1&subarticlenbr=248

Batson, G., Quin, E., & Wilson, M. (2012). Integrating somatics and science. *Journal of Dance & Somatic Practices, 3*(1-2), 183-193.

Dowd, I. (1990). *Taking root to fly* (2nd ed.). North Hampton, MA: Contact Collaborations.

Eddy, M. (2009). A brief history of somatic practices and dance: Historical development of the field of somatic education and its relationship to dance. *Journal of Dance and Somatic Practices*, *1*(1), 5-27.

Eddy, M. (2012). The ongoing development of "Past Beginnings": A further discussion of neuromotor development: Somatic links between Bartenieff Fundamentals, Body-Mind Centering® and Dynamic Embodiment©. *The Journal of Laban Movement Studies, 3*(1), 54-79.

Enghauser, R. (2007). The quest for an ecosomatic approach to dance pedagogy. *Journal of Dance Education, 7*(3), 80-90.

Feldenkrais, M. (1991). *Awareness through movement.* London: Thorsons.

Fortin, S. (1993). When dance science and somatics enter the dance technique class. *Kinesiology and Medicine for Dance, 15*(2), 88-107.

Fortin, S. (1995). Toward a new generation: Somatic dance education in academia. *Impulse, 3,* 253-262.

Fortin, S., Long, W., & Lord, M. (2002). Three voices: Researching how somatic education informs contemporary dance technique classes. *Research in Dance Education, 3*(2), 155-179.

Geber, P., & Wilson, M. (2010). Teaching at the interface of dance science and somatics. *Journal of Dance Medicine & Science, 14*(2), 50-57.

Hackney, P. (1993). Remembering Irmgard. *Contact Quarterly, 18*(1), 13-20.

Hanna, T. (1983). *Somatics: Journal of Bodily Arts and Sciences,* inside cover.

Haywood, K.M., & Getchell, N. (2009). *Life span motor development* (5th ed.). Champaign, IL: Human Kinetics.

Magill, R.A. (2011). *Motor learning and control* (9th ed.). New York: McGraw-Hill.

Magill, R.A., & Anderson, D. (2014). *Motor learning and control* (10th ed.). New York: McGraw-Hill.

Matt, P.H. (1991/1992). Ideokinesis: Integrating the science and somatics of dance. *Kinesiology and Medicine for Dance, 14*(1), 68-77.

Schmidt, R.A., & Lee, T.D. (2011). *Motor control and learning: A behavioral emphasis* (5th ed.). Champaign, IL: Human Kinetics.

Spiesman, M.C. (1960). Dance education pioneers: Colby, Larson, H'Doubler. *Journal of Health, Physical Education, Recreation, 31*(1), 25-76.

Sweigard, L.E. (1974). *Human movement potential: Its ideokinetic facilitation.* Lanham, MD: University Press of America.

Todd, M.E. (1937). *The thinking body.* New York: Paul B. Hoeber.

Zhu, L. (2012). *The translator-centered multidisciplinary construction: Douglas Robinson's translation theories explored.* Bern, Switzerland: International Academic.

Chapter 2

Bandura, A. (1977). *Social learning theory.* Upper Saddle River, NJ: Prentice Hall.

Burke, R.E. (2007). Sir Charles Sherrington's "The integrative action of the nervous system: a centenary appreciation." *Brain, 130,* 887-894. doi:10.1093/brain/awm022

Cherry, K. (2013). Social learning theory: An overview of Bandura's social learning theory. http://psychology.about.com/od/developmental psychology/a/sociallearning.htm

Gesell, A., & Amatruda, C.S. (1947). *Developmental diagnosis* (2nd ed.). New York: Paul B. Hoeber.

Gibson, J. (1979). *An ecological approach to visual perception.* Boston: Houghton Mifflin.

Haywood, K.M., & Getchell, N. (2009). *Life span motor development* (5th ed.). Champaign, IL: Human Kinetics.

Haywood, K.M., Robertson, M.A., & Getchell, N. (2012). Advanced analysis of motor development. Champaign, IL: Human Kinetics.

Kugler, P.N., Kelso, J.A.S., & Turvey, M.T. (1982). On the control and coordination of naturally developing systems. In J.A.S. Kelso & J.E. Clark (Eds.), *The development of movement control and coordination.* New York: Wiley.

Magnus, R. (1925). Animal posture (The Croonian Lecture). *Proceedings of the Royal Society of London, 98,* 339-352.

McGraw, M. (1945). *Neuromuscular maturation of the human infant.* New York: Hafner Press.

Rose, D.J., & Christina, R.W. (2006). *A multilevel approach to the study of motor control and learning* (2nd ed.). San Francisco: Benjamin Cummings.

Schaltenbrand, G. (1928). The development of human motility and motor disturbances. *Archives of Neurology and Psychology, 20*(4), 720-730. doi: 10.1001/archneurpsyc.1928.02210160059003

Shumway-Cook, A., & Woollacott, M. (2001). Motor control: *Theory and practical applications* (2nd ed.). Baltimore: Williams & Wilkins.

Shumway-Cook, A., & Woollacott, M.H. (2012). *Motor control: Translating research into clinical practice* (4th ed.). Philadelphia: Lippincott Williams & Wilkins.

Skinner, B.F. (1974). *About behaviorism.* New York: Alfred A. Knopf.

Weisz, S. (1938). Studies in equilibrium reaction. *Journal of Nervous and Mental Disease, 88,* 150-162.

Woollacott, M.H., & Shumway-Cook, A. (Eds.). (1989). *Development of posture and gait across the life span.* Columbia: University of South Carolina Press.

Chapter 3

Batson, G. (2008). *Proprioception.* Resource Paper. International Association for Dance Medicine & Science. www.iadms.org/displaycommon .cfm?an=1&subarticlenbr=210

Bengtsson, S.L., Csíkszentmihályi, M., & Ullén, F. (2007). Cortical regions involved in the generation of musical structures during improvisations in pianists. *Journal of Cognitive Neuroscience, 19*(5), 830-842.

Berkowitz, A., & Ansari, D. (2008). Generation of novel motor sequences: The neural correlates of musical improvisation. *NeuroImage, 41*(2), 535-543.

Bertenthal, B.I. (1996). Origins and early development of perception, action, and orientation. *Annual Review of Psychology, 47,* 431-459.

Bertenthal, B.I., & Bai, D.L. (1989). Infants' sensitivity to optical flow for controlling posture. *Developmental Psychology, 25*(6), 936-945. doi: 10.1037/0012-1649.25.6.936

Cordo, P.J., & Nashner, L.M. (1982). Properties of postural adjustments associated with rapid arm movements. *Journal of Neurophysiology, 47*(2), 287-302.

Dietz, M., Trippel, M., & Hortsmann, G.A. (1991). Significance of proprioceptive and vestibule-spinal reflexes in the control of stance and gait. In A.E. Patla (Ed.), *Adaptability of human gait.* Amsterdam: Elsevier.

Education Committee, IADMS. (2000). *The challenge of the adolescent dancer.* Resource paper. International Association for Dance Medicine & Science. www.iadms.org/displaycommon.cfm?an=1& subarticlenbr=1

Einspieler, C., Marschik, P.B., & Prechtl, F.R. (2008). Human motor behavior: Prenatal origin and early postnatal development. *Journal of Psychology, 216*(3), 148-154. doi: 10.1027/0044-3409.216.3.147

Fink, A., Graif, B., & Neubauer, A.C. (2009). Brain correlates underlying creative thinking: EEG alpha activity in professional vs. novice dancers. *NeuroImage, 46,* 854-862.

Forssberg, H. (1987). Anticipatory postural adjustments during human locomotion. *Electroencephalography and Clinical Neurophysiology. Supplement, 39,* 72-76.

Foster, E.C., Sveistrup, H., & Woollacott, M.H. (1996). Transitions in visual proprioception: A cross-sectional developmental study of the effect of visual flow on postural control. *Journal of Motor Behavior, 28*(2), 101-112.

Ghez, C. (1991). Posture. In E.R. Kandel, J.H. Schwartz, & T.M. Jessell (Eds.), *Principles of neural science* (3rd ed., pp. 596-607). New York: McGraw-Hill.

Golomer, E., Dupui, P., & Monod, H. (1997). The effects of maturation on self-induced dynamic body sway frequencies of girls performing acrobatics or classical dance. *European Journal of Applied Physiology and Occupational Physiology, 76*(2), 140-144.

Hansen, P.D., Wollacott, M.H., & Debu, B. (1988). Postural responses to changing task conditions. *Experimental Brain Research, 73*(3), 627-636.

Haywood, K.M., & Getchell, N. (2009). *Life span motor development* (5th ed.). Champaign, IL: Human Kinetics.

Haywood, K.M., Robertson, M.A., & Getchell, N. (2012). *Advanced analysis of motor development.* Champaign, IL: Human Kinetics.

Hirabayashi, S., & Iwasaki, Y. (1994). Developmental perspective of sensory organization on postural control. *Brain & Development, 17*(2), 111-113.

Horak, F.B., Diener, H.C., & Nashner, L.M. (1989). Influence of central set on human postural responses. *Journal of Neurophysiology, 62*(4), 841-853.

Horak, F.B., & Nashner, L.M. (1986). Central programming of postural movements: Adaptations to altered support surface configurations. *Journal of Neurophysiology, 55*(6), 1369-1381.

Jouen, F. (1984). Visual-vestibular interactions in infancy. *Infant Behavior and Development, 7*(2), 135-145.

Jouen, F. (1990). Early visual-vestibular interactions and postural development. In H. Bloch & B. Bertenthal (Eds.), *Sensory-motor organizations and development in infancy and early childhood* (pp. 199-215). Dordrecht, Netherlands: Martinus Nijhoff.

Kandel, E.R., Schwartz, J.H., & Jessell, T.M. (2000). *Principles of neural science* (4th ed.). New York: McGraw-Hill.

Krasnow, D. (2010). Improvisation as a tool for enhanced motor learning in dance. *The Twenty-Eighth Annual Symposium of Medical Problems of Performing Artists,* July 29-August 1, 2010, Snowmass, Colorado.

Lee, D.N., & Aronson, E. (1974). Visual proprioceptive control of standing in human infants. *Perception & Psychophysics, 15*(3), 529-532.

McCollum, G., & Leen, T. (1989). The form and exploration of mechanical stability limits in erect stance. *Journal of Motor Behavior, 21*(3), 225-244.

Moore, S.P., Rushmer, D.S., Windus, S.L., & Nashner, L.M. (1988). Human automatic postural responses: Responses to horizontal perturbations of stance in multiple directions. *Experimental Brain Research, 73*(3), 648-658.

Myklebust, B.M, & Gottlieb, G.L. (1993). Development of the stretch reflex in the newborn: Reciprocal excitation and reflex irradiation. *Child Development, 64*(4), 1036-1045.

Myklebust, B.M., Gottlieb, G.L., & Agarawal, G.C. (1986). Stretch reflexes of the normal infant. *Developmental Medicine and Child Neurology, 28*(4), 440-449.

Nashner, L. (1976). Adapting reflexes controlling the human posture. *Experimental Brain Research, 26*(1), 59-72.

Nashner, L.M. (1977). Fixed patterns of rapid postural responses among leg muscles during stance. *Experimental Brain Research, 30*(1), 13-24.

Nashner, L.M. (1982). Adaptation of human movement to altered environments. *Trends in Neurosciences, 5,* 358-361. doi: 10.1016/0166-2236(82)90204-1

Nolan, L., Grigorenko, A., & Thorstensson, A. (2005). Balance control: Sex and age differences in 9- to 16-year-olds. *Developmental Medicine and Child Neurology, 47*(7), 449-454.

Pappas, E., & Hagins, M. The effects of "raked" stages on the standing posture of dancers. *Journal of Dance Medicine & Science, 12*(2), 54-58.

Peterson, M.L., Christou, E., & Rosengren, K.S. (2006). Children achieve adult-like sensory integration during stance at 12-years-old. *Gait Posture, 23*(4), 455-463.

Prechtl, H.F.R. (1984). *Continuity of neural functions from prenatal to postnatal life: Clinics in developmental medicine,* 94. Oxford, UK: Blackwell Scientific.

Prechtl, H.F.R. (1986a). New perspectives in early human development. *European Journal of Obstetrics & Gynecology and Reproductive Biology, 21*(5-6), 347-355.

Prechtl, H.F.R. (1986b). Prenatal motor development. In M.C. Wade & H.T.A. Whiting (Eds.), *Motor development in children: Aspects of coordination and control* (pp. 53-64). Dordrecht, Netherlands: Martinus Nighoff.

Rose, D.J., & Christina, R.W. (2006). *A multilevel approach to the study of motor control and learning* (2nd ed.). San Francisco: Benjamin Cummings.

Schmid, M., Conforto, S., Lopez, L., & D'Alessio, T. (2007). Cognitive load affects postural control in children. *Experimental Brain Research, 179*(3), 375-385.

Shumway-Cook, A., & Woollacott, M. (2001). *Motor control: Theory and practical applications* (2nd ed.). Baltimore: Williams & Wilkins.

Shumway-Cook, A., & Woollacott, M.H. (2012). *Motor control: Translating research into clinical practice* (4th ed.). Philadelphia: Lippincott Williams & Wilkins.

Sparto, P.J., Redfern, M.S., Jasko, J.G., Casselbrant, M.L., Mandel, E.M., & Furman, J.M. (2006). The influence of dynamic visual cues for postural control in children aged 7-12 years. *Experimental Brain Research, 168*(4), 505-516.

Steindl, R., Kunz, K., Schrott-Fischer, A., & Scholtz, A.W. (2006). Effect of age and sex on maturation of sensory systems and balance control. *Developmental Medicine & Child Neurology, 48*, 477-482.

Sveistrup, H., Foster, E. & Woollacott, M.H. (1992). Changes in the effect of visual flow on postural control across the life span. In M.H. Woollacott & F.B. Horak (Eds.), *Posture and gait: Control mechanisms* (pp. 224-227). Eugene, OR: Institute of Neuroscience, University of Oregon.

Thelen, E., Ulrich, B.D., & Jensen, J.L. (1989). The developmental origins of locomotion. In M.H. Woollacott & A. Shumway-Cook (Eds.), *Development of posture and gait across the life span,* (pp. 25-47). Columbia: University of South Carolina Press.

Wilmerding, V. & Krasnow, D. (2009). *Motor learning and teaching dance.* Resource Paper. International Association for Dance Medicine & Science. www.iadms.org/displaycommon.cfm?an=1&subarticlenbr=250

Woollacott, M.H., Debû, B., & Mowatt, M. (1987). Neuromuscular control of posture in the infant and child: Is vision dominant? *Journal of Motor Behavior, 19*(2), 167-186.

Woollacott, M.H., & Shumway-Cook, A. (Eds.). (1989). *Development of posture and gait across the life span.* Columbia: University of South Carolina Press.

Woollacott, M.H., Shumway-Cook, A., & Nasher, L.M. (1986). Aging and posture control: Changes in sensory organization and muscular coordination. *The International Journal of Aging and Human Development, 23*(2), 97-114.

Chapter 4

Arain, M., Haque, M., Johal, L., Mathur, P., Nel, W., Rais, A., Sandhu, R., & Sharma, S. (2013). Maturation of the adolescent brain. *Neuropsychiatric Disease and Treatment, 9*, 449-461.

Assaiante, C., & Amblard, B. (1995). An ontogenetic model for the sensorimotor organization of balance control in humans. *Human Movement Science, 14*(1), 13-43.

Bayley, N. (1936). The development of motor abilities during the first three years: A study of sixty-one infants tested repeatedly. *Monographs of the Society for Research in Child Development, 1*(1), 1-26.

Bainbridge Cohen, B. (2008). *Sensing, feeling, and action: The experiential anatomy of Body-Mind Centering* (3rd ed.). Northhampton, MA: Contact Collaborations.

Bartenieff, I., with Lewis, D. (1980). *Body movement: Coping with the environment.* New York: Gordon and Breach Science.

Bayley, N. (1969). *Scales of infant development.* San Antonio: Psychological Corporation.

Bernstein, N. (1967). *The coordination and regulation of movements.* Oxford: Pergamon Press.

Chandler, L.S., Skillen, M.A., & Swanson, M.W. (1980). *Movement assessment of infants: A manual.* Rolling Bay, WA: Authors.

Clark, J.E., & Whitall, J. (1989). Changing patterns of locomotion: From walking to skipping. In M.H. Woollacott & A. Shumway-Cook (Eds.), *Development of posture and gait across the life span* (pp. 128-151). Columbia: University of South Carolina Press.

Clark, J.E., Whitall, J., & Phillips, S.J. (1988). Human interlimb coordination: The first six months of independent walking. *Developmental Psychobiology, 21*(5), 445-456.

Diamond, A. (2000). Close interrelation of motor development and cognitive development and of the cerebellum and prefrontal cortex. *Child Development, 71*(1), 44-56.

Dominici, N., Ivanenko, Y.P., Cappellini, G., Zampagni, M.L., & Lacquaniti, F. (2010). Kinematic strategies in newly walking toddlers stepping over different support surfaces. *Journal of Neurophysiology, 103*(3), 1673-1684. doi:10.1152/jn.00945.2009

Eddy, M. (2012). The ongoing development of "Past Beginnings": A further discussion of neuromotor development: Somatic links between Bartenieff Fundamentals, Body-Mind Centering® and Dynamic Embodiment©. *The Journal of Laban Movement Studies, 3*(1), 54-79.

Education Committee, IADMS. (2000). *The challenge of the adolescent dancer.* Resource paper. International Association for Dance Medicine & Science. www.iadms.org/displaycommon.cfm?an=1&subarticlenbr=1

Folio, R.M., & Fewell, R.R. (1983). *Peabody developmental motor scales.* Allen, TX: DLM Teaching Resources.

Franchak, J.M., Kretch, K.S., Soska, K.C., Babcock, J.S., & Adolph, K.E. (2010). Head-mounted eye-tracking of infants' natural interactions: A new method. *Proceedings of the 2010 Symposium on Eye-Tracking Research & Applications* (pp. 21-27). New York: Association for Computing Machinery. doi: 10.1145/1743666.1743671

Gesell, A. (1946). The ontogenesis of infant behavior. In L. Carmichael (Ed.), *Manual of child psychology* (pp. 335-373). New York: Wiley.

Gesell, A., & Amatruda, C.S. (1947). *Developmental diagnosis* (2nd ed.). New York: Paul B. Hoeber.

Gutteridge, M.V. (1939). A study of motor achievements in young children. *Archives of Psychology, 244*, 1-178.

Haywood, K.M., & Getchell, N. (2009). *Life span motor development* (5th ed.). Champaign, IL: Human Kinetics.

Haywood, K.M., Robertson, M.A., & Getchell, N. (2012). *Advanced analysis of motor development.* Champaign, IL: Human Kinetics.

Held, R., & Hein, A. (1963). Movement-produced stimulation in the development of visually guided behavior. *Journal of Comparative and Physiological Psychology, 56*(5), 872-876. doi: 10.1037/h0040546

Hirabayashi, S., & Iwasaki, Y. (1994). Developmental perspective of sensory organization on postural control. *Brain & Development, 17*(2), 111-113.

Jensen, J.L., Schneider, K., Ulrich, B.D., Zernicke R.F., & Thelen, E. (1994). Adaptive dynamics of the leg movement patterns of human infants: I. The effects of posture on spontaneous kicking. *Journal of Motor Behavior, 26*(4), 303-312.

Jensen, J.L., Schneider, K., Ulrich, B.D., Zernicke R.F., & Thelen, E. (1994). Adaptive dynamics of the leg movement patterns of human infants: II. Treadmill stepping in infants and adults. *Journal of Motor Behavior, 26*(4), 313-324.

Jensen, J.L., Thelen, E., Ulrich, B.D., Schneider, K., & Zernicke, R.F. (1995). Adaptive dynamics of the leg movement patterns of human infants: III. Age-related differences in limb control. *Journal of Motor Behavior, 27*(4), 366-374.

Krasnow, D. (2010). Improvisation as a tool for enhanced motor learning in dance. *The Twenty-Eighth Annual Symposium of Medical Problems of Performing Artists,* July 29-August 1, 2010, Snowmass, CO.

McGraw, M.B. (1932). From reflex to muscular control in the assumption of an erect posture and ambulation in the human infant. *Child Development, 3*(4), 291-297.

McGraw, M.B. (1943). *The neuromuscular maturation of the human infant.* New York: Columbia University Press.

Purcell Cone, T., & Cone, S. (2012). *Teaching children dance* (3rd ed.). Champaign, IL: Human Kinetics.

Quatman-Yates, C.C., Quatman, C.E., Meszaros, A.J., Paterno, M.V., & Hewett, T.E. (2012). A systematic review of sensorimotor function during adolescence: A developmental stage of increased motor awkwardness? *British Journal of Sports Medicine, 46*(9), 649-655. doi:10.1136/bjsm.2010.079616

Roberton, M.A., & Halverson, L.E. (1984). *Developing children: Their changing movement.* Philadelphia: Lea & Febiger.

Roncesvalles, M.N., Woollacott, M.H., & Jensen, J.L. (2001). Development of lower extremity kinetics for balance control in infants and young children. *Journal of Motor Behavior, 33*(1), 180-192.

Rose, D.J., & Christina, R.W. (2006). *A multilevel approach to the study of motor control and learning* (2nd ed.). San Francisco: Benjamin Cummings.

Russell, D.J., Rosenbaum, P.L., Cadman, D.T., Gowland, C., Hardy, S., & Jarvis, S. (1989). The gross motor function measure: A means to evaluate the effects of physical therapy. *Developmental Medicine & Child Neurology, 31*(3), 341-352.

Shirley, M.M. (1963). The motor sequence. In D. Dwayne (Ed.). *Readings in child psychology.* Englewood Cliffs, NJ: Prentice Hall.

Shumway-Cook, A., & Woollacott, M. (2001). *Motor control: Theory and practical applications* (2nd ed.). Baltimore: Williams & Wilkins.

Shumway-Cook, A., & Woollacott, M.H. (2012). *Motor control: Translating research into clinical practice* (4th ed.). Philadelphia: Lippincott Williams & Wilkins.

Spencer, J.P., Clearfield, M., Corbetta, D., Ulrich, B., Buchanan, P., & Schöner, G. (2006). Moving toward a grand theory of development: In memory of Esther Thelen. *Child Development, 77*(6), 1521-1538.

Sundermier, L., & Woollacott, M.H. (1998). The influence of vision on the automatic postural muscle responses of newly standing and newly walking infants. *Experimental Brain Research, 120*(4), 537-540.

Thelen, E. (1985). Developmental origins of motor coordination: Leg movements in human infants. *Developmental Psychobiology, 18*(1), 1-22.

Thelen, E. (1998). The improvising infant: Learning about learning to move. In J.S. DeLoache, S.C. Mangelsdorf, & E. Pomerantz (Eds.), *Current readings in child development* (3rd ed., pp. 26-42). Boston: Allyn & Bacon.

Thelen, E., & Corbetta, D. (1994). Exploration and selection in the early acquisition of skills. *International Review of Neurobiology, 37*, 75-102.

Thelen, E., & Fisher, D.M. (1982). Newborn stepping: An explanation for a "disappearing" reflex. *Developmental Psychology, 18*(5), 760-775. doi: 10.1037/0012-1649.18.5.760

Thelen, E., Fisher, D.M., & Ridley-Johnson, R. (1984). The relationship between physical growth and a newborn reflex. *Infant Behavior and Development, 7*(4), 479-493.

Thelen, E., Kelso, J.A.S., & Fogel, A. (1987). Self-organizing systems and infant motor development. *Developmental Review, 7*(1), 39-65.

Thelen, E., & Ulrich, B.D. (1991). Hidden skills: A dynamic systems analysis of treadmill stepping during the first year. *Monographs of the Society for Research in Child Development, 56* (1, Serial No. 223).

Thelen, E., Ulrich, B.D., & Jensen, J.L. (1989). The developmental origins of locomotion. In M. H. Woollacott & A. Shumway-Cook (Eds.), *Development of posture and gait across the life span (pp. 25-47)*. Columbia: University of South Carolina Press.

Whitall, J., & Getchell, N. (1995). From walking to running: Using a dynamical systems approach to the development of motor skills. *Child Development, 66*(5), 1541-1553.

Wilmerding, V., & Krasnow, D. (2009). *Motor learning and teaching dance.* Resource Paper. International Association for Dance Medicine & Science. www.iadms.org/displaycommon.cfm?an=1&subarticlenbr=250

Woollacott, M.H., & Shumway-Cook, A. (Eds.). (1989). *Development of posture and gait across the life span.* Columbia: University of South Carolina Press.

Chapter 5

Barroso, R., Tricoli, V., Dos Santos Gil, S., Ugrinowitsch, C., & Roschel, H. (2012). Maximal strength, number of repetitions, and total volume are differently affected by static-, ballistic-, and proprioceptive neuromuscular facilitation stretching. *Journal of Strength and Conditioning Research, 26*(9), 2432-2437.

Behm, D.G., Bambury, A., Cahill, F., & Power, K. (2004). Effect of acute static stretching on force, balance, reaction time, and movement time. *Medicine & Science in Sports & Exercise, 36*(8), 1397-1402.

Bird, H.A., & Foley, E.C. (2012). Hypermobility in dancers: Asset or liability? *Rheumatology.* Published online. doi: 10.1093/rheumatology/kes291

Branta, C., Haubenstricker, J., & Seefeldt, V. (1984). Age changes in motor skill during childhood and adolescence. *Exercise and Sport Sciences Reviews, 12*(1), 467-520.

Bronner, S., & Ojofeitimi, S. (2011). Pelvis and hip three-dimensional kinematics in grand battement movements. *Journal of Dance Medicine & Science, 15*(1), 23-30.

Cornwell A., Nelson, A.G., Heise, G.D., & Sidaway, B. (2001). Acute effects of passive muscle stretching on vertical jump performance. *Journal of Human Movement Studies, 40*(4), 307-324.

Cramer, J.T., Housh, T.J., Weir, J.P., & Johnson, G.O. (2005). The acute effects of static stretching on peak torque, mean power output, electromyogra-

phy and mechanomyography. *European Journal of Applied Physiology, 93,* 530-539. doi: 10.1007/s00421-004-1199-x

Critchfield, B. (2011). *Stretching for dancers.* Resource Paper. International Association for Dance Medicine & Science. www.iadms.org/displaycommon.cfm?an=1&subarticlenbr=353

Harley, Y.X.R., Gibson, A.S., Harley, E.H., Lambert, M.I., Vaughan, C.L., & Noakes, T.D. (2002). Quadriceps strength and jumping efficiency in dancers. *Journal of Dance Medicine & Science, 6*(3), 87-94.

Haywood, K.M., & Getchell, N. (2009). *Life span motor development* (5th ed.). Champaign, IL: Human Kinetics.

Haywood, K.M., Robertson, M.A., & Getchell, N. (2012). *Advanced analysis of motor development.* Champaign, IL: Human Kinetics.

Juras, G., Slomka, K., & Latash, M. (2009). Violations of Fitts' Law in a ballistic task. *Journal of Motor Behavior, 41*(6), 525-528.

Köster, B., Deuschl, G., Lauk, M., Timmer, J., Guschlbauer, B., & Lücking, C.H. (2002). Essential tremor and cerebellar dysfunction: Abnormal ballistic movements. *Journal of Neurology, Neurosurgery, and Psychiatry, 73*(4), 400-405. doi:10.1136/jnnp.73.4.400

Krasnow, D., Ambegaonkar, J.P., Wilmerding, M.V., Stecyk, S., Koutedakis, Y., & Wyon, M. (2012). Electromyographic comparison of grand battement devant at the barre, in the center, and traveling. *Medical Problems of Performing Artists, 27*(3), 143-155.

Krasnow, D., Wilmerding, M.V., Stecyk, S., Wyon, M., & Koutedakis, Y. (2012). Examination of weight transfer strategies during the execution of grand battement devant at the barre, in the center, and traveling. *Medical Problems of Performing Artists, 27*(2), 74-84.

Marques-Bruna, P. & Grimshaw, P.N. (1997). 3-dimensional kinematics of overarm throwing action of children age 15 to 30 months. *Perceptual and Motor Skills, 84*(3c), 1267-1283. doi: 10.2466/pms.1997.84.3c.1267

McCormack, M., Briggs, J., Hakim, A., & Grahame, R. (2004). Joint laxity and benign joint hypermobility syndrome in student and professional ballet dancers. *The Journal of Rheumatology, 31*(1), 173-178.

Morrin, N., & Redding, E. (2013). Acute effects of warm-up stretch protocols on balance, vertical jump height, and range of motion in dancers. *Journal of Dance Medicine & Science, 17*(1), 34-40.

Palmer, E., Cafarelli, E., & Ashby, P. (1994). The processing of human ballistic movements explored by stimulation over the cortex. *Journal of Physiology, 481*(2), 509-520.

Power K., Behm, D., Cahill, F., Carroll, M., & Young, W. (2004). An acute bout of static stretching: Effects on force and jumping performance. *Medicine & Science in Sports & Exercise, 36*(8), 1389-1396.

Roberton, M.A., & Halverson, L.E. (1984). *Developing children: Their changing movement.* Philadelphia: Lea & Febiger.

Samuel, M.N., Holcomb, W.R., Guadagnoli, M.A., Rubley, M.D., & Wallmann, H. (2008). Acute effects of static and ballistic stretching on measures of strength and power. *Journal of Strength and Conditioning Research, 22*(5), 1422-1428.

Schmidt, R.A., & Lee, T.D. (2011). *Motor control and learning: A behavioral emphasis* (5th ed.). Champaign, IL: Human Kinetics.

Vanderka, M. (2011). Acute effects of stretching on explosive power. *Acta Facultatis Educationis Physicae Universitatis Comenianae, 51*(2), 23-34.

Van Zandwijk, J.P., Bobbert, M.F., Munneke, M., & Oas, P. (2000). Control of maximal and submaximal vertical jumps. *Medicine and Science in Sports and Exercise, 32*(2), 477-485.

Wadman, W.J., Denier van der Gon, J.J., Geuze, R.H., & Mol, C.R. (1979). Control of fast goal-directed arm movements. *Journal of Human Movement Studies, 5*, 3-17.

Chapter 6

Clippinger, K. (2007). *Dance anatomy and kinesiology.* Champaign, IL: Human Kinetics.

Franklin, E. (2004). *Conditioning for dance.* Champaign, IL: Human Kinetics.

Ghez, C., & Krakauer, J. (2000). The organization of movement. In E.R. Kandel, J.H. Schwartz, & T.M. Jessell (Eds.), *Principles of neural science* (4th ed., pp. 653-673). New York: McGraw-Hill.

Haywood, K.M., & Getchell, N. (2009). *Life span motor development* (5th ed.). Champaign, IL: Human Kinetics.

Haywood, K.M., Robertson, M. A., & Getchell, N. (2012). *Advanced analysis of motor development.* Champaign, IL: Human Kinetics.

Huwyler, J.S. (2009). *The dancer's body: A medical perspective on dance and dance training* (2nd ed.). Binsted, Hampshire, UK: Dance Books.

Krasnow, D., & Deveau, J. (2010). *Conditioning with imagery for dancers.* Toronto: Thompson Educational.

Magill, R.A. (2011). *Motor learning and control* (9th ed.). New York: McGraw-Hill.

Moore, M. (2007). Golgi tendon organs (GTOs): Neuroscience update with relevance to stretching and proprioception in dancers. *Journal of Dance Medicine & Science, 11*(3), 85-92.

Rose, D.J., & Christina, R.W. (2006). *A multilevel approach to the study of motor control and learning* (2nd ed.). San Francisco: Benjamin Cummings.

Schmidt, R.A., & Lee, T.D. (2011). *Motor control and learning: A behavioral emphasis* (5th ed.). Champaign, IL: Human Kinetics.

Shumway-Cook, A., & Woollacott, M. (2001). *Motor control: Theory and practical applications* (2nd ed.). Baltimore: Williams & Wilkins.

Shumway-Cook, A., & Woollacott, M.H. (2012). *Motor control: Translating research into clinical practice* (4th ed.). Philadelphia: Lippincott Williams & Wilkins.

Stephens, R.E. (2005). The neuroanatomical and biomechanical basis of flexibility exercises in dance. In R. Solomon, J. Solomon, & S.C. Minton (Eds.), *Preventing dance injuries* (2nd ed., pp. 151-163). Champaign, IL: Human Kinetics.

Sweigard, L.E. (1974). *Human movement potential: Its ideokinetic facilitation.* Lanham, MD: University Press of America.

Todd, M.E. (1929). *The balancing of forces in the human being: Its application to postural patterns.* New York: Author.

Todd, M.E. (1997). *The thinking body* (3rd ed.). Binsted, Hampshire, UK: Dance Books.

Welsh, T. (2009). *Conditioning for dancers.* Gainesville, FL: University Press of Florida.

Chapter 7

Barrell, G.M. & Terry, P.C. (2003). Trait anxiety and coping strategies among ballet dancers. *Medical Problems of Performing Artists, 18*(2), 59-64.

Batson, G. (1996). Conscious use of the human body in movement: The peripheral neuroanatomic basis of the Alexander Technique. *Medical Problems of Performing Artists, 11*(1), 3-11.

Bernstein, N.A. (1996). On dexterity and its development. In M.L. Latash & M.T. Turvey (Eds.), *Dexterity and its development* (pp. 3-244). Mahwah, NJ: Erlbaum.

Broadbent, D.E. (1958). *Perception and communication.* London: Pergamon Press.

Cattell, J.M. (1893). Aufmerksamkeit und reaction. *Philosophische Studien, 8*, 403-406. English translation in R.S. Woodworth (1947), *Psychological Research* (Vol. 1, pp. 252-255). Lancaster, PA: Science Press.

Cherry, E.C. (1953). Some experiments on the recognition of speech, with one and two ears. *Journal of the Acoustical Society of America, 25*(5), 975-979. doi: 10.1121/1.1907229

Cohen, A., Ivry, R.I., & Keele, S.W. (1990). Attention and structure in sequence learning. *Journal of Experimental Psychology: Learning, Memory, and Cognition, 16*(1), 17-30.

Dearborn, K., Harring, K., Young, C., & O'Rourke, E. (2006). Mirror and phrase difficulty influence dancer attention and body satisfaction. *Journal of Dance Education, 6*(4), 116-123.

Deutsch, J.A., & Deutsch, D. (1963). Attention: Some theoretical considerations. *Psychological Review, 70*(1), 80-90.

Dowd, I. (1990). *Taking root to fly* (2nd ed.). North Hampton, MA: Contact Collaborations.

Enghauser, R. (2003). Motor learning and the dance technique class: Science, tradition, and pedagogy. *Journal of Dance Education, 3*(3), 87-95.

Feigenberg, I.M., & Latash, L.P. (1996). N.A. Bernstein: The reformer of neuroscience. In M.L. Latash and M.T. Turvey (Eds.), *Dexterity and its development* (pp. 247-275). Champaign, IL: Human Kinetics.

Fortin, S., Long, W., & Lord, M. (2002). Three voices: Researching how somatic education informs contemporary dance technique classes. *Research in Dance Education, 3*(2), 155-179.

Franklin, E. (2012). *Dynamic alignment through imagery* (2nd ed.). Champaign, IL: Human Kinetics.

Friedenberg, J., & Silverman, G. (2006). *Cognitive science: An introduction to the study of mind.* Thousand Oaks, CA: Sage.

Harris, D.A. (2001). Using \gb\-blockers to control stage fright: A dancer's dilemma. *Medical Problems of Performing Artists, 16*(2), 72-76.

Ivry, R.B., Mayr, U., Corcos, D.M., & Poster, M.I. (2006). Psychological processes and neural mechanism for action: The legacy of Steven W. Keele. *Journal of Motor Behavior, 38*(1), 3-6.

James, W. (1890). *The principles of psychology* (Vol. 1). New York: Holt.

Kahneman, D. (1973). *Attention and effort.* Englewood Cliffs, NJ: Prentice Hall.

Keele, S.W. (1973). *Attention and human performance.* Pacific Palisades, CA: Goodyear.

Krasnow, D., & Deveau, J. (2010). *Conditioning with imagery for dancers.* Toronto: Thompson Educational.

Krasnow, D., Mainwaring, L., & Kerr, G. (1999). Injury, stress, and perfectionism in young dancers and gymnasts. *Journal of Dance Medicine and Science, 3*, 51-58.

Laufer, Y., Rotem-Lehrer, N., Ronen, Z., Khayutin, G., & Rozenberg, I. (2007). Effect of attention focus on acquisition and retention of postural control following ankle sprain. *Archives of Physical Medicine and Rehabilitation, 88*(1), 105-108.

Liederbach, M., & Compagno, J.M. (2001). Psychological aspects of fatigue-related injuries in dancers. *Journal of Dance Medicine & Science, 5*(4), 116-120.

Magill, R.A. (2011). *Motor learning and control* (9th ed.). New York: McGraw-Hill.

Mainwaring, L., Krasnow, D., & Kerr, G. (2001). And the dance goes on: Psychological impact of injury. *Journal of Dance Medicine and Science, 5*, 105-115.

Mainwaring, L., Krasnow, D., & Young, L. (2003). A teacher's guide to helping young dancers cope with psychological aspects of hip injuries. *Journal of Dance Education, 3*, 57-64.

Nagel, J.J. (1993). Stage fright in musicians: A psychodynamic perspective. *Bulletin of the Menninger Clinic, 57*(4), 492-503.

Neisser, U., & Becklen, R. (1975). Selective looking: Attending to visually specified events. *Cognitive Psychology, 7*(4), 480-494.

Nideffer, R.M. (1995). *Focus for success.* San Diego: Enhanced Performance Services.

Noh, Y.-E., Morris, T., & Anderson, M.B. (2007). Psychological intervention programs for reduction of injury in ballet dancers. *Research in Sports Medicine, 15*(1), 13-32.

Posner, M.I., & Snyder, C.R. (1975). Attention and cognitive control. In R.L. Solso (Ed.), *Information processing and cognition* (pp. 205-223). Hillsdale, NJ: Erlbaum.

Prinz, W. (1997). Perception and action planning. *European Journal of Cognitive Psychology, 9*(2), 129-154. doi: 10.1080/713752551

Schmidt, R.A., & Lee, T.D. (2011). *Motor control and learning: A behavioral emphasis* (5th ed.). Champaign, IL: Human Kinetics.

Schmidt, R.A., & Lee, T.D. (2014). *Motor learning and performance: From principles to application* (5th ed.). Champaign, IL: Human Kinetics.

Schneider, W., & Shiffrin, R.M. (1977). Controlled and automatic human information processing: I. Detection, search, and attention. *Psychological Review, 84*(1), 1-66.

Stroop, J.R. (1935). Studies of interference in serial verbal reactions. *Journal of Experimental Psychology, 18*(6), 643-662.

Sweigard, L.E. (1974). *Human movement potential: Its ideokinetic facilitation.* Lanham, MD: University Press of America.

Todd, M.E. (1937). *The thinking body.* New York: Paul B. Hoeber.

Todd, M.E. (1997). *The thinking body* (3rd ed.). Binsted, Hampshire, UK: Dance Books.

Walker, I.J., & Nordin-Bates, S.M. (2010). Performance anxiety experiences of professional ballet dancers: The importance of control. *Journal of Dance Medicine & Science, 14*(4), 133-145.

Welford, A.T. (1952). The "psychological refractory period" and the timing of high-speed performance—a review and a theory. *British Journal of Psychology, 43*(1), 2-19.

Wickens, C.D. (1991). Processing resources and attention. In D.L. Damos (Ed.), *Multi-task performance* (pp. 3-34). London: Taylor & Francis.

Wilmerding, V., & Krasnow, D. (2009). *Motor learning and teaching dance.* Resource Paper. International Association for Dance Medicine & Science. www.iadms.org/displaycommon.cfm?an=1&subarticlenbr=250

Wulf, G., & Prinz, W. (2001). Directing attention to movement effects enhances learning: A review. *Psychonomic Bulletin & Review, 8*(4), 648-660.

Chapter 8

Batson, G. (2008). *Proprioception.* Resource Paper. International Association for Dance Medicine & Science. www.iadms.org/displaycommon.cfm?an=1&subarticlenbr=210

Golomer, E., Cremieux, J., Dupui, P., Isableu, B., & Ohlmann, T. (1999). Visual contribution to self-induced body sway frequencies and visual perception of male professional dancers. *Neuroscience Letters, 267*(3), 189-192.

Haywood, K.M., & Getchell, N. (2009). *Life span motor development* (5th ed.). Champaign, IL: Human Kinetics.

Helsen, W.F., Elliott, D., Starkes, J.L., & Ricker, K.L. (1998). Temporal and spatial coupling of point of gaze and hand movements in aiming. *Journal of Motor Behavior, 30*(3), 249-259.

Helsen, W.F., Elliott, D., Starkes, J.L., & Ricker, K.L. (2000). Coupling of eye, finger, elbow, and shoulder movements during manual aiming. *Journal of Motor Behavior, 32*(3), 241-248.

Herdman, S.J. (2007). *Vestibular rehabilitation.* Philadelphia: F.A. Davis.

Inglis, J.T., Kennedy, P.M., Wells, C., & Chua, R. (2002). The role of cutaneous receptors in the foot. *Advances in Experimental Medicine and Biology, 508*, 111-117.

Konczak, J. (1994). Effects of optical flow on the kinematics of human gait: A comparison of young and older adults. *Journal of Motor Behavior, 26*(3), 225-236. doi: 10.1080/00222895.1994.9941678

Krasnow, D., & Deveau, J. (2010). *Conditioning with imagery for dancers.* Toronto: Thompson Educational.

Lee, D.N. (1980). Visuo-motor coordination in space-time. In G.E. Stelmach & J. Requin (Eds.), *Tutorials in Motor Behavior* (pp. 281-295). Amsterdam: North Holland.

Lee, D.N. (2009). General tau theory: Evolution to date. *Perception, 38*(6), 837-850.

Magill, R.A. (2011). *Motor learning and control* (9th ed.). New York: McGraw-Hill.

Moore, M. (2007). Golgi tendon organs (GTOs): Neuroscience update with relevance to stretching and proprioception in dancers. *Journal of Dance Medicine & Science, 11*(3), 85-92.

Proske, U., & Gandevia, S.C. (2012). The proprioceptive senses: Their roles in signaling body shape, body position and movement, and muscle force. *Physiological Reviews, 92*(4), 1651-1697.

Proske, U., Schaible, H.-G., & Schmidt, R.F. (1988). Joint receptors and kinesthesia. *Experimental Brain Research, 72*, 219-224.

Ramsay, J.R., & Riddoch, M.J. (2001). Position-matching in the upper limb: Professional ballet dancers perform with outstanding accuracy. *Clinical Rehabilitation, 18*(3), 324-330.

Rose, D.J., & Christina, R.W. (2006). *A multilevel approach to the study of motor control and learning* (2nd ed.). San Francisco: Benjamin Cummings.

Schmidt, R.A., & Lee, T.D. (2011). *Motor control and learning: A behavioral emphasis* (5th ed.). Champaign, IL: Human Kinetics.

Schmidt, R.A., & Lee, T.D. (2014). *Motor learning and performance: From principles to application* (5th ed.). Champaign, IL: Human Kinetics.

Shumway-Cook, A., & Woollacott, M.H. (2012). *Motor control: Translating research into clinical practice* (4th ed.). Philadelphia: Lippincott Williams & Wilkins.

Simmons, R.W. (2005). Sensory organization determinants of postural stability in trained ballet dancers. *International Journal of Neuroscience, 115*(1), 87-97.

Sivak, B., & MacKenzie, C.L. (1990). Integration of visual information and motor output in reaching and grasping: The contributions of peripheral and central vision. *Neuropsychologia, 28*(10), 1095-1116.

Trevarthen, C.B. (1968). Two mechanisms of vision in primates. *Psychologische Forschung, 31,* 299-337. http://link.springer.com/article/10.1007/BF00422717#page-2

Woodworth, R.S. (1899). The accuracy of voluntary movement. *The Psychological Review, 3*(3), i-114. doi: 10.1037/h0092992

Chapter 9

Carter, M.C., & Shapiro, D.C. (1984). Control of sequential movements: Evidence for generalized motor programs. *Journal of Neurophysiology, 52*(5), 787-796.

Enghauser, R. (2003). Motor learning and the dance technique class: Science, tradition, and pedagogy. *Journal of Dance Education, 3*(3), 87-95.

Golubitsky, M., Stewart, I., Buono, P.L., & Collins, J.J. (1999). Symmetry in locomotor central pattern generators and animal gaits. *Nature, 401*(6754), 693-695.

Gordon, J., Ghilardi, M.F., & Ghez, C. (1995). Impairments of reaching movements in patients without proprioception. I. Spatial errors. *Journal of Neurophysiology, 73*(1), 347-360.

Haywood, K.M., Robertson, M.A., & Getchell, N. (2012). *Advanced analysis of motor development.* Champaign, IL: Human Kinetics.

James, W. (1890). *The principles of psychology* (Vol. 1). New York: Holt.

Keele, S.W., Cohen, A., & Ivry, R. (1990). Motor programs: Concepts and issues. In M. Jeannerod (Ed.), *Attention and performance XIII.* Hillsdale, NJ: Erlbaum.

Lai, Q., Shea, C.H., Wulf, G., & Wright, D.L. (2000). Optimizing generalized motor programs and parameter learning. *Research Quarterly for Exercise and Sport, 71*(1), 10-24. doi: 10.1080/02701367.2000.10608876

Laszlo, J.I. (1967). Training of fast tapping with reduction of kinaesthetic, tactile, visual and auditory sensations. *Quarterly Journal of Experimental Psychology, 19*(4), 344-349. doi: 10.1080/14640746708400113

Magill, R.A. (2011). *Motor learning and control* (9th ed.). New York: McGraw-Hill.

Puretz, S. (1988). Psychomotor research and the dance teacher. In P.M. Clarkson & M. Skrinar (Eds.), *Science of dance training* (pp. 279-287). Champaign, IL: Human Kinetics.

Schmidt, R.A. (2003). Motor schema theory after 27 years: Reflections and implications for a new theory. *Research Quarterly for Exercise and Sport, 74*(4), 366-375.

Schmidt, R.A., & Lee, T.D. (2011). *Motor control and learning: A behavioral emphasis* (5th ed.). Champaign, IL: Human Kinetics.

Schneider, S., Askew, C.D., Abel, T., & Strüder, H.K. (2010). Exercise, music, and the brain: Is there a central pattern generator? *Journal of Sports Sciences, 23*(12), 1337-1343. doi: 10.1080/02640414.2010.507252

Shapiro, D.C., Zernicke, R.F., Gregor, R.J., & Diestel, J.D. (1981). Evidence for generalized motor programs using gait pattern analysis. *Journal of Motor Behavior, 13*(1), 33-47.

Summers, J.J. (1975). The role of timing in motor program representation. *Journal of Motor Behavior, 7*(4), 229-241.

Wadman, W.J., Denier van der Gon, J.J., Geuze, R.H., & Mol, C.R. (1979). Control of fast goal-directed arm movements. *Journal of Human Movement Studies, 5,* 3-17.

Zehr, E.P. (2005). Neural control of rhythmic human movement: The common core hypothesis. *Exercise and Sport Sciences Reviews, 33*(1), 54-60.

Zehr, E.P., & Stein, R.B. (1999). What functions do reflexes serve during human locomotion? *Progress in Neurobiology, 58*(2), 185-205.

Chapter 10

Aschersleben, G. (2002). Temporal control of movements in sensorimotor synchronization. *Brain and Cognition, 48*(6), 66-79.

Augustyn, J.S., & Rosenbaum, D.A. (2005). Metacognitive control of action: Preparation for aiming reflects knowledge of Fitts's law. *Psychonomic Bulletin & Review, 12*(5), 911-916.

Bernstein, N.A. (1967). *The co-ordination and regulation of movements.* Oxford: Pergamon Press.

Cerritelli, B., Maruff, P., Wilson, P., & Currie, J. (2000). The effect of an external load on the force and timing components of mentally represented actions. *Behavioural Brain Research, 108*(1), 91-96.

Coker, C.A. (2013). *Motor learning & control for practitioners* (3rd ed.). Scottsdale, AZ: Holcomb Hathaway.

Drury, C.G., & Woolley, S.M. (1995). Visually-controlled leg movements embedded in a walking task. *Ergonomics, 38*(4), 714-722.

Fitts, P.M. (1954). The information capacity of the human motor system in controlling the amplitude of movement. *Journal of Experimental Psychology, 47,* 381-391.

Fitts, P.M., & Peterson, J.R. (1964). Information capacity of discrete motor responses. *Journal of Experimental Psychology, 48*(2), 483-492.

Franz, E.A., Zelaznik, H.N., & McCabe, G. (1991). Spatial topological constraints in a bimanual task. *Acta Psychologica, 76*(2), 137-151.

Franz, E.A., Zelaznik, H.N., Swinnen, S.P., & Walter, C.B. (2001). Spatial conceptual influences on the coordination of bimanual actions: When a dual task becomes a single task. *Journal of Motor Behavior, 33*(1), 103-112.

Hay, L. (1981). The effect of amplitude and accuracy requirements on movement time in children. *Journal of Motor Behavior, 13*(3), 177-186.

Haywood, K.M., Robertson, M.A., & Getchell, N. (2012). *Advanced analysis of motor development.* Champaign, IL: Human Kinetics.

Heuer, H., Schmidt, R.A., & Ghodsian, D. (1995). Generalized motor programs for rapid bimanual tasks: A two-level multiplicative-rate model. *Biological Cybernetics, 73*, 343-356.

Hodges, N.J., Hayes, S.H., Horn, R.R., & Williams, A.M. (2005). Changes in coordination, control and outcome as a result of extended practice on a novel motor skill. *Ergonomics, 48*(11-14), 1672-1685.

Hodges, N., & Williams, M.A. (2012). *Skill acquisition in sport: Research, theory and practice* (2nd ed.). New York: Routledge.

Holland, S., Bouwer, A.J., Dalgelish, M., & Hurtig, T.M. (2010). Feeling the beat where it counts: Fostering multi-limb rhythm skills with the haptic drum kit. In *Proceedings of the Fourth International Conference on Tangible, Embedded, and Embodied Interaction*, January 2010, Cambridge, MA, pp. 21-28.

Jiang, J., Shen, Y., & Neilson, P.E. (2002). A simulation study of the degrees of freedom of movement in reaching and grasping. *Human Movement Science, 21*(5-6), 881-904.

Kelso, B.A. (1984). The effects of extended practice on aiming movements in terms of Fitts' Law. Unpublished masters' thesis, York University, Toronto, Canada.

Kelso, J.A.S. (1992). Theoretical concepts and strategies for understanding perceptual-motor skill: From information capacity enclosed systems to self-organization in open, nonequilibrium systems. *Journal of Experimental Psychology: General, 121*(3), 260-261.

Konczak, J., Velden, H., & Jaeger, L. (2009). Learning to play the violin: Motor control by freezing, not freeing degrees of freedom. *Journal of Motor Behavior, 4*(3), 243-252.

Magill, R.A. (2011). *Motor learning and control* (9th ed.). New York: McGraw-Hill.

Mouchnino, L., Aurenty, R., Massion, J., & Pedotti, A. (1992). Coordination between equilibrium and head-trunk orientation during leg movement: A new strategy built up by training. *Journal of Neurophysiology, 67*(6), 1587-1598.

Newell, K.M., Broderick, M.P., Deutsch, K.M., & Slifkin, A.B. (2003). Task goals and change in dynamical degrees of freedom with motor learning. *Journal of Experimental Psychology: Human Perception and Performance, 29*(2), 379-387.

Newell, K.M., Hoshizaki, L.E., & Carlton, L.G. (1979). Movement time and velocity as determinants of movement timing accuracy. *Journal of Motor Behavior, 11*(1), 49-58.

Peters, M. (1977). Simultaneous performance of two motor activities: The factor of timing. *Neuropsychologica, 15*(3), 461-464. doi: 10.1016/0028-3932(77)90099-9

Phillips-Silver, J., Aktipis, C.A., & Bryant, G.A. (2010). The ecology of entrainment: Foundations of coordinated rhythmic movement. *Music Perception, 28*(1), 3-14.

Rose, D.J., & Christina, R.W. (2006). *A multilevel approach to the study of motor control and learning* (2nd ed.). San Francisco: Benjamin Cummings.

Schellekens, J.M., Kalverboer, A.F., & Scholten C.A. (1984). The micro-structure of tapping movements in children. *Journal of Motor Behavior, 16*(1), 20-39.

Schmidt, R.A., & Lee, T.D. (2011). *Motor control and learning: A behavioral emphasis* (5th ed.). Champaign, IL: Human Kinetics.

Schmidt, R.A., & Lee, T.D. (2014). *Motor learning and performance: From principles to application* (5th ed.). Champaign, IL: Human Kinetics.

Schmidt, R.A., Zelaznik, H.N., & Frank, J.S. (1978). Sources of inaccuracy in rapid movement. In G.E. Stelmach (Ed.), *Information processing in motor control and learning* (pp. 183-203). New York: Academic Press.

Schmidt, R.A., Zelaznik, H.N., Hawkins, B., Frank, J.S., & Quinn, J.T., Jr. (1979). Motor-output variability: A theory for the accuracy of rapid motor acts. *Psychological Review, 86*(5), 415-451.

Summers, J.J., Todd, J.A., & Kim, Y.H. (1993). The influence of perceptual and motor factors on bimanual coordination in a polyrhythmic tapping task. *Psychological Research, 55*, 107-115.

Thompson, A.A. & Henriques, D.Y.P. (2011). The coding and updating of visuospatial memory for goal-directed reaching and pointing. *Vision Research, 51*(8), 819-826.

Todorov, E., & Jordan, M.I. (2002). Optimal feedback control as a theory of motor coordination. *Nature Neuroscience, 5*(11), 1226-1235.

Turvey, M.T. (1990). Coordination. *American Psychologist, 45*(8), 938-953.

Woodworth, R.S. (1899). The accuracy of voluntary movement. *The Psychological Review, 3*(3), i-114. doi: 10.1037/h0092992

Chapter 11

Adams, J.A. (1971). A closed-loop theory of motor learning. *Journal of Motor Behavior, 3*(2), 111-150.

Enghauser, R. (2003). Motor learning and the dance technique class: Science, tradition, and pedagogy. *Journal of Dance Education, 3*(3), 87-95.

Fitts, P.M., & Posner, M.I. (1967). *Human performance.* Belmont, CA: Brooks/Cole.

Gardner, H. (1983). *Frames of mind: The theory of multiple intelligences.* New York: Basic Books.

Gentile, A.M. (1972). A working model of skill acquisition with application to teaching. *Quest, 17*(1), 3-23. doi: 10.1080/00336297.1972.10519717

Higgins, J.R., & Spaeth, R.A. (1979). Relationship between consistency of movement and environmental conditions. *Quest, 17*(1), 61-69.

Kandel, E.R., Schwartz, J.H., & Jessell, T.M. (2000). *Principles of neural science* (4th ed.). New York: McGraw-Hill.

Kolb, D.A. (1985). *Learning-style inventory* (revised). Boston: McBer.

Magill, R.A., & Hall, K.G. (1990). A review of the contextual interference effect in motor skill acquisition. *Human Movement Science, 9*(3-5), 241-289.

McCarthy, B. (1987). The 4MAT system: *Teaching to learning styles with right/left mode techniques.* Barrington, IL: Excel.

Newell, K.M. (1991). Motor skill acquisition. *Annual Review of Psychology, 42*, 213-237.

Rose, D.J., & Christina, R.W. (2006). *A multilevel approach to the study of motor control and learning* (2nd ed.). San Francisco: Benjamin Cummings.

Schmidt, R.A. (1975). A schema theory of discrete motor skill learning. *Psychological Review, 82*(4), 225-260.

Schmidt, R.A. (2003). Motor schema theory after 27 years: Reflections and implications for a new theory. *Research Quarterly for Exercise and Sport, 74*(4), 366-375.

Schmidt, R.A., & Lee, T.D. (2011). *Motor control and learning: A behavioral emphasis* (5th ed.). Champaign, IL: Human Kinetics.

Schmidt, R.A., & Lee, T.D. (2014). *Motor learning and performance: From principles to application* (5th ed.). Champaign, IL: Human Kinetics.

Shumway-Cook, A., & Woollacott, M.H. (2012). *Motor control: Translating research into clinical practice* (4th ed.). Philadelphia: Lippincott Williams & Wilkins.

Van Rossum, J.H.A. (1990). Schmidt's schema theory: The empirical base of the variability of practice hypothesis: A critical analysis. *Human Movement Science, 9*(3-5), 387-435.

Waterhouse, L. (2006). Inadequate evidence for multiple intelligences, Mozart effect, and emotional intelligence theories. *Educational Psychologist, 41*(4), 247-255.

Wilmerding, V., & Krasnow, D. (2009). *Motor learning and teaching dance.* Resource Paper. International Association for Dance Medicine & Science. www.iadms.org/displaycommon.cfm?an=1&subarticle nbr=250

Chapter 12

Abernethy, B., & Zawi, K. (2007). Pickup of essential kinematics underpins expert perception of movement patterns. *Motor Behavior, 39*(5), 353-367.

Bandura, A. (1986). The explanatory and predictive scope of self-efficacy theory. *Journal of Social and Clinical Psychology, 4*(3), 359-373. doi: 10.1521/jscp.1986.4.3.359

Barr, S. (2009). Examining the technique class: Re-examining feedback. *Research in Dance Education, 10*(1), 33-45.

Blake, R., & Shiffrar, M. (2007). Perception of human motion. *Annual Review of Psychology, 58*, 47-73. doi: 10.1146/annurev.psych.57.102904.190152

Blandin, Y., & Proteau, L. (2000). On the cognitive basis of observational learning: Development of mechanisms for the detection and correction of errors. *The Quarterly Journal of Experimental Psychology, Section A: Human Experimental Psychology, 53*(3), 846-867. doi: 10.1080/713755917

Enghauser, R. (2003). Motor learning and the dance technique class: Science, tradition, and pedagogy. *Journal of Dance Education, 3*(3), 87-95.

Fishman, S., & Tobey, C. (1978). Augmented feedback. In W.G. Anderson, & G.T. Barrette (Eds.), *What's going on in gym: Descriptive studies of physical education classes* (pp. 51-62). *Motor Skills: Theory into Practice, Monograph 1.*

Iacoboni, M., & Mazziotta, J.C. (2007). Mirror neuron system: Basic findings and clinical applications. *Annals of Neurology, 62*(3), 213-218.

Kimmerle, M., & Côté, P. (2003). *Teaching dance skills: A motor learning and developmental approach.* Andover, NJ: J. Michael Ryan.

Krasnow, D., Ambegaonkar, J.P., Wilmerding, M.V., Stecyk, S., Koutedakis, Y., & Wyon, M. (2012). Electromyographic comparison of grand battement devant at the barre, in the center, and traveling. *Medical Problems of Performing Artists, 27*(3), 143-155.

Krasnow, D., Wilmerding, M.V., Stecyk, S., Wyon, M., & Koutedakis, Y. (2012). Examination of weight transfer strategies during the execution of grand battement devant at the barre, in the center, and traveling. *Medical Problems of Performing Artists, 27*(2), 74-84.

Magill, R.A. (2011). *Motor learning and control* (9th ed.). New York: McGraw-Hill.

Magill, R.A., & Anderson, D. (2014). *Motor learning and control* (10th ed.). New York: McGraw-Hill.

Magill, R.A., & Schoenfelder-Zohdi, B. (1996). A visual model and knowledge of performance as sources of information for learning a rhythmic gymnastics skill. *International Journal of Sport Psychology, 27*(1), 7-22.

Masters, R.S.W., & Poolton, J.M. (2012). Advances in implicit motor learning. In N.J. Hodges & A.M. Williams (Eds.), *Skill acquisition in sport: Research, theory and practice* (2nd ed., pp. 59-76). New York: Routledge.

Rose, D.J., & Christina, R.W. (2006). *A multilevel approach to the study of motor control and learning* (2nd ed.). San Francisco: Benjamin Cummings.

Salmoni, A.W., Schmidt, R.A., & Walter, C.B. (1984). Knowledge of results and motor learning: A review and reappraisal. *Psychological Bulletin, 95*(3), 355-386.

Schmidt, R.A., & Lee, T.D. (2011). *Motor control and learning: A behavioral emphasis* (5th ed.). Champaign, IL: Human Kinetics.

Schmidt, R.A., & Lee, T.D. (2014). *Motor learning and performance: From principles to application* (5th ed.). Champaign, IL: Human Kinetics.

Selder, D.J., & Del Rolan, N. (1979). Knowledge of performance, skill level and performance on the balance beam. *Canadian Journal of Applied Sport Sciences, 4*(3), 226-229.

Shumway-Cook, A., & Woollacott, M. (2001). *Motor control: Theory and practical applications* (2nd ed.). Baltimore: Williams & Wilkins.

Shumway-Cook, A., & Woollacott, M.H. (2012). *Motor control: Translating research into clinical practice* (4th ed.). Philadelphia: Lippincott Williams & Wilkins.

Skrinar, M. (1988). Selected motor learning applications to the technique class. In P.M. Clarkson & M. Skrinar (Eds.), *Science of dance training* (pp. 269-277). Champaign, IL: Human Kinetics.

Skully, D.M., & Newell, K.M. (1985). Observational learning and the acquisition of motor skills: Toward a visual perception perspective. *Journal of Human Movement Studies, 11*, 169-186.

Smith, R.E. (2006). Positive reinforcement, performance feedback, and performance enhancement. In J.M. Williams (Ed.), *Applied sport psychology: Personal growth to peak performance* (5th ed., pp. 40-56). Dubuque, IA: McGraw-Hill.

Weeks, D.L., & Anderson, L.P. (2000). The interaction of observational learning with overt practice: Effects on motor learning. *Acta Psychologica, 104*(2), 259-271. doi: 10.1016/S0001-6918(00)00039-1

Wilmerding, M.V., & Krasnow, D. (2011). Dance pedagogy: Myth versus reality. In A. Williamon, D. Edwards, & L. Bartel (Eds.), *Proceedings of the International Symposium on Performance Science* (pp. 283-289). The Netherlands: Association Européenne des Conservatoires, Académies de Musique et Musikhochschulen.

Wilmerding, V., & Krasnow, D. (2009). *Motor learning and teaching dance.* Resource Paper. International Association for Dance Medicine & Science. www.iadms.org/displaycommon.cfm?an=1&subarticlenbr=250

Winstein, C.J., & Schmidt, R.A. (1990). Reduced frequency of knowledge of results enhances motor skill learning. *Journal of Experimental Psychology: Learning, Memory, and Cognition, 16*(4), 677-691.

Wulf, G., McConnel, N., Gartner, M., & Schwarz, A. (2002). Enhancing the learning of sport skills through external-focus feedback. *Journal of Motor Behavior, 34*(2), 171-182.

Wulf, G., & Prinz, W. (2001). Directing attention to movement effects enhances learning: A review. *Psychonomic Bulletin & Review, 8*(4), 648-660.

Wulf, G., & Weigelt, C. (1997). Instructions about physical principles in learning a complex skill: To tell or not to tell . . . *Research Quarterly for Exercise and Sport, 68*(4), 362-367.

Wuyts, I.J., & Buekers, M.J. (1995). The effects of visual and auditory models on the learning of a rhythmical synchronization dance skill. *Research Quarterly for Exercise and Sport, 66*(2), 105-115.

Chapter 13

Bandura, A. (1997). *Self-efficacy: The exercise of control.* New York: Freeman.

Brophy, J.E. (1981). Teacher praise: A functional analysis. *Review of Educational Research, 51*(1), 5-32.

Carr, S., & Wyon, M. (2003). The impact of motivational climate on dance students' achievement goals, trait anxiety, and perfectionism. *Journal of Dance Medicine & Science, 7*(4), 105-114.

Chiviacowsky, S., & Wulf, G. (2007). Feedback after good trials enhances learning. *Research Quarterly for Exercise and Sport, 78*(2), 40-47. doi: 10.1080/02701367.2007.10599402

Csíkszentmihályi, M. (1975). *Beyond boredom and anxiety: Experiencing flow in work and play.* San Francisco: Jossey-Bass.

Csíkszentmihályi, M. (1990). *Flow: The psychology of optimal experience.* New York: Harper Perennial.

Duda, J.L., & Treasure, D.C. (2006). Motivational processes and the facilitation of performance, persistence, and well-being in sport. In J.M. Williams (Ed.), *Applied sport psychology: Personal growth to peak performance* (pp. 57-81). New York: McGraw-Hill.

Enghauser, R. (2003). Motor learning and the dance technique class: Science, tradition, and pedagogy. *Journal of Dance Education, 3*(3), 87-95.

Erez, M., & Zidon, I. (1984). Effect of goal acceptance on the relationship of goal difficulty to performance. *Journal of Applied Psychology, 69*(1), 69-78.

Erikson, E.H. (1959). *Identity and the life cycle.* New York: International Universities Press.

Fox, K.R., & Corbin, C.B. (1989). The physical self-perception profile: Development and preliminary validation. *Journal of Sport and Exercise Psychology, 11*(4), 408-430.

Gould, D., Feltz, D., & Weiss, M.R. (1985). Motives for participating in competitive youth swimming. *International Journal of Sports Psychology, 6*(2), 126-140.

Harter, S. (1981). A model of intrinsic mastery motivation in children: Individual differences and developmental change. In W.A. Collins (Ed.), *Minnesota Symposium on Child Psychology* (Vol. 14, pp. 215-225). Hillsdale, NJ: Earlbaum.

Haywood, K.M., & Getchell, N. (2009). *Life span motor development* (5th ed.). Champaign, IL: Human Kinetics.

Lazaroff, E.M. (2001). Performance and motivation in dance education. *Arts Education Policy Review, 103*(2), 23-29.

Lewthwaite, R., & Wulf, G. (2010). Social-comparative feedback affects motor skill learning. *The Quarterly Journal of Experimental Psychology, 63*(4), 738-749. doi: 10.1080/17470210903111839

Locke, E.A., & Latham, G.P. (1985). The application of goal setting to sports. *Sport Psychology, 7*(3), 205-222.

Magill, R.A. (2011). *Motor learning and control* (9th ed.). New York: McGraw-Hill.

Magill, R.A., & Anderson, D. (2014). *Motor learning and control* (10th ed.). New York: McGraw-Hill.

Mainwaring, L.M., & Krasnow, D.H. (2010). Teaching the dance class: Strategies to enhance skill acquisition, mastery and positive self-image. *Journal of Dance Education, 10*(1), 14-21.

Montessori, M. (1912). *The Montessori method: Scientific pedagogy as applied to child education in "The Children's Houses" with additions and revisions by the author* (2nd ed.). Translated from the Italian by A.E. George. New York: Frederick A. Stokes.

O'Donoghue, P.L., & Jones, E.L. (2007). Motivated behavior in a university dance environment. In *Proceedings of the 17th Annual Meeting of the International Association of Dance Medicine & Science*, Canberra, Australia.

Orlick, T. (2008). *In pursuit of excellence* (4th ed.). Champaign, IL: Human Kinetics.

Orlick, T.D. (1974). The athlete drop-out: A high price for inefficiency. *Canadian Association for Health, Physical Education, and Recreation Journal, 41*(2), 21-27.

Quested, E., & Duda, J.L. (2009). Perceptions of the motivational climate, need satisfaction, and indices of well- and ill-being among hip hop dancers. *Journal of Dance Medicine & Science, 13*(1), 10-19.

Rose, D.J., & Christina, R.W. (2006). *A multilevel approach to the study of motor control and learning* (2nd ed.). San Francisco: Benjamin Cummings.

Rosenberg, M. (1965). *Society and the adolescent self-image.* Princeton, NJ: Princeton University Press.

Schmidt, R.A., & Lee, T.D. (2011). *Motor control and learning: A behavioral emphasis* (5th ed.). Champaign, IL: Human Kinetics.

Schmidt, R.A., & Lee, T.D. (2014). *Motor learning and performance: From principles to application* (5th ed.). Champaign, IL: Human Kinetics.

Skrinar, M. (1988). Who's teaching the dance class? In P.M. Clarkson & M. Skrinar (Eds.), *Science of dance training* (pp. 289-297). Champaign, IL: Human Kinetics.

Slavin, R.E. (1991). Synthesis of research of cooperative learning. *Educational Leadership, 48*(5), 71-82.

Taylor, J., & Taylor, C. (1995). *Psychology of dance.* Champaign, IL: Human Kinetics.

Weiner, B. (1972). *Theories of motivation: From mechanism to cognition.* Chicago: Markham.

Wilmerding, V., & Krasnow, D. (2009). *Motor learning and teaching dance.* Resource paper. International Association for Dance Medicine and Science. www.iadms.org/displaycommon.cfm?an=1&subarticlenbr=250

Chapter 14

Annett, J., & Piech, J. (1985). The retention of a skill following distributed training. *Programmed Learning and Educational Technology, 22*(2), 182-186.

Batson, G. (1996). Conscious use of the human body in movement: The peripheral neuroanatomic basis of the Alexander Technique. *Medical Problems of Performing Artists, 11*(1), 3-11.

Batson, G. (2007). Revisiting overuse injuries in dance in view of motor learning and somatic models of distributed practice. *Journal of Dance Medicine & Science, 11*(3), 70-75.

Batson, G. (2008). *Proprioception.* Resource Paper. International Association for Dance Medicine & Science. www.iadms.org/displaycommon.cfm?an=1&subarticlenbr=210

Batson, G. (2009). *Somatic studies and dance.* Resource Paper. International Association for Dance Medicine & Science. www.iadms.org/displaycommon.cfm?an=1&subarticlenbr=248

Batson, G. (2009). The somatic practice of intentional rest in dance education: Preliminary steps towards a method of study. *Journal of Dance and Somatic Practices, 1*(2), 177-197.

Battig, W.F. (1979). The flexibility of human memory. In L.S. Cermak & F.I.M. Craik (Eds.), *Levels of processing in human memory* (pp. 23-44). Hillsdale, NJ: Erlbaum.

Bengtsson, S.L., Csíkszentmihályi, M., & Ullén, F. (2007). Cortical regions involved in the generation of musical structures during improvisations in pianists. *Journal of Cognitive Neuroscience, 19*(5), 830-842.

Berkowitz, A., & Ansari, D. (2008). Generation of novel motor sequences: The neural correlates of musical improvisation. *NeuroImage, 41*(2), 535-43.

Brashers-Krug, T., Shadmehr, R., & Bizzi, E. (1996). Consolidation in human motor memory. *Nature, 382,* 252-255.

Dail, T.K., & Christina, R.W. (2004). Distribution of practice and metacognition in learning and long-term retention. *Research Quarterly for Exercise and Sport, 75*(2), 148-155.

Dearborn, K., Harring, K., Young, C., & O'Rourke, E. (2006). Mirror and phrase difficulty influence dancer attention and body satisfaction. *Journal of Dance Education, 6*(4), 116-123.

Dearborn, K., & Ross, R. (2006). Dance learning and the mirror: Comparison study of dance phrase learning with and without the mirror. *Journal of Dance Education, 6*(4), 109-115.

Driskell, J.E., Willis, R.P., & Copper, C. (1992). Effect of overlearning on retention. *Journal of Applied Psychology, 77*(5), 615-622.

Dudai, Y. (2004). The neurobiology of consolidations, or, how stable is the engram? *Annual Review of Psychology, 55,* 51-86.

Eddy, M. (2012). The ongoing development of "Past Beginnings": A further discussion of neuromotor development: Somatic links between Bartenieff Fundamentals, Body-Mind Centering® and Dynamic Embodiment©. *The Journal of Laban Movement Studies, 3*(1), 54-79.

Edwards, R.V., & Lee, A.M. (1985). The relationship of cognitive style and instructional strategy to learning and transfer of motor skills. *Research Quarterly for Exercise and Sport, 56*(3), 286-290.

Enghauser, R. (2003). Motor learning and the dance technique class: Science, tradition, and pedagogy. *Journal of Dance Education, 3*(3), 87-95.

Ericsson, K.A., Krampe, R.T., & Tesch-Römer, C. (1993). The role of deliberate practice in the acquisition of expert performance. *Psychological Review, 100*(3), 363-406.

Ericsson, K.A., Prietula, M.J., & Cokely, E.T. (2007). The making of an expert. *Harvard Business Review* (July-August).

Fink, A., Graif, B., & Neubauer, A.C. (2009). Brain correlates underlying creative thinking: EEG alpha activity in professional vs. novice dancers. *NeuroImage, 46*(3), 854-862.

Gentile, A.M. (1972). A working model of skill acquisition with application to teaching. *Quest, 17*(1), 3-23. doi: 10.1080/00336297.1972.10519717

Hagendoorn, I.G. (2003). Cognitive dance improvisation: How study of the motor system can inspire dance (and vice versa). *Leonardo, 36*(3), 221-227.

Hansen, S., Tremblay, L., & Elliott, D. (2005). Part and whole practice: Chunking and online control in the acquisition of a serial motor task. *Research Quarterly for Exercise and Sport, 76*(1), 60-66.

Kandel, E.R., Schwartz, J.H., & Jessell, T.M. (2000). *Principles of neural science* (4th ed.). New York: McGraw-Hill.

Kimmerle, M., & Côté, P. (2003). *Teaching dance skills: A motor learning and developmental approach.* Andover, NJ: J. Michael Ryan.

Krasnow, D. (2010). Improvisation as a tool for enhanced motor learning in dance. *The Twenty-Eighth Annual Symposium of Medical Problems of Performing Artists,* July 29-August 1, 2010, Snowmass, Colorado.

Krasnow, D., Monasterio, R., & Chatfield, S.J. (2001). Emerging concepts of posture and alignment. *Medical Problems of Performing Artists, 16*(1), 8-16.

Lee, T.D., Magill, R.A., & Weeks, D.J. (1985). Influence of practice schedule on testing schema theory predictions in adults. *Journal of Motor Behavior, 17*(3), 283-299.

Mackrous, I. & Proteau, L. (2007). Specificity of practice results from differences in movement planning strategies. *Experimental Brain Research, 183*(2), 181-193.

Magill, R.A. (2011). Motor learning and control (9th ed.). New York: McGraw-Hill.

Magill, R.A., & Anderson, D. (2014). *Motor learning and control* (10th ed.). New York: McGraw-Hill.

Mermier, C.M., Zuhl, M.N., Wilmerding, M.V., Beam, J.R., White, A.C., Salgado, R.M., & Beverly, J.M. (2013). The effects of a harness safety system during maximal treadmill run testing in collegiate middle and long distance runners. *Journal of Strength & Conditioning Research, 27*(11), 2934-2938. doi: 10.1519/JSC.0b013e318289e463

Naylor, J., & Briggs, G. (1963). Effects of task complexity and task organization on the relative efficiency of part and whole training methods. *Journal of Experimental Psychology, 65*(3), 217-244.

Radell, S.A. (2012). Body image and mirror use in the ballet class. *The IADMS Bulletin for Teachers, 4*(1), 10-13.

Radell, S.A. (2013). *Mirrors in the dance class: Help or hindrance?* Resource paper. International Association for Dance Medicine and Science. http://www.iadms.org/displaycommon.cfm?an=1&subarticlenbr=400

Radell, S.A., Adame, D.D., & Cole, S.P. (2003). Effect of teaching with mirrors on ballet dance performance. *Perceptual & Motor Skills, 97,* 960-4.

Radell, S.A., Adame, D.D., & Cole, S.P. (2004). The impact of mirrors on body image and classroom performance in female college ballet dancers. *Journal of Dance Medicine & Science, 8*(2), 47-52.

Radell, S.A., Adame, D.D., Cole, S.P., & Blumenkehl, N.J. (2011). The impact of mirrors on body image and performance in high and low performing female ballet students. *Journal of Dance Medicine & Science, 15*(3), 108-115.

Ribeiro, M.M., & Fonseca, A. (2011). The empathy and the structuring sharing modes of movement sequences in the improvisation of contemporary dance. *Research in Dance Education, 12*(2), 71-85.

Rose, D.J., & Christina, R.W. (2006). *A multilevel approach to the study of motor control and learning* (2nd ed.). San Francisco: Benjamin Cummings.

Schmidt, R.A., & Lee, T.D. (2011). *Motor control and learning: A behavioral emphasis* (5th ed.). Champaign, IL: Human Kinetics.

Schmidt, R.A., & Lee, T.D. (2014). *Motor learning and performance: From principles to application* (5th ed.). Champaign, IL: Human Kinetics.

Shea, C.H., & Wright, D.L. (1995). Contextual dependencies: Influence on response latency. *Memory, 3*(1), 81-95.

Shea, J.B., & Morgan, R.L. (1979). Contextual interference effects on the acquisition, retention, and transfer of a motor skill. *Journal of Experimental Psychology: Human Learning and Memory, 5*(2), 179-187.

Shumway-Cook, A., & Woollacott, M. (2001). *Motor control: Theory and practical applications* (2nd ed.). Baltimore: Williams & Wilkins.

Skrinar, M. (1988). Who's teaching the dance class? In P.M. Clarkson & M. Skrinar (Eds.), *Science of dance training* (pp. 289-297). Champaign, IL: Human Kinetics.

Stickgold, R. (2005). Sleep-dependent memory consolidation. *Nature, 437,* 1272-1278.

Tremblay, L., & Proteau, L. (1998). Specificity of practice: The case of powerlifting. *Research Quarterly for Exercise and Sport, 69*(3), 284-289.

Walker, M.P., Brakefield, T., Morgan, A., & Hobson, J.A. (2002). Practice with sleep makes perfect: Sleep-dependent motor skill learning. *Neuron, 35*(1), 205-211.

Walker, M.P., Brakefield, T., Seidman, J., Morgan, A., Hobson, J.A., & Stickgold, R. (2003). Sleep and the time course of motor skill learning. *Learning and Memory, 10,* 275-284.

Walter, C.B., & Swinnen, S.P. (1992). Adaptive tuning of interlimb attraction to facilitate bimanual coupling. *Journal of Motor Behavior, 24*(1), 95-104.

Whittenburg, Z. (2011). The mirror mystique: Allegra Kent muses on the mirror as both friend and foe. *Dance Magazine, 85*(11), 40-45. www.dancemagazine.com/issues/November-2011/The-Mirror-Mystique

Wightman, D.C., & Lintern, G. (1985). Part-task training strategies for tracking and manual control. *Human Factors: The Journal of the Human Factors and Ergonomics Society, 27*(3), 267-283.

Wilmerding, V., & Krasnow, D. (2009). *Motor learning and teaching dance.* Resource paper. International Association for Dance Medicine and Science. www.iadms.org/displaycommon.cfm?an=1&subarticlenbr=250

Yagura, H., Hatakenaka, M., & Miyai, I. (2006). Does therapeutic facilitation add to locomotor outcome of body weight-supported treadmill training in nonambulatory patients with stroke? A randomized controlled trial. *Archives of Physical Medicine and Rehabilitation, 87*(4), 529-535.

Chapter 15

Atkinson, R.C., & Shiffrin, R.M. (1971). The control of short-term memory. *Scientific American, 225,* 82-90.

Baddeley, A. (2003). Working memory: Looking back and looking forward. *Nature Reviews: Neuroscience, 4,* 829-839.

Baddeley, A. D., & Hitch, G. (1974). Working memory. In G.H. Bower (Ed.), *The psychology of learning and motivation: Advances in research and theory* (Vol. 8, pp. 47-89). New York: Academic Press.

Cook, T.W. (1936). Studies in cross education: V. Theoretical. *Psychological Review, 43*(2), 149-178.

Cowan, N., Chen, Z., & Rouder, J.N. (2004). Constant capacity in an immediate serial-recall task: A logical sequel to Miller (1956). *Psychological Science, 15*(9), 634-640.

De Bartolomeo, O., Sette, M.M., Sloten, J.V., & Albisetti, W. (2007). Electromyographic study on the biomechanics of the lower limb during the execution of technical fundamentals of dance: The relevé [poster]. *Journal of Biomechanics, 40*(2), S789.

Enghauser, R. (2003). Motor learning and the dance technique class: Science, tradition, and pedagogy. *Journal of Dance Education, 3*(3), 87-95.

Farrar-Baker, A., & Wilmerding, V. (2006). Prevalence of lateral bias in the teaching of beginning and advanced ballet classes. *Journal of Dance Medicine & Science, 10*(3-4), 81-84.

Harley, Y.X.R., Gibson, A.S., Harley, E.H., Lambert, M.I., Vaughan, C.L., & Noakes, T.D. (2002). Quadriceps strength and jumping efficiency in dancers. *Journal of Dance Medicine & Science, 6*(3), 87-94.

James, W. (1890). *Principles of psychology* (Vol. 2). New York: Holt.

Kimmerle, M. (2001). Lateral bias in dance teaching. *Journal of Physical Education, Recreation, & Dance, 72*(5), 34-37.

Kimmerle, M. (2010). Lateral bias, functional asymmetry, dance training and dance injuries. *Journal of Dance Medicine & Science, 14*(2), 58-66.

Kimmerle, M., & Côté, P. (2003). *Teaching dance skills: A motor learning and developmental approach.* Andover, NJ: J. Michael Ryan.

Krasnow, D., Ambegaonkar, J.P., Wilmerding, M.V., Stecyk, S., Koutedakis, Y., & Wyon, M. (2012). Electromyographic comparison of grand battement devant at the barre, in the center, and traveling. *Medical Problems of Performing Artists, 27*(3), 143-155.

Krasnow, D.H., Chatfield, S.J., Barr, S., Jenson, J.L., & Dufek, J.S. (1997). Imagery and conditioning practices for dancers. *Dance Research Journal, 29*(1), 43-64.

Krasnow, D., & Deveau, J. (2010). *Conditioning with imagery for dancers.* Toronto: Thompson Educational.

Krasnow, D., Wilmerding, M.V., Stecyk, S., Wyon, M., & Koutedakis, Y. (2011). Biomechanical research in dance: A literature review. *Medical Problems of Performing Artists, 26*(1), 3-23.

Krasnow, D., Wilmerding, M.V., Stecyk, S., Wyon, M., & Koutedakis, Y. (2012). Examination of weight transfer strategies during the execution of grand battement devant at the barre, in the center, and traveling. *Medical Problems of Performing Artists, 27*(2), 74-84.

Lee, T.D. (1988). Testing for motor learning: A focus on transfer-appropriate processing. In O. G. Meijer & K. Roth (Eds.), *Complex motor behaviour: The motor-action controversy* (pp. 210-215). Amsterdam: Elsevier.

Magill, R.A. (2011). *Motor learning and control* (9th ed.). New York: McGraw-Hill.

Magill, R.A., & Anderson, D. (2014). *Motor learning and control* (10th ed.). New York: McGraw-Hill.

McLain, S., Carter, C.L., & Abel, J. (1997). The effect of a conditioning and alignment program on the measurement of supine jump height and pelvic alignment when using the Current Concepts Reformer. *Journal of Dance Medicine & Science, 1*(4), 149-154.

Poggini, L., Losasso, S., Cerreto, M., & Cesari, L. (1997). Jump ability in novice ballet dancers before and after training. *Journal of Dance Medicine & Science, 1*(2), 46-50.

Puretz, S. (1988). Psychomotor research and the dance teacher. In P.M. Clarkson & M. Skrinar (Eds.), *Science of dance training* (pp. 279-287). Champaign, IL: Human Kinetics.

Puretz, S.L. (1983). Bilateral transfer: The effects of practice on transfer of complex dance movement patterns. *Research Quarterly for Exercise and Sport, 54*(1), 48-54.

Rose, D.J., & Christina, R.W. (2006). *A multilevel approach to the study of motor control and learning* (2nd ed.). San Francisco: Benjamin Cummings.

Ryman, R., & Ranney, D. (1978/79). A preliminary investigation of two variations of the grand battement devant. *Dance Research Journal, 11*(1/2), 2-11.

Schmidt, R.A., & Lee, T.D. (2011). *Motor control and learning: A behavioral emphasis* (5th ed.). Champaign, IL: Human Kinetics.

Schmidt, R.A., & Lee, T.D. (2014). *Motor learning and performance: From principles to application* (5th ed.). Champaign, IL: Human Kinetics.

Schmidt, R.A., & Young, D.E. (1987). Transfer of movement control in motor learning. In S.M. Cormier & J.D. Hagman (Eds.), *Transfer of learning* (pp. 47-79). Orlando, FL: Academic Press.

Shea, J.B., & Morgan, R.L. (1979). Contextual interference effects on the acquisition, retention, and transfer of a motor skill. *Journal of Experimental Psychology: Human Learning and Memory, 5*(2), 179-187.

Sidaway, B., Ahn, S., Boldeau, P., Griffin, S., Noyes, B., & Pelletier, K. (2008). A comparison of manual guidance and knowledge of results in the learning of a weight-bearing skill. *Journal of Neurologic Physical Therapy, 32*(1), 32-38.

Simmering, V.R., Peterson, C., Darling, W., & Spencer, J P. (2008). Location memory biases reveal the challenges of coordinating visual and kinesthetic reference frames. *Experimental Brain Research, 184*(2), 165-178.

Smyth, M.M., & Pendleton, L.R. (1990). Space and movement in working memory. *The Quarterly Journal of Experimental Psychology Section A: Human Experimental Psychology, 42*(2), 291-304.

Starkes, J.L., Deakin, J.M., Lindley, S., & Crisp, F. (1987). Motor versus verbal recollection of ballet sequences by young expert dancers. *Journal of Sport Psychology, 9*(3), 222-230.

Sweigard, L.E. (1974). *Human movement potential: Its ideokinetic facilitation.* Lanham, MD: University Press of America.

Thorndike, E.L. (1914). *Educational psychology: Briefer course.* New York: Columbia University Press.

Torres-Zavala, C., Henriksson, J., & Henriksson, M. (2005). The influence of the barre on movement pattern during performance of développé [abstract]. In R. Solomon & J. Solomon (Eds.), *Proceedings of the 15th Annual Meeting of the International Association for Dance Medicine and Science* (pp. 147-148). Stockholm, Sweden: IADMS.

Trepman, E., Gellman, R.E., Micheli, L.J, & De Luca, C.J. (1998). Electromyographic analysis of grand-plié in ballet and modern dancers. *Medicine and Science in Sports and Exercise, 30*(12), 1708-1720.

Trepman, E., Gellman, R.E., Solomon, R., Murthy, K.R., Micheli, L.J., & De Luca, C.J. (1994). Electromyographic analysis standing posture and demi-plié in ballet and modern dancers. *Medicine and Science in Sports and Exercise, 26*(6), 771-782.

Tsutsui, S., & Imanaka, K. (2003). Effect of manual guidance on acquiring a new bimanual coordination pattern. *Research Quarterly for Exercise and Sport, 74*(1), 104-109.

Tulving, E. (1985). How many memory systems are there? *American Psychologist, 40*(4), 385-398.

Tulving, E., & Thomson, D.M. (1973). Encoding specificity and retrieval processes in episodic memory. *Psychological Review, 80*(5), 352-373.

Wilmerding, V., Heyward, V.T., King, M., Fiedler, K.J., Stidley, C.A., Pett, S.B., & Evans, B. (2001). Electromyographic comparison of the développé devant at barre and centre. *Journal of Dance Medicine & Science, 5*(3), 69-74.

Winther, K.T., & Thomas, J.R. (1981). Developmental differences in children's labeling of movement. *Journal of Motor Behavior, 13*(3), 77-90.

Woodhull-McNeal, A.P., Clarkson, P.M., James, R., Watkins, A., & Barrett, S. (1990). How linear is dancers' posture? *Medical Problems of Performing Artists, 5*(4), 151-154.

Chapter 16

Bartenieff, I., with Lewis, D. (1980). *Body movement: Coping with the environment.* New York: Gordon and Breach Science.

Batson, G. (2009). *Somatic studies and dance.* Resource Paper. International Association for Dance Medicine & Science. www.iadms.org/displaycommon.cfm?an=1&subarticlenbr=248

Denis, M. (1985). Visual imagery and the use of mental practice in the development of motor skills. *Canadian Journal of Applied Sport Sciences, 10*(4), 4S-15S.

Dowd, I. (1990). *Taking root to fly* (2nd ed.). North Hampton, MA: Contact Collaborations.

Eddy, M. (2012). The ongoing development of "Past Beginnings": A further discussion of neuromotor development: Somatic links between Bartenieff Fundamentals, Body-Mind Centering® and Dynamic Embodiment©. *The Journal of Laban Movement Studies, 3*(1), 54-79.

Fairweather, M.M., & Sidaway, B. (1993). Ideokinetic imagery as a postural development technique. *Research Quarterly for Exercise and Sport, 64*(4), 385-392.

Feltz, D.L., & Landers, D.M. (1983). The effects of mental practice on motor skill learning and performance: A meta-analysis. *Journal of Sport Psychology, 5,* 25-27.

Feltz, D.L., & Landers, D.M. (2007). The effects of mental practice on motor skill learning and performance: A meta-analysis. In D. Smith & M. Bar-Eli (Eds.), *Essential readings in sport and exercise psychology* (pp. 219-230). Champaign, IL: Human Kinetics.

Fish, L., Hall, C., & Cumming, J. (2004). Investigating the use of imagery by elite ballet dancers. *Journal of Dance Medicine & Science, 10*(3), 26-39.

Frank, J.S., & Earl, M. (1990). Coordination of posture and movement. *Physical Therapy: Journal of the American Physical Therapy Association, 70*(12), 855-863.

Franklin, E. (2012). *Dynamic alignment through imagery* (2nd ed.). Champaign, IL: Human Kinetics.

Hall, C.R., & Martin, K.A. (1997). Measuring movement imagery abilities: A revision of the Movement Imagery Questionnaire. *Journal of Mental Imagery, 21*(1-2), 143-154.

Hall, C.R., & Pongrac, J. (1983). Movement Imagery Questionnaire. London, Ontario, Canada: University of Western Ontario.

Hanrahan, C. (1995). Creating dance images: Basic principles for teachers. *Journal of Physical Education, Recreation & Dance, 66*(1), 33-40.

Hanrahan, C., & Salmela, J.H. (1986). Mental imagery as a facilitator in dance movement skills. In L.E. Unestaehl (Ed.), *Contemporary Sport Psychology: Proceedings from the VI World Congress in Sport Psychology* (pp. 131-141). Orebro, Sweden: VEJE.

Hanrahan, C. & Salmela, J.H. (1990). Dance images—do they really work or are we just imagining things? *Journal of Physical Education, Recreation & Dance, 61*(2), 18-21.

Hanrahan, C., Tétreau, B., & Sarrazin, C. (1995). Use of imagery while performing dance movement. *International Journal of Sport Psychology, 26,* 413-430.

Hanrahan, C., & Vergeer, I. (2000-2001). Multiple uses of mental imagery by professional modern dancers. *Imagination, Cognition, and Personality, 20*(3), 231-255.

Hird, J.S., Landers, D.M., Thomas, J.R., & Horan, J.J. (1991). Physical practice is superior to mental practice in enhancing cognitive and motor task performance. *Journal of Sport & Exercise Psychology, 13*(3), 281-293.

Kimmerle, M., & Côté, P. (2003). *Teaching dance skills: A motor learning and developmental approach.* Andover, NJ: J. Michael Ryan.

Krasnow, D.H., Chatfield, S.J., Barr, S., Jenson, J.L., & Dufek, J.S. (1997). Imagery and conditioning practices for dancers. *Dance Research Journal, 29*(1), *43-64.*

Krasnow, D., & Deveau, J. (2010). *Conditioning with imagery for dancers.* Toronto: Thompson Educational.

Lafleur, M.F., Jackson, P.L., Malouin, F., Richards, C.L., Evans, A.C., & Doyon, J. (2002). Motor learning produces parallel dynamic functional changes during the execution and imagination of sequential foot movements. *Neuro-Image, 16*(1), 142-157.

Magill, R.A. (2011). *Motor learning and control* (9th ed.). New York: McGraw-Hill.

Magill, R.A., & Anderson, D. (2014). *Motor learning and control* (10th ed.). New York: McGraw-Hill.

Martin, K.A., Moritz, S.A., & Hall, C.R. (1999). Imagery use in sport: A literature review and applied model. *The Sport Psychologist, 13*(3), 245-268.

Matt, P.H. (1991/1992). Ideokinesis: Integrating the science and somatics of dance. *Kinesiology and Medicine for Dance, 14*(1), 68-77.

Minton, S. (1990). Enhancement of alignment through imagery. *Journal of Physical Education, Recreation & Dance, 61*(2), 28-29.

Minton, S. (1991/1992). Exploring the mind/body connection with imagery. *Kinesiology and Medicine for Dance, 14*(1), 29-32.

Monsma, E.V., & Overby, L. (2004). The relationship between imagery and competitive anxiety in ballet auditions. *Journal of Dance Medicine & Science, 8*(1), 11-18.

Moran, A., Campbell, M., Holmes, P. & MacIntyre, T. (2012). Mental imagery, action observation, and skill learning. In N. Hodges & M.A. Williams (Eds.), *Skill acquisition in sport: Research, theory, and practice* (2nd ed., pp. 94-111). London: Routledge.

Murphy, S.M., Nordin, S., & Cumming, J. (2008). Imagery in sport, exercise and dance. In T.S. Horn (Ed.), *Advances in sport psychology* (3rd ed., pp. 297-324). Champaign, IL: Human Kinetics.

Nordin, S., & Cumming, J. (2005). Professional dancers describe their imagery: Where, what, why and how. *Sport Psychologist, 19,* 395-416.

Nordin, S., & Cumming, J. (2006). The development of imagery in dance: Part I: Quantitative findings from a mixed sample of dancers. *Journal of Dance Medicine & Science, 10*(1&2), 21-27.

Nordin, S., & Cumming, J. (2006). The development of imagery in dance: Part II: Quantitative findings from a mixed sample of dancers. *Journal of Dance Medicine & Science, 10*(1&2), 28-34.

Overby, L.Y. (1990). The use of imagery by dance teachers--development and implementation of two research instruments. *Journal of Physical Education, Recreation & Dance, 61*(2), 24-27.

Overby, L.Y. (1991/1992). Principles of motor learning applied to the teaching of dance technique. *Kinesiology and Medicine for Dance, 14*(1), 113-118.

Overby, L.Y., & Dunn, J. (2011). The history and research of dance imagery: Implications for teachers. *IADMS Bulletin for Teachers, 3*(2), 9-11.

Overby, L.Y., Hall, C., & Haslem, I. (1998). A comparison of imagery used by dance teachers, figure skating coaches, and soccer coaches. *Imagination, Cognition, and Personality, 17*(4), 323-337.

Rose, D.J., & Christina, R.W. (2006). *A multilevel approach to the study of motor control and learning* (2nd ed.). San Francisco: Benjamin Cummings.

Sawada, M., Mori, S., & Ishii, M. (2002). Effect of metaphorical verbal instruction on modeling of sequential dance skills by young children. *Perceptual and Motor Skills, 95*, 1097-1105.

Schmidt, R.A., & Lee, T.D. (2011). *Motor control and learning: A behavioral emphasis* (5th ed.). Champaign, IL: Human Kinetics.

Schmidt, R.A., & Lee, T.D. (2014). *Motor learning and performance: From principles to application* (5th ed.). Champaign, IL: Human Kinetics.

Smith, K.L. (1990). Dance and imagery: The link between movement and imagination. *Journal of Physical Education, Recreation & Dance, 61*(2), 17.

Sweigard, L.E. (1974). *Human movement potential: Its ideokinetic facilitation.* Lanham, MD: University Press of America.

Todd, M.E. (1937). *The thinking body.* New York: Paul B. Hoeber.

Van Gyn, G.H., Wenger, H.A., & Gaul, C.A. (1990). Imagery as a method of enhancing transfer from training to performance. *Journal of Sport & Exercise Psychology, 12*(4), 366-375.

About the Authors

Donna Krasnow is a professor emerita in the department of dance at York University in Toronto, Canada, and is a member of the special faculty at California Institute of the Arts in the United States. She specializes in dance science research, concentrating on dance kinesiology, injury prevention and care, conditioning for dancers, and motor learning and motor control, with a special emphasis on the young dancer. Donna has published numerous articles in the *Journal of Dance Medicine & Science* and *Medical Problems of Performing Artists*, as well as resource papers in collaboration with M. Virginia Wilmerding for the International Association for Dance Medicine & Science (IADMS). She was the conference director for IADMS from 2004 to 2008 as well as serving on the board of directors. Donna is currently the associate editor for dance for *Medical Problems of Performing Artists*. She conducts workshops for dance faculty in alignment and healthy practices for dancers, including the Teachers Day Seminars at York University, and is a nine-time resident guest artist at Victorian College of the Arts and VCA Secondary School, University of Melbourne, Australia. Donna has created a specialized body conditioning system for dancers called C-I Training (conditioning with imagery). She has produced a DVD series of this work, and in 2010 she coauthored the book *Conditioning with Imagery for Dancers* with professional dancer Jordana Deveau. She offers courses for teachers in Limón technique pedagogy and C-I Training. Information can be found at www.citraining.com.

M. Virginia ("Ginny") Wilmerding danced professionally in New York City in her early professional career, and is now a research professor at the University of New Mexico in Albuquerque, New Mexico, United States, where she teaches for both the exercise science and dance programs. Courses include kinesiology, research design, exercise physiology, exercise prescription, exercise and disease prevention, and conditioning. She also teaches at the Public Academy for Performing Arts, a charter school. Ginny is currently the chief executive officer (CEO) of the International Association for Dance Medicine & Science (IADMS) and the chair of the IADMS Annual Meeting Program Committee. She is past president of IADMS and served on the IADMS board of directors from 2001 to 2011. Ginny serves as associate editor for science for the *Journal of Dance Medicine & Science*. She has published original research in *Journal of Dance Medicine & Science*, *Medical Problems of Performing Artists*, *Medicine & Science in Sports & Exercise*, *Journal of Strength and Conditioning Research*, and *IDEA Today*. She has also coauthored resource papers for IADMS with Donna Krasnow. Research interests include body composition, training methodologies, injury incidence and prevention, pedagogical considerations in technique class, and the physiological requirements of various dance idioms.

You'll find other outstanding
dance resources at
www.HumanKinetics.com